Kalevala
The Land of the Heroes

KALEVALA
The Land of the Heroes

Translated by W.F. Kirby
Introduced by M.A. Branch

THE ATHLONE PRESS
London and Dover, New Hampshire

Published in Great Britain in 1985
by The Athlone Press, 44 Bedford Row, London WC1R 4LY
and in North America
by The Athlone Press, 51 Washington Street, Dover NH 03820

The translation of *Kalevala* was first published in 1907
in the Everyman's Library, by J.M. Dent & Co and E.P. Dutton & Co.
Copyright©1985 M.A. Branch, Preface, Introduction,
Notes, Glossary and Further Reading

British Library Cataloguing in Publication Data
Kirby, W.F.
  Kalevala.
  I. Title   II. Kalevala. *English*
  894'.5411   PH324.E5

  ISBN 0–485–11258–2
  ISBN 0–485–12048–8 Pbk

Library of Congress Cataloging in Publication Data
Kalevala. English
  Kalevala.

  Translation of: Kalevala.
  Originally published: 1907.
  Includes bibliographical references.
  I. Kirby, W.F. (William Forsell), 1844–1912.
II. Branch, M.A. (Michael Arthur)
PH324.E5K5 1985 894'.54111 84–21619
ISBN 0–485–11258–2
ISBN 0–485–12048–8 (pbk.)

Printed in Great Britain by Redwood Burn, Trowbridge

Contents

Runos

Contents

Preface

W.F. Kirby's translation of the 1849 *Kalevala* first appeared in 1907. It had been a long time in the making. In 1888 William Forsell Kirby (1844–1913), an entomologist at the Natural History Museum in London, circulated an announcement of his intention to prepare an English version of the *Kalevala* on the basis of Anton Schiefner's German translation which had appeared in 1852. The announcement provoked a series of indignant articles in the columns of *The Athenaeum*. Sir Edmund Gosse, Andrew Lang and Max Müller were among the eminent scholars who insisted that a new translation had to be based on the original Finnish text. To his credit Kirby heeded these views. He put aside his publication plans and set about learning Finnish. Indeed he went further and also learnt Estonian, one of the languages most closely related to Finnish; before returning to his work on the *Kalevala* Kirby published selections from the Estonian national epic, *Kalevipoeg*, in his two-volume *Hero of Esthonia and other studies in the romantic literature of that country* (London, 1895). The thoroughness of Kirby's linguistic and scholarly preparations is evident in the quality of his translation of the *Kalevala* and in his own *Notes* and *Glossary* which follow the work.

Kirby's translation stands as a document of its age. He followed the example of John Martin Crawford, who published the first translation of the *Kalevala* in English in 1888, and eminent translators into other languages in attempting to reproduce the distinctive metre of the Finnish text. The transparent relationship between this metre and that of *Hiawatha* demonstrates the influence of *Kalevala* on Longfellow, who had read it in Schiefner's German translation. In this printing Kirby's translation is reproduced without significant change. Where a possibly misleading translation error occurs, I have suggested an alternative translation in the *Notes*; dilutions of the original Finnish text and even small errors of translation which do not distort the underlying meaning have been left untouched.

The *Introduction* is new. It replaces that by J.B.C. Grundy which in turn had replaced Kirby's own introductory text. The various *Introductions* to translations of the *Kalevala* offer some insight into the changing reasons for its lasting hold on our attention. The present *Introduction* aims to throw some light on the nature and significance of Finnish oral poetry, and to show how the poems of a dying tradition were transformed into a work of literature that was to become a foundation stone of a Finnish national culture and identity.

Changes and omissions have been made in the *Notes* and *Glossary* only where research has subsequently rendered an observation incorrect or irrelevant. In order not to change the character of these sections, I have retained the method used by Kirby to integrate the observations of his two Finnish advisers, Professor Kaarle Krohn and Madame Aino Malmberg, and allowed myself to intrude in their scholarly exchanges, *sotto voce*, only where unavoidable. In offering alternative translations and observations I found valuable guidance in the English prose translation of the *Kalevala* by Professor Francis Peabody Magoun, Jr (Harvard) and the German verse translation of Professor Hans Fromm (Munich). The encyclopaedic *Kalevala* handbook of Professor Aimo Turunen (*Kalevalan sanat*, 1979) has been a constant and most valuable source of information. The responsibility for any errors in the use of these sources is of course mine alone.

The folk poems quoted in the *Introduction* and followed by the abbreviation FFPE for *Finnish Folk Poetry: Epic* (Helsinki, 1977), were translated by Mr Keith Bosley; these translations, together with the map and notes on pronunciation, are reproduced by kind permission of the Finnish Literature Society of Helsinki. To Mr Bosley I am also indebted for permission to quote his translation of the Finnish poem *Jos mun tuttuni tulisi* ('If the one I know came now') from the forthcoming anthology of poetry in the Finno–Ugrian languages, *The Great Bear*.

Bloomsbury
August 1984   *M.A. Branch*

Pronunciation

The orthography of Finnish is phonetic. Each letter represents a single sound. If a letter is written twice, it indicates in the case of vowels that the sound is double the length of the single sound; where consonants are written twice, they are at syllable boundaries and should be pronounced twice. In normal spoken Finnish, the main stress always falls on the first syllable of the word, with decreasing secondary stress on the third and fifth syllables (provided they do not mark the end of a word when they are unstressed); the requirements of the Kalevala metre, however, can alter this stress pattern.

Vowels
a as in *father*; **e** as in *pet*; **i** as in *hit*; **o** as in *hot*; **u** as in *pull*; **y** as in French *tu*, German *über*; **ä** as in *bad*; **ö** like its German counterpart, or as in French *peu*.

Consonants
l, m, n, r are similar to the corresponding sounds of English but without aspiration; **g** occurs in loanwords when it is pronounced as in *goat*, in the cluster **ng** as the combined sound in *singer*; **h** at the beginning of a syllable as in *hat* and at the end of a syllable as in *loch*; **j** as **y** in *yoke*; **v** as in *very* but with more labialization than in English.

Introduction

In 1849 the Finnish Literature Society in Helsinki published a work which was soon to become synonymous around the world with Finnish folklore. *Kalevala*, the compilation of Elias Lönnrot (1802–84), a doctor of medicine and later Professor of Finnish at the University of Helsinki, has come to represent for the world the quintessence of Finnish traditional culture, frequently compared in form and content to other great epics of world literature. Translated into more than thirty languages, the 1849 edition remains 135 years later the best-known work of Finnish literature outside Finland; in English alone there have been three full translations and several prose adaptations.

The European heritage

Close examination of the contents of the *Kalevala* and the circumstances in which the epic took shape show, paradoxically, that its full significance is not to be understood solely as a Finnish phenomenon. Its compiler belonged to a generation of young intellectuals who were profoundly influenced by a philosophy of nationalism which had come to Finland from various parts of eighteenth-century Europe. It is most closely associated with the German thinker J.G. Herder (1744–1803), who argued the need for a nation to possess a distinctive cultural identity which was founded in the language and oral literature of the ordinary, unlettered people. In Finland, at the end of the eighteenth century, such thinking fell on fertile ground, coinciding with ideas which the eminent Finnish historian H.G. Porthan (1739–1804) had himself been teaching. Following the annexation of the Swedish Province of Finland by Russia in 1808–9 and the beginning of a new phase in Finland's history as a Grand Duchy in the Empire interest in Herder's and Porthan's ideas gained greatly in strength, and the cultivation of a national identity became a veritable duty for many educated Finns. Moreover, in the early years of the Grand Duchy their efforts met with tolerance, often support, from the imperial authorities in St Petersburg who saw an emerging Finnish national consciousness as a sure means of weakening age-old and potentially dangerous links with Sweden.

For the young Finnish nationalists at the beginning of the eighteenth century the 'ordinary people' were the Finns of the Grand Duchy. Their interest soon turned, however, to the linguistically related Karelians and Ingrians across the frontier in Russia, and later it also spread to the remaining Baltic–Finnish peoples, the Vepsians, Votes, Estonians and Livonians. As these young Finnish scholars set about recording the culture of the ordinary people, they began to discover a wealth of oral literature about an ancient world in which animistic powers governed man's environment. They collected myths about the origin of the world and forces essential to man's existence: light, fertility, fire, metals. They listened to stories of how heroes had regulated and determined the annual cycle of growth at the beginning of time and brought order into the primeval world. They saw the use of magic to evoke help from the Otherworld when the resources of ordinary men failed.

With the advantage of hindsight we know that these discoveries are the essence of folk tradition everywhere in the world. But as man's empirical understanding of the world extends, so old customs and beliefs fade. The accompanying oral tradition finds new functions before passing into darkness. It may be absorbed or transformed into new cultural traditions, some of it finds its way into the motifs and themes of high culture, some finds a new lease of life in children's lore. The special importance of the materials in the Baltic–Finnish languages is that the process of decay began much later than in most other parts of Europe.

The reasons for this lie partly in geographical and economic factors, partly in language and partly in religion. From the date of their settlement on the shores of the Gulf of Finland, at least 3000 years ago, until recent times the Baltic–Finns have lived on the periphery of European political, trading and cultural influence. It was only with Swedish and Russian expansion in the eleventh and twelfth centuries that the division, governance and taxation of the territories inhabited by the Baltic–Finns began to be firmly established. Similarly, regular trade with the area came only with the eastward thrust of the Hanseatic League in the thirteenth century. Even after the development of more regular contacts with Western and Central Europe, particularly through the spread of Christianity, the transmission of European high culture through education reached only the tiny handful of urban centres where the language of communication was not the Baltic–Finnish vernacular but Russian, Swedish or German. Indeed, until well into the nineteenth century, education and government in most of the area inhabited by the Baltic–Finnish peoples were conducted in languages which hardly any of the ordinary people understood.

The spread of Christianity was the most crucial single factor in determining the rate at which the old beliefs and practices were abandoned. The ancient beliefs and customs were weakened first in those areas, mainly in Finland, where the Lutheran Church was heir to the Roman Catholic Church. Ironically, the earliest printed specimen of Finnish folk poetry is contained in a condemnation, published in 1542, of the lewdness of pagan practices. Although some materials did survive the attempts of the Lutheran Church to eradicate them, they are for the most part fragmentary and lack the stature of the ancient tradition. The substance of the latter was preserved mainly in those areas under the fief of the Russian Orthodox Church. Because its priests were less concerned about the threat the old beliefs might hold for the souls of their parishioners and because the Orthodox areas were even more isolated for reasons of geography or language, or both, the performance of the old oral poems still flourished as a vigorous popular tradition in the nineteenth century. Remote on the periphery of Europe, isolated by a barrier of language, there survived this precious treasury of ancient poetic tradition. It was upon the motifs and themes of that tradition that Lönnrot drew in the creation of his *Kalevala*.

Oral poetry and the Kalevala tradition

The explanations of the origin of the world, the system of gods and other supernatural beings which govern man's environment in the poems recorded in the Baltic–Finnish area contain much that is universal in quality. Similarly their mode of performance, in the form of sung poetry, is also common practice in many parts of the world. On the other hand, the particular metrical and structural form of Baltic–Finnish oral poetry is a local, distinctive feature of great antiquity. The material collected by Lönnrot and his successors shows that there once existed throughout the Baltic–Finnish area – from the scattered communities of Archangel Karelia far in the north, west and south-west into Finland, south to Lake Ladoga, and in a wide swath south-west around the Gulf of Finland into Estonia – a body of sung poetry consistent in form and structure and sharing a common stock of motifs and themes. This remarkable consistency has led many scholars to conclude that this poetry, like the languages in which it was performed, shares a common origin in an ancient past.

Lönnrot's *Kalevala* has given its name to the distinctive unrhymed, non-strophic trochaic tetrameter in which this type of traditional poetry was cast. The Kalevala tetrameter was either normal or broken. In the normal tetrameter, the natural stress of speech and the foot-stress in the line of poetry coincide, and a caesura is placed between the second and third feet:

Noŭsĭ / siĭtă / /Väină̈/möĭnĕn   (Runo II:1)

In the broken tetrameter a syllable not normally stressed in speech occurs in the stressed part of the foot; no caesura occurs in such lines:

saărĕ/hén sĕ/läĭlli/séhĕn   (Runo II:3)

Outside Finland this verse form is most familiar in Longfellow's imitation in *Hiawatha*. But it is a pale and sometimes laughable imitation, for the quantitive nature of Finnish invests the Kalevala metre, in authentic performance, with a flexibility and liveliness, further heightened by a performer's dexterity in handling various patterns of consonant–vowel or vowel–consonant alliteration (a feature that does not appear contrived in a language with only thirteen consonant sounds). After alliteration, the most common stylistic device is parallellism, the elaboration or variation in one or successive lines of the idea in the preceding line:

Ahti oli saarella asuva	Ahti dwelt upon an island,
Kaukoniemen kainalossa.	By the bay near Kauko's headland,
Oli pellon kynnännässä,	And his fields he tilled industrious,
vainion vakoannassa.	ånd the fields he trenched with ploughing,
	And his ears were of the finest,
Korvalta ylen korea,	And his hearing of the keenest.
kovin tarkka kuulennalta.	Heard he shouting in the village,
Kuulevi jumun kylältä,	From the lake came sounds of hammering,
järyn järvien takoa,	On the ice the sound of footsteps,
jalan iskun iljeneltä,	On the heath a sledge was rattling.
reen kapinan kankahalta.	Therefore in his mind he fancied,
Juohtui juoni mielehensä,	In his brain the notion entered,
tuuma aivohon osasi:	That at Pohjola was wedding,
häitä Pohjola pitävi,	And a drinking-bout in secret.
salajoukko juominkia!	

Runo XXVI:1–14

Although alliteration, parallellism and other repetitive character-
istics of oral literature do not always sit comfortably in a literary text,
in the living tradition they were employed by skilful singers to tease
the audience and to heighten the excitement by delaying the dénoue-
ment. Such structural devices also reflect the mode of performance of
Kalevala poetry, particularly of epic poems. From early records and
surviving nineteenth-century practices we know that poems were
performed by two singers, or two groups of singers. A fore-singer, or
singers, would sing the first line with an after-singer, or singers,
joining in at the third or fourth foot and continuing with the following
line, while the fore-singer prepared to sing the next line. Certain
particular styles of performance became associated with particular
areas. In Archangel Karelia, for example, epic poetry was generally
performed by two men sitting side by side with their right hands
clasped, swaying backwards and forwards in time with the rhythm.
In Ingria, epic was more commonly sung by groups of women, often
as the accompaniment to ring or long dances. Musical accompaniment was sometimes provided by the *kantele*, a five-stringed
instrument comparable in appearance and mode of playing to the
zither.

Despite local developments over many centuries affecting the reper-
toires of individual singers and despite new styles of presentation
adopted in different regions, Kalevala poetry retains a stock of poems
which are remarkably consistent in form and content. The same
heroes perform the same deeds throughout the Baltic–Finnish area.
There is a common currency of stock epithets and motifs. The great
hero Väinämöinen is 'old and steadfast' or 'eternal sage'; his usual
companion Ilmarinen is 'everlasting smith'. An unsuccessful venture
brings the hero 'weeping home, his hat askew', while the rich man's
daughter rejects suitors year after year until 'the floor-beam was
trampled by her high-heeled shoes' and 'the threshold-timber was
worn away by her fine skirt-hem'. Frequently, the same figurative
expressions and metaphors denote throughout the Baltic–Finnish
area a stock situation; the journey to the Otherworld, for example, is
frequently signalled by the following lines:

> He trod for a day clinking
> upon men's sword-blades
> he trod a day, another
> upon women's needle-points
> FFPE 28:38–41

In those Russian Orthodox areas where Kalevala poetry survived into the nineteenth century, its performance retained a freshness and purpose vividly recorded in the diaries and memoirs of numerous collectors. Apart from spells, the ancient ritual functions of Kalevala poetry had been largely forgotten and the vast body of texts owed their continuing popularity to their function as both entertainment and art. Men and women sang, either in groups or alone, as they worked in the fields, hunted or fished. In the evenings the men and women sang and amused each other as they performed their household tasks, the women spinning or weaving, the men carving or mending their nets. Boys and girls teased each other with songs that once formed part of elaborate wedding rites. Some poems retained a distant association with a particular festival and were performed when neighbouring groups met to celebrate the festival.

At the time when most of this poetry was collected, singers usually performed the poems from memory. Although there were still individual singers in the nineteenth century whose performance was widely recognized by Karelian and Ingrian communities for its brilliance, the era of the poet-singer who consciously improvised, created or re-created materials in the Kalevala style, extending the common stock of poems, is thought to have ended in the fifteenth century in Finland and by the seventeenth century in most other parts of the Baltic–Finnish area.

In seeking to understand the work of successive generations of anonymous creative poet-singers, the term 'folk' is deceptive. We have before us fragments of the work of men and women who in other parts of Europe could have risen to prominence as poets and authors in the high tradition. Such were the demands of handling the Kalevala metre that only people of special talent could excel in its practice. Very little will ever be known about the personalities of the great poet-singers to whom we owe the surviving stock of material; indeed, frustratingly little is known even of the outstanding nineteenth-century singers. A few attacted particular attention on account of their unusual skills and prodigious memories. But after being fêted for short periods of their lives, commemorated by painters and sculptors, they soon slipped back into their own backwoods communities leaving only their poems to posterity. Even less is known about the thousands of informants who provided the bulk of the material housed in the vast archival collections of oral poetry in Finland, Russia and Estonia; 'singer unknown' is the recurrent designation in source indexes.

Against this background it is possible to offer no more than certain careful generalizations about the final, nineteenth-century phase of the Kalevala-poetry tradition. Men tended to sing heroic poetry, while women favoured lyric, legends and ballads. Heroic epic survived most powerfully in the northern parts of Archangel Karelia, where the great singers customarily combined stories of the traditional heroes to produce long narrative sequences (a technique adopted by Lönnrot in compiling his *Kalevala*). Such a performance was vividly described by Lönnrot himself in 1834: 'Frequently, when several singers were present at a festival, a singing contest would be held, and friends and acquaintances would lay bets on who would win. Arhippa Perttunen said that the people of his village often persuaded him to take part in contests and he could not remember ever being beaten.' On these occasions the first contestant sang a poem, after which the other contestant had to sing a poem about the same theme and of about equal length; they continued in this way until one of the singers had exhausted his stock of poems. 'If the singers performed badly,' Lönnrot continued, 'the audience would laugh at their struggles to have the last word. Such a contest is like a squabble between two hens: the one who clucks longer claims to have won.' When the singers were more skilful, the contest would continue until one of them fell asleep from exhaustion.

Further south different social systems led to different emphases. In the Ladoga Karelia region, the tradition was cultivated for the most part by the womenfolk. Social life in the extended Karelian family dominates the surviving poetry, producing a wide variety of work songs, miniature family sagas, and powerful, subjective lyric. The following example, which spread to many parts of the Baltic–Finnish area (and was first published in English in 1802), retains its power to move us even today:

If the one I know came now
the one I've seen were in sight
I'd go a mile to meet him
by boat across the water
upon skis through the backwoods
lifting up the fence
unlatching the gate:
I would tear brushwood fences
iron fences I'd bring down.

> I would grasp him by the hand
> though a snake were in his palm
> I'd throw myself on his neck
> though death were upon his neck
> I'd snatch a kiss from his mouth
> though his mouth bled from a wolf
> and to his side I would go
> though his side were all bloody.
> (Trs. Keith Bosley)

Further south, in Ingria, the efforts of serfdom and other aspects of Russian life are reflected in the themes and tenor of the poems. There, too, Kalevala poetry was almost wholly cultivated by women, but it is characterized by an improvisatory style which draws on traditional stock passages as allusive symbols to convey themes which are often meaningless to anyone not present at the moment of performance:

> Where had my bird gone
> my favourite bird?
> 'She got iron boots
> a crutch for a third.'
> She went in search of the bird
> She travelled a little way
> walked a short distance.
> Listened: heard a hum.
> Looked: Katti at the roadside.
> She was weaving cloth
> a girl was holding the reed
> the goose there winding.
> FFPE 133:27–56

Kalevala poetry

The 22,795 lines of the 1849 *Kalevala* represent only a small part of the oral poetry in the Kalevala metre saved by collectors before the old style of singing died out. Only estimates can be made of the amount of surviving material. Some 1,270,000 lines of the Kalevala poetry housed in the archives of the Finnish Literature Society have been published in the 33-volume *Suomen kansan vanhat runot* ('Ancient poems of the Finnish people', Helsinki, 1908–48); half as much again remains unpublished in the Society's archives. Large archival collections also exist in the Estonian Academy of Sciences and in the Petrozavodsk branch of the Soviet Academy of Sciences.

Examination of this material in the light of facts and assumptions about the ancient history of the Baltic–Finnish area advanced by experts from many fields, from archaeology to linguistics and literature, allows certain tentative hypotheses to be made about the nature and function of Kalevala poetry some two-and-a-half millennia or more ago, and about the course of its subsequent evolution. To go back two-and-a-half millennia is to establish an arbitrary but convenient starting point. Comparative evidence suggests that Kalevala poetry already existed then as a specific art form common to the ancestors of the Baltic–Finnish peoples; certain metrical features may indeed date from an earlier period before the language of the ancestors of the Baltic–Finns had completely separated from an even older form of Finno–Ugrian language. Moreover, the corpus of motifs and themes assumed to have made up the common stock of Kalevala poetry two-and-a-half millennia ago already comprised items known in widely separate parts of the world. Whether these universals can be accounted for by transmission from other areas or by creation in more than one area where similar conditions prevailed, or by something of each, will never be known. It is clear, however, that even in this early period Kalevala poetry had already assimilated tradition and poetry from neighbouring tribes of different background and origin. Similarity of Baltic–Finnish themes with those in Balt oral poetry leaves no doubt of the importance of contacts with ancient Balts in shaping the material which made up the common stock (it is curious to note, for example, that the Baltic–Finnish *kantele* and the names of several god–figures derive from ancient Balt words).

It may also be assumed that at this time numerous ritual activities – such as calendar rites, particularly those connected with the fertility of man, beast and the earth – were accompanied by the performance of Kalevala poetry. Acts beset by danger or which exposed man to circumstances over which he had no control, such as hunting, particularly of the bear, or the evocation of supernatural forces to effect cures or to ward off disease, all required the performance of appropriate poems. Rites of passage were accompanied by elaborate and often dramatic ritual; in the case of marriage and death these evolved into extended performances lasting many days.

When did singers begin to perform this poetry purely for its artistic or entertainment value? These latter functions may long have existed in some measure side by side with a ritual function, the emphasis shifting between the two functions, changing in step with man's growing understanding of the conditions governing his environment; as a result, events and characters in ritual poetry were gradually adapted for new poems and shaped into the adventures and acts of heroes and, later, of ordinary men and women. Thus the common stock of epic, lyric and magic poems grew as they were created, re-created, and combined in ever-increasing configurations from one generation to the next.

Myth poems

Baltic–Finnish epic poetry of the type recorded by Lönnrot and his successors can be divided into four main types. Myth poetry describes acts of creation at the beginning of time, the creation of the world and of human, animal and plant life (cf. Runos I, II, VI). This is probably the oldest stratum of Kalevala poetry; it is also the stratum in which universal features are most common. Baltic–Finnish poems about the origin of the celestial bodies and the earth from an egg are part of a tradition known from the Eastern Mediterranean to the Pacific; another belief attributing the forging of the heavens to a smith, Ilmarinen, also has its counterpart in many parts of the world. The shaping of the primeval seabed by the drifting, new-born god Väinämöinen recalls the performance of the same tasks by a boar in an Indian myth. Similarly the Baltic–Finnish myth of how fire was brought to man by animals can be compared with myths recorded in Bengal and in North-West America. The Baltic–Finns' 'world tree' myth is also known over the same area as myths about the egg-origin of the world. Tales of the primeval bear who comes down from the heavens, its life and death on earth and its return to its father in the heavens are known in most parts of the far North (cf. Runo XLVI). The two predominant characters in this early Baltic–Finnish poetry are Väinämöinen and the smith Ilmarinen. Their origins are obscure. They may have been gods of water and land respectively; in the surviving material from this early period their roles are variously those of gods and culture heroes. The milieu in which they move is a misty North Land peopled by featureless god-like beings who exist in their acts rather than as personalities.

Magic and Shaman poems

The second phase in the evolution of Baltic–Finnish epic comprises in large measure magic and shaman poetry; some scholars date this phase to the centuries immediately before the birth of Christ through to AD 500–600. The evidence of vocabulary borrowings by the Baltic–Finnish languages shows this to have been a time of contacts with ancient East Germanic and Scandinavian tribes from whom the Baltic–Finns borrowed numerous technical concepts (e.g. plough, spear, sword, gold, iron, trade) and adopted the organization of society (e.g. power, king, to govern, to judge). Evidence of early Scandinavian contacts is also present in motifs and themes about journeys and conflict. In the poetry from this second phase the milieu becomes unmistakably North European: forested, close to water, inhabited by small communities whose heroes struggle for brides and other possessions. The universe becomes more ordered. The god-heroes Väinämöinen and Ilmarinen are reduced in scale to become shamans and tribal leaders; they are joined by other characters – Lemminkäinen, a young, reckless, tempestuous shaman (cf. Runos XI–XV, XXVI–XXVII), and Joukahainen, a feeble aspiring shaman whose hubris brings about his downfall (cf. Runo III).

Women also acquire a more prominent role as mothers, wives, lovers, servants, who not infrequently outsmart their rumbustious menfolk. Outstanding among the women is Louhi, Mistress of Pohjola (cf. Runo VII), the land to the north of the homes of Väinämöinen, Ilmarinen and Lemminkäinen (a land to which Lönnrot gave the name 'Kalevala'). When Louhi's daughter is sought in marriage by the heroes from the south, Louhi demands as the bride-price the manufacture of the *sampo*, an object that brings its possessor everlasting wealth. Although Ilmarinen succeeds in forging the *sampo* and later marries Louhi's daughter, she is soon lost (cf. Runos X, XVI–XX, XXVI–XXVIII). When Väinämöinen, Ilmarinen and Lemminkäinen try to take back the *sampo*, a bitter struggle ensues between Louhi, transformed into an avenging flying monster, and the fleeing men of the south. As they fight the *sampo* is smashed to pieces and lost at sea (cf. Runos XXXIX–XLIII).

The poems which took shape during the second phase of development provide some insight into how the ancient Finns and their Baltic–Finnish neighbours understood the world around them. A division of the universe into three parts can be discerned. There are hints of a more clearly understood upper world or heaven indicated by references to two supreme deities, *Ukko* and *Jumala*. The former is a typical thunder god; although the character of the latter is less clearly defined in surviving poems, his importance is demonstrated by the fact that the early Christian missionaries were later to adopt his name for the Christian God.

Natural phenomena in the world of the living were governed by animistic powers. Man shared his world with a host of unseen spirit forces to which he attributed the functioning of all natural phenomena for which he lacked empirical knowledge. The spirit forces (*haltijat*, female *haltijattaret*) were perceived in hierarchies and had to be propitiated through ritual acts. The most important spirits were personified (e.g. Ahti, master of the waters, Tapio, master of the forests), while the lesser spirits were denoted by the name of the object or phenomenon they were thought to govern.

Also close at hand was the third part of the universe, Tuonela, the Otherworld, where Tuoni ruled over the spirits of the dead. The spirits, especially those of one's own ancestors, had to be treated with special reverence and celebrated at appropriate anniversaries, For, as possessors of the knowledge essential to the effective working of magic, the spirits were able to influence the life of mortal man, even intervening in the acts of the *haltijat*. Communication between the living and the dead was the task of the shaman. Contact with the Otherworld was thought to occur after the shaman had fallen into a trance, often induced by dance and rhythmic chanting, enabling his soul to leave his body and cross the Otherworld River to Tuonela. The poetry of this period illuminates how the shaman's soul journeyed to the Otherworld with vivid descriptions of the dangers as 'iron-clawed, iron-fingered' daughters of the Master of Tuonela:

> . . . treated the man as man
> the hero like a hero:
> they gave him food, gave him drink –
>   some serpent-venom
>   and some lizard heads.
> They even laid him to rest
>   on a bed of silk
> which was of serpent-venom.
> Then the old Väinämöini,
>   felt his doom coming,
> his day of distress dawning . . .
>   FFPE 30:80–90 (cf. Runos XVI,
>   XVII, XXV)

Adventure poems

During the third phase in the evolution of Kalevala poetry –
approximately AD 600–1000 – the Baltic–Finns began to have contacts with the East Vikings and may indeed have taken part in some of
their expeditions. Themes and motifs familiar in the earlier Scandinavian sagas increase in number in the Baltic–Finnish materials.
Further localization occurs in the imagery and language of poetry.
The shamans take on the role of Viking warriors, journeys to the
Otherworld evolve into daring adventures on land and sea. The deeds
of the warriors are cast against a background that preserves a wealth of
ethnographic detail, from the description of duelling etiquette and the
ornamentation of a spearhead to boat design and sailing techniques.

The boisterous poetry of the Viking phase also brings into greater
prominence the male–female relationship. One of the outstanding
poems of this period, the stormy courtship and marriage of Ahti and
Kyllikki, depicts the conflict arising from the irreconcilability of the
wife's desire for a stable family life and the husband's irrepressible
longing for adventure at sea, mocking even the most intimate side of
married life. Ahti seizes on the merest rumour of an indiscretion by
Kyllikki as grounds for breaking his oath to forgo his roving ways,
and summons together the crew of his ship. His companion Teuri
responds with alacrity to Ahti's summons, leaving his newly-wedded
wife on her bed as he rushes out to the waiting boat:

> The nipple's still unfingered
> the buttocks unwhipped
> the loins untickled.
> FFPE 40:357 (cf. Runos XI, XII)

As the corpus of poetry was augmented through the composition of
new poems and the re-creation of older material, syncretism – the
combining of material from different phases to create new poems
– becomes increasingly important. This can be seen by comparing
the Lemminkäinen shaman poems of the second phase with the
Kaukamoinen Viking of the third phase. The story of how Lemminkäinen, the precocious shaman, is punished by death for going
uninvited to the revels of the gods became confused with the tale
of a Viking, Kaukamoinen, who attends a feast univited, insults his
host and kills him in a duel. Kaukamoinen seeks safety from his
enemy's folk by fleeing across the seas to the 'Island'. Ribald poems

about sexual abandon became associated with the adventures of Kaukamoinen, a rascally philanderer (cf. Runos XXVII, XXVIII) and in successive re-creations of his adventures became an integral part of the Kaukamoinen cycle of poems. The effect of syncretism is apparent in later re-creations of some Lemminkäinen poems, in which the two shamans' duel of spells acquires a new ending: Lemminkäinen defeats his opponent and flees to the Island, where it is he who engages in Herculean sexual adventures. In other versions of the poem, Kaukamoinen plays the shaman's role. Lönnrot, following the example of his informants, takes the syncretic process even further, merging the Lemminkäinen and Kaukamoinen poems and incorporating fragments of several others to create the wholly new composite Lemminkäinen of the *Kalevala*.

Poems of the Christian period

The Viking adventure period overlaps with the poetry of the period of approximately 900–1450 AD, the fourth development phase when the arrival and establishment of Christianity exerted a profound effect on the subject matter and function of Kalevala poetry. Although the Church of Rome was officially established in Finland as a result of the Crusade of King Eric Jedvardsson of Sweden in 1155, features of Christian teaching had been current in Finland several centuries earlier, in a period known as 'Barbarian Christianity'. Missionaries of the Greek Orthodox Church were also active in Finland long before King Eric's Crusade, as the Old Slavonic origin of the Finnish words for 'priest', 'cross' and 'pagan' indicates.

   In the early phases of the Christian influence, both during the 'Barbarian' period and after the official establishment of the Church in Finland in the twelfth century, the missionaries and priests did not hesitate to borrow the form and content of Kalevala poetry to communicate the new doctrine. Väinämöinen continues to visit the Otherworld in search of knowledge to work his magic but on his safe return, having overcome great dangers, he advises the abandonment of such practices:

> 'Do not, young men, go
> to Mana unless you're killed,
> to Tuonela unless dead.'
> Then the old Väinämöini
> drove off to church, resplendent
> above the other proud folk.
> FFPE 30:96–101 (cf. Runo XVI)

Greek Orthodox and Roman Catholic legends come together in the priests' long accounts of the life of the Messiah; local northern features are introduced to make the unfamiliar landscape of the Holy Land comprehensible. The cherry tree becomes a giant whortleberry; Mary skis over the winter snow to the stable in Nazareth. Even the Immaculate Conception assumes a new form because of the common belief that impregnation could be caused by eating a small object such as a berry. This early phase of established Christianity in Finland saw the translation into Kalevala poetry of the most popular legends of both the Eastern and Western Churches. The Kalevala verse form was also used to propagate a local legend about the life and martyr- dom of the patron saint of Finland, Bishop Henry (*d.*1156), hailing, according to legend, from England.

The strength of the old beliefs was not easily overcome. The need to employ the old poetry with all its pagan associations as a vehicle for conveying the new beliefs tells its own story. Frequently, the old pagan characters feature in the Christian priests' poems, either in an exemplary role or, later, to denote wicked or pitiable characters. In some poems Väinämöinen becomes a parallel figure to Herod as the symbol of all that is evil; Herod and Väinämöinen together, for example, stand in for the Emperor Maxentius as the tormentors of St Catherine of Alexandria. As the Christian priests grew in confidence they began to use the old poetry to denigrate ancient practices and heroes. One poem attacks the practice of fertility rites by suggesting that they make the 'forests wither' and that only Christian rites can restore them to life. An old ritual healing poem of magnificent imagery describing the slaughter of a great ox by a dwarf from the sea was parodied by a Christian priest in a new poem about a great pig. When Ukko, the supreme diety in the pagan hierarchy, approaches the rooting pig:

> with a golden club
> a copper hammer
> a silver mallet:
> the porker turned its snout round
> and gaped at its tail.
> Ukko fled up a spruce-tree
> other gods up other trees
> the little lords up pine-trees.
> FFPE 52:17–24 (cf. Runo XX)

Väinämöinen became the object of the Christian priests' sharpest abuse. They mocked him in the eyes of the people for his senility – a man who could not tell the difference between a fish and a miraculous young woman come to care for him in his old age (cf. Runo V). More bitterly, borrowing the French legend of St Goar, they accused him of hypocrisy and of concealing an evil past. When Väinämöinen condemns Mariatta's two-week-old fatherless son to death, the child accuses Väinämöinen of incest with his mother. The priest thereupon christened the child *Metsolan kuningas*, 'King of the Forest Land', while Väinämöinen sailed away for ever, in a 'copper-bottomed boat', to be swallowed up by the Maelstrom:

> plunged to the depths of the sea
> to the earth-mothers below
> up to the heavens above
> into the whirlpool's gullet.
> FFPE 57:28–31 (cf. Runo L)

Decay

For reasons explained above, Kalevala poetry began to lose its vigour as a creative form at the end of the Middle Ages. There is some evidence of works composed in the Kalevala metre during the sixteenth and seventeenth centuries – propaganda chronicles of wars between Russia and Sweden by Finnish and Karelian poets on opposite sides – although they lack the poetic quality and sensitivity of the poems of the earlier periods. The last substantial body of epic created in the Kalevala style appears to be a set of Ingrian plaints, probably composed in the eighteenth century and performed as the young men of the village were taken away as conscripts to the Russian army.

Lyric and spell poetry continued to be composed until more recently, giving us today a huge collection of material about the perception of daily life in the Baltic–Finnish area. Work and family poems recall the vicissitudes of life as a serf, or as a member of an extended Karelian family; subjective lyrical poems offer some insight into the tenor of daily life, its fears and hopes; fantasy poems acquaint us with the terror of the unknown world which one entered on leaving the security of the village; spells and the thousands of protective formulas which men and women concocted to protect themselves against the power of envious, malicious and demanding spirits bring home to us the uncertainty of every aspect of life and the lurking fear of death.

The making of the Kalevala

Within a short time of its publication in 1849 the *Kalevala* had come to the attention of the world outside Finland as a carefully constructed epic of major proportions which critics did not hesitate to rank alongside the *Iliad*, the *Poetic Edda* or the *Niebelungenlied*. In the circles in which Lönnrot moved, however, it was regarded as the final stage in the completion of an undertaking which had its roots in the 1820s and could not have been achieved without the support and efforts of many scholars and enthusiasts.

As a result of the collection of oral poetry that had begun very soon after the annexation of Finland by Russia in 1808–9, several short works about the nature and significance of the poems appeared in the following decade. By 1820, material had been collected in several of the more remote parts of Finland and also among the Finnish-speaking communities established in central Sweden by migrants from Savo in Eastern Finland in the sixteenth and seventeenth centuries. During the 1820s, as authentic material began to accumulate in increasing quantities, a debate about the poetics and significance of the traditional poetry began in scholarly circles at the university in Turku, Åbo Akademi, and in the columns of the newly established Finnish press. An important contribution to this debate was the publication in several parts of *Suomen kansan vanhoja runoja ynnä myös nykyisempiä lauluja* ('Some ancient poems of the Finnish people together with some more recent songs', 1822–31), collected and compiled by Zachris Topelius the elder (1781–1831), partly from published material and partly from poems sung to him by itinerant pedlars visiting Finland from villages in Archangel Karelia on the Russian side of the frontier. Topelius was quick to realize how much richer the pedlars' poems were in quality and substance than the sources that had hitherto been available; in the final volume of his collection he urged admirers of folk poetry to concentrate their attention henceforth on the vllages of Archangel Karelia.

Thus, when Lönnrot arrived in Turku in 1822 to begin his studies at the Akademi, there already existed a substantial corpus of material together with some critical thought about its significance. Lönnrot's interest in the study of traditional poetry was guided right from the beginning by Reinhold von Becker (1788–1858), a historian, journalist and publicist devoted to the Finnish national cause. Von Becker had himself already collected poems in the field and in 1820 had used them to reconstruct the character of Väinämöinen.

As Lönnrot acknowledged in the Preface to the 1849 *Kalevala*, it was to von Becker's reconstruction of Väinämöinen that he owed the idea of assembling oral poems into a longer work. Some years later, in 1827, Lönnrot chose Väinämöinen as the subject of the dissertation for his first degree, which he wrote under the supervision of von Becker. As Professor Magoun has demonstrated, 'The scale is microscopic, but in it one sees a kind of foetal *Kalevala*'. In the immediately following years Lönnrot established himself as a leading authority on oral poetry, and even his dissertation for the degree of doctor of medicine took as its subject Finnish folk medicine. In 1828, he had undertaken his first extended fieldwork in Finland and the following year saw the publication of the first of a series of four volumes, *Kantele*, in which he brought together poems from earlier published sources and those he had collected himself.

Lönnrot's pioneer work took place against a background of great change and upheaval in Finnish intellectual life. After the destruction of Åbo Akademi and much of Turku by fire in 1827, the teachers and students of the Akademi had moved in the following year to the new Alexander's University in Helsinki. Far from arresting the development of a national culture, the move to a new home gave it a new vigour and new directions. Shortly after the University in Helsinki had opened its doors, a group of intellectuals formed an informal discussion group which became known as the 'Saturday Society'. Its members, of whom Lönnrot was one, came from university and administration circles, and also included women. At the Society's regular meetings much time was devoted to the consideration of how to further national interests, particularly in education and culture

From these discussions emerged the idea of founding a learned society to further the creation of a national culture. Established in 1831, the Finnish Literature Society (Suomalaisen Kirjallisuuden Seura) decided at one of its first meetings to support Lönnrot's study of Kalevala poetry by providing him with the means to travel and write. With this support Lönnrot travelled to Archangel Karelia in 1832, returning there in each of the three following years.

Early in 1835 he completed a preliminary work, the so-called *Alku-Kalevala* ('Proto-Kalevala'), consisting of 5,052 lines arranged in sixteen poems. The principal themes of the definitive 1849 *Kalevala* are already present: the creation of the cosmos; the ransom of Väinämöinen from Pohjola; Lemminkäinen's adventures and death; the rivalry of Ilmarinen and Väinämöinen for the hand of the

daughter of Louhi, Mistress of Pohjola; Ilmarinen's wedding feast in
Pohjola; the tragic story of Kullervo; the theft of the *sampo* and the
ensuing struggle between the land of Kalevala and Pohjola; the origin
of the first *kantele*; the singing competition between the upstart
Joukahainen and Väinämöinen leading to the suicide of Joukahainen's sister, Aino, promised in ransom to Väinämöinen; and finally
the miraculous birth of a son to Marjatta and the banishment of
Väinämöinen.

When the first edition of the *Kalevala* (known as the *Old Kalevala*)
appeared later the same year, the difference was one of size (12,078
lines arranged in 32 poems) and emphasis. In structure, the *Old
Kalevala* differs little from the 1849 edition. The Joukahainen episode
and Aino's subsequent suicide were shifted from the final part of the
epic to the opening cycle of poems in order to emphasize the wife-
acquisition theme, a recurrent feature in Kalevala poetry. Apart from
the difference in length (22,795 lines arranged in 50 poems), however,
the 1849 *Kalevala* incorporates substantial changes in the selection
and arrangement of material used to convey each of the themes
outlined above. These changes reveal how confident Lönnrot had
grown in the command of his material. He now felt able to mould it for
a specific purpose – to reconstruct the heroic age of the Finns.

From the First to the Second Edition

The differences between the *Kalevala* of 1835 and the 1849 edition are
explained by various factors: the large increase in the quantity of
material available to Lönnrot, the reception of the *Old Kalevala* by
scholars and critics, particularly those abroad, and cultural and
political developments in Finland as the idea of a Finnish nation-state
took root in Helsinki and St Petersburg and its significance was
grasped.

Following the publication of the 1835 *Kalevala* Lönnrot had continued to collect oral poetry in the field, but his journeys now took
him in other directions, including Lapland and Olonets Karelia. As
interest among his contemporaries grew in the cultures of other
Finno–Ugrian peoples (all of whom, with the exception of the Hun-
garians, live in Russia), many scholars – no small number inspired by
Lönnrot's example – travelled east to collect oral poetry, especially in
Ladoga Karelia and Ingria, and made their material available to him.
Thus when he began to revise the 1835 *Kalevala* he had at his disposal
a much expanded corpus which included numerous poems belonging

to the genres of lyric and magic. So extensive was this new material that Lönnrot was able to incorporate it not only in the new edition of the *Kalevala* but also in a series of companion volumes. In 1840–41, he published 686 poems – lyric, work, festive and ceremonial – in the *Kanteletar* ('Spirit of the *Kantele*'). A collection of folk proverbs followed in 1842 and riddles in 1844; his magic poems had to wait until 1880 foi publication.

This new material was used in profusion in the 1849 *Kalevala*, and indeed some duplication with the contents of the companion volumes is noticeable. The collection of new material also led to the replacement of some of the poems in the 1835 edition by variants which Lönnrot believed more complete or historically more informative. The richness and abundance of the new material are especially obvious in passages describing the performance of spells, where Lönnrot always presents a prodigious selection of all the spells that he had collected for the magic act in question. Nowhere are the fruits of later collection more apparent than in Lönnrot's rendering of the wedding of Ilmarinen to the daughter of the Mistress of Pohjola (Runos XX–XXV): Ilmarinen and his bride seemingly fade out of the narrative as the reader shares Lönnrot's beguilement at the poetic beauty, the rich fantasy and fertile imagination of the oral accompaniment to each ritual phase of the extended East Finnish–Karelian rite of passage.

A comparison of the 1835 and 1849 editions of the *Kalevala* shows at once how much closer the contents of the earlier edition are to the poems as they were sung to Lönnrot in the field. Although in the 1849 edition Lönnrot reproduced most lines in the form in which he had collected them (hardly more than 600 lines were composed by Lönnrot himself), his arrangement of themes and ordering of individual lines in a narrative sequence frequently show considerable licence. In part this was a result of his own observations of the singers whose poems he had recorded. Seeing that some of the most skilful singers combined familiar material in a new narrative sequence at each performance, Lönnrot allowed himself the same freedom. In this he was also encouraged by contemporary theories about the compilation of the epics of classical Greek literature which suggested that 'Homer' was the collector and arranger of local myths and tales rather than their creator. Lönnrot adapted this technique in order to give the individual episodes of the *Kalevala* greater depth and internal coherence.

The two characters of the *Kalevala*, for example, the girl Aino and

the boy Kullervo, who take their own lives owe their fuller development to Lönnrot's bolder manipulation of his material. While the
individual lines which make up the *Aino* and *Kullervo* cycles were
collated from authentic material, neither cycle was ever sung in the
form presented by Lönnrot. The *Aino* cycle (Runos III–V) combines
material from two separate poem types: the Christian denigration of
the senile Väinämöinen (which Lönnrot also used for Runo L) and
lyrical epic poems performed by women (possibly in protest at
society's indifference to their own wishes in the choice of husband).
Even the girl's name – which at the height of the *fin-de-siècle*
Kalevala Romantic Movement became one of the most popular
Finnish forenames – was invented by Lönnrot. Similarly the *Kullervo*
cycle (Runos XXXI–XXXVI), which exerted an even greater influence on Finnish *fin-de-siècle* art and music, lacks a real counterpart in
authentic tradition. Kullervo is a composite character compiled from
ancient stories about an unnaturally strong child (the European
'strong John' motif), ballads of Germanic origin about a young robber
who unwittingly commits incest with his long-lost sister, and medieval fantasies about a soldier away at war. Incest plays no part in the
Kullervo story of the 1835 *Kalevala*; here the death of Ilmarinen's wife
through the acts of the superhuman child sets in train the bitter
rivalry between the land of Kalevala and Pohjola. While it retains this
function in the 1849 edition, Lönnrot has transformed Kullervo into a
hero comparable to Oedipus and Hamlet, and condemned by the
fates to destruction.

For the most part Lönnrot handled his oral poetry material with
great care and respect, following the example of the Archangel
Karelian singers as he brought variants together to form a coherent
story, allowing one variant to introduce another. His Väinämöinen
and Ilmarinen behave for the most part like their counterparts
in authentic poetry; their changing roles – god, shaman, Viking
– reflect the centuries of recomposition. Lönnrot's Lemminkäinen is a composite of several different characters, as described
above. Louhi and Kyllikki and other lesser female characters are
largely true to their counterparts in the various strata of authentic
tradition. Marjatta and her Christ-like child are based on two
separate stories in authentic tradition: the Holy Mother and Child
from poems about the Messiah and the early Christian legend of St
Goar.

Events and milieu – be they from myth or late Viking poetry –
are depicted with authentic material much as Lönnrot and his

contemporaries recorded them. To make the language of the texts comprehensible, Lönnrot standardized the many dialects in which the poems were sung, adopting an archaic style of Finnish suggestive of Karelian but purged of lexical and syntactical features unfamiliar to his readers (for many of whom Finnish itself was a linguistic challenge). Lönnrot did not imitate his informants' frequent disregard of repetition and parallellism devices which they used choosingly to vary the pace of the narrative or to create special effects; in Lönnrot's *Kalevala* these formulas are followed with an almost slavish reverence. If Lönnrot is to be criticized for his compilation technique, it is because he does not always apply it with complete regularity. Features from one poem are not always brought into line with features from another when the two are combined, allowing internal inconsistencies and occasional contradictions to enter the text, as the translator reminds us in his *Notes*.

Two other features of the *Kalevala* should be mentioned which are not typical of the authentic material on which it was based. Apart from the final poem of the 1849 *Kalevala*, the frequent allusions in authentic materials to Christian features are noticeably absent from Lönnrot's epic; where they do occur, it is because Lönnrot did not perceive them as Christian in character (e.g. *Kuippana*, Runo XXXII:493, whom Lönnrot treats as a pagan figure but is probably St Hubert). This 'paganization' is especially noticeable in spell material which in its original form is full of allusions to and evocations of the Christian saints and other legendary characters; workers of magic did not scorn the new, more powerful beliefs in their efforts to ensure the effectiveness of their spells and incantations.

The second untypical feature, not unconnected with the first, is the cultivation of 'Kalevala', a term occurring only occasionally in authentic Finnish epic tradition, where it refers to the land or home of Kaleva (a male name). According to West Finnish and Estonian tradition Kaleva was a powerful hero or giant; Lönnrot appears to have seized on this as further evidence of a heroic age in Finland's past: Hegel's *Heroenzeit*. Lönnrot and his contemporaries shared the view that without a heroic age there could be no national epic, and without that no real 'national spirit'.

For to understand Lönnrot's purpose in compiling the 1849 *Kalevala*, it has to be seen against the background of the emerging Finnish nation-state. Ever since Porthan's day, successive generations of nationalists had been seeking a historical past in which to root their national culture. They had speculated about the significance of references in the Scandinavian sagas to *Bjarmia* and in the Russian chronicles to *Perm*, a land said to be inhabited by people of great wealth, speaking neither Norse nor Russian, and whose god *Jomali* was worshipped in a temple richly ornamented in gold.

The attempt to identify that land as the ancient home of the Finns occupied several young nationalists of Lönnrot's generation. While Lönnrot was collecting and shaping his poems, others were studying the evidence of history, language and place-names in the search for the ancient homeland. In the early 1830s a Finnish historian, A.J. Sjögren (1794–1855), who had travelled for five years in Northern Finland and Russia, published the results of his explorations. He set out a theory of the migration of the ancestors of the Baltic–Finns from deep inside Russia and established to the satisfaction of himself and many contemporaries that a large expanse of Northern Russia, including the regions corresponding to *Bjarmia–Perm*, had been inhabited by their ancestors.

These ideas are present in several of Lönnrot's works. In the Foreword to his *Kalevala* Lönnrot explains how the poems had taken shape in 'ancient Permia', between the banks of the Dvina and the Gulf of Finland, and recorded the struggles between the two groups into which the Finnish inhabitants of the region were divided, the people of Kalevala in the south and those of Pohjola in the north. The poems, he argued, told how the people of Kalevala under the leadership of Väinämöinen, Ilmarinen and Lemminkäinen, towards the end of the first millennium after the birth of Christ, were freed once and for all from the obligation to pay tribute to the people of Pohjola. 'The unifying feature of the poems is their account of how Kalevala gradually grew in wealth to be like Pohjola and finally overcame it.' Thus Lönnrot offered to his countrymen in the *Kalevala* the chronicle of a heroic age that was to provide for Lönnrot's contemporaries an essential foundation-stone in the construction of a Finnish national culture and nation-state.

Yet the *Kalevala* possesses a lasting power to fascinate and inspire, long after its early purpose in the ethnogenesis of the Finns was achieved. Successive generations have enjoyed the *Kalevala* for its poetry and for the intrinsic interest of the tales it tells. Nowadays, as attention focuses on the nature and quality of oral tradition, not as evidence of a heroic past but for what it can reveal of pre-literate art, so the *Kalevala* has yet a new role to play by illuminating the process of how the fantasy and imagination of ordinary unlettered people came to shape the high culture of a later age, leaving behind great epic and lyric as their collective but anonymous memorial. While Lönnrot, a man of great modesty, would scarcely have relished the epithet of a latter-day Homer, which some have sought to force upon him as the author of *Kalevala*, he must surely stand as one of the last great 'singers of tales'.

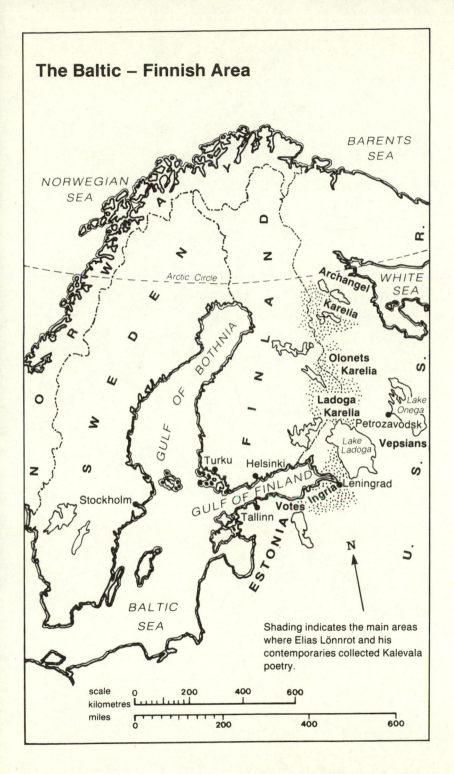

The Baltic – Finnish Area

BARENTS SEA

NORWEGIAN SEA

N O R W A Y

Arctic Circle

Archangel

Karelia

WHITE SEA

R.

S W E D E N

GULF OF BOTHNIA

F I N L A N D

Olonets Karelia

Ladoga Karelia

Lake Onega

Petrozavodsk

Vepsians

U. S. S. R.

Turku

Helsinki

Lake Ladoga

Leningrad

Stockholm

GULF OF FINLAND

Votes

Ingria

Tallinn

E S T O N I A

N

BALTIC SEA

Shading indicates the main areas where Elias Lönnrot and his contemporaries collected Kalevala poetry.

scale
kilometres
miles

0   200   400   600

0   200   400   600

I Birth of Väinämöinen

Prelude (1–102). The Virgin of the Air descends into the sea, where she is fertilized by the winds and waves and becomes the Water-Mother (103–76). A teal builds its nest on her knee, and lays eggs (177–212). The eggs fall from the nest and break, but the fragments form the earth, sky, sun, moon and clouds (213–44). The Water-Mother creates capes, bays, sea-shores, and the depths and shallows of the ocean (245–80). Väinämöinen is born from the Water-Mother, and is tossed about by the waves for a long time until he reaches the shore (281–344).

I am driven by my longing,
And my understanding urges
That I should commence my singing,
And begin my recitation.
I will sing the people's legends,
And the ballads of the nation.
To my mouth the words are flowing,
And the words are gently falling,
Quickly as my tongue can shape them,
And between my teeth emerging.   10

Dearest friend, and much-loved brother,
Best beloved of all companions!
Come and let us sing together,
Let us now begin our converse,
Since at length we meet together,
From two widely sundered regions.
Rarely can we meet together,
Rarely one can meet the other,
In these dismal Northern regions,
In the dreary land of Pohja.   20

Let us clasp our hands together,
Let us interlock our fingers;
Let us sing a cheerful measure,
Let us use our best endeavours,
While our dear ones hearken to us,
And our loved ones are instructed,
While the young are standing round us,
Of the rising generation,
Let them learn the words of magic,
And recall our songs and legends,   30
Of the belt of Väinämöinen,
Of the forge of Ilmarinen,
And of Kaukomieli's sword-point,
And of Joukahainen's crossbow:
Of the utmost bounds of Pohja,
And of Kalevala's wide heathlands.

These my father sang aforetime,
As he carved his hatchet's handle,
And my mother taught me likewise,
As she turned around her spindle,   40
When upon the floor, an infant,
At her knees she saw me tumbling,
As a helpless child, milk-bearded,
As a babe with mouth all milky.
Tales about the Sampo failed not,
Nor the magic spells of Louhi.
Old at length became the Sampo;
Louhi vanished with her magic;
Vipunen while singing perished;
Lemminkäinen in his follies.   50

There are many other legends;
Songs I learned of magic import;
Some beside the pathway gathered;
Others broken from the heather;
Others wrested from the bushes;
Others taken from the saplings,
Gathered from the springing verdure,
Or collected from the by-ways,
As I passed along as herd-boy,
As a child in cattle-pastures,   60

On the hillocks, rich in honey,
On the hills, for ever golden,
After Muurikki, the black one,
By the side of dappled Kimmo.

Then the Frost his songs recited,
And the rain its legends taught me;
Other songs the winds have wafted,
Or the ocean waves have drifted;
And their songs the birds have added,
And the magic spells the tree-tops.   70

In a ball I bound them tightly;
And arranged them in a bundle;
On my little sledge I laid it,
On my sleigh I laid the bundle;
Home upon the sledge I brought it,
Then into the barn conveyed it;
In the storehouse loft I placed it,
In a little box of copper.

In the cold my song was resting,
Long remained in darkness hidden.   80
I must draw the songs from Coldness,
From the Frost must I withdraw them,
Bring my box into the chamber,
On the bench-end lay the casket,
Underneath this noble gable,
Underneath this roof of beauty.
Shall I ope my box of legends,
And my chest where lays are treasured?
Is the ball to be unravelled,
And the bundle's knot unfastened?   90
Then I'll sing so grand a ballad,
That it wondrously shall echo,
While the rye-bread I am eating,
And the beer of barley drinking.
But though ale should not be brought me,
And though beer should not be offered,
I will sing, though dry my throttle,
Or will sing, with water only,
To enhance our evening's pleasure,

Celebrate the daylight's beauty,   100
Or the beauty of the daybreak,
When another day is dawning.

I have often heard related,
And have heard the song recited,
How the nights closed ever lonely,
And the days were shining lonely.
Only born was Väinämöinen,
And revealed the bard immortal,
Sprung from the divine Creatrix,
Born of Ilmatar, his mother.   110

Air's young daughter was a virgin,
Fairest daughter of Creation.
Long did she abide a virgin,
All the long days of her girlhood,
In the Air's own spacious mansions,
In those far extending regions.

Wearily the time passed ever,
And her life became a burden,
Dwelling evermore so lonely,
Always living as a maiden,   120
In the Air's own spacious mansions,
In those far-extending deserts.

After this the maid descending,
Sank upon the tossing billows,
On the open ocean's surface,
On the wide expanse of water.

Then a storm arose in fury,
From the East a mighty tempest,
And the sea was wildly foaming,
And the waves dashed ever higher.   130

Thus the tempest rocked the virgin,
And the billows drove the maiden,
O'er the ocean's azure surface,
On the crest of foaming billows,

Till the wind that blew around her,
And the sea woke life within her.

Then she bore her heavy burden,
And the pain it brought upon her,
Seven long centuries together,
Nine times longer than a lifetime.   140
Yet no child was fashioned from her,
And no offspring was perfected.

Thus she swam, the Water-Mother,
East she swam, and westward swam she,
Swam to north-west and to south-west,
And around in all directions,
In the sharpness of her torment,
In her body's fearful anguish;
Yet no child was fashioned from her,
And no offspring was perfected.   150

Then she fell to weeping gently,
And in words like these expressed her:
"O how wretched is my fortune,
Wandering thus, a child unhappy!
I have wandered far already,
And I dwell beneath the heaven,
By the tempest tossed for ever,
While the billows drive me onward,
O'er this wide expanse of water,
On the far-extending billows.   160

Better were it had I tarried,
Virgin in aërial regions,
Then I should not drift for ever,
As the Mother of the Waters.
Here my life is cold and dreary,
Every moment now is painful,
Ever tossing on the billows,
Ever floating on the water.

Ukko, thou of Gods the highest,
Ruler of the whole of heaven!   170

Hasten here, for thou art needed;
Hasten here at my entreaty.
Free the damsel from her burden,
And release her from her tortures.
Quickly haste, and yet more quickly,
Where I long for thee so sorely!"

Short the time that passed thereafter,
Scarce a moment had passed over,
Ere a beauteous teal came flying
Lightly hovering o'er the water,   180
Seeking for a spot to rest in,
Searching for a home to dwell in.

Eastward flew she, westward flew she,
Flew to north-west and to southward,
But the place she sought she found not,
Not a spot, however barren,
Where her nest she could establish,
Or a resting-place could light on.

Then she hovered, slowly moving,
And she pondered and reflected: 190
"If my nest in wind I 'stablish
Or should rest it on the billows,
Then the winds will overturn it,
Or the waves will drift it from me."

Then the Mother of the Waters,
Water-Mother, maid aërial,
From the waves her knee uplifted,
Raised her shoulder from the billows,
That the teal her nest might 'stablish,
And might find a peaceful dwelling.   200
Then the teal, the bird so beauteous,
Hovered slow, and gazed around her,
And she saw the knee uplifted
From the blue waves of the ocean,
And she thought she saw a hillock,
Freshly green with springing verdure.
There she flew, and hovered slowly,
Gently on the knee alighting;

And her nest she there established,
And she laid her eggs all golden, 210
Six gold eggs she laid within it,
And a seventh she laid of iron.

O'er her eggs the teal sat brooding,
And the knee grew warm beneath her;
And she sat one day, a second,
Brooded also on the third day;
Then the Mother of the Waters,
Water-Mother, maid aërial,
Felt it hot, and felt it hotter,
And she felt her skin was heated, 220
Till she thought her knee was burning,
And that all her veins were melting.
Then she jerked her knee with quickness,
And her limbs convulsive shaking,
Rolled the eggs into the water,
Down amid the waves of ocean;
And to splinters they were broken,
And to fragments they were shattered.

In the ooze they were not wasted,
Nor the fragments in the water, 230
But a wondrous change came o'er them,
And the fragments all grew lovely.
From the cracked egg's lower fragment,
Now the solid earth was fashioned,
From the cracked egg's upper fragment,
Rose the lofty arch of heaven,
From the yolk, the upper portion,
Now became the sun's bright lustre;
From the white, the upper portion,
Rose the moon that shines so brightly; 240
Whatso in the egg was mottled,
Now became the stars in heaven,
Whatso in the egg was blackish,
In the air as cloudlets floated.

Now the time passed quickly over,
And the years rolled quickly onward,

In the new sun's shining lustre,
In the new moon's softer beaming.
Still the Water-Mother floated,
Water-Mother, maid aërial,   250
Ever on the peaceful waters,
On the billows' foamy surface,
With the moving waves before her,
And the heaven serene behind her.

When the ninth year had passed over,
And the summer tenth was passing,
From the sea her head she lifted,
And her forehead she uplifted,
And she then began Creation,
And she brought the world to order,   260
On the open ocean's surface,
On the far extending waters.

Wheresoe'er her hand she pointed,
There she formed the jutting headlands;
Wheresoe'er her feet she rested,
There she formed the caves for fishes;
When she dived beneath the water,
There she formed the depths of ocean;
When towards the land she turned her,
There the level shores extended,   270
Where her feet to land extended,
Spots were formed for salmon-netting;
Where her head the land touched lightly,
There the curving bays extended.
Further from the land she floated,
And abode in open water,
And created rocks in ocean,
And the reefs that eyes behold not,
Where the ships are often shattered,   280
And the sailors' lives are ended.

Now the isles were formed already,
In the sea the rocks were planted;
Pillars of the sky established,
Lands and continents created;
Rocks engraved as though with figures,

And the hills were cleft with fissures.
Still unborn was Väinämöinen;
Still unborn, the bard immortal.

Väinämöinen, old and steadfast,
Rested in his mother's body 290
For the space of thirty summers,
And the sum of thirty winters,
Ever on the placid waters,
And upon the foaming billows.

So he pondered and reflected
How he could continue living
In a resting-place so gloomy,
In a dwelling far too narrow,
Where he could not see the moonlight,
Neither could behold the sunlight. 300

Then he spoke the words which follow,
And expressed his thoughts in this wise:
"Aid me Moon, and Sun release me,
And the Great Bear lend your counsel,
Through the portal that I know not,
Through the unaccustomed passage.
From the little nest that holds me,
From a dwelling-place so narrow!
To the land conduct the roamer,
To the open air conduct me, 310
To behold the moon in heaven,
And the splendour of the sunlight;
See the Great Bear's stars above me,
And the shining stars in heaven!"

When the moon no freedom gave him,
Neither did the sun release him,
Then he wearied of existence,
And his life became a burden.
Thereupon he moved the portal,
With his finger, fourth in number, 320
Opened quick the bony gateway,
With the toes upon his left foot,

With his nails beyond the threshold,
With his knees beyond the gateway.

Headlong in the water falling,
With his hands the waves repelling,
Thus the man remained in ocean,
And the hero on the billows.

In the sea five years he sojourned,
Waited five years, waited six years,   330
Seven years also, even eight years,
On the surface of the ocean,
By a nameless promontory,
Near a barren, treeless country.
On the land his knees he planted,
And upon his arms he rested,
Rose that he might view the moonbeams,
And enjoy the pleasant sunlight,
See the Great Bear's stars above him,
And the shining stars in heaven.   340

Thus was ancient Väinämöinen,
He, the ever famous minstrel
Born of the divine Creatrix,
Born of Ilmatar, his mother.

II Väinämöinen's sowing

Väinämöinen lands on a treeless country and directs Sampsa Pellervoinen to sow trees (1–42). At first the oak will not grow, but after
repeated sowings it springs up, overshadows the whole country, and
hides the sun and moon (43–110). A little man rises from the sea, who
fells the oak and permits the sun and moon to shine again (111–224).
Birds sing in the trees; herbs and flowers and berries grow on the
ground; only the barley will not spring up (225–56). Väinämöinen
finds some barleycorns in the sand on the shore, and fells the forest,
leaving only a birch-tree as a resting-place for the birds (257–64). The
eagle, grateful for this, strikes fire, and the felled trees are consumed
(265–84. Väinämöinen sows the barley, prays to Ukko for its increase,
and it grows and flourishes (285–378).

Then did Väinämöinen, rising,
Set his feet upon the surface
Of a sea-encircled island,
In a region bare of forest.

There he dwelt, while years passed over,
And his dwelling he established
On the silent, voiceless island,
In a barren, treeless country.

Then he pondered and reflected,
In his mind he turned it over: 10
"Who shall sow this barren country,
Thickly scattering seeds around him?"

Pellervoinen, earth-begotten,
Sampsa, youth of smallest stature,
Came to sow the barren country,
Thickly scattering seeds around him.

Down he stooped the seeds to scatter,
On the land and in the marshes,
Both in flat and sandy regions,
And in hard and rocky places.   20
On the hills he sowed the pine-trees,
On the knolls he sowed the fir-trees,
And in sandy places heather;
Leafy saplings in the valleys.

In the dales he sowed the birch-trees,
In the loose earth sowed the alders,
Where the ground was damp the cherries,
Likewise in the marshes, sallows.
Rowan-trees in holy places,
Willows in the fenny regions,   30
Juniper in stony districts,
Oaks upon the banks of rivers.

Now the trees sprang up and flourished,
And the saplings sprouted bravely.
With their bloom the firs were loaded,
And the pines their boughs extended.
In the dales the birch was sprouting,
In the loose earth rose the alders,
Where the ground was damp the cherries,
Juniper in stony districts,   40
Loaded with its lovely berries;
And the cherries likewise fruited.

Väinämöinen, old and steadfast,
Came to view the work in progress,
Where the land was sown by Sampsa,
And where Pellervoinen laboured:
While he saw the trees had flourished,
And the saplings sprouted bravely,
Yet had Jumala's tree, the oak-tree,
Not struck down its root and sprouted.   50

Therefore to its fate he left it,
Left it to enjoy its freedom,
And he waited three nights longer,
And as many days he waited.

Then he went and gazed around him,
When the week was quite completed.
Yet had Jumala's tree, the oak-tree,
Not struck down its root and sprouted.

Then he saw four lovely maidens;
Five, like brides, from water rising;   60
And they mowed the grassy meadow,
Down they cut the dewy herbage,
On the cloud-encompassed headland,
On the peaceful island's summit,
What they mowed, they raked together,
And in heaps the hay collected.

From the ocean rose up Tursas,
From the waves arose the hero,
And the heaps of hay he kindled,
And the flames arose in fury.   70
All was soon consumed to ashes,
Till the sparks were quite extinguished.

Then among the heaps of ashes,
In the dryness of the ashes,
There a tender germ he planted,
Tender germ, of oak an acorn
Whence the beauteous plant sprang upward,
And the sapling grew and flourished,
As from earth a strawberry rises,
And it forked in both directions.   80
Then the branches wide extended,
And the leaves were thickly scattered,
And the summit rose to heaven,
And its leaves in air expanded.

In their course the clouds it hindered,
And the driving clouds impeded,
And it hid the shining sunlight,
And the gleaming of the moonlight.

Then the aged Väinämöinen,
Pondered deeply and reflected: 90
"Is there none to fell the oak-tree,

And o'erthrow the tree majestic?
Sad is now the life of mortals,
And for fish to swim is dismal,
Since the air is void of sunlight,
And the gleaming of the moonlight."

But they could not find a hero,
Nowhere find a man so mighty,
Who could fell the giant oak-tree,
With its hundred spreading branches.   100

Then the aged Väinämöinen,
Spoke the very words which follow:
"Noble mother, who hast borne me,
Luonnotar, who me hast nurtured!
Send me powers from out the ocean:
(Numerous are the powers of ocean)
So that they may fell the oak-tree,
And destroy the tree so baneful,
That the sun may shine upon us,
And the pleasant moonlight glimmer."   110

Then a man arose from ocean,
From the waves a hero started;
Not the hugest of the hugest,
Nor the smallest of the smallest:
As a man's thumb was his stature,
Lofty as the span of woman.

Decked his head a helm of copper,
On his feet were boots of copper,
On his hands were copper gauntlets,
Gloves adorned with copper tracings;   120
Round his waist his belt was copper;
In his belt his axe was copper;
And the haft thereof was thumb-long,
And the blade thereof was nail-long.

Väinämöinen, old and steadfast,
Deeply pondered and reflected:
"While he seems a man in semblance,

And a hero in appearance,
Yet his height is but a thumb-length,
Scarce as lofty as an ox-hoof!"   130

Then he spoke the words which follow,
And expressed himself in this wise:
"Who are you, my little fellow,
Most contemptible of heroes,
Than a dead man scarcely stronger;
Or one perished scarcely fairer."

Then the puny man from ocean,
Hero of the floods, made answer:
"I'm a man as you behold me,
Small, but mighty water-hero,   140
I have come to fell the oak-tree,
And to splinter it to fragments."

Väinämöinen, old and steadfast,
Answered in the words which follow:
"You have hardly been created,
Neither made, nor so proportioned,
As to fell this mighty oak-tree,
Overthrow the tree stupendous."

Scarcely had the words been spoken,
While his gaze was fixed upon him,   150
When the man transformed before him,
And became a mighty hero.
While his feet the earth were stamping,
To the clouds his head he lifted,
To his knees his beard was flowing,
To his spurs his locks descended.
Fathom-wide his eyes were parted,
Fathom-wide his trousers measured;
Round his knee the girth was greater,
And around his hip 'twas doubled.   160
Then he sharpened keen the axe-blade,
Brought the polished blade to sharpness;
Six the stones on which he ground it,
Seven the stones on which he whet it.

Then the man stepped forward lightly,
Hastened on to do his mission;
Wide his trousers, and they fluttered
Round his legs as onward strode he,
And the first step taken, brought him
To the shore so soft and sandy;   170
With the second stride he landed
On the dun ground further inland,
And the third step brought him quickly,
Where the oak itself was rooted.

With his axe he smote the oak-tree,
With his sharpened blade he hewed it;
Once he smote it, twice he smote it,
And the third stroke wholly cleft it.
From the axe the flame was flashing,
Flame was bursting from the oak-tree,   180
As he strove to fell the oak-tree,
Overthrow the tree stupendous.

Thus the third blow was delivered,
And the oak-tree fell before him,
For the mighty tree was shattered,
And the hundred boughs had fallen,
And the trunk extended eastward,
And the summit to the north-west,
And the leaves were scattered southward,
And the branches to the northward.   190

He who took a branch from off it,
Took prosperity unceasing;
What was broken from the summit,
Gave unending skill in magic;
He who broke a leafy branchlet,
Gathered with it love unending.
What remained of fragments scattered,
Chips of wood, and broken splinters,
On the bright expanse of ocean,
On the far-extending billows,   200
In the breeze were gently rocking,
On the waves were lightly drifted,
Like the boats on ocean's surface,
Like the ships amid the sea-waves.

Northward drove the wind the fragments,
Where the little maid of Pohja,
Stood on beach, and washed her head-dress,
And she washed her clothes and rinsed them,
On the shingle by the ocean,
On a tongue of land projecting.   210

On the waves she saw the fragments,
Put them in her birch-bark wallet,
In her wallet took them homeward;
In the well-closed yard she stored them,
For the arrows of the sorcerer,
For the chase to furnish weapons.
When the oak at last had fallen,
And the evil tree was levelled,
Once again the sun shone brightly,
And the pleasant moonlight glimmered,   220
And the clouds extended widely,
And the rainbow spanned the heavens,
O'er the cloud-encompassed headland,
And the island's hazy summit.

Then the wastes were clothed with verdure,
And the woods grew up and flourished;
Leaves on trees and grass in meadows.
In the trees the birds were singing,
Loudly sang the cheery throstle;
In the tree-tops called the cuckoo.   230

Then the earth brought forth her berries;
Shone the fields with golden blossoms;
Herbs of every species flourished,
Plants and trees of all descriptions;
But the barley would not flourish,
Nor the precious seed would ripen.

Then the aged Väinämöinen,
Walked around, and deeply pondered,
By the blue waves' sandy margin,
On the mighty ocean's border,   240
And six grains of corn he found there,

Seven fine seeds of corn he found there,
On the borders of the ocean,
On the yielding sandy margin.
In a marten's skin he placed them,
From the leg of summer squirrel.

Then he went to sow the fallows;
On the ground the seeds to scatter,
Near to Kaleva's own fountain,
And upon the field of Osmo.   250

From a tree there chirped the titmouse:
"Osmo's barley will not flourish,
Nor will Kaleva's oats prosper,
While untilled remains the country,
And uncleared remains the forest,
Nor the fire has burned it over."

Väinämöinen, old and steadfast,
Ground his axe-blade edge to sharpness
And began to fell the forest,
Toiling hard to clear the country.   260
All the lovely trees he levelled,
Sparing but a single birch-tree,
That the birds might rest upon it,
And from thence might call the cuckoo.

In the sky there soared an eagle,
Of the birds of air the greatest,
And he came and gazed around him:
"Wherefore is the work unfinished,
And the birch-tree still unfallen?
Wherefore spare the beauteous birch-tree?"   270

Said the aged Väinämöinen,
"Therefore is the birch left standing,
That the birds may perch upon it;
And the birds of air may rest there."

Said the bird of air, the eagle,
"Very wisely hast thou acted,
Thus to leave the birch-tree standing
And the lovely tree unfallen,

That the birds may perch upon it,
And that I myself may rest there."   280

Then the bird of air struck fire,
And the flames rose up in brightness,
While the north wind fanned the forest,
And the north-east wind blew fiercely.
All the trees were burned to ashes,
Till the sparks were quite extinguished.

Then the aged Väinämöinen,
Took the six seeds from his satchel,
And he took the seven small kernels,
From the marten's skin he took them,   290
From the leg of summer squirrel,
From the leg of summer ermine.

Then he went to sow the country,
And to scatter seeds around him,
And he spoke the words which follow:
"Now I stoop the seeds to scatter,
As from the Creator's fingers,
From the hand of Him Almighty,
That the country may be fertile,
And the corn may grow and flourish.   300

Patroness of lowland country,
Old one of the plains; Earth-Mother!
Let the tender blade spring upward,
Let the earth support and cherish.
Might of earth will never fail us,
Never while the earth existeth,
When the Givers are propitious,
And Creation's daughters aid us.

Rise, O earth, from out thy slumber,
Field of the Creator, rouse thee,   310
Make the blade arise and flourish,
Let the stalks grow up and lengthen,
That the ears may grow by thousands,
Yet a hundredfold increasing,
By my ploughing and my sowing,
In return for all my labour!

Ukko, thou of Gods the highest,
Father, thou in heaven abiding,
Thou to whom the clouds are subject,
Of the scattered clouds the ruler!   320
All thy clouds do thou assemble,
In the light make clear thy counsel,
Send thou forth a cloud from eastward,
In the north-west let one gather,
Send thou others from the westward,
Let them drive along from southward,
Send the light rain forth from heaven,
Let the clouds distill with honey,
That the corn may sprout up strongly,
And the stalks may wave and rustle!"   330

Ukko, then, of Gods the highest,
Father of the highest heaven,
Heard, and all the clouds assembled,
In the light made clear his counsel,
And he sent a cloud from eastward,
In the north-west let one gather,
Others, too, he sent from westward,
Let them drive along from southward,
Linked them edge to edge together,
And he closed the rifts between them.   340
Then he sent the rain from heaven,
And the clouds distilled sweet honey,
That the corn might sprout up stronger,
And the stalks might wave and rustle.
Thus the sprouting germ was nourished,
And the rustling stalks grew upward,
From the soft earth of the cornfield,
Through the toil of Väinämöinen.

After this, two days passed over,
After two nights, after three nights,   350
When the week was full completed,
Väinämöinen, old and steadfast,
Wandered forth to see the progress;
How his ploughing and his sowing
And his labours had resulted.
There he found the barley growing,

And the ears were all six-cornered,
And the stalks were all three-knotted.

Then the aged Väinämöinen
Wandered on and gazed around him,   360
And the cuckoo, bird of springtime,
Came and saw the birch-tree growing:
"Wherefore is the birch left standing,
And unfelled the slender birch-tree?"

Said the aged Väinämöinen:
"Therefore is the birch left standing,
And unfelled the slender birch-tree,
As a perch for thee, O Cuckoo;
Whence the cuckoo's cry may echo.
From thy sand-hued throat cry sweetly,   370
With thy silver voice call loudly,
With thy tin-like voice cry clearly,
Call at morning, call at evening,
And at noontide call thou likewise,
To rejoice my plains surrounding,
That my woods may grow more cheerful,
That my coast may grow more wealthy,
And my region grow more fruitful!"

III Väinämöinen and Joukahainen

Väinämöinen increases in wisdom and composes songs (1–20). Joukahainen sets out to contend with him in wisdom; but as he cannot overcome him, he challenges him to a duel, whereupon Väinämöinen grows angry, and sinks him in a swamp by his magic songs (21–330). Joukahainen, in great distress, finally offers his sister Aino in marriage to Väinämöinen, who accepts the offer and releases him (331–476). Joukahainen returns home discomfited, and relates his misfortunes to his mother (477–524). The mother rejoices at the prospect of such an alliance, but the daughter laments and weeps (525–80).

Väinämöinen, old and steadfast
Passed the days of his existence
Where lie Väinölä's sweet meadows,
Kalevala's extended heathlands:
There he sang his songs of sweetness,
Sang his songs and proved his wisdom.

Day by day he sang unwearied,
Night by night discoursed unceasing,
Sang the songs of by-gone ages,
Hidden words of ancient wisdom,   10
Songs which all the children sing not,
All beyond men's comprehension,
In these ages of misfortune,
When the race is near its ending.

Far away the news was carried,
Far abroad was spread the tidings
Of the songs of Väinämöinen,
Of the wisdom of the hero;
In the south was spread the rumour;
Reached to Pohjola the tidings.   20

Here dwelt youthful Joukahainen,
He, the meagre youth of Lapland;
And, when visiting the village,
Wondrous tales he heard related,
How there dwelt another minstrel,
And that better songs were carolled,
Far in Väinölä's sweet meadows,
Kalevala's extended heathlands;
Better songs than he could compass;
Better than his father taught him.   30

This he heard with great displeasure,
And his heart was filled with envy
That the songs of Väinämöinen
Better than his own were reckoned.
Then he went to seek his mother;
Sought her out, the aged woman,
And declared that he would journey,
And was eager to betake him,
Unto Väinölä's far dwellings,
That he might contend with Väinö.   40

But his father straight forbade him,
Both his father and his mother,
Thence to Väinölä to journey,
That he might contend with Väinö:
"He will surely sing against you,
Sing against you, and will ban you,
Sink your mouth and head in snow-drifts,
And your hands in bitter tempest:
Till your hands and feet are stiffened,
And incapable of motion."   50

Said the youthful Joukahainen,
"Good the counsel of my father,
And my mother's counsel better;
Best of all my own opinion;
I will set myself against him,
And defy him in a contest,
I myself my songs will sing him,
I myself will speak my mantras;

Sing until the best of minstrels
Shall become the worst of singers.   60
Shoes of stone will I provide him,
Wooden trousers on his haunches;
On his breast a stony burden,
And a rock upon his shoulders;
Stony gloves his hands shall cover,
And his head a stony helmet."

Then he went his way unheeding,
Went his way, and fetched his gelding,
From whose mouth the fire was flashing,
'Neath whose legs the sparks were flying.   70
Then the fiery steed he harnessed,
To the golden sledge he yoked him,
In the sledge himself he mounted,
And upon the seat he sat him,
O'er the horse his whip he brandished,
With the beaded whip he smote him,
From the place the horse sprang quickly,
And he darted lightly forwards.

On he drove with thundering clatter,
As he drove a day, a second,   80
Driving also on the third day,
And at length upon the third day,
Came to Väinölä's sweet meadows,
Kalevala's extended heathlands.

Väinämöinen, old and steadfast,
He, the oldest of magicians,
As it chanced was driving onward,
Peacefully his course pursuing
On through Väinölä's sweet meadows,
Kalevala's extended heathlands.   90

Came the youthful Joukahainen
Driving on the road against him,
And the shafts were wedged together,
And the reins were all entangled,
And the collar jammed with collar,
And the runners dashed together.

Thus their progress was arrested,
Thus they halted and reflected;
Sweat dropped down upon the runners;
From the shafts the steam was rising.   100

Asked the aged Väinämöinen,
"Who are you, and what your lineage,
You who drive so reckless onward,
Utterly without reflection?
Broken are the horses' collars,
And the wooden runners likewise;
You have smashed my sledge to pieces,
Broke the sledge in which I travelled."

Then the youthful Joukahainen
Answered in the words which follow: 110
"I am youthful Joukahainen;
But yourself should also tell me,
What your race, and what your nation,
And from what vile stock you issue?"

Väinämöinen, old and steadfast,
Told his name without concealment,
And began to speak as follows:
"Youth, if you are Joukahainen,
You should move aside a little,
For remember, you are younger!"   120

But the youthful Joukahainen
Answered in the words which follow:
"Here of youthfulness we reck not;
Nought doth youth or age concern us,
He who highest stands in knowledge,
He whose wisdom is the greatest,
Let him keep the path before him,
And the other yield the passage.
If you are old Väinämöinen,
And the oldest of the minstrels,   130
Let us give ourselves to singing,
Let us now repeat our sayings,
That the one may teach the other,
And the one surpass the other!"

Väinämöinen, old and steadfast,
Answered in the words which follow:
"What can I myself accomplish
As a wise man or a singer?
I have passed my life in quiet,
Here among these very moorlands,   140
On the borders of my home-field
I have heard the cuckoo calling.
But apart from this at present,
I will ask you to inform me
What may be your greatest wisdom;
And the utmost of your knowledge?"

Said the youthful Joukahainen,
"Many things I know in fulness,
And I know with perfect clearness,
And my insight shows me plainly,   150
In the roof we find the smoke-hole,
And the fire is near the hearthstone.

Joyful life the seal is leading,
In the waves there sports the sea-dog,
And he feeds upon the salmon,
And the powans round about him.

Smooth the water loved by powans,
Smooth the surface, too, for salmon;
And in frost the pike is spawning,
Slimy fish in wintry weather.   160
Sluggish is the perch, the humpback,
In the depths it swims in autumn,
But it spawns in drought of summer,
Swimming slowly to the margin.

If this does not yet suffice you,
I am wise in other matters,
And of weighty things can tell you:
In the north they plough with reindeer,
In the south the mare is useful,
And the elk in furthest Lapland.   170

Trees I know on Pisa mountain,
Firs upon the rocks of Horna,
Tall the trees on Pisa mountain,
And the firs on rocks of Horna.

Three great waterfalls I know of,
And as many lakes extensive,
And as many lofty mountains,
Underneath the vault of heaven:
Hälläpyörä is in Häme,
Karjala has Kaatrakoski,   180
But they do not match the Vuoksi,
There where Imatra is rushing."

Said the aged Väinämöinen,
"Childish tales, and woman's wisdom,
But for bearded men unsuited,
And for married men unfitted.
Tell me words of deepest wisdom,
Tell me now of things eternal!"

Then the youthful Joukahainen
Answered in the words which follow: 190
"Well I know whence comes the titmouse,
That the titmouse is a birdie,
And a snake the hissing viper,
And the ruffe a fish in water.
And I know that hard is iron,
And that mud when black is pungent.
Painful, too, is boiling water,
And the heat of fire is hurtful,
Water is the oldest medicine,
Cataract's foam a magic potion;   200
The Creator's self a sorcerer,
Jumala the Great Magician.

From the rock springs forth the water,
And the fire from heaven descendeth,
And from ore we get the iron,
And in hills we find the copper.

Marshy country is the oldest,
And the first of trees the willow.
Pine-roots were the oldest houses,
And the earliest pots were stone ones."   210

Väinämöinen, old and steadfast,
Answered in the words which follow:
"Is there more that you can tell me,
Or is this the end of nonsense?"

Said the youthful Joukahainen,
"Many little things I wot of,
And the time I well remember
When 'twas I who ploughed the ocean,
Hollowed out the depths of ocean,
And I dug the caves for fishes,   220
And I sank the deep abysses,
When the lakes I first created,
And I heaped the hills together,
And the rocky mountains fashioned.

Then I stood with six great heroes,
I myself the seventh among them.
When the earth was first created,
And the air above expanded;
For the sky I fixed the pillars,
And I reared the arch of heaven,   230
To the moon assigned his journey,
Helped the sun upon his pathway,
To the Bear his place appointed,
And the stars in heaven I scattered."

Said the aged Väinämöinen,
"Ay, indeed, a shameless liar!
You at least were never present
When the ocean first was furrowed,
And the ocean depths were hollowed,
And the caves were dug for fishes,   240
And the deep abysses sunken,
And the lakes were first created,
When the hills were heaped together,
And the rocky mountains fashioned.

No one ever yet had seen you,
None had seen you, none had heard you,
When the earth was first created,
And the air above expanded,
When the posts of heaven were planted,
And the arch of heaven exalted,   250
When the moon was shown his pathway,
And the sun was taught to journey,
When the Bear was fixed in heaven,
And the stars in heaven were scattered."

But the youthful Joukahainen
Answered in the words which follow:
"If I fail in understanding,
I will seek it at the sword-point.
O thou aged Väinämöinen,
O thou very broad-mouthed minstrel,   260
Let us measure swords together,
Let the blade decide between us!"

Said the aged Väinämöinen,
"I have little cause to fret me
Either for your sword or wisdom,
For your sword-point or your judgment.
But, apart from this at present,
I will draw no sword upon you,
So contemptible a fellow,
And so pitiful a weakling."   270

Then the youthful Joukahainen
Shook his head, his mouth drawn crooked,
And he tossed his locks of blackness,
And he spoke the words which follow:

"He who shuns the sword's decision,
Nor betakes him to his sword-blade,
To a swine I soon will sing him,
To a snouted swine transform him.
Heroes I have thus o'erpowered,
Hither will I drive and thither.   280
And will pitch them on the dunghill,
Grunting in the cowshed corner."

Angry then was Väinämöinen,
Filled with wrath and indignation,
And himself commenced his singing,
And to speak his words of wisdom;
But he sang no childish ditties,
Children's songs and women's jesting,
But a song for bearded heroes,
Such as all the children sing not,   290
Nor a half the boys can master,
Nor a third can lovers compass,
In the days of dark misfortune,
When our life is near its ending.

Sang the aged Väinämöinen;
Lakes swelled up, and earth was shaken,
And the coppery mountains trembled,
And the mighty rocks resounded.
And the mountains clove asunder;
On the shore the stones were shivered.   300

Then he sang of Joukahainen,
Changed his runners into saplings,
And to willows changed the collar,
And the reins he turned to alder,
And he sang the sledge all gilded,
To the lake among the rushes,
And the whip, with beads embellished,
To a reed upon the water,
And the horse, with front white-spotted
To a stone beside the torrent.   310

Then he sang his sword, gold-hilted,
To a lightning-flash in heaven,
And his ornamented crossbow,
To a rainbow o'er the water,
And he sang his feathered arrows,
Into hawks that soar above him;
And his dog, with upturned muzzle,
Stands a stone in earth embedded.

From his head, his cap, by singing,
Next became a cloud above him,   320

From his hands, his gloves, by singing,
Next were changed to water-lilies,
And the blue coat he was wearing,
Floats as fleecy cloud in heaven,
And the handsome belt that girt him,
In the sky as stars he scattered.

As he sang, sank Joukahainen
Waist-deep in the swamp beneath him,
Hip-deep in the marshy meadow,
To his arm-pits in a quicksand.   330
Then indeed young Joukahainen
Knew at last, and comprehended;
And he knew his course was finished,
And his journey now was ended.
For in singing he was beaten,
By the aged Väinämöinen.

He would raise his foot to struggle,
But he could no longer lift it;
Then he tried to lift the other,
But as shod with stone he felt it.   340

Then the youthful Joukahainen
Felt the greatest pain and anguish,
And he fell in grievous trouble,
And he spoke the words which follow:
"O thou wisest Väinämöinen,
O thou oldest of magicians,
Speak thy words of magic backwards,
And reverse thy songs of magic.
Loose me from this place of terror,
And release me from my torment.   350
I will pay the highest ransom,
And the fixed reward will give thee!"

Said the aged Väinämöinen,
"What do you propose to give me,
If I turn my words of magic,
And reverse my songs of magic,
Loose you from this place of terror,
And release you from your torment?"

Said the youthful Joukahainen,
"I've two crossbows I could give you,   360
Ay, a pair of splendid crossbows,
One shoots forth with passing quickness,
Surely hits the mark the other.
If it please you, choose between them!"

Said the aged Väinämöinen,
"No, your bows I do not covet,
For the wretched bows I care not;
I myself have plenty of them.
All the walls are decked with crossbows,   370
All the pegs are hung with crossbows;
In the woods they wander hunting,
Nor a hero needs to span them."

Then the youthful Joukahainen
In the swamp he sank yet deeper.

Said the youthful Joukahainen,
"I have yet two boats to offer;
Splendid boats, as I can witness,
One is light, and fit for racing,
Heavy loads will bear the other;
If it please you, choose between them!"   380

Said the aged Väinämöinen,
"No, your boats I do not covet,
And I will not choose between them,
I myself have plenty of them.
All the staves are full already,
Every creek is crowded with them,
Boats to face the gale adapted,
Boats against the wind that travel."

Then the youthful Joukahainen,
In the swamp he sank yet deeper.   390

Said the youthful Joukahainen,
"I have still two noble stallions;
Ay, a pair of handsome horses;
One of these of matchless swiftness,

And the other best in harness.
If it please you, choose between them!"

Said the aged Väinämöinen,
"No, I do not want your horses;
Do not need your steeds, white-footed.
I myself have plenty of them.   400
Every stall has now its tenant,
Every stable's filled with horses,
With their backs like water shining;
Lakes of fat upon their haunches."

Then the youthful Joukahainen,
In the swamp he sank yet deeper.

Said the youthful Joukahainen,
"O thou aged Väinämöinen,
Speak thy words of magic backwards,
And reverse thy songs of magic.   410
I will give a golden helmet,
And a hat filled up with silver,
Which my father won in warfare,
Which he won in battle-struggle!"

Said the aged Väinämöinen,
"No, I do not want your silver,
And for gold, I only scorn it.
I myself have both in plenty.
Every store-room crammed with treasure,
Every chest is overflowing.   420
Gold as ancient as the moonlight,
Silver with the sun coeval."

Then the youthful Joukahainen
In the swamp he sank yet deeper.

Said the youthful Joukahainen,
"O thou aged Väinämöinen,
Loose me from this place of terror,
And release me from my torment.
All my stacks at home I'll give thee,
And my fields I likewise promise,   430

All to save my life I offer,
If you will accept my ransom!"

Said the aged Väinämöinen,
"No, your barns I do not covet,
And your fields are 'neath my notice.
I myself have plenty of them.
Fields are mine in all directions,
Stocks are reared on every fallow,
And my own fields please me better,
And my stacks of corn are finest."   440

Then the youthful Joukahainen
In the swamp he sank yet deeper.

Then the youthful Joukahainen,
Felt at length the greatest anguish,
Chin-deep in the swamp while sinking,
In the mud his beard was draggled,
In the moss his mouth was sunken,
And his teeth among the tree-roots.

Said the youthful Joukahainen,
"O thou wisest Väinämöinen,   450
O thou oldest of magicians,
Sing once more thy songs of magic,
Grant the life of one so wretched,
And release me from my prison.
In the stream my feet are sunken,
With the sand my eyes are smarting!

Speak thy words of magic backwards,
Break the spell that overwhelms me!
You shall have my sister Aino,
I will give my mother's daughter.   460
She shall dust your chamber for you,
Sweep the flooring with her besom,
Keep the milk-pots all in order;
And shall wash your garments for you.
Golden fabrics she shall weave you,
And shall bake you cakes of honey."

Then the aged Väinämöinen,
Heard his words, and grew full joyful,
Since to tend his age was promised
Joukahainen's lovely sister.   470

On the stone of joy he sat him,
On the stone of song he rested,
Sang an hour, and sang a second,
And again he sang a third time:
Thus reversed his words of magic,
And dissolved the spell completely.

Then the youthful Joukahainen
From the mud his chin uplifted,
And his beard he disentangled,
From the rock his steed led forward,   480
Drew his sledge from out the bushes,
From the reeds his whip unloosing.

Then upon his sledge he mounted,
And upon the seat he sat him,
And with gloomy thoughts he hastened,
With a heart all sad and doleful,
Homeward to his dearest mother,
Unto her, the aged woman.

On he drove with noise and tumult,
Home he drove in consternation,   490
And he broke the sledge to pieces,
At the door the shafts were broken.

Then the noise alarmed his mother,
And his father came and asked him,
"Recklessly the sledge was broken;
Did you break the shafts on purpose?
Wherefore do you drive so rashly,
And arrive at home so madly?"

Then the youthful Joukahainen
Could not keep his tears from flowing;   500
Sad he bowed his head in sorrow,

And his cap awry he shifted,
And his lips were dry and stiffened,
O'er his mouth his nose was drooping.

Then his mother came and asked him
Wherefore was he sunk in sorrow:
"Oh my son, why weep so sadly?
O my darling, why so troubled,
With thy lips so dry and stiffened,
O'er thy mouth thy nose thus drooping?"   510

Said the youthful Joukahainen,
"O my mother, who hast borne me,
There is cause for what has happened,
For the sorcerer has o'ercome me.
Cause enough have I for weeping,
And the sorcerer's brought me sorrow.
I myself must weep for ever,
And must pass my life in mourning,
For my very sister Aino,
She, my dearest mother's daughter,   520
I have pledged to Väinämöinen,
As the consort of the minstrel,
To support his feeble footsteps,
And to wait upon him always."

Joyous clapped her hands his mother,
Both her hands she rubbed together,
And she spoke the words which follow:
"Do not weep, my son, my dearest,
For thy tears are quite uncalled for.
Little cause have we to sorrow,   530
For the hope I long have cherished,
All my lifetime I have wished it,
And have hoped this high-born hero
Might akin to us be reckoned,
And the minstrel Väinämöinen
Might become my daughter's husband."

But when Joukahainen's sister
Heard, she wept in deepest sorrow,

Wept one day, and wept a second,
At the threshold ever weeping,   540
Wept in overwhelming sorrow,
In the sadness of her spirit.

Then her mother said consoling,
"Wherefore weep, my little Aino?
You have gained a valiant bridegroom,
And the home of one most noble,
Where you'll look from out the window,
Sitting on the bench and talking."

But her daughter heard and answered,
"Oh my mother, who hast borne me,   550
Therefore have I cause for weeping,
Weeping for the beauteous tresses,
Now my youthful head adorning,
And my hair so soft and glossy,
Which must now be wholly hidden,
While I still am young and blooming.

Then must I through lifetime sorrow
For the splendour of the sunlight,
And the moonbeam's charming lustre
And the glory of the heavens,   560
Which I leave, while still so youthful,
And as child must quite abandon,
I must leave my brother's work-room,
Just beyond my father's window."

Said the mother to the daughter,
To the girl the crone made answer,
"Cast away this foolish sorrow,
Cease your weeping, all uncalled for,
Little cause have you for sorrow,
Little cause for lamentation!   570
God's bright sun is ever shining
On the world in other regions,
Shines on other doors and windows
Than your father's or your brother's;
Berries grow on every mountain,

Strawberries on the plains are growing,
You can pluck them in your sorrow
Wheresoe'er your steps may lead you;
Not alone on father's acres,
Or upon your brother's clearings."   580

IV   The fate of Aino

Väinämöinen meets Aino in the woods and addresses her (1–20). Aino hurries home weeping, and informs her mother (21–116). Her mother forbids her to weep, and tells her to rejoice, and to adorn herself handsomely (117–88). Aino continues to weep, and declares that she will never take a very old man as her husband (189–254). She wanders sorrowfully into the wild woods, and reaches the banks of a strange unknown lake, where she goes to bathe, and is lost in the water (255–370). The animals commission the hare to carry the tidings of Aino's death to her home (371–434). Her mother weeps for her night and day (435–518).

Then the little maiden Aino,
Youthful Joukahainen's sister,
Went for besoms to the greenwood,
Sought for bath-whisks in the bushes;
One she gathered for her father,
And a second for her mother,
And she gathered yet another,
For her young and ruddy brother.

As she turned her footsteps homeward,
Pushing through the alder-bushes,   10
Came the aged Väinämöinen,
And he saw her in the thicket,
Finely clad among the herbage,
And he spoke the words which follow:

"Maiden, do not wear for others,
But for me alone, O maiden,
Round thy neck a beaded necklace,
And a cross upon thy bosom.
Plait for me thy beauteous tresses,
Bind thy hair with silken ribands!"   20

But the young maid gave him answer:
"Not for thee, and not for others,
Rests the cross upon my bosom,
And my hair is bound with ribands.
Nought I care for sea-borne raiment;
Wheaten bread I do not value.
I will walk in home-spun garments,
And with crusts will still my hunger,
In my dearest father's dwelling,
And beside my much-loved mother."   30

From her breast she took the crosslet,
Drew the rings from off her fingers,
From her neck the beaded necklace,
From her head the scarlet ribands.
Down upon the ground she threw them,
Scattered them among the bushes;

Then she hastened, ever weeping,
Loud lamenting, to the homestead.

At the window sat her father,
While he carved a hatchet-handle: 40
"Wherefore weepest thou, my daughter,
Young, and yet so full of sadness?"

"Cause enough have I for weeping,
Cause for weeping and lamenting.
Therefore weep I, dearest father,
Weep, and feel so full of sorrow.
From my breast I lost the crosslet,
From my belt I dropped the buckle,
From my breast my silver crosslet,
From my waist the copper girdle."   50

At the gate, her brother sitting,
For the sledge was shaping runners.
"Wherefore weepest thou, my sister,
Young, and yet so full of sorrow?"

"Cause enough have I for weeping,
Cause for weeping and lamenting.

Therefore do I weep, poor brother,
Weep, and feel so full of sorrow.
Rings I lost from off my fingers,
From my neck my beaded necklace,   60
And my finger-rings were golden,
And my necklace-beads were silver."

At the window sat her sister,
And she wove a golden girdle:
"Wherefore weepest thou, poor sister,
Young, and yet so full of sorrow?"

"Cause enough have I for weeping,
Cause for weeping and lamenting.
Therefore do I weep, poor sister,
Weep and feel so full or sorrow.   70
From my brow the gold has fallen,
From my hair I lost the silver,
Tore the blue bands from my temples,
From my head the scarlet braiding."

On the threshold of the storehouse,
Skimming milk, she found her mother.
"Wherefore weepest thou, my daughter,
Young, and yet so full of sorrow?"

"O my mother, who hast borne me,
O my mother, who hast nursed me,   80
Cause enough have I for anguish,
Cause enough for bitter sorrow.
Therefore do I weep, poor mother,
Therefore grieve I, O my mother,
To the wood I went for besoms,
Gathered bath-whisks from the bushes;
One I gathered for my father,
One I gathered for my mother,
And I gathered yet another,
For my young and ruddy brother.   90
As I turned my footsteps homeward,
And across the heath was tripping,
From the dell there called Osmoinen,
From the field cried Kalevainen,

'Do not wear, fair maid, for others,
But for me alone, poor maiden,
Round thy neck a beaded necklace,
And a cross upon thy bosom.
Plait for me thy beauteous tresses,
Braid thy hair with silken ribands!'   100

From my breast I took the crosslet,
From my neck the beaded necklace,
Tore the blue bands from my temples,
From my head the scarlet ribands,
Then upon the ground I threw them,
Scattered them among the bushes,
And I answered him in this wise:
'Not for thee, and not for others,
Rests my cross upon my bosom,
And my hair is bound with ribands.   110
Nought I care for sea-borne raiment,
Wheaten bread I do not value,
I will walk in home-spun garments,
And with crusts will still my hunger,
In my dearest father's dwelling,
And beside my much-loved mother.' "

And her mother answered thus wise,
Said the old crone to the maiden,
"Do not weep, my dearest daughter,
Do not grieve my youthful daughter,   120
Eat a whole year long fresh butter,
That your form may grow more rounded,
Eat thou pork the second season,
That your form may grow more charming,
And the third year eat thou cream-cakes,
That you may become more lovely.
Seek the storehouse on the mountain,
There the finest chamber open.
There are coffers piled on coffers,
Chests in heaps on chests are loaded,   130
Open then the finest coffer,
Raise the painted lid with clangour,
There you'll find six golden girdles,
Seven blue robes of finest texture,

Woven by the Moon's own daughter,
By the Sun's own daughter fashioned.

In the days when I was youthful,
In my youthful days of girlhood,
In the wood I sought for berries,
Gathered raspberries on the mountain,   140
Heard the moonlight's daughter weaving,
And the sunlight's daughter spinning,
There beside the wooded island,
On the borders of the greenwood.

Thereupon I softly neared them,
And beside them took my station,
And began to ask them gently,
In the words that I repeat you:
'Give you of your gold, O Kuutar,   150
And your silver give, Päivätär,
To the maiden poorly dowered,
To the child who now implores you!'

Then her gold did Kuutar give me,
And her silver gave Päivätär.
With the gold I decked my temples,
And adorned my head with silver,
Homeward like a flower I hastened,
Joyful, to my father's dwelling.

These I wore one day, a second,   160
Then upon the third day after
Took the gold from off my temples,
From my head removed the silver,
Took them to the mountain storehouse;
In the chest with care I laid them,
There until this day I left them,
And since then I have not seen them.

On thy brows bind silken ribands,
On thy temples gold adornments,
Round thy neck a beaded necklace,
On thy breast a golden crosslet.   170
Put thou on a shift of linen,

Of the finest flax that's woven,
Lay thou on a robe of woollen,
Bind it with a silken girdle,
Then the finest silken stockings,
And of shoes the very finest,
Then in plaits thy hair arranging,
Bind it up with silken ribands,
Slip the gold rings on thy fingers,
Deck thy wrists with golden bracelets!   180
After this return thou homewards
From thy visit to the storehouse,
As the joy of all thy kindred,
And of all thy race the fairest,
Like a floweret by the wayside,
Like a raspberry on the mountain,
Far more lovely than aforetime,
Fairer than in former seasons."

Thus the mother urged her counsel,
Thus she spoke unto her daughter,   190
But the daughter did not heed her,
Heeded not her mother's counsel.
From the house she wandered weeping,
From the homestead went in sorrow,
And she said the words which follow,
And expressed herself in this wise:
"What may be the joyous feelings,
And the thoughts of one rejoicing?
Such may be the joyous feelings,
And the thoughts of one rejoicing;   200
Like the dancing of the water
On the waves when gently swelling.
What do mournful thoughts resemble?
What the long-tailed duck may ponder?
Such may mournful thoughts resemble,
Thus the long-tailed duck may ponder,
As 'neath frozen snow embedded,
Water deep in well imprisoned.

Often now my life is clouded,
Often is my childhood troubled,   210
And my thoughts like withered herbage,

As I wander through the bushes,
Wandering on through grassy meadows,
Pushing through the tangled thickets,
And my thoughts are pitch for blackness
And my heart than soot not brighter.

Better fortune had befell me,
And it would have been more happy,
Had I not been born and nurtured,
And had never grown in stature,   220
Till I saw these days of sorrow,
And this joyless time o'ertook me,
Had I died in six nights only,
Or upon the eighth had perished.
Much I should not then have needed,
But a shroud a span-long only,
And of earth a tiny corner.
Little then had wept my mother,
Fewer tears had shed my father,
And my brother not a tearlet."   230

Thus she wept a day, a second,
And again her mother asked her,
"Wherefore dost thou weep, poor maiden,
Wherefore thus lament and sorrow?"

"Therefore weep I, hapless maiden,
Therefore do I weep for ever,
That yourself have pledged me, hapless,
And your daughter you have promised
Thus to be an old man's comfort,
As a solace to the old man,   240
To support his feeble footsteps,
And to wait upon him always.
Better were it had you sent me
Deeply down beneath the billows,
There to be the powan's sister,
And companion of the fishes.
In the lake 'tis surely better
There beneath the waves to sojourn,
There to be the powan's sister,
And companion of the fishes,   250

Than to be an old man's comfort,
To support his aged footsteps,
So that I can mend his stockings,
And may be a staff to prop him."

Then she sought the mountain storehouse,
And the inner room she entered;
And the finest chest she opened,
Raised the painted lid with clangour,
And she found six golden girdles,
Seven blue robes of finest texture,   260
And she robed her in the finest,
And completed her adornment.
Set the gold upon her temples,
On her hair the shining silver,
On her brow the sky-blue ribands,
On her head the bands of scarlet.

Then she wandered from the storehouse,
And across the fields she wandered,
Past the marshes, and the heathlands,
Through the shady, gloomy forests.   270
Thus she sang, as on she hastened,
Thus she spoke, as on she wandered:
"All my heart is filled with trouble;
On my head a stone is loaded.
But my trouble would not vex me,
And the weight would less oppress me,
If I perished, hapless maiden,
Ending thus my life of sorrow,
In the burden of my trouble,
In the sadness of my sorrow!   280

Now my time perchance approaches,
From this weary world to hasten,
Time to seek the world of Mana,
Time to Tuonela to hasten;
For my father will not mourn me,
Nor my mother will lament me,
Nor my sister's cheeks be moistened,
Nor my brother's eyes be tearful,
If I sank beneath the waters,

Sinking where the fish are sporting,   290
To the depths beneath the billows,
Down amid the oozy blackness."

On she went, one day, a second,
And at length, upon the third day,
Came she to a lake's broad margin,
To the bank, o'ergrown with rushes;
And she reached it in the night-time,
And she halted in the darkness.

In the evening wept the maiden,
Through the darksome night lamented,   300
On the rocks that fringed the margin,
Where a bay spread wide before her;
At the earliest dawn of morning,
As she gazed from off a headland,
Just beyond she saw three maidens,
Bathing there amid the waters,
Aino made the fourth among them,
And the fifth a slender sapling!

Then her shift she cast on willows,
And her dress upon the aspens,   310
On the open ground her stockings,
Threw her shoes upon the boulders,
On the sand her beads she scattered,
And her rings upon the shingle.

In the waves a rock was standing,
Brightly hued and golden shining;
And she swam and sought to reach it,
As a refuge in her trouble.

When at length she stood upon it,
And would rest upon the summit,   320
On the stone of many colours,
On the rock so smooth and shining,
In the waves it sank beneath her,
Sinking to the very bottom.
With the rock, the maiden Aino
Sank beneath the water's surface.

There the dove for ever vanished,
Thus the luckless maiden perished,
She herself exclaimed in dying,
When she felt that she was sinking: 330
"To the lake I went to bathe me,
And to swim upon its surface,
But, like tender dove, I vanished,
Like a bird by death o'ertaken.
Never may my dearest father,
Never while his life endureth,
Cast his net amid the waters,
In these waves, so wide extending!

To the shore I went to wash me,
To the lake I went to bathe me,   340
But, like tender dove, I vanished,
Like a bird by death o'ertaken;
Never may my dearest mother,
Never while her life endureth,
Fetch the water for her baking,
From the wide bay near her dwelling!

To the shore I went to wash me,
To the lake I went to bathe me,
But, like tender dove, I vanished,
Like a bird by death o'ertaken;   350
Never may my dearest brother,
Never while his life endureth,
Water here his prancing courser,
Here upon the broad lake's margin!

To the shore I went to wash me,
To the lake I went to bathe me,
But, like tender dove, I vanished,
Like a bird by death o'ertaken;   360
Never may my dearest sister,
Never while her life endureth,
Hither stay to wash her eyebrows,
On the bridge so near her dwelling.
In the lake the very water
Is as blood that leaves my veinlets;

Every fish that swims this water,
Is as flesh from off my body;
All the bushes on the margin
Are as ribs of me unhappy;
And the grass upon the margin
As my soiled and tangled tresses." 370

Thus the youthful maiden perished,
And the dove so lovely vanished.

Who shall now the tidings carry,
And repeat the mournful story,
At the dwelling of the maiden,
At the homestead of the fair one?

First the bear would take the tidings,
And repeat the mournful story;
But the bear conveyed no tidings,
For he strayed among the cattle. 380

Who shall now the tidings carry,
And repeat the mournful story,
At the dwelling of the maiden,
At the homestead of the fair one?

Then the wolf would take the message,
And repeat the mournful story;
But the wolf conveyed no tidings,
For among the sheep he wandered.

Who shall now the tidings carry,
And repeat the mournful story, 390
At the dwelling of the maiden,
At the homestead of the fair one?

Then the fox would take the message,
And repeat the mournful story;
But the fox conveyed no tidings,
For among the geese he wandered.

Who shall now the tidings carry,
And repeat the mournful story,

At the dwelling of the maiden,
At the homestead of the fair one?   400

'Twas the hare who took the tidings,
And conveyed the mournful story;
For the hare replied discreetly,
"I will not forget the message!"

Then the hare sprang quickly onward,
Sped the Long-ear with his story,
On his crooked legs he hastened,
With his cross-like mouth he hurried,
To the dwelling of the maiden,
To the homestead of the fair one.   410

Thus he hastened to the sauna,
And he crouched upon the threshold.
Full of maidens is the bath-house,
In their hands the bath-whisks holding:
"Scamp, come here; and shall we boil you,
Or, O Broad-eye, shall we roast you,
Either for the master's supper,
Or perchance the mistress' breakfast,
For the luncheon of the daughter,
Or perchance the son to dine on?"   420

Thereupon the hare responded,
And the Round-eye answered boldly,
"Would that Lempo might come hither
For the cooking in the kettle!
I am come to give you tidings,
And to bring a message to you:

Vanished from you is the fair one,
Perished has the tin-adorned one,
Sunken with her silver buckle,
Drowning with her belt of copper,   430
Diving in the muddy water,
To the depths below the billows,
There to be the powan's sister,
And companion of the fishes."

Then her mother fell to weeping,
And her bitter tears flowed freely,
And she loud lamented, speaking
In her grief the words which follow:
"Never, O unhappy mothers,
Never while your life endureth,   440
Never may you urge your daughters,
Or attempt to force your children
To a marriage that repels them,
Like myself, O wretched mother,
Urging vainly thus my daughter,
Thus my little dove I fostered!"

Thus the mother wept, lamenting,
And her bitter tears flowed freely
From her blue eyes in her sadness,
O'er her cheeks, so pale with sorrow.   450

After one tear flowed another,
And her bitter tears flowed freely
From her cheeks, so pale with sorrow,
To her breast, so sadly heaving.

After one tear flowed another,
And her bitter tears flowed freely
From her breast, so sadly heaving,
On the borders of her garments.

After one tear flowed another,
And her bitter tears flowed freely   460
From the borders of her garments
Down upon her scarlet stockings.

After one tear flowed another,
And her bitter tears flowed freely
Down from off her scarlet stockings
To her shoes, all gold-embroidered.

After one tear flowed another,
And her bitter tears flowed freely
From her shoes, all gold-embroidered,

On the ground where she was standing.   470
As they flowed, the ground they moistened,
And they swelled to streams of water.

On the ground the streams were flowing,
And became the source of rivers;
Thence arose three mighty rivers
From the tears of bitter weeping,
Which were ever ceaseless flowing
From the weeping mother's eyelids.

From each stream that thus was fashioned,
Rushed three waterfalls in fury,   480
And amid each cataract's flowing,
Three great rocks arose together,
And on every rocky summit
There arose a golden mountain,
And on every mountain summit
Up there sprang three beauteous birch-trees,
In the crown of every birch-tree,
Golden cuckoos three were perching.

All at once they called together,
And the first cried, "Sweetheart, sweetheart!"   490
And the second, "Lover, lover!"
And the third cried, "Gladness, gladness!"

He who cried out, "Sweetheart, sweetheart!"
Sang his song for three months running,
For the young and loveless maiden,
Resting now beneath the water.

He who cried out, "Lover, lover!"
Sang his song for six months running,
Sang to the unhappy suitor,
Who must sorrow through his lifetime.   500

He who cried out, "Gladness, gladness!"
Sang his song for all a lifetime;
Sang to the unhappy mother,
Who must daily weep for ever.

And the mother spoke as follows,
As she listened to the cuckoo:
"Never may a hapless mother
Listen to the cuckoo crying!
When I hear the cuckoo calling,
Heavy beats my heart within me.
From my eyes the tears are falling,
O'er my cheeks are waters rolling,
And the drops like peas are swelling,
Than the largest broad-beans larger.
By an ell my life is shortened,
By a span-length I am older,
And my strength has wholly failed me,
Since I heard the cuckoo calling."

510

V Väinämöinen's fishing

Väinämöinen fishes for Joukahainen's sister in the lake, and draws her into his boat in the form of a fish (1–72). He is about to cut her to pieces when she slips from his hand into the lake, and tells him who she is (73–133). Väinämöinen tries to persuade her to return to him, and then fishes for her, but in vain (134–63). He returns home disconsolate, and his dead mother advises him to woo the Maiden of Pohja (164–241).

Now the tidings were repeated,
And the news was widely rumoured,
How the youthful maid had perished,
And the fair one had departed.

Väinämöinen, old and steadfast,
Deeply sorrowed at the tidings;
Wept at evening, wept at morning,
Spent the livelong night in weeping,
For the fair one who had perished,
For the maiden who had slumbered,   10
In the muddy lake downsunken
To the depths below the billows.

Then he went, in sorrow sighing,
While his heart was filled with anguish,
To the blue lake's rocky margin,
And he spoke the words which follow:
"Tell me, Untamo, thou sleeper,
Tell me all thy dreams, O idler,
Where to find the realm of Ahto,
Where dwell Vellamo's fair maidens?"   20

Sleeper Untamo made answer,
And his dreams he thus repeated:
"There has Ahto fixed his country,
There dwell Vellamo's fair maidens,   30
Near the cloud-encompassed headland,
Near the ever-hazy island,
In the depths below the billows,
On the black ooze at the bottom.

There has Ahto fixed his country,
There dwell Vellamo's fair maidens,
Living in a narrow chamber,
In a little room abiding,
With the walls of varied marble,
In the depths beside the headland."

Then the aged Väinämöinen
Hastened to his little vessel,
And he scanned his fishing-tackle,
And his hooks with care inspected;
Put the tackle in his pocket,
And the barbed hooks in his wallet.   40
Through the waves his boat he ferried,
Making for the jutting headland,
To the cape, with clouds encompassed,
And the ever-hazy island.

Then he set about his fishing,
And he watched his angle closely,
And he held his hand-net ready,
Dropped his angle in the water,
And he fished, and tried his fortune,
While the rod of copper trembled,   50
And the thread of silver whistled,
And the golden line whirred loudly.

And at length one day it happened,
Very early in the morning,
On his hook a fish was hanging,
And a salmon-trout was captured.
In the boat he drew it quickly,
And upon the planks he cast it.

Then he scanned the fish, and turned it,
And he spoke the words which follow: 60
"'Tis a fish, among the fishes,
For I never saw its equal,
Smoother is it than a powan,
Than a salmon-trout more yellow,
Greyer than a pike I deem it,
For a female fish too finless,
For a male 'tis far too scaleless;
Has no tresses, like a maiden,
Nor, like water-nymphs, 'tis belted;
Nor is earless like a pigeon;   70
It resembles most a salmon,
Or a perch from deepest water."

In his waistband Väinämöinen
Bore a case-knife, silver-hafted,
And he drew the knife of sharpness,
Drew the case-knife silver-hafted,
And prepared to slit the salmon,
And to cut the fish to pieces,
Thought to eat it for his breakfast,
Or a snack to make his luncheon,   80
To provide him with a dinner,
And a plenteous supper likewise.

As he would have slit the salmon,
And would cut the fish to pieces,
Sprang the salmon in the water,
For the beauteous fish jumped sideways,
From the planking of the red boat,
From the boat of Väinämöinen.

Thereupon her head she lifted,
Raised her shoulders from the water,   90
On the fifth wave's watery hillock,
From the sixth high wave emerging,
Then her hands in air uplifted,
And displayed her left foot also,
When the seventh wave rose, upswelling,
And upon the ninth wave's summit.

Thereupon the fish addressed him,
And it spoke, and thus protested:
"O thou aged Väinämöinen!
Surely I have not come hither,   100
Like a salmon, to be slaughtered,
Or a fish, to cut to pieces,
Only to become your breakfast,
Or a snack to make your luncheon,
To provide you with a dinner,
And a plenteous supper likewise."

Said the aged Väinämöinen,
"Wherefore didst thou then come hither?"

"Therefore 'tis that I have sought thee,
In thine arm like dove to nestle,   110
By thy side to sit for ever,
On thy knee, as consort sitting,
To prepare the couch to rest thee,
And to smooth thy pillow for thee,
Keep thy little room in order,
And to sweep the flooring for thee,
In thy room to light the fire,
And to fan the flames up brightly,
There large loaves of bread to bake thee,
Cakes of honey to prepare thee,   120
And thy jug of beer to fill thee,
And thy dinner set before thee.

I am not a water-salmon,
Not a perch from deepest water;
But a young and lovely maiden,
Youthful Joukahainen's sister,
Whom thou all thy life hast longed for,
Whom thou hast so long desired.

O thou pitiful old creature,
Väinämöinen, void of wisdom,   130
Thou hadst not the wit to hold me,
Vellamo's young water-maiden,
Me, the darling child of Ahto!"

Said the aged Väinämöinen,
Head bowed down, and deeply grieving,
"Sister thou of Joukahainen,
Once again return, I pray thee!"

But she never more came near him,
Ne'er again throughout his lifetime;
For she turned away, and, diving,   140
Vanished from the water's surface
Down among the rocks so varied,
In a liver-coloured crevice.

Väinämöinen, old and steadfast,
Pondered deeply, and reflected,
What to do, and what was needful.
Quick he wove a net all silken,
And he drew it straight and crossways,
Through the reach, and then across it,
Drew it through the quiet waters,   150
Through the depths beloved by salmon,
And through Väinölä's deep waters,
And by Kalevala's sharp headlands,
Through the deep, dark watery caverns,
And the wide expanse of water,
And through Joukola's great rivers,
And across the bays of Lapland.

Other fish he caught in plenty,
All the fishes of the waters,
Only not the fish he sought for,   160
Which he kept in mind for ever,
Never Vellamo's fair maiden,
Not the dearest child of Ahto.

Then the aged Väinämöinen,
Bowed his head, lamenting deeply,
With his cap so sadly askew,
And he spoke the words which follow:
"O how grievous is my folly,
Weak am I in manly wisdom!
Once indeed was understanding,   170
Insight too, conferred upon me,

And my heart was great within me;
Such in former times my portion.
But in days that now are passing,
In the evil days upon me,
Now my strength with age is failing,
All my understanding weakens
And my insight has departed,
All my judgment is perverted.

She for whom long years I waited,   180
Whom for half my life I longed for,
Vellamo's fair water-maiden,
Youngest daughter of the surges,
Who should be my friend for ever,
And my wife throughout my lifetime,
Came and seized the bait I offered,
In my boat sprang unresisting;
But I knew not how to hold her,
To my home I could not take her,
But she plunged amid the waters,   190
Diving to the depths profoundest!"

Then he wandered on a little,
And he walked, in sadness sighing,
To his home direct returning,
And he spoke the words which follow:
"Once indeed the birds were singing,
And my joyous cuckoo hailed me,
Both at morning and at evening,
Likewise, too, in midday hours.
What has stilled their lively music,   200
And has hushed their charming voices?
Care has stilled their lively music,
Sorrow checked their cheerful voices,
Therefore do they sing no longer,
Neither at the sun's declining,
To rejoice me in the evening,
Nor to cheer me in the morning.

Now no more can I consider
How to shape my course of action,
How upon the earth to sojourn,   210

How throughout the world to travel.
Would my mother now were living,
And my aged mother waking!
She would surely tell me truly
How to best support my trouble,
That my grief may not o'erwhelm me,
And my sorrow may not crush me,
In these weary days of evil,
In this time of deep depression."

In her grave his mother wakened,   220
Answered from beneath the billows:
"Still thy mother lives and hears thee,
And thy aged mother wakens,
That she plainly may advise thee,
How to best support thy trouble,
That thy grief may not o'erwhelm thee,
And thy sorrow may not crush thee,
In these weary days of evil,
In these days of deep depression.
Seek thou out the maids of Pohja,   230
Where the daughters are more handsome,
And the maidens twice as lovely,
And are five or six times nimbler,
Not like lazy girls of Jouko,
Lapland's fat and sluggish daughters.

Thence a wife, O son, provide thee,
From the fairest maids of Pohja;
Choose a maid of fair complexion,
Lovely, too, in every feature,
One whose feet are always nimble,   240
Always active in her movements!"

VI Joukahainen's crossbow

Joukahainen cherishes hatred against Väinämöinen and lies in wait for him on his journey to Pohjola (1–78). He sees him riding past and shoots at him, but only kills his horse (79–182). Väinämöinen falls into the water and is driven out to sea by a tempest, while Joukahainen rejoices, because he thinks he has at last overcome Väinämöinen (183–234).

Väinämöinen, old and steadfast,
Now resolved upon a journey
To the cold and dreary regions
Of the gloomy land of Pohja.

Then he took his straw-hued stallion
Like a pea-stalk in his colour,
And the golden bit adjusted,
Bridle on his head of silver,
On his back himself he seated,
And he started on his journey;   10
And he trotted gently onward,
At an easy pace he journeyed,
Mounted on the straw-hued courser,
Like a pea-stalk in his colour.

Thus through Väinölä he journeyed,
Over Kalevala's wide heathlands,
And the horse made rapid progress,
Home behind, and journey shortened;
Then across the sea he journeyed,
O'er the far-extending billows,   20
With the horse's hoofs unwetted,
And his feet unsunk in water.

But the youthful Joukahainen,
He, the puny son of Lapland,
Long had cherished his resentment,
And had long indeed been envious
Of the aged Väinämöinen,
Of the ever-famous minstrel.

Then he wrought a mighty crossbow,
And a splendid bow he fashioned,   30
And he formed the bow of iron,
Overlaid the back with copper,
And with gold inlaid it also,
And with silver he adorned it.

Where did he obtain the bowstring?
Whence a cord to match the weapon?
Sinews from the elk of Hiisi,
And the hempen cord of Lempo.

Thus at length the bow was finished,
And the stock was quite completed,   40
And the bow was fair to gaze on,
And its value matched its beauty:
On its back a horse was standing,
On the stock a foal was running,
On the curve a sleeping woman,
At the catch a hare was couching.

Shafts of wood he likewise fashioned,
Every arrow triply feathered,
And the shafts were formed of oakwood,
And he made the heads of pinewood;   50
Thus the arrows were completed,
And he fixed the feathers on them,
From the swallows' plumage taken,
Likewise from the tails of sparrows.

After this, the points he sharpened,
And the arrow-points he poisoned,
In the black blood of the serpent,
In the blood of hissing adders.

Thus he made his arrows ready,
And his bow was fit for bending,   60
And he watched for Väinämöinen,
Waited for Suvantolainen,
Watched at morning, watched at evening,
Waited also through the noontide.

Long he watched for Väinämöinen,
Waited long, and wearied never,
Sitting gazing from the window,
Or behind the sheds he waited,
Sometimes lurking by the pathway,
Sometimes watching in the meadow,   70
On his back his well-filled quiver,
'Neath his arm his crossbow ready.

Then he waited further onwards,
Lurking near another building,
On the cape that juts out sharply,
Where the tongue of land curves outward,
Near a waterfall, all foaming,
Past the banks of sacred rivers.

And at length one day it happened,
Very early in the morning,   80
As he turned his eyes first westward,
And he turned his head then eastward
Something dark he spied on ocean,
Something blue upon the billows.
"Is a cloud in east arising,
Or the dawn of day appearing?"

In the east no cloud was rising,
Nor the dawn of day appearing.
'Twas the aged Väinämöinen,
'Twas the ever-famous minstrel,   90
Who to Pohjola was hastening,
As to Pimentola he journeyed,
Mounted on his straw-hued courser,
Like a pea-stalk in his colour.

Then the youthful Joukahainen,
He, the meagre son of Lapland,
Spanned in haste his mighty crossbow,
And he aimed the splendid weapon
At the head of·Väinämöinen,
Thus to kill Suvantolainen.   100

Then his mother came and asked him,
And the aged one inquired,
"Wherefore do you span your weapon,
Bending thus the iron crossbow?"

Then the youthful Joukahainen
Answered in the words which follow:
"Therefore do I span the weapon,
Bending thus the iron crossbow,
For the head of Väinämöinen,
Thus to kill Suvantolainen;   110
I will shoot old Väinämöinen,
Strike the ever-famous minstrel,
Through the heart, and through the liver,
'Twixt the shoulders I will shoot him."

But his mother straight forbade him,
And dissuaded him from shooting:
"Do not shoot at Väinämöinen,
Do not Kalevalainen slaughter.
Of a noble race is Väinö,
He's my sister's son, my nephew.   120

If you shoot at Väinämöinen,
And should Kalevalainen slaughter,
Gladness from the world will vanish,
And from earth will song be banished;
In the world is gladness better,
And on earth is song more cheerful,
Than to Manala if banished,
Or to Tuoni's darkest regions."

Then the youthful Joukahainen
Paused a moment and reflected,   130

And he pondered for an instant,
Though his hands to shoot were ready;
One would shoot, and one restrained him,
But his sinewy fingers forced him.

And at length these words he uttered,
And expressed his own decision:
"What if twice from earth in future
Every gladness should be banished?
Let all songs for ever vanish;
I will shoot my arrows, heedless!"   140

Then he spanned the mighty crossbow,
And he drew the bow of copper,
And against his left knee bent it,
Steady with his foot he held it,
Took an arrow from his quiver,
Chose a triple-feathered arrow,
Took the strongest of his arrows,
Chose the very best among them,
Then upon the groove he laid it,
On the hempen cord he fixed it.   150

Then his mighty bow he lifted,
And he placed it to his shoulder,
Ready now to shoot the arrow,
And to shoot at Väinämöinen.
And he spoke the words which follow:
"Do thou strike, O birchwood arrow,
Strike thou in the back, O pinewood.
Twang thy best, O hempen bowstring!
If my hand is leaning downward,
Let the arrow then strike higher,   160
If my hand is bending upward,
Let the arrow then strike downward!"

Quickly then he drew the trigger,
Shot the first among his arrows.
Far too high the shaft flew upward,
High above his head to skyward,
And it whizzed among the cloudlets,
Through the scattered clouds it wandered.

Thus he shot, in reckless fashion,
Shot the second of his arrows.   170
Far too low the shot flew downwards,
Deep in Mother Earth 'twas sunken;
Earth was almost sunk to Mana,
And the hills of sand were cloven.

Then he shot again, a third time,
And the third shaft, straighter flying,
In the blue elk's spleen was buried,
Under aged Väinämöinen.
Thus he shot the straw-hued courser,
Like a pea-stalk in his colour;   180
Through the flesh beneath his shoulder,
In the left side deep he pierced him.

Then the aged Väinämöinen
Plunged his fingers in the water,
With his hands the waves he parted,
Grasping at the foaming billows,
From the blue elk's back he tumbled,
From the steed of pea-stalk colour.

Then a mighty wind arising
Raised upon the sea a billow,   190
And it bore old Väinämöinen,
Swimming from the mainland further,
O'er the wide expanse of water,
Out into the open ocean.

Then the youthful Joukahainen
Uttered words of boastful triumph:
"Now thou ancient Väinämöinen,
Never while thy life endureth,
In the course of all thy lifetime,
While the golden moon is shining,   200
Walk in Väinölä's fair meadows,
Or on Kalevala's broad heathlands!

May you toss for six years running,
Seven long summers ever drifting,
Tossed about for over eight years,

On the wide expanse of water,
On the surface of the billows,
Drift for six years like a pine-tree,
And for seven years like a fir-tree,
And for eight years like a tree-stump!"   210

Then the house again he entered,
And at once his mother asked him,
"Have you shot at Väinämöinen?
Slaughtered Kaleva's famous offspring?"

Then the youthful Joukahainen
Answered in the words which follow:
"I have shot at Väinämöinen,
And have o'erthrown Kalevalainen,
Sent him swimming in the water,
Swept him out upon the billows,   220
On the restless waves of ocean
Where the waves are wildly tossing,
And the old man plunged his fingers
And his palms amid the waters,
Then upon his side he tumbled,
And upon his back he turned him,
Drifting o'er the waves of ocean,
Out upon the foaming billows."

But his mother made him answer:
"Very evil hast thou acted,   230
Thus to shoot at Väinämöinen,
And to o'erthrow Kalevalainen.
Of Suvantola the hero,
Kalevala's most famous hero!"

VII   Väinämöinen and Louhi

Väinämöinen swims for several days on the open sea (1–88). The eagle, grateful to him for having spared the birch-tree for him to rest on, when he was felling the trees, takes Väinämöinen on his wings, and carries him to the borders of Pohjola, where the Mistress of Pohjola takes him to her abode, and receives him hospitably (89–274). Väinämöinen desires to return to his own country, and the Mistress of Pohjola permits him to depart, and promises him her daughter in marriage if he will forge the *Sampo* in Pohjola (275–322). Väinämöinen promises that when he returns home he will send the smith Ilmarinen to forge the *Sampo*, and the Mistress of Pohjola gives him a horse and a sledge to convey him home (323–68).

Väinämöinen, old and steadfast,
Swam upon the open ocean,
Drifting like a fallen pine-tree,
Like a rotten branch of fir-tree,
During six days of the summer,
And for six nights in succession,
While the sea spread wide before him,
And the sky was clear above him.

Thus he swam for two nights longer,
And for two days long and dreary.   10
When the ninth night darkened round him,
And the eighth day had passed over,
Sudden anguish came upon him,
And his pain grew ever greater.
From his toes his nails were dropping,
And the joints from off his fingers.

Then the aged Väinämöinen
Spoke in words like those which follow:

"Woe to me, unhappy creature,
Overburdened with misfortune!   20
I have wandered from my country,
And my ancient home abandoned.
'Neath the open sky for ever,
Driven along in sun and moonlight,
Rocked about by winds for ever,
Tossed about by every billow,
On the wide expanse of water,
Out upon the open ocean,
Here I live a cold existence,
And 'tis painful thus to wallow,   30
Always tossing on the billows,
On the surface of the waters.

Now, alas, I know no longer
How to lead this life of sadness
In this everlasting trouble,
In an age when all is fleeting:
Shall I rear in wind a dwelling,
Build a house upon the waters?

If I rear in wind a dwelling,
Then the wind would not sustain it;   40
If I build a house on water,
Then the waves will drift it from me."

Came a bird from Lapland flying,
From the north-east came an eagle,
Not the largest of the eagles,
Nor was he among the smallest;
With one wing he swept the water,
To the sky was swung the other;
On the sea his tail he rested,
On the cliffs his beak he rattled.   50

Slowly back and forwards flying,
Turning all around, and gazing,
Soon he saw old Väinämöinen
On the blue waves of the ocean.
"What has brought you here, O hero,
Wandering through the waves of ocean?"

Väinämöinen, old and steadfast,
Answered in the words which follow:
"This has brought the man to ocean,
Plunged the hero in the sea-waves;   60
I would seek the maid of Pohja,
Woo the maiden of Pimentola.

On my journey swift I hastened,
On the ocean's watery surface,
Till about the time of daybreak,
Came I, after many mornings,
Where is Luotola's deep embayment,
Hard by Joukola's rapid river,
When my horse was shot beneath me,
By an arrow launched against me.   70

Thus I fell into the water,
In the waves I plunged my fingers,
And the wind impels me onward,
And the billows drift me forward.

Then there came a gale from north-west,
From the east a mighty tempest,
Far away the tempest drove me,
Swimming from the land still further;
Many days have I been floating,
Many days have I been swimming,   80
On this wide expanse of water,
Out upon the open ocean.
And I cannot now conjecture,
Cannot guess, nor e'en imagine,
How I finally shall perish,
And what death shall overtake me
Whether I shall die of hunger,
Or shall sink beneath the waters."

Said the bird of air, the eagle,
"Let thy heart be free from trouble;   90
Climb upon my back, and seat thee,
Standing up upon my wing-tips,
From the sea will I transport thee,
Wheresoever thou may'st fancy.

For the day I well remember,
And recall a happier season,
When fell Kaleva's green forest,
Cleared was Osmola's famed island,
But thou didst protect the birch-tree,
And the beauteous tree left'st standing,   100
That the birds might rest upon it,
And that I myself might sit there."

Then the aged Väinämöinen
Raised his head from out the water,
From the sea the man sprang upward,
From the waves the hero mounted,
On the eagle's wings he sat him,
On the wing-tips of the eagle.

Then the bird of air, the eagle,
Raised the aged Väinämöinen;   110
Through the path of wind he bore him,
And along the east-wind's pathway,
To the utmost bounds of Pohja,
Onwards to the misty Sariola,
There abandoned Väinämöinen,
Soared into the air, and left him.

There stood Väinämöinen weeping,
There stood weeping and lamenting,
On the borders of the ocean,
On a land whose name he knew not,   120
With a hundred wounds upon him,
By a thousand winds belaboured,
And his beard was much disordered,
And his hair was all entangled.

Thus he wept for two, and three nights,
For as many days stood weeping,
For the country round he knew not,
And no path could he discover,
Which perchance might lead him homeward,
Back to a familiar country,   130
To his own, his native country,
Where he passed his days aforetime.

But the little maid of Pohja,
Fair-haired damsel of the household,
With the sun had made agreement,
And both sun and moon had promised,
They would always rise together,
And they would awake together.
She herself arose before them,
Ere the sun or moon had risen,   140
Long before the time of cockcrow,
Or the chirping of a chicken.

From five sheep she shore the fleeces,
Clipped the wool from off six lambkins,
In her loom she wove the fleeces,
And the whole with care she carded,
Long before the dawn of morning,
Long before the sun had risen.

After this she washed the tables,
Swept the wide-extended flooring,   150
With the broom of twigs all leafless,
Then with broom of leafy branches.
Then the sweepings she collected
In the dustpan made of copper;
Out of doors she took the rubbish,
To the field beyond the farmyard,
To the field's extremest limit,
Where the lowest fence has opening.
There she stood upon the sweepings,
And she turned around, and listened.   160
From the lake she heard a weeping,
Sounds of woe across the river.

Quickly then she hastened homeward,
And she hurried to the parlour.
As she came, she told her tidings,
In such words as those which follow:
"From the lake I hear a weeping,
Sounds of woe across the river."

Louhi, Pohjola's old Mistress,
Old and gap-toothed dame of Pohja,   170

Hastened forth into the farmyard,
Hurried to the fence's opening,
Where she bent her ear to listen,
And she spoke the words which follow:
"This is not like children weeping
Nor like women's lamentation,
But a bearded hero's weeping;
Thus weep men whose chins are bearded."

Three planks high the boat was builded,
Which she pushed into the water,   180
And herself began to row it,
And she rowed, and hastened onward
To the spot where Väinämöinen,
Where the hero was lamenting.
There was Väinämöinen weeping,
There Uvanto's swain lamented,
By the dreary clumps of willow,
By the tangled hedge of cherry.
Moved his mouth, his beard was shaking,
But his lips he did not open.   190

Then did Pohjola's old Mistress,
Speak unto, and thus addressed him:
"O thou aged man unhappy,
Thou art in a foreign country!"

Väinämöinen, old and steadfast,
Lifted up his head and answered
In the very words that follow:
"True it is, and well I know it,
I am in a foreign country,
Absolutely unfamiliar.   200
I was better in my country,
Greater in the home I came from."

Louhi, Pohjola's old Mistress,
Answered in the words which follow:
"In the first place you must tell me,
If I may make bold to ask you,
From what race you take your lineage,
And from what heroic nation?"

Väinämöinen, old and steadfast,
Answered in the words which follow: 210
"Well my name was known aforetime,
And in former days was famous,
Ever cheerful in the evening,
Ever singing in the valleys,
There in Väinölä's sweet meadows,
And on Kalevala's broad heathlands;
But my grief is now so heavy
That I know myself no longer."

Louhi, Pohjola's old Mistress,
Answered in the words which follow: 220
"Rise, O man, from out the marshes,
Hero, seek another pathway.
Tell me now of thy misfortunes,
And relate me thy adventure!"

Thus she made him cease his weeping,
Made the hero cease lamenting,
And into her boat she took him,
Bade him at the stern be seated,
And herself resumed the oars,
And she then began to row him   230
Unto Pohjola, o'er water,
And she brought him to her dwelling.
Then she fed the famished stranger,
And she dried his dripping garments,
Then she rubbed his limbs all stiffened,
And she warmed him and massaged him,
Till she had restored his vigour,
And the hero had recovered.
After this, she spoke and asked him,
In the very words which follow: 240
"Why did'st weep, O Väinämöinen,
Why lament, Uvantolainen,
In that miserable region,
On the borders of the lakelet?"

Väinämöinen, old and steadfast,
Answered in the words which follow:
"Cause enough have I for weeping,

Reason, too, for lamentation,
In the sea I long was swimming,
Tossed about upon the billows,   250
On the wide expanse of water,
Out upon the open ocean.

I must weep throughout my lifespan,
And lament throughout my lifetime,
That I swam beyond my country,
Left the country so familiar,
And have come to doors I know not,
And to hedge-gates that I know not,
All the trees around me pain me,
All the pine-twigs seem to pierce me,   260
Every birch-tree seems to flog me,
Every alder seems to wound me,
But the wind is friendly to me,
And the sun still shines upon me,
In this unaccustomed country,
And within the doors I know not."

Louhi, Pohjola's old Mistress,
Answered in the words which follow:
"Do not weep, O Väinämöinen,
Nor lament, Uvantolainen.   270
Here 'tis good for thee to sojourn,
And to pass thy days in comfort.
Salmon you can eat at table,
And beside it pork is standing."

But the aged Väinämöinen
Answered in the words which follow:
"Foreign food I do not relish,
In the best of strangers' houses.
In his land a man is better,
In his home a man is greater.   280
Grant me, Jumala most gracious,
O compassionate Creator,
Once again to reach my country,
And the land I used to dwell in!
Better is a man's own country,
Water from beneath the sabot,

Than in unfamiliar countries,
Mead to drink from golden goblets."

Louhi, Pohjola's old Mistress,
Answered in the words which follow: 290
"What are you prepared to give me,
If I send you to your country,
To the borders of your cornfields,
Or the bath-house of your dwelling?"

Said the aged Väinämöinen,
"Tell me then what I shall give you,
If you send me to my country,
To the borders of my cornfields,
There to hear my cuckoo calling,
And my birds so sweetly singing.   300
Will you choose a gold-filled helmet,
Or a hat filled up with silver?"

Louhi, Pohjola's old Mistress,
Answered in the words which follow:
"O thou wisest Väinämöinen,
Thou the oldest of the sages,
Golden gifts I do not ask for,
And I wish not for thy silver.
Gold is but a toy for children,
Silver bells adorn the horses,   310
But if you can forge a Sampo,
Weld its many-coloured cover,
From the tips of swan's white wing-plumes,
From the milk of barren heifer,
From a single grain of barley,
From a single fleece of ewe's wool,
Then will I my daughter give you,
Give the maiden as your guerdon,
And will bring you to your country,
There to hear the birds all singing,   320
There to hear your cuckoo calling,
On the borders of your cornfields."

Väinämöinen, old and steadfast,
Answered in the words which follow:

"No, I cannot forge a Sampo,
Nor can weld its pictured cover.
Only bring me to my country,
And I'll send you Ilmarinen,
Who shall forge a Sampo for you,
Weld its many-coloured cover.   330
He perchance may please the maiden,
Win your daughter's young affections.

He's a smith without an equal,
None can wield the hammer like him,
For 'twas he who forged the heaven,
And who wrought the air's foundations,
Yet we find no trace of hammer,
Nor the trace of tongs discover."

Louhi, Pohjola's old Mistress,
Answered in the words which follow: 340
"I will only yield my daughter,
And my child I promise only
To the man who welds a Sampo
With its brilliant-coloured cover,
From the tips of swan's white wing-plumes,
From the milk of barren heifer,
From a single grain of barley,
From a single fleece of ewe's wool."

Thereupon the colt she harnessed,
In the front she yoked the bay one,   350
And she placed old Väinämöinen
In the sledge behind the stallion.
And she spoke and thus addressed him,
In the very words which follow:
"Do not raise your head up higher,
Turn it not to gaze about you,
That the steed may not be wearied,
Till the evening shall have gathered;
If you dare to raise your head up,
Or to turn to gaze around you,   360
Then misfortune will o'ertake you,
And an evil day betide you."

Then the aged Väinämöinen
Whipped the horse, and urged him onward,
And the white-maned courser hastened
Noisily upon the journey,
Forth from Pohjola's dark regions,
Sariola for ever misty.

VIII   Väinämöinen's wound

On his journey Väinämöinen encounters the magnificently clad
Maiden of Pohja, and makes advances to her (1–50). The maiden at
length consents to his wishes if he will make a boat from the splinters of
her spindle, and move it into the water without touching it (51–132).
Väinämöinen sets to work, but wounds his knee severely with his axe,
and cannot staunch the flow of blood (133–204). He goes in search of
some magic remedy and finds an old man who promises to stop the
bleeding (205–82).

> Lovely was the maid of Pohja,
> Famed on land, on water peerless,
> On the arch of air high-seated,
> Brightly shining on the rainbow,
> Clad in robes of dazzling lustre,
> Clad in raiment white and shining.
> There she wove a golden fabric,
> Interwoven all with silver,
> And her shuttle was all golden,
> And her comb was all of silver.   10
>
> From her hand flew swift the shuttle,
> In her hands the reel was turning,
> And the copper shafts they clattered,
> And the silver comb resounded,
> As the maiden wove the fabric,
> And with silver interwove it.
>
> Väinämöinen, old and steadfast,
> Thundered on upon his journey,
> From the gloomy land of Pohja,
> Sariola for ever misty.   20
> Short the distance he had travelled,
> Short the way that he had journeyed,
> When he heard the shuttle whizzing,
> High above his head he heard it.

Thereupon his head he lifted,
And he gazed aloft to heaven,
And beheld a glorious rainbow;
On the arch the maiden seated,
As she wove a golden fabric,
As the silver comb resounded.   30

Väinämöinen, old and steadfast,
Stayed his horse upon the instant,
And he raised his voice, and speaking,
In such words as these addressed her:
"Come into my sledge O maiden,
In the sledge beside me seat thee."

Then the maiden made him answer,
And in words like these responded:
"Wherefore should the maiden join you,
In the sledge beside you seated?"   40

Väinämöinen, old and steadfast,
Heard her words, and then responded:
"Therefore should the maiden join me,
In the sledge beside me seat her;
Bread of honey to prepare me,
And the best of beer to brew me,
Singing blithely on the benches,
Gaily talking at the window,
When in Väinölä I sojourn,
At my home in Kalevala."   50

Then the maiden gave him answer,
And in words like these addressed him:
"As I wandered through the bedstraw,
Tripping o'er the yellow meadows,
Yesterday, in time of evening,
As the sun was slowly sinking,
In the bush a bird was singing,
And I heard the fieldfare trilling,
Singing of the whims of maidens,
And the whims of new-wed damsels.   60
Thus the bird was speaking to me,
And I questioned it in this wise:

'Tell me O thou little fieldfare,
Sing thou, that my ears may hear it,
Whether it indeed is better,
Whether thou hast heard 'tis better,
For a girl in father's dwelling,
Or in household of a husband?'

Thereupon the bird made answer,
And the fieldfare answered chirping: 70
"Brilliant is the day in summer,
But a maiden's lot is brighter.
And the frost makes cold the iron,
Yet the new bride's lot is colder;
In her father's house a maiden
Lives like berry in the garden,
But a bride in house of husband,
Lives like house-dog tightly fettered.
To a slave comes rarely pleasure;
To a wedded damsel never.'"   80

Väinämöinen, old and steadfast,
Answered in the words which follow:
"Song of birds is idle chatter,
And the throstle's, merely chirping;
As a child a daughter's treated,
But a maid must needs be married.
Come into my sledge, O maiden,
In the sledge beside me seat thee.
I am not a man unworthy,
Duller not than other heroes!"   90

But the maid gave crafty answer,
And in words like these responded:
"As a man I will esteem you,
And as hero will regard you,
If you can split up a horsehair
With a blunt and pointless knife-blade,
And an egg in knots you tie me,
Yet no knot is seen upon it."

Väinämöinen, old and steadfast,
Then the hair in twain divided,   100

With a blunt and pointless knife-blade,
With a knife completely pointless,
And an egg in knots he twisted,
Yet no knot was seen upon it;
Then again he asked the maiden
In the sledge to sit beside him.

But the maid gave crafty answer:
"I perchance at length may join you,
If you'll peel the stone I give you,
And a pile of ice will hew me,   110
But no splinter scatter from it,
Nor the smallest fragment loosen."

Väinämöinen, old and steadfast,
Did not find the task a hard one.
From the stone the rind he severed,
And a pile of ice he hewed her,
But no splinters scattered from it,
Nor the smallest fragment loosened;
Then again he asked the maiden
In the sledge to sit beside him.   120

But the maid gave crafty answer,
And she spoke the words which follow:
"No, I will not yet go with you,
If a boat you cannot carve me,
From the splinters of my spindle, .
From the fragments of my shuttle,
And shall launch the boat in water,
Push it out upon the billows,
But no knee shall press against it,
And no hand must even touch it;   130
And no arm shall urge it onward,
Neither shall a shoulder guide it."

Väinämöinen, old and steadfast,
Answered in the words which follow:
"None in any land or country,
Under all the vault of heaven,

Like myself can build a vessel,
Or so deftly can construct it."

Then he took the spindle-splinters,
Of the reel he took the fragments,   140
And began the boat to fashion,
Fixed a hundred planks together,
On a mount of steel he built it,
Built it on the rocks of iron.

At the boat with zeal he laboured,
Toiling at the work unresting,
Working thus one day, a second,
On the third day likewise working,
But the rocks his axe-blade touched not,
And upon the hill it rang not.   150

But at length, upon the third day,
Hiisi turned aside the axe-shaft,
Lempo turned the edge against him,
And an evil stroke delivered:
On the rocks the axe-blade glinted,
On the hill the blade rang loudly,
From the rock the axe rebounded,
In the flesh the steel was buried,
In the victim's knee 'twas buried,
In the toes of Väinämöinen,   160
In the flesh did Lempo drive it,
To the veins did Hiisi guide it,
From the wound the blood flowed freely,
Bursting forth in streaming torrents.

Väinämöinen, old and steadfast,
He, the oldest of magicians,
Uttered words like those which follow,
And expressed himself in this wise:
"O thou evil axe ferocious,
With thy edge of gleaming sharpness,   170
Thou hast thought to hew a tree-trunk,
And to strike upon a pine-tree,

Match thyself against a fir-tree,
Or to fall upon a birch-tree.
'Tis my flesh that thou hast wounded,
And my veins thou hast divided!"

Then his magic spells he uttered,
And himself began to speak them,
Spells of origin, for healing,
And to close the wound completely.   180
But he could not think of any
Words of origin of iron,
Which might serve to bind the evil,
And to close the gaping edges
Of the great wound from the iron,
By the blue edge deeply bitten.

But the blood gushed forth in torrents,
Rushing like a foaming river,
O'er the berry-bearing bushes,
And the heath the ground that covered.   190
There remained no single hillock,
Which was not completely flooded
By the overflowing blood-stream,
Which came rushing forth in torrents
From the knee of one most worthy,
From the toes of Väinämöinen.

Väinämöinen, old and steadfast,
Gathered from the rocks the lichen,
From the swamps the moss collected,
Earth he gathered from the hillocks,   200
Hoping thus to stop the outlet
Of the wound that bled so freely,
But he could not check the bleeding,
Nor restrain it in the slightest.

And the pain he felt oppressed him,
And the greatest trouble seized him.
Väinämöinen, old and steadfast,
Then began to weep full sorely.
Thereupon his horse he harnessed,
In the sledge he yoked the chestnut,   210

On the sledge himself he mounted,
And upon the seat he sat him.

O'er the horse his whip he brandished,
With the bead-decked whip he lashed him,
And the horse sped quickly onward.
Rocked the sledge, the way grew shorter,
And they quickly reached a village,
Where the path in three divided.

Väinämöinen, old and steadfast,
Drove along the lowest pathway,   220
To the lowest of the homesteads,
And he asked upon the threshold,
"Is there no one in this household,
Who can cure the wounds of iron,
Who can soothe the hero's anguish,
And can heal the wound that pains him?"

On the floor a child was playing,
By the stove a boy was sitting,
And he answered him in this wise:
"There is no one in this household   230
Who can heal the wounds of iron,
Who can soothe the hero's anguish,
To the rock can fix it firmly,
And can heal the wound that pains him.
Such may dwell in other houses:
Drive away to other houses!"

Väinämöinen, old and steadfast,
O'er the horse his whip then brandished,
And the sledge went rattling onward.
Thus a little way he travelled,   240
On the midmost of the pathways,
To the midmost of the houses,
And he asked upon the threshold,
And beseeching at the window:
"Is there no one in this household,
Who can heal the wounds of iron,
Who can stanch the blood when flowing,
And can check the rushing bloodstream?"

'Neath the quilt a crone was resting,
By the stove there sat a gossip,   250
And she spoke and answered plainly,
As her three teeth gnashed together:
"There is no one in this household,
Who can heal the wounds of iron,
None who knows efficient blood-spells,
And can close the wound that pains you.
Such may dwell in other houses:
Drive away to other houses!"

Väinämöinen, old and steadfast,
O'er the horse his whip then brandished,   260
And the sledge went rattling onward.
Thus a little way he travelled,
On the highest of the pathways,
To the highest of the houses,
And he asked upon the threshold,
Calling from beside the doorpost:
"Is there any in this household,
Who can heal the wounds of iron,
Who can check this rushing bloodstream,
And can stay the dark red torrent?"   270

By the stove an old man rested,
On the stove-bed lay a greybeard,
From the stove the old man mumbled,
And the greybeard cried in answer:
"Stemmed before were greater torrents,
Greater floods than this were hindered,
By three words of the Creator,
By the mighty words primeval.
Brooks and streams were checked from flowing,
Mighty streams in rapids falling,   280
Bays were formed in rocky headlands,
Tongues of land were linked together."

IX   The origin of iron

Väinämöinen repeats to the old man the legend of the origin of iron (1–266). The old man reviles the iron and repeats spells for the stopping of blood, and the flow of blood is stayed (267–416). The old man directs his son to prepare a salve, and dresses and binds up the wound. Väinämöinen is cured, and thanks Jumala for his merciful assistance (417–586).

Then the aged Väinämöinen
In the sledge at once stood upright,
From the sledge he sprang unaided,
And courageously stood upright.
To the room he hastened quickly,
And beneath the roof he hurried.

There they brought a silver beaker,
And a golden goblet likewise,
But they proved by far too little,
Holding but the smallest measure   10
Of the blood of aged Väinö,
From the hero's foot that spouted.

From the stove the old man mumbled,
Cried the greybeard when he saw him:
"Who among mankind may'st thou be,
Who among the roll of heroes?
Seven large boats with blood are brimming,
Eight large tubs are overflowing
From your knee, O most unhappy,
On the floor in torrents gushing!   20
Other words I well remember,

But the oldest I recall not,
How the iron was first created,
And the unworked ore was fashioned."

Then the aged Väinämöinen
Answered in the words that follow:
"Well I know the birth of Iron,
And how steel was first created:
Air is the primeval mother,
Water is the eldest brother,   30
Iron is the youngest brother,
And the Fire in midst between them.

Ukko, mightiest of Creators,
He, the God above in heaven,
From the Air the Water parted,
And the continents from water,
When unborn was evil Iron,
Uncreated, undeveloped.

Ukko, God of realms supernal,
Rubbed his mighty hands together.   40
Both his hands he rubbed together,
On his left knee then he pressed them,
And three maidens were created,
Three fair Daughters of Creation,
Mothers of the rust of Iron,
And of blue-mouthed steel the fosterers.

Strolled the maids with swinging footsteps
On the borders of the cloudlets,
And their full breasts were o'erflowing,
And their nipples pained them sorely.   50
Down on earth their milk ran over,
From their breasts' o'erflowing fulness,
Milk on land, and milk on marshes,
Milk upon the peaceful waters.

Black milk from the first was flowing,
From the eldest of the maidens,
White milk issued from another,
From the second of the maidens,   60

Red milk by the third was yielded,
By the youngest of the maidens.

Where the black milk had been dropping,
There was found the softest Iron,
Where the white milk had been flowing,
There the hardest steel was fashioned,
Where the red milk had been trickling,
There was undeveloped Iron.

But a short time had passed over,
When the Iron desired to visit
Him, its dearest elder brother,
And to make the Fire's acquaintance.   70

But the Fire arose in fury,
Blazing up in greatest anger,
Seeking to consume its victim,
E'en the wretched Iron, its brother.

Then the Iron sought out a refuge,
Sought for refuge and protection
From the hands of furious Fire,
From his mouth, all bright with anger.

Then the Iron took refuge from him,
Sought both refuge and protection   80
Down amid the quaking marshes,
Where the springs have many sources,
On the level mighty marshes,
On the void and barren mountains,
Where the swans their eggs deposit,
And the goose her brood is rearing.

In the swamps lay hid the Iron,
Stretched beneath the marshy surface,
Hid for one year and a second,
For a third year likewise hidden,   90
Hidden there between two tree-stumps,
'Neath three roots of birch-trees hidden
But it had not yet found safety
From the fierce hands of the Fire,

And a second time it wandered
To the dwelling of the Fire,
That it should be forged to weapons,
And to sword-blades should be fashioned.

On the marshes wolves were running,
On the heath the bears came trooping.   100
'Neath the wolves' feet quaked the marshes,
'Neath the bears the heath was shaken,
Thus was ore of iron uncovered,
And the bars of steel were noticed,
Where the claws of wolves had trodden,
And the paws of bears had trampled.

Then was born smith Ilmarinen,
Thus was born, and thus was nurtured,
Born upon a hill of charcoal,
Reared upon a plain of charcoal,   110
In his hands a copper hammer,
And his little pincers likewise.

Ilmari was born at night-time,
And at day he built his smithy,
Sought a place to build his smithy,
Where he could construct his bellows;
In the swamp he found a land-ridge,
And a small place in the marshes,
So he went to gaze upon it,
And examined the surroundings,   120
And erected there his bellows,
And his anvil there constructed.

Then he hastened to the wolf-tracks,
And the bear-tracks also followed,
And the ore of iron he saw there,
And the lumps of steel he found there,
In the wolves' enormous footprints;
Where the bears' paws left their imprints.
Then he spoke the words which follow:
'O thou most unlucky Iron,   130
In an ill abode thou dwellest,
In a very lowly station,

'Neath the wolf-prints in the marshes,
And the imprints of the bear-paws!'

Then he pondered and reflected,
'What would be the upshot of it,
If I cast it in the fire,
And I laid it on the anvil?'

Sore alarmed was hapless Iron,
Sore alarmed, and greatly startled,   140
When of Fire it heard him speaking,
Speaking of the furious Fire.

Said the smith, said Ilmarinen,
'But indeed it cannot happen;
Fire his friends will never injure,
Nor will harm his dear relations!
If you seek the Fire's red chamber,
All illumined with its brightness,
You will greatly gain in beauty,
And your splendour greatly increase.   150
Fitted thus for men's keen sword-blades
Or as clasps for women's girdles.'

Therefore when the day was ended,
Was the Iron from out the marshes,
Delved from all the swampy places,
Carried homeward to the smithy.

Then he cast it in the furnace,
And he laid it on the anvil,
Blew a blast, and then a second,
And he blew again a third time,   160
Till the Iron was fully softened,
And the ore completely melted,
Like to wheaten dough in softness,
Soft as dough for rye-bread kneaded,
In the furnace of the smithy,
By the bright flame's softening power.

Then exclaimed the Iron unhappy:
'O thou smith, O Ilmarinen,

Take me quickly from this furnace,
From the red flames that torment me!'   170

Said the smith, said Ilmarinen,
'If I take you from the furnace,
Perhaps you might become outrageous,
And commit some furious action.
Perhaps you might attack your brother,
And your mother's child might injure.'

Therefore swore the wretched Iron,
By the oaths of all most solemn,
By the forge and by the anvil,
By the hammer and the mallet,   180
And it said the words which follow,
And expressed itself in this wise:
'Give me trees that I can bite them,
Give me stones that I may break them,
I will not assault my brother,
Nor my mother's child will injure.
Better will be my existence,
And my life will be more happy,
If I dwell among companions,
As the tools of handicraftsmen,   190
Than to wound my own relations,
And disgrace my own connections.'

Then the smith, e'en Ilmarinen,
He, the great primeval craftsman,
From the fire removed the Iron;
Laid it down upon the anvil,
Welded it till it was wearied,
Shaped it into pointed weapons,
Into spears, and into axes,
Into tools of all descriptions.   200
Still there was a trifle wanting,
And the Iron still defective,
For the tongue of Iron had hissed not,
And its mouth of steel was formed not,
For the Iron was not yet hardened,
Nor with water had been tempered.

Then the smith, e'en Ilmarinen,
Pondered over what was needed,
Mixed a small supply of ashes,
And some lye he added to it,   210
To the blue steel's smelting mixture,
For the tempering of the Iron.

With his tongue he tried the liquid,
Tasted it if it would please him,
And he spoke the words which follow:
'Even yet it does not please me
For the blue steel's smelting mixture,
And perfecting of the Iron.'

From without a bee came flying,
Blue-winged from the grassy hillocks,   220
Flitting hither, flitting thither,
Flying all around the smithy.

Then the smith spoke up as follows:
'O thou bee, my nimble comrade,
Honey on thy wings convey me,
On thy tongue from out the forest,
From the summits of six flowerets,
And from seven tall grass-stems bring it,
For the blue steel's smelting mixture,
And the tempering of the Iron!'   230

But the hornet, Bird of Hiisi,
Looked around him, and he listened,
Gazing from beside the roof-tree,
Looking from below the birch-bark,
At the tempering of the Iron,
And the blue steel's smelting mixture.

Thence he flew on whirring pinions,
Scattering all of Hiisi's terrors,
Brought the hissing of the serpents,
And of snakes the dusky venom,   240
And of ants he brought the acid,
And of toads the hidden poison,

That the steel might thus be poisoned,
In the tempering of the Iron.

Then the smith, e'en Ilmarinen,
He, the greatest of the craftsmen,
Was deluded, and imagined
That the bee returned already,
And had brought the honey needed,
Brought the honey that he wanted,   250
And he spoke the words which follow:
'Here at last is what will please me,
For the blue steel's smelting mixture,

And the tempering of the Iron.'
Thereupon the steel he lifted,
In he plunged the luckless Iron,
As from out the fire he took it,
And he took it from the anvil.

Then indeed the steel was angry,
And the Iron was seized with fury.   260
And its oath the wretch has broken,
Like a dog has soiled its honour,
Brutally its brother bitten,
Striking at its own relations,
Let the blood rush forth in torrents,
From the wound in torrents gushing."

From the stove the old man mumbled,
Shook his beard, his head he nodded:
"Now I know whence comes the Iron,
And of steel the evil customs.   270

O thou most unhappy Iron,
Wretched Iron, slag most worthless,
Steel thou art of evil witchcraft,
Thou hast been for nought developed,
But to turn to evil courses,
In the greatness of thy power!

Once thou wast devoid of greatness;
Neither wast thou great nor little,

Neither noted for thy beauty,
Nor remarkable for evil,   280
When as milk thou wast created,
When the sweet milk trickled over
From the breasts of youthful maidens,
From the maidens' swelling bosoms,
On the borders of the cloudland,
'Neath the broad expanse of heaven.

Thou wast then devoid of greatness,
Thou wast neither great nor little,
When thou in the mud wast resting,
Sunk below the sparkling water,   290
Overspreading all the marshland,
At the base of rocky mountains,
And in loose earth thou wast altered,
And to iron-ore converted.

Thou wast still devoid of greatness,
Thou wast neither great nor little,
When the elks were trampling o'er thee,
And the reindeer, in the marshes,
When the wolves' claws trod upon thee,
And the bears' paws passed above thee.   300

Thou wast still devoid of greatness,
Thou wast neither great nor little,
When thou from the marsh wast gathered,
From the ground with care uplifted,
Carried thence into the smithy,
To the forge of Ilmarinen.

Thou wast still devoid of greatness,
Thou wast neither great nor little,
When as ore thou there wast hissing,
Plunged amid the boiling water,   310
Or amid the fiery furnace,
When the mighty oath thou sworest,
By the forge and by the anvil,
By the hammer and the mallet,
Where the smith himself was standing,
On the flooring of the smithy.

Now that thou hast grown to greatness,
Thou hast wrought thyself to frenzy,
And thy mighty oath hast broken,
Like a dog hast soiled thy honour,   320
For thy kinsman thou hast wounded,
Raised thy mouth against thy kinsman!

Who hast led thee to this outrage,
To this wickedness incited?
Perhaps thy father or thy mother,
Or the eldest of thy brothers,
Or the youngest of thy sisters,
Or some other near relation?

Not thy father, not thy mother,
Nor the eldest of thy brothers,   330
Nor the youngest of thy sisters
Nor some other near relation.
Thou thyself hast wrought the evil,
And hast done a deadly outrage.

Come thyself to see the mischief,
And to remedy the evil.
Come, before I tell thy mother,
And complain unto thy parents;
More will be thy mother's trouble,
Great the anguish of thy parents,   340
That their son had wrought this evil,
And their son had wrought this folly.

Hear me, Blood, and cease thy flowing,
O thou Bloodstream, rush no longer,
Nor upon my head spurt further,
Nor upon my breast down-trickle.
Like a wall, O Blood, arrest thee,
Like a fence, O Bloodstream, stand thou,
As a sword in sea is standing,
Like a reed in moss-grown country,   350
Like the bank that bounds the cornfield,
Like a rock in raging torrent!

But thy own sense ought to teach thee
How that thou should'st run more smoothly.
In the flesh should'st thou be moving,
With thy current smoothly flowing.
In the body it is better,
Underneath the skin more lovely
Through the veins to trace thy pathway,
With thy current smoothly flowing, 360
Than upon the earth rush downward,
And among the dust to trickle.

Flow not, milk, upon the flooring,
Soil thou not, O Blood, the meadows,
Nor the grass, O crown of manhood,
Nor the hillocks, gold of heroes.
In the heart should be thy dwelling,
And among the lungs' dark cellars.
Thither then withdraw thou quickly,
There withdraw upon the instant. 370
Do not issue like a river,
Nor as pond extend thy billows,
Trickling forth from out the marshes,
Nor to leak like boats when damaged.

Therefore, dear one, cease thy flowing,
Crimson Blood, drip down no longer,
Not impeded, but contented.
Dry were once the Falls of Tyrjä,
Likewise Tuonela's dread river,
Dry the lake and dry the heaven, 380
In the mighty droughts of summer,
In the evil times of bush-fires.

If thou wilt not yet obey me,
Still I know another method,
And resort to fresh enchantments:
And I call for Hiisi's caldron,
And will boil the blood within it
All the blood that forth has issued,
So that not a drop escapes me,
That the red blood flows no longer, 390

Nor the blood to earth drops downward,
And the blood no more may issue.
But if manly strength has failed me,
Nor is Ukko's son a hero,
Who can stop this inundation,
Stem the swift arterial torrent,
Thou our Father in the heavens,
Jumala, the clouds who rulest,
Thou hast manly strength sufficient,
Thou thyself the mighty hero,   400
Who shall close the blood's wide gateway,
And shall stem the blood escaping.

Ukko, O thou great Creator,
Jumala, aloft in heaven!
Hither come where thou art needed,
Hither come where we implore thee,
Press thy mighty hands upon it,
Press thy mighty thumbs upon it,
And the painful wound close firmly,
And the door whence comes the evil,   410
Spread the tender leaves upon it,
Leaves of golden water-lily,
Thus to close the path of bleeding,
And to stem the rushing torrent,
That upon my beard it spurts not,
Nor upon my rags may trickle!"

Thus he closed the bleeding opening,
Sent his son into the smithy,
To prepare a healing ointment   420
From the blades of magic grasses,
From the thousand-headed yarrow,
And from dripping mountain-honey,
Falling down in drops of sweetness.
Then the boy went to the smithy,
To prepare the healing ointment,
On the way he passed an oak-tree,
And he stopped and asked the oak-tree,
"Have you honey on your branches?
And beneath your bark sweet honey?"   430

And the oak-tree gave him answer:
"Yesterday, throughout the evening,
Dripped the honey on my branches,
On my summit splashed the honey,
From the clouds dropped down the honey,
From the scattered clouds distilling."

Then he took the slender oak-twigs,
From the tree the broken fragments,
Took the best among the grasses,
Gathered many kinds of herbage,   440
Herbs one sees not in this country;
Such were mostly what he gathered.

Then he placed them o'er the furnace,
And the mixture brought to boiling;
Both the bark from off the oak-tree,
And the finest of the grasses.

Thus the pot was boiling fiercely,
Three long nights he kept it boiling,
And for three days of the springtime,
While he watched the ointment closely,   450
If the salve was fit for using,
And the magic ointment ready.

But the salve was still unfinished,
Nor the magic ointment ready;
Grasses to the mass he added,
Added herbs of many species,
Which were brought from other places,
Gathered on a hundred pathways,
These were culled by nine magicians,
And by eight wise seers discovered.   460

Then for three nights more he boiled it,
And for nine nights in succession;
Took the pot from off the furnace,
And the salve with care examined,
If the salve was fit for using,
And the magic ointment ready.

Here there grew a branching aspen,
On the borders of the cornfield,
And in twain he broke the aspen,
And the tree completely severed;   470
With the magic salve he smeared it,
Carefully the ointment tested,
And he spoke the words which follow:
"As I with this magic ointment
Smear the injured crown all over,
Let no harm be left upon it,
Let the aspen stand uninjured,
Even as it stood aforetime!"

Then at once was healed the aspen,
Even as it stood aforetime,   480
And its crown was far more lovely,
And the trunk below was healthy.
Then again he took the ointment,
And the salve again he tested,
And on broken stones he tried it,
And on shattered rocks he rubbed it,
And the stone with stone knit firmly,
And the cracks were fixed together.

From the forge the boy came homeward,
When the salve was fit for using,   490
With the ointment quite perfected,
In the old man's hands he placed it:
"Here I bring a perfect ointment,
And the magic salve is ready.
It could fuse the hills together,
In a single rock unite them."

With his tongue the old man tried it,
With his mouth the liquid tasted,
And the ointment tasted perfect,
And the salve was most efficient.   500

This he smeared on Väinämöinen,
And with this he healed the sufferer;
Stroked him downward, stroked him upward,
Rubbed him also on the middle,

And he spoke the words which follow,
And expressed himself in this wise:
"Tis not I who use my muscles,
But 'tis the Creator moves them;
With my own strength do not labour,
But with strength from the Almighty.   510
With my mouth I speak not to you;
Jumala's own mouth speaks with you,
If my speech is sweet unto you,
Jumala's own speech is sweeter.
Even if my hands are lovely,
The Creator's hands are fairer."

When the salve was rubbed upon him,
And the healing ointment touched him,
Almost fainting with the anguish,
Väinämöinen writhed and struggled;   520
Turning this way, turning that way,
Seeking ease, but never finding.

Then the old man banned the suffering,
Far away he drove the anguish,
To the central Hill of Tortures,
To the topmost Mount of Suffering,
There to fill the stones with anguish,
And the slabs of rock to torture.

Then he took a silken fabric,
And in strips he quickly cut it;   530
From the edge he tore the fragments,
And at once he formed a bandage;
Then he took the silken bandage,
And with utmost care he wound it,
Round the knees he wound it deftly,
Round the toes of Väinämöinen.

Then he spoke the words which follow,
And expressed himself in this wise:
"Thus I use God's silken bandage,
The Creator's mantle wind I   540
Round the great knees of the patient,
Round the toes of one most noble!

Watch thou, Jumala most gracious,
Give thy aid, O great Creator,
That we fall not in misfortune,
That no evil may o'ertake us!"

Then the aged Väinämöinen
Felt he had regained his vigour,
And that he was healed completely,
And his flesh again was solid,   550
And beneath it all was healthy.
In his body he was painless,
And his sides were quite uninjured,
From above the wounds had vanished,
Stronger felt he than aforetime,
Better than in former seasons.
On his feet he now was walking
And could bend his knees in stamping;
Not the least of pain he suffered,
Not a trace remained of aching.   560

Then the aged Väinämöinen,
Lifted up his eyes to heaven,
Gazing up to God most gracious,
Lifting up his head to heaven,
And he spoke the words which follow,
And expressed himself in this wise:
"Thence all mercy flows for ever,
Thence comes aid the most effective,
From the heaven that arches o'er us,
From the omnipotent Creator.   570

Praise to Jumala most gracious,
Praise to thee, O great Creator,
That thy aid thou hast vouchsafed me,
Granted me thy strong protection,
When my suffering was the greatest,
From the edge of sharpest Iron!"

Then the aged Väinämöinen
Further spoke these words of warning:
"People, henceforth in the future
On your present welfare build not,   580

Make no boat in mood of boasting,
Nor confide too much in boat-ribs.
God foresees the course of by-ways,
The Creator orders all things;
Not the foresight of the heroes,
Nor the might of all the great ones!"

X The forging of the *Sampo*

Väinämöinen reaches home and urges Ilmarinen to depart to woo the Maiden of Pohja, because he would be able to forge a *Sampo* (1–100). Ilmarinen refuses to go to Pohjola, but Väinämöinen conveys him thither without his consent by a stratagem (101–200). Ilmarinen arrives in Pohjola, where he is very well received, and promises to forge a *Sampo* (201–80). He forges the *Sampo*, and the Mistress of Pohjola conceals it in the Rocky Mountain of Pohjola (281–432). Ilmarinen asks for the maiden as his reward, but she makes excuses, saying that she is not yet ready to leave home (433–62). Ilmarinen receives a boat, returns home, and informs Väinämöinen that he has forged the *Sampo* in Pohjola (463–510).

Väinämöinen, old and steadfast,
Took his horse of chestnut colour,
And between the shafts he yoked him,
Yoked before the sledge the chestnut,
On the sledge himself he mounted,
And upon the seat he sat him.

Quickly then his whip he flourished,
Cracked his whip, all bead-embroidered,
Quick he sped upon his journey,
Lurched the sledge, the way was shortened,   10
Loudly rang the birchwood runners,
And the rowan cumber rattled.

On he rushed with speed tremendous,
Through the swamps and open country,
O'er the heaths, so wide extending.
Thus he drove a day, a second,
And at length, upon the third day,
Reached the long bridge-end before him
Kalevala's extended heathlands,
Bordering on the field of Osmo.   20

Then he spoke the words which follow,
And expressed himself in this wise:
"Wolf, do thou devour the dreamer,
Seize the Laplander, O sickness!
He who said that I should never
In my lifetime reach my homestead,
Nor again throughout my lifetime,
Nor as long as shines the moonlight,
Neither tread Väinölä's meadows,
Kalevala's extended heathlands."   30

Then the aged Väinämöinen,
Spoke aloud his songs of magic,
And a flower-crowned fir grew upward,
Crowned with flowers, and limbs all golden,
And its summit reached to heaven,
To the very clouds uprising.
In the air the boughs extended,
And they spread themselves to heaven.

Then he sang his songs of magic,
And he sang a moon all shining,   40
On the fir-tree's golden summit,
And the Great Bear in the branches.

On he drove with speed tremendous,
Straight to his beloved homestead,
Head bowed down, and thoughts all gloomy,
With his cap so sad askew,
For the great smith Ilmarinen,
He the great primeval craftsman,
He had promised as his surety,
That his own head he might rescue   50
Out of Pohjola's dark regions,
Sariola for ever misty.

Presently his horse he halted
At the new-cleared field of Osmo,
And the aged Väinämöinen,
In the sledge his head uplifted,
Heard the noise within the smithy,
And the clatter in the coal-shed.

Väinämöinen, old and steadfast,
Then himself the smithy entered,   60
And he found smith Ilmarinen,
Wielding mightily his hammer.

Said the smith, said Ilmarinen:
"O thou aged Väinämöinen,
Where have you so long been staying,
Where have you so long been living?"

Väinämöinen, old and steadfast,
Answered in the words which follow:
"There have I so long been staying,
There have I so long been living,   70
In the gloomy land of Pohja,
Sariola for ever misty.
Long I coursed on Lapland snowshoes,
With the world-renowned magicians."

Then the smith, e'en Ilmarinen,
Answered in the words which follow:
"O thou aged Väinämöinen,
Thou the great primeval sorcerer,
Tell me of your journey thither;
Tell me of your homeward journey."   80

Said the aged Väinämöinen,
"Much indeed have I to tell you:
Lives in Pohjola a maiden,
In that village cold a virgin,
Who will not accept a suitor,
Mocks the very best among them.
Half of all the land of Pohja
Praises her surpassing beauty:
From her temples shines the moonlight,
From her breasts the sun is shining,   90
And the Great Bear from her shoulders,
From her back the starry Seven.

Thou thyself, smith Ilmarinen,
Thou, the great primeval craftsman,
Go thyself to woo the maiden,

And behold her shining tresses!
If you can but forge a Sampo,
With its many-coloured cover,
You will then receive the maiden,
And the fair maid be your guerdon."   100

Said the smith, e'en Ilmarinen,
"O thou aged Väinämöinen,
You have perhaps already pledged me
To the gloomy land of Pohja,
That your own head you might rescue,
And might thus secure your freedom!
Not in course of all my lifetime,
While the golden moon is shining,
Hence to Pohjola I'll journey,
Huts of Sariola so dreary,   110
To the land where men are devoured,
Where the heroes will be drowned."

Then the aged Väinämöinen,
Answered in the words which follow:
"There is wonder after wonder;
There's a spruce with flowery summit,
Flowery summit, leaves all golden,
Near where Osmo's field is bordered;
On the crown the moon is shining,
In the boughs the Bear is resting."   120

Said the smith, e'en Ilmarinen,
"This I never can believe in,
If I do not go to see it,
And my own eyes have not seen it."

Said the aged Väinämöinen,
"If you cannot then believe it,
We will go ourselves, and witness
Whether true or false the story!"

Then they both went forth to see it,
View the spruce with flowery summit,   130
First walked aged Väinämöinen,
And smith Ilmarinen second.

When they reached the spot they sought for,
On the edge of Osmo's cornfield,
Then the smith his steps arrested,
In amazement at the spruce-tree,
With the Great Bear in the branches,
And the moon upon its summit.

Then the aged Väinämöinen,
Spoke the very words which follow: 140
"Now thou smith, my dearest brother,
Climb and fetch the moon above us.
Bring thou, too, the Great Bear shining
On the spruce-tree's golden summit!"

Then the smith, e'en Ilmarinen,
Climbed aloft into the spruce-tree,
Up he climbed into the daylight,
Climbed to fetch the moon above him,
And the Great Bear, shining brightly,
On the spruce-tree's golden summit.   150

Said the spruce-tree's golden summit,
Said the widely-branching spruce-tree,
"Mighty man, of all most foolish,
O most thoughtless of the heroes!
In my branches, fool, thou climbest,
To my summit, as a boy might,
And would'st grasp the moon's reflection,
And the false stars thou beholdest!"

Then the aged Väinämöinen,
Lifted up his voice in singing.   160
As he sang uprose a tempest,
And the wind rose wildly furious,
And he spoke the words which follow,
And expressed himself in this wise:
"In thy boat, O wind, convey him,
In thy skiff, O breeze, convey him,
Bear him to the distant regions
Of the gloomy land of Pohja!"

Then there rose a mighty tempest,
And the wind so wildly furious 170
Carried off smith Ilmarinen,
Hurried him to distant regions,
To the gloomy land of Pohja,
Sariola for ever misty.

Then the smith, e'en Ilmarinen,
Journeyed forth, and hurried onwards,
On the tempest forth he floated,
On the pathway of the breezes,
Over moon, and under sunray,
On the shoulders of the Great Bear, 180
Till he reached the halls of Pohja,
Baths of Sariola the gloomy,
Yet the tailed-dogs were not barking,
And the watch-dogs were not yelping.

Louhi, Pohjola's old Mistress,
Old and gap-toothed dame of Pohja,
In the house she stood and listened,
And at length she spoke as follows:
"Who then are you among mortals,
Who among the roll of heroes, 190
On the tempest-path who comest,
On the sledgeway of the breezes,
Yet the dogs ran forth not, barking,
And the shaggy-tailed ones barked not!"

Said the smith, e'en Ilmarinen,
"Surely I have not come hither
That the village dogs should shame me,
Or the shaggy-tailed ones hurt me,
Here behind these foreign portals,
And behind these unknown fences." 200

Then did Pohjola's old Mistress
Question thus the new-come stranger:
"Have you ever on your travels,
Heard reports of, or encountered

Him, the great smith Ilmarinen,
Most accomplished of the craftsmen?
Long have we been waiting for him,
Long been anxious for his coming
Here to Pohjola's dark regions,
That a Sampo he might forge us."   210

Then the smith, e'en Ilmarinen,
Answered in the words which follow:
"I have met upon my journey
With the smith named Ilmarinen;
I myself am Ilmarinen,
And a most accomplished craftsman."

Louhi, Pohjola's old Mistress,
Old and gap-toothed dame of Pohja,
Hurried back into her dwelling,
And she spoke the words which follow: 220
"Come my daughter, thou the youngest,
Thou the fairest of my children,
Robe thyself in choicest raiment,
Clothe thee in the brightest-coloured,
In the finest of your dresses,
Brightest beads upon thy bosom,
Round thy neck the very finest,
And upon thy temples shining.
See thou that thy cheeks are rosy,
And thy countenance is cheerful!   230
Here's the smith named Ilmarinen,
He the great primeval craftsman,
Who will forge the Sampo for us,
With its brightly-pictured cover."

Then the lovely maid of Pohja,
Famed on land, on water peerless,
Took the choicest of her dresses,
And the brightest of her garments,
And the fifth at last selected.
Then her headdress she adjusted,   240
And her copper belt girt round her,
And her wondrous golden girdle.

Back she came from out the storeroom,
Dancing back into the courtyard,
And her eyes were brightly shining.
As she moved, her earrings jingled,
And her countenance was charming,
And her lovely cheeks were rosy.
Gold was shining on her bosom,
On her head was silver gleaming.   250

Then did Pohjola's old Mistress,
Lead the smith named Ilmarinen,
Into Pohjola's great castle,
Rooms of Sariola the gloomy.
There she set a meal before him,
Gave the hero drink in plenty,
And she feasted him profusely,
And at length she spoke as follows:

"O thou smith, O Ilmarinen,
Thou the great primeval craftsman,   260
If you can but forge a Sampo,
With its brightly-coloured cover,
From the tips of swans' white wing-plumes,
From the milk of barren heifer,
From a little grain of barley,
From the wool of sheep of summer,
Will you then accept this maiden,
As reward, my charming daughter?"

Then the smith named Ilmarinen
Answered in the words which follow: 270
"I will go to forge the Sampo,
Weld its brightly-coloured cover,
From the tips of swans' white wing-plumes,
From the milk of barren heifer,
From a little grain of barley,
From the wool of sheep of summer,
For 'twas I who forged the heavens,
And the vault of air I hammered,
Ere the air had yet beginning,
Or a trace of aught was present."   280

Then he went to forge the Sampo,
With its brightly-coloured cover,
Sought a station for a smithy,
And he needed tools for labour;
But no place he found for smithy,
Nor for smithy, nor for bellows,
Nor for furnace, nor for anvil,
Not a hammer, nor a mallet.

Then the smith, e'en Ilmarinen,
Spoke aloud the words which follow: 290
"None despair, except old women,
Scamps may leave their task unfinished;
Not a man, how weak soever,
Not a hero of the laziest!"

For his forge he sought a station,
And a wide place for the bellows,
In the country round about him,
In the outer fields of Pohja.

So he sought one day, a second,
And at length upon the third day   300
Found a stone all streaked with colours,
And a mighty rock beside it;
Here the smith his search abandoned,
And the smith prepared his furnace,
On the first day fixed the bellows,
And the forge upon the second.

Thereupon smith Ilmarinen,
He the great primeval craftsman,
Heaped the fuel upon the fire,
And beneath the forge he thrust it,   310
Made his servants work the bellows,
To the half of all their power.

So the servants worked the bellows,
To the half of all their power.
During three days of the summer,
During three nights of the summer.
Corns beneath their heels were growing,
And upon their toes were blisters.

On the first day of their labour
He himself, smith Ilmarinen,   320
Stooped him down, intently gazing,
To the bottom of the furnace,
If perchance amid the fire
Something brilliant had developed.

From the flames there rose a crossbow,
Golden bow from out the furnace;
'Twas a gold bow tipped with silver,
And the shaft shone bright with copper.

And the bow was fair to gaze on,
But of evil disposition: 330
And a head each day demanded,
And on feast-days two demanded.

He himself, smith Ilmarinen,
Was not much delighted with it,
So he broke the bow to pieces,
Cast it back into the furnace,
Made his servants work the bellows,
To the half of all their power.

So again upon the next day,
He himself, smith Ilmarinen,   340
Stooped him down, intently gazing
To the bottom of the furnace,
And a boat rose from the furnace,
From the heat rose up a red boat,
And the prow was golden-coloured,
And the rowlocks were of copper.

And the boat was fair to gaze on,
But of evil disposition;
It would go to needless combat,
And would fight when cause was lacking.   350

Therefore did smith Ilmarinen
Take no slightest pleasure in it.
And he smashed the boat to splinters,
Cast it back into the furnace;

Made his servants work the bellows,
To the half of all their power.
Then upon the third day likewise,
He himself, smith Ilmarinen,
Stooped him down, intently gazing
To the bottom of the furnace,   360
And a heifer then rose upward,
With her horns all golden-shining,
With the Bear-stars on her forehead;
On her head appeared the Sun-disc.

And the cow was fair to gaze on,
But of evil disposition;
Always sleeping in the forest,
On the ground her milk she wasted.

Therefore did smith Ilmarinen
Take no slightest pleasure in her,   370
And he cut the cow to fragments,
Cast her back into the furnace,
Made his servants work the bellows,
To the most of all their power.

So again upon the fourth day,
He himself, smith Ilmarinen
Stooped him down, and gazed intently
To the bottom of the furnace,
And a plough rose from the furnace,
With the ploughshare golden-shining,   380
Golden share, and frame of copper,
And the handles tipped with silver.

And the plough was fair to gaze on,
But of evil disposition,
Ploughing up the village cornfields,
Ploughing up the open meadows.

Therefore did smith Ilmarinen
Take no slightest pleasure in it;
And he broke the plough to pieces,

Cast it back into the furnace,   390
Called the winds to work the bellows
To the utmost of their power.

Then the winds arose in fury,
Blew the east wind, blew the west wind,
And the south wind yet more strongly,
And the north wind howled and blustered.
Thus they blew one day, a second,
And upon the third day likewise.
Fire was flashing from the windows,
From the door the sparks were flying   400
And the dust arose to heaven;
With the clouds the smoke was mingled.

Then again smith Ilmarinen,
On the evening of the third day,
Stooped him down, and gazed intently
To the bottom of the furnace;
And he saw the Sampo forming,
With its brightly-coloured cover.

Thereupon smith Ilmarinen,
He the great primeval craftsman,   410
Welded it and hammered at it,
Heaped his rapid blows upon it,
Forged with cunning art the Sampo:
On one side there was a corn-mill,
On another side a salt-mill,
And upon the third a coin-mill.

Now was grinding the new Sampo,
And revolved the pictured cover,
Chestfuls did it grind till evening,
First for food it ground a chestful,   420
And another ground for barter,
And a third it ground for storage.

Now rejoiced the Crone of Pohja,
And conveyed the bulky Sampo,

To the rocky hills of Pohja,
And within the Mount of Copper,
And behind nine locks secured it;
There it struck its roots around it,
Fathoms nine in depth that measured,
One in Mother Earth deep-rooted,   430
In the strand the next was planted,
In the nearest mount the third one.

Afterwards smith Ilmarinen,
Asked the maiden as his guerdon,
And he spoke the words which follow:
"Will you give me now the maiden,
For the Sampo is completed,
With its beauteous pictured cover?"

Then the lovely maid of Pohja
Answered in the words which follow: 440
"Who in years that this shall follow,
For three summers in succession,
Who shall hear the cuckoo calling,
And the birds all sweetly singing,
If I seek a foreign country,
As in foreign lands a berry?

If the dove had thus departed,
And the maiden thus should wander,
Strayed away the mother's darling,
Likewise would the cranberries vanish,   450
All the cuckoos vanish with them,
And the nightingales would migrate,
From the summit of this mountain,
From the summits of these uplands.

Not as yet can I abandon
My delightful life as maiden,
And my toils and my employments
In the glowing heat of summer:
All unplucked the mountain-berries,
And the lakeshore will be songless,   460
And unvisited the meadows,
And in woods I sport no longer.

Thereupon smith Ilmarinen,
He the great primeval craftsman,
Sad, and with his head down-hanging,
And his cap in grief askew,
Presently began to ponder,
In his head long time debating
How he now should journey homeward,
To his own familiar country,   470
From the gloomy land of Pohja,
Sariola for ever misty.

Then said Pohjola's old Mistress:
"O thou smith, O Ilmarinen
Wherefore is thy mind so saddened,
And thy cap in grief pushed sideways?
Are you thinking how to journey,
Homeward to your native country?"

Said the smith, e'en Ilmarinen:
"Yes, my thoughts are there directed   480
To my home that I may die there,
And may rest in scenes familiar."

Then did Pohjola's old Mistress
Set both meat and drink before him,
At the boat-stern then she placed him,
There to work the copper paddle,
And she bade the wind blow strongly,
And the north wind fiercely bluster.

Thus it was smith Ilmarinen,
He the great primeval craftsman,   490
Travelled homeward to his country,
O'er the blue sea's watery surface.

Thus he voyaged one day, a second,
And at length upon the third day,
Reached the smith his home in safety,
In the land where he was nurtured.

Asked the aged Väinämöinen,
When he saw smith Ilmarinen:
"Ilmarinen, smith and brother,

Thou the great primeval craftsman,   500
Hast thou forged a new-made Sampo,
With its brightly-coloured cover?"

Then replied smith Ilmarinen,
Ready with a fitting answer:
"Grinds forth meal, the new-made Sampo,
And revolves the pictured cover,
Chestfuls does it grind till evening,
First for food it grinds a chestful,
And another grinds for barter,
And a third it grinds for storage."   510

XI Lemminkäinen and Kyllikki

Lemminkäinen goes to seek a wife among the noble maidens of Saari (1–110). At first they laugh at him, but afterwards become very friendly (111–56). But Kyllikki, on whose account he has come, will not listen to him, and at length he carries her off by force, drags her into his sledge, and drives away with her (157–222). Kyllikki weeps, and especially reproaches Lemminkäinen with his fondness for war, and Lemminkäinen promises not to go to war if Kyllikki promises never to go to the village dances, and both swear to observe these conditions (223–314). Lemminkäinen drives home, and mother rejoices in her young daughter-in-law (315–402).

Now 'tis time to speak of Ahti,
Of that lively youth to gossip.
Ahti, dweller in the island,
He the scapegrace son of Lempi,
In a noble house was nurtured,
By his dear and much-loved mother,
Where the bay spread out most widely,
Where the cape extended furthest.

Kauko fed himself on fishes,
Ahti was reared up on perches,   10
And he grew a man most handsome,
Very bold and very ruddy,
And his head was very handsome,
And his form was very shapely,
Yet he was not wholly faultless,
But was careless in his morals:
Passing all his time with women,
Wandering all around at night-time,
When the maidens took their pleasure
In the dance, with locks unbraided.   20

Kylli, beauteous maid of Saari,
Saari's maiden, Saari's flower,
In a noble house was nurtured,
And her stature grew most graceful,
Sitting in her father's dwelling,
Resting there in seat of honour.

Long she grew, and wide was famous:
Suitors came from distant regions,
To the far-famed maiden's homestead,
To the dwelling of the fair one.   30

For his son, the Sun had wooed her;
But she would not go to Sunland,
Where the Sun is ever shining
In the burning heats of summer.

For his son, the Moon had wooed her;
But she would not go to Moonland,
Where the Moon is ever shining,
In the realms of air to wander.

For his son, a Star had wooed her;
But she would not go to Starland,   40
Through the live-long night to glimmer,
In the open skies of winter.
Many suitors came from Viro,
And from Ingerland came others;
None among them pleased the maiden,
And she answered all as follows:
"'Tis for nought your gold you squander,
And your silver waste for nothing.
Never will I go to Viro,
Neither go, nor in the future   50
Row a boat through Viro's waters,
Nor will move a punt from Saari,
Nor will eat the fish of Viro,
Nor the fish-soup eat of Viro.

Nor to Ingerland I'll travel,
Nor its slopes and shores will visit.

There is hunger, nought but hunger,
Want of trees, and want of timber,
Want of water, want of wheatfields,
There is even want of ryebread." 60

Then the lively Lemminkäinen,
He the handsome Kaukomieli,
Now resolved to make a journey
And to woo the Flower of Saari,
Seek at home the peerless fair one,
With her beauteous locks unbraided.

But his mother would dissuade him,
And the aged woman warned him:
"Do not seek, my son, my darling,
Thus to wed above your station. 70
There are none would think you noble
Of the mighty race of Saari!"

Said the lively Lemminkäinen,
Said the handsome Kaukomieli,
"If my house is not as noble,
Nor my race esteemed so mighty,
For my handsome shape they'll choose me,
For my noble form will take me."

But his mother still opposed her
Unto Lemminkäinen's journey, 80
To the mighty race of Saari,
To the clan of vast possessions:
"There the maidens all will scorn you,
And the women ridicule you."

Little heeded Lemminkäinen,
And in words like these he answered:
"I will check the women's laughter,
And the giggling of their daughters;
Sons I'll give unto their bosoms,
Children in their arms to carry; 90
Then they will no longer scorn me,
Thus I'll stop their foolish jesting."

Then his mother made him answer:
"Woe to me, my life is wretched!
If you mock the Saari women,
Bring to shame the modest maidens,
You will bring yourself in conflict,
And a dreadful fight will follow.
All the noble youths of Saari,
Full a hundred skilful swordsmen,   100
All shall rush on thee unhappy,
Standing all alone amidst them."

Little heeded Lemminkäinen
All the warnings of his mother;
Chose the best among his stallions.
And the steed he quickly harnessed,
And he drove away with clatter,
To the village famed of Saari,
There to woo the Flower of Saari,
She, the peerless maid of Saari.   110

But the women ridiculed him,
And the maidens laughed and jeered him.
In the lane he drove most strangely,
Strangely to the farm came driving,
Turned the sledge all topsy-turvy,
At the gate he overturned it.

Then the lively Lemminkäinen
Mouth awry, and head downsunken,
While his black beard he was twisting,
Spoke aloud the words which follow: 120
"Never aught like this I witnessed,
Never saw I, never heard I,
That the women laughed about me,
And the maidens ridiculed me."

Little troubled Lemminkäinen,
And he spoke the words which follow:
"Is there not a place in Saari,
On the firm ground of the island,
For the sport that I will show you,

And for dancing on the greensward,   130
With the joyous girls of Saari,
With their fair unbraided tresses?"

Then the Saari maidens answered,
Spoke the maidens of the headland:
"There is room enough in Saari,
On the firm ground of the island,
For the sport that you shall show us,
And for dancing on the greensward,
For the milkmaids in the meadows,
And the herd-boys in their dances;   140
Very lean are Saari's children,
But the foals are sleek and fattened."

Little troubled Lemminkäinen,
But engaged himself as herd-boy,
Passed his days among the meadows,
And his nights 'mid lively maidens,
Sporting with the charming maidens,
Toying with their unbound tresses.

Thus the lively Lemminkäinen,
He the handsome Kaukomieli,   150
Ended soon the women's laughter,
And the joking of the maidens;
There was not a single daughter,
Not a maid, however modest,
But he did not soon embrace her,
And remain awhile beside her.

One alone of all the maidens,
Of the mighty race of Saari,
Would not list to any lover,
Not the greatest man among them;   160
Kyllikki, the fairest maiden,
Loveliest flower of all in Saari.

Then the lively Lemminkäinen,
He the handsome Kaukomieli,
Wore a hundred boots to tatters,

Rowed in twain a hundred oars,
As he strove to win the maiden,
Kyllikki herself to conquer.

Kyllikki the lovely maiden
Answered him in words that follow: 170
"Wherefore wander here, O weakling,
Racing round me like a plover,
Always seeking for a maiden,
With her tin-adorned girdle?
I myself will never heed you
Till the stone is ground to powder,
Till the pestle's stamped to pieces,
And the mortar smashed to atoms.

Nought I care for such a milksop,
Such a milksop, such a humbug;   180
I must have a graceful husband,
I myself am also graceful;
I must have a shapely husband,
I myself am also shapely;
And a well-proportioned husband,
I myself am also handsome."

But a little time thereafter,
Scarce had half a month passed over,
On a certain day it happened,
As was usual in the evenings,   190
All the girls had met for pleasure,
And the beauteous maids were dancing,
In a grove near open country,
On a lovely space of heathland.
Kyllikki was first among them,
She the far-famed Flower of Saari.
Thither came the ruddy scoundrel,
There drove lively Lemminkäinen,
With the best among his horses,
With the horse that he had chosen,   200
Right into the open playground,
Where the beauteous maids were dancing.
Kyllikki he seized and lifted,
Then into the sledge he pushed her,

And upon the bearskin sat her,
That upon the sledge was lying.

With his whip he lashed the stallion,
And he cracked the lash above him,
And he started on his journey,
And he cried while driving onward: 210
"O ye maidens, may ye never
In your lives betray the secret,
Speak of how I drove among you,
And have carried off the maiden!

But if you will not obey me,
You will fall into misfortune;
To the war I'll sing your lovers,
And the youths beneath the sword-blades,
That you hear no more about them,
See them not in all your lifetime,   220
Either on the paths when walking,
Or across the fields when driving!"

Kyllikki lamented sorely,
Sobbed the beauteous Flower of Saari:
"Let me but depart in safety,
Let the child depart quite freely,
Set me free to journey homeward
To console my weeping mother!

If you will not now release me,
Set me free to journey homeward,   230
O then I have five strong brothers,
And my uncle's sons are seven,
Who can run with hare-like swiftness,
And will haste the maid to rescue."

When she could not gain her freedom,
She began to weep profusely,
And she spoke the words which follow:
"I, poor maid, was born for nothing,
And for nought was born and fostered,
And my life was lived for nothing,   240
Since I fall to one unworthy,

In a worthless fellow's clutches,
One for battle always ready,
And a rude ferocious warrior!"

Answered lively Lemminkäinen,
Said the handsome Kaukomieli:
"Kyllikki, my dearest heart-core,
Thou my sweetest little berry,
Do not vex yourself so sorely,
Do not thus give way to sadness.   250
I will cherish you when eating,
And caress you on my journeys,
Whether sitting, whether standing,
Always near when I am resting!

Wherefore then should you be troubled,
Wherefore should you sigh for sorrow?
Are you therefore grieved so sorely,
Therefore do you sigh for trouble,
Lest the cows or bread might fail you,
Or provisions be deficient?   260

Do not vex yourself so sorely,
I have cows enough and plenty,
Plenty are there, milk to yield me:
Some, Muurikkis, in the marshes,
Some, Mansikkis, on the hillsides,
Some, Puolukkas, on the clearing.
Sleek they are, although unfoddered.
Fine they are, although untended.
In the evening none need bind them,
In the evening none need loose them,   270
No one need provide them fodder,
Nor give salt in morning hours.

Or perchance are you lamenting,
Sighing thus so full of trouble,
That I am not high descended,
Nor was born of noble lineage?

If I am not high descended,
Nor was born of noble lineage,

Yet have I a sword of keenness,
Gleaming brightly in the battle.   280
This is surely high descended,
And has come of noble lineage:
For the blade was forged by Hiisi,
And by Jumala 'twas polished,
Thus am I so high descended,
And I come of noblest lineage,
With my sword so keenly sharpened
Gleaming brightly in the battle."

But the maiden sighed with anguish,
And in words like these made answer: 290
"O thou Ahti, son of Lempi,
If you would caress the maiden,
Keep her at your side for ever,
Dove-like in thy arms for ever,
Pledge thyself by oaths eternal,
Not again to join in battle,
Whether love of gold may lure you,
Or your wish is fixed on silver!"

Then the lively Lemminkäinen
Answered in the words which follow: 300
"Here I swear, by oaths eternal,
Not again to join in battle,
Whether love of gold may lure me,
Or my wish is fixed on silver.
But thyself on oath must pledge thee,
Not to wander to the village,
Whether for the love of dancing,
Or to loiter in the pathways!"

Then they took the oaths between them,
And with oaths eternal bound them,   310
There in Jumala's high presence,
In the sight of the Almighty,
Ahti should not go to battle,
Nor should Kylli seek the village.

Then the lively Lemminkäinen
Whipped his steed to faster running,

Shook the reins to urge him onward,
And he spoke the words which follow:
"Now farewell to Saari's meadows,
Roots of pine, and trunks of fir-trees,   320
Where I wandered for a summer,
Where I tramped throughout the winter,
And on cloudy nights took shelter,
Hiding from the stormy weather,
While I waited for my dear one,
And to bear away my darling!"

On he urged his prancing courser,
Till he saw his home before him,
And the maiden spoke as follows,
And in words like these addressed him: 330
"Lo, I see a hut before us,
Looking like a place of famine.
Tell me whose may be the cottage,
Whose may be this wretched dwelling?"

Then the lively Lemminkäinen
Answered in the words which follow:
"Do not grieve about the hovel,
Sigh not for the hut before you!
We will build us other houses,
And establish better dwellings,   340
Built of all the best of timber,
With the very best of planking."

Thus the lively Lemminkäinen
Reached again his home in safety,
Finding there his dearest mother,
She, his old and much-loved mother,

And his mother spoke as follows,
And expressed herself in thiswise:
"Long, my son, have you been absent,
Long in foreign lands been roaming."   350

Said the lively Lemminkäinen,
And he spoke the words which follow:
"I have brought to shame the women,

With the modest girls have sported,
And have well repaid the laughter,
And the jests they heaped upon me.
To my sledge the best I carried,
And upon the rug I sat her,
And between the runners laid her,
And beneath the rug I hid her;   360
Thus repaid the laughing women,
And the joking of the maidens.

O my mother, who hast borne me,
O my mother, who hast reared me,
I have gained what I have sought for,
And have won what most I longed for.
Now prepare the best of bolsters,
And the softest of the cushions,
In my native land to rest me,
With my young and lovely maiden!"   370

Then his mother spoke as follows,
And in words like these expressed her:
"Now to Jumala he praises,
Praise to thee, O great Creator,
For the daughter thou hast sent me,
Who can fan the flames up brightly,
Who can work at weaving deftly,
And is skilful, too, in spinning,
And accomplished, too, in washing,
And can bleach the clothes to whiteness!   380

For thy own weal thank him also;
Good is won, and good brought homeward:
Good decreed by the Creator,
Good that's granted by his mercy.
On the snow is fair the bunting,
Fairer yet is she beside thee;
White the foam upon the water,
Whiter yet this noble lady:
On the lake the duck is lovely,
Lovelier yet thy cherished darling;   390
Brilliant is a star in heaven,
Brighter yet thy promised fair one.

Let the floors be wide expanded,
And the windows widened greatly,
Let new walls be now erected,
All the house be greatly bettered,
And the threshold new-constructed,
Place new doors upon the threshold,
For the youthful bride beside you,
She, of all the very fairest,   400
She, the best of all the maidens,
And the noblest in her lineage!"

XII Lemminkäinen's first expedition to Pohjola

Kyllikki forgets her oath and goes to the village, whereupon Lemminkäinen is enraged and resolves to divorce her immediately, and to set
forth to woo the Maiden of Pohja (1–128). His mother does her
utmost to dissuade him, telling him that he will very probably be
killed. Lemminkäinen, who is brushing his hair, throws the brush
angrily out of his hand and declares that blood shall flow from the
brush if he should come to harm (129–212). He makes ready, starts
on his journey, comes to Pohjola, and sings all the men out of the
homestead of Pohjola; and only neglects to enchant one wicked
cowherd (213–504).

Then did Ahti Lemminkäinen,
He the handsome Kaukolainen
Live awhile a life of quiet
With the young bride he had chosen,
And he went not forth to battle,
Nor went Kylli to the village.

But at length one day it happened
In the early morning hours,
Forth went Ahti Lemminkäinen
To the place where spawn the fishes,   10
And he came not home at evening,
And at nightfall he returned not.
Kyllikki then sought the village,
There to dance with sportive maidens.

Who shall now the tidings carry,
Who will now convey a message?
Ainikki 'twas, Ahti's sister,
She it was who brought the tidings,
She it was conveyed the message:
"Ahti, O my dearest brother,   20

Kyllikki has sought the village,
Entered there the gates of strangers,
Where the village girls are sporting,
Dancing with unbraided tresses."

Ahti then, for ever boyish,
He the lively Lemminkäinen,
Grew both sorrowful and angry,
And for long was wild with fury,
And he spoke the words which follow:
"O my mother, aged woman,   30
Wash my shirt, and wash it quickly
In the black snake's deadly venom,
Dry it then, and dry it quickly
That I may go forth to battle,
And contend with youths of Pohja,
And o'erthrow the youths of Lapland.
Kyllikki has sought the village,
Entered there the gates of strangers,
There to dance with sportive maidens,
With their tresses all unbraided."   40

Kyllikki made answer promptly,
She his favoured bride responded:
"Ahti, O my dearest husband,
Do not now depart to battle!
I beheld while I was sleeping,
While my slumber was the deepest,
From the hearth the flames were flashing,
Flashing forth with dazzling brightness,
Leaping up below the windows,
To the furthest walls extending,   50
Then throughout the house blazed fiercely,
Like a cataract in its fury,
O'er the surface of the flooring,
And from window unto window."

But the lively Lemminkäinen
Answered in the words which follow:
"Nought I trust in dreams of women,
Nor rely on woman's insight.
O my mother who hast borne me,

Bring me here my war-shirt quickly,　　　60
Bring me, too, my mail for battle!
For my inclination leads me
Hence to drink the beer of battle,
And to taste the mead of combat."

Then his mother spoke in answer:
"O my son, my dearest Ahti,
Do thou not go forth to battle!
In the house is beer in plenty,
In the barrels made of alder,
And behind the taps of oakwood.　　　70
It is seasoned now for drinking,
And all day canst thou be drinking."

Said the lively Lemminkäinen,
"But for home-brewed ale I care not,
Rather would I drink stream-water,
From the end of tarry rudder,
And this drink were sweeter to me
Than the beer in all our cellars.
Bring me here my war-shirt quickly,
Bring me, too, my mail for battle!　　　80
I will seek the homes of Pohja,
And o'erthrow the youths of Lapland,
And for gold will ask the people,
And I will demand their silver."

Then said Lemminkäinen's mother,
"O my son, my dearest Ahti,
We ourselves have gold in plenty,
Silver plenty in the storeroom.
Only yesterday it happened,
In the early hours of morning,　　　90
Ploughed the slave a field of vipers,
Full of twining, twisting serpents,
And a chest-lid raised the ploughshare,
And the chest was full of money.
Coins by hundreds there were hidden,
Thousands there were squeezed together,
To our stores the chest was carried,
In the loft we stored it safely."

Said the lively Lemminkäinen,
"Nought I care for home-stored treasures.   100
I will win me marks in battle,
Treasures won by far are better,
Than the gold in all our storerooms,
Or the silver found in ploughing.
Bring me here my war-shirt quickly,
Bring me, too, my mail for battle,
I will go to war in Pohja,
To destroy the sons of Lapland!

There my inclination leads me
And my understanding drives me,   110
And my own ears shall inform me,
And my own eyes show me truly,
If in Pohjola a maiden,
In Pimentola a maiden,
Is not longing for a lover,
For the best of men desirous."

Then said Lemminkäinen's mother,
"O my son, my dearest Ahti,
Kyllikki at home is with thee,
Fairest she of all the housewives.   120
Strange it were to see two women
In a bed beside one husband."

Said the lively Lemminkäinen,
"Kyllikki has sought the village.
Let her go to all the dances,
Let her sleep in all the houses,
Where the village girls are sporting,
Dancing with unbraided tresses!"

Still his mother would dissuade him,
And the aged woman warned him: 130
"Yet beware, my son, and go not
Unto Pohjola's dread homestead,
Destitute of magic knowledge,
Destitute of all experience,
There to meet the youths of Pohja,

And to conquer Lapland's children!
There the Laplanders will sing you,
And the Turja men will thrust you,
Head in clay, and mouth in charcoal,
With your arms where sparks are flying,   140
And your hands in glowing embers,
There upon the burning hearthstones."

Lemminkäinen heard and answered:
"Once some sorcerers would enchant me,
Wizards charm, and snakes would blast me,
As three Laplanders attempted
Through the night in time of summer,
On a rock all naked standing,
Wearing neither clothes nor waistband;
Not a rag was twisted round them,   150
But they got what I could give them,
So much got those wretched creatures,
Like the axe from stone that's battered,
Or against the rock the auger,
Or on slippery ice a sabot,
Or like Death in empty houses.

Otherwise indeed they threatened,
Otherwise events had happened,
For they wanted to o'erthrow me,
Threatened they would sink me deeply   160
In the swamp when I was walking,
That in mire I might be sunken,
In the mud my chin pushed downward,
And my beard in filthy places.
But indeed a man they found me,
And they did not greatly fright me.
I myself put forth my magic,
And began my spells to mutter,
Sang the wizards with their arrows,
And the archers with their weapons,   170
Sorcerers with their knives of iron,
Soothsayers with their pointed weapons,
Under Tuoni's mighty Cataract,
Where the surge is most terrific,

Underneath the highest cataract,
'Neath the worst of all the whirlpools.
There the sorcerers now may slumber,
There repose beneath their blankets,
Till the grass may spring above them,
Through their heads and caps sprout upward,   180
Through the arm-pits of the sorcerers,
Piercing through their shoulder-muscles,
While the wizards sleep in soundness,
Sleeping there without protection."

Still his mother would restrain him,
Hinder Lemminkäinen's journey,
Once again her son dissuaded,
And the dame held back the hero:
"Do not go, O do not venture
To that cold and dreary village,   190
To the gloomy land of Pohja!
There destruction sure awaits you,
Evil waits for thee, unhappy,
Ruin, lively Lemminkäinen!
Hadst thou hundred mouths to speak with,
Even so, one could not think it,
Nor that by thy songs of magic
Lapland's sons would be confounded,
For you know not Turja's language,
Not the tongue they speak in Lapland."   200

Then the lively Lemminkäinen,
He the handsome Kaukomieli,
As it chanced, his hair was brushing,
And with greatest neatness brushed it.
To the wall his brush then cast he,
To the stove the comb flung after,
And again he spoke and answered,
In the very words which follow:
"Then ruin falls on Lemminkäinen,
Evil waits for him unhappy,   210
When the brush with blood is running,
And the comb with blood is streaming."

Then went lively Lemminkäinen,
To the gloomy land of Pohja,
'Spite the warnings of his mother,
'Gainst the aged woman's counsel.

First he armed him, and he girt him,
In his coat of mail he clad him,
With a belt of steel encompassed,
And he spoke the words which follow: 220
"Stronger feels a man in armour,
In the best of iron mail-coats,
And of steel a magic girdle,
As a wizard 'gainst magicians.
Then no trouble need alarm him,
Nor the greatest evil fright him."

Then he grasped his sword so trusty,
Took his blade, like flame that glittered,
Which by Hiisi's self was whetted,
And by Jumala was polished.   230
By his side the hero girt it,
Thrust in sheath with leather lining.

How shall now the man conceal him,
And the mighty hero hide him?
There a little time he hid him,
And the mighty one concealed him,
'Neath the beam above the doorway,
By the doorpost of the chamber,
In the courtyard by the hayloft,
By the gate of all the furthest.   240

Thus it was the hero hid him
From the sight of all the women;
But such art is not sufficient,
And such caution would not serve him,
For he likewise must protect him
From the heroes of the people,
There where two roads have their parting,
On a blue rock's lofty summit,

And upon the quaking marshes,
Where the waves are swiftly coursing,   250
Where the waterfall is rushing,
In the winding of the rapids.

Then the lively Lemminkäinen
Spoke the very words which follow:
"Rise ye up from earth, O swordsmen,
You, the earth's primeval heroes,
From the wells arise, ye warriors,
From the rivers rise, ye bowmen!
With thy dwarfs arise, O woodland,
Forest, come with all thy people,   260
Mountain-Ancient, with thy forces,
Water-Hiisi, with thy terrors,
Water-Mistress, with thy people,
With thy scouts, O Water-Father,
All ye maidens from the valleys,
Richly robed, among the marshes,
Come ye to protect a hero,
Comrades of a youth most famous,
That the sorcerers' arrows strike not,
Nor the swords of the magicians,   270
Nor the knife-blades of enchanters,
Nor the weapons of the archers!

If this be not yet sufficient,
Still I know of other measures,
And implore the very Highest,
Even Ukko in the heavens,
He of all the clouds the ruler,
Of the scattered clouds conductor.

Ukko, thou of Gods the highest,
Aged Father in the heavens,   280
Thou amidst the clouds who breathest,
Thou amid the air who speakest!
Give me here a sword of fire,
By a sheath of fire protected,
That I may resist misfortune,
And I may avoid destruction,

Overthrow the powers infernal,
Overcome the water-sorcerers,
That all foes who stand before me,
And the foes who stand behind me,   290
And above me and beside me,
May be forced to own my power.
Crush the sorcerers, with their arrows,
The magicians, with their knife-blades,
And the wizards with their sword-blades,
All the scoundrels with their weapons!"

Then the lively Lemminkäinen,
He the handsome Kaukomieli,
From the bush his courser whistled,
From the grass, the gold-maned courser.   300
Thereupon the horse he harnessed,
In the shafts the fiery courser,
In the sledge himself he seated,
And the sledge began to rattle.
O'er the horse his whip he flourished,
Cracked the whip, and urged him onward,
Started quickly on his journey.
Rocked the sledge, the way grew shorter,
And the silver sand was scattered,
And the golden heather crackled.   310

Thus he drove one day, a second,
Drove upon the third day likewise,
And at length upon the third day
Came the hero to a village.

Then the lively Lemminkäinen
Drove the rattling sledge straight onward
Forth along the furthest pathway,
To the furthest of the houses,
And he asked upon the threshold,
Speaking from behind the window: 320
"Is there some one in this household
Who can loose my horse's harness,
And can sink the shaft-poles for me,
And can loose the horse's collar?"

From the floor a child made answer,
And a boy from out the doorway:
"There is no one in this household,
Who can loose your horse's harness,
Or can sink the shaft-poles for you,
Or can loose the horse's collar."   330

Little troubled Lemminkäinen,
O'er the horse his whip he brandished,
With the beaded whip he smote him,
Drove the rattling sledge straight onward,
On the midmost of the pathways
To the midmost of the houses,
And he asked upon the threshold,
And beneath the eaves he shouted:
"Is there no one in this household
Who will hold the horse-reins for me,   340
And the chest-bands will unloosen,
That the foaming steed may rest him?"

From the stove a crone responded
From the stove-bench cried a gossip:
"There are plenty in this household
Who can hold the horse-reins for you,
And the chest-bands can unloosen,
And can sink the shaft-poles for you.
Perhaps ten men may be sufficient,
Or a hundred if you need them,   350
Who would raise their sticks against you,
Give you, too, a beast of burden,
And would drive you homeward, rascal,
To your country, wretched creature,
To the household of your father,
To the dwelling of your mother,
To the gateway of your brother,
To the threshold of your sister,
Ere this very day is ended,
Ere the sun has reached its setting."   360

Little heeded Lemminkäinen,
And he spoke the words which follow:

"May they shoot the crone, and club her,
On her crooked chin, and kill her."
Then again he hurried onward,
Thundering on upon his journey,
On the highest of the pathways,
To the highest of the houses.

Then the lively Lemminkäinen
Reached the house to which he journeyed,   370
And he spoke the words which follow,
And expressed himself in thiswise:
"Stop the barker's mouth, O Hiisi,
And the dog's jaws close, O Lempo,
And his mouth securely muzzle,
That his gagged teeth may be harmless,
That he may not bark a warning
When a man is passing by him!"

As he came into the courtyard,
On the ground he slashed his whiplash,   380
From the spot a cloud rose upward,
In the cloud a dwarf was standing,
And he quickly loosed the chest-bands,
And the shafts he then let downward.
Then the lively Lemminkäinen
Listened with his ears attentive,
But no person there observed him,
So that no one present knew it.
Out of doors he heard a singing,
Through the moss he heard them speaking,   390
Through the walls heard music playing,
Through the shutters heard a singing.

In the house he cast his glances,
Gazed into the room in secret,
And the house was full of wizards,
And the benches full of singers,
By the walls there sat musicians.
Seers were sitting in the doorway,
On the upper benches sorcerers,
By the hearth were soothsayers seated,   400

There a Lapland bard was singing,
Hoarsely singing songs of Hiisi.

Then the lively Lemminkäinen
Thought it wise to change his figure,
To another shape transformed him,
Left his hiding place, and entered,
Thrust himself into the chamber,
And he spoke the words which follow:
"Fine a song may be when ended,
Grandest are the shortest verses,   410
Wisdom better when unspoken,
Than in midmost interrupted."

Then came Pohjola's old Mistress,
On the floor advancing swiftly,
Till she reached the chamber's middle,
And she spoke these words in answer:
"Once there was a dog among us,
Shaggy iron-haired puppy,
Eating flesh, of bones a biter,
One who licked the blood when freshest;   420
Who among mankind may you be,
Who among the list of heroes,
Boldly thus the house to enter,
Pushing right into the chamber,
Yet the dogs have never heard you,
Nor have warned us with their barking?"

Said the lively Lemminkäinen,
"Surely I have not come hither,
Void of art and void of knowledge,
Void of strength and void of cunning,   430
Taught not magic by my father,
And without my parents' counsel,
That your dogs should now devour me,
And the barkers should attack me.

But it was my mother washed me,
When a boy both small and slender,
Three times in the nights of summer,
Nine times in the nights of autumn,

And she taught me all the pathways,
And the knowledge of all countries, 440
And at home sang songs of magic,
Likewise too in foreign countries."

Then the lively Lemminkäinen,
He the handsome Kaukomieli,
Soon began his songs of magic,
All at once began his singing;
Fire flashed from his fur-cloak's borders,
And his eyes with flame were shining,
With the songs of Lemminkäinen,
As he sang his spells of magic. 450

Sang the very best of singers
To the worst of all the singers,
And he fed their mouths with pebbles,
And he piled up rocks above them,
On the best of all the singers,
And most skilful of magicians.

Then he sang the men thereafter
Both to one side and the other:
To the plains, all bare and treeless,
To the lands, unploughed for ever, 460
To the ponds, devoid of fishes,
Where no perch has ever wandered,
To the dreadful falls of Rutja,
And amid the roaring whirlpools,
Underneath the foaming river,
To the rocks beneath the cataract,
There to burn as if 'mid fire,
And to scatter sparks around them.

Then the lively Lemminkäinen
Sang his songs against the swordsmen. 470
Sang the heroes with their weapons,
Sang the young men, sang the old men,
And the men of age between them,
And his songs spared one man only:
And he was a wicked cowherd,
Old, with eyes both closed and sightless.

Märkähattu then, the cowherd,
Spoke the very words which follow:
"O thou lively son of Lempi,
Thou hast banned the young and old men,   480
Banned the men of age between them,
Wherefore hast not banned me likewise?"

Said the lively Lemminkäinen,
"Therefore 'tis that I have spared thee,
That thou dost appear so wretched,
Pitiful without my magic.
In the days when thou wast younger,
Thou wast worst of all the cowherds,
Hast destroyed thy mother's children,
And disgraced thy very sister,   490
All the horses hast thou crippled,
All the foals hast thou outwearied,
In the swamps or stony places,
Plashing through the muddy waters."

Märkähattu then, the cowherd,
Greatly vexed, and greatly angry,
Through the open door went quickly,
Through the yard to open country,
Ran to Tuonela's deep river,
To the sacred river's whirlpool,   500
Waited there for Kaukomieli,
Waited there for Lemminkäinen,
Till on his return from Pohja,
He should make his journey homeward.

XIII   Hiisi's elk

Lemminkäinen asks the old woman of Pohja for her daughter, but she demands that he should first capture the Elk of Hiisi on snowshoes (1–30). Lemminkäinen starts off in high spirits to hunt the elk, but it escapes, and he breaks his snowshoes and spear (31–270).

Then the lively Lemminkäinen
Said to Pohjola's old Mistress,
"Give me, old one, now your maiden,
Bring me here your lovely daughter,
She the best of all among them,
She the tallest of the maidens!"

Then did Pohjola's old Mistress
Answer in the words which follow:
"Nay, I will not give my maiden,
And you shall not have my daughter,   10
Not the best or worst among them,
Not the tallest, not the shortest;
For you have a wife already,
Long the mistress of your household."

Said the lively Lemminkäinen,
"Kylli in the town lies fettered,
At the steps before the village,
By the gate where strangers enter,
So a better wife I wish for;
Therefore give me now your daughter,   20
She the fairest of your daughters,
Loveliest among the maidens!"

Then said Pohjola's old Mistress,
"Never will I give my daughter

To a vain and worthless fellow,
To a hero good for nothing.
Therefore you may woo my daughter,
Win the flower-crowned maiden,
If you hunt the elk on snowshoes,
In the distant field of Hiisi."   30

Then the lively Lemminkäinen
Fixed the point upon his javelin,
And his bowstring made of sinew,
And with bone he tipped his arrows,
And he said the words which follow:
"Now my javelin I have pointed,
All my shafts with bone have pointed,
And have strung my bow with sinew,
Not the snowshoe left for gliding,
Nor the right one to kick forward."   40

Then the lively Lemminkäinen
Pondered deeply and reflected,
How he should procure his snowshoes,
How they best should be constructed.

Then to Kauppi's house he hastened,
And to Lyylikki's forge hurried:
"O thou wisest Vuojalainen,
Thou the handsome Lapland Kauppi,
Make me snowshoes that will suit me,
Fitted with the finest leather;   50
I must chase the elk of Hiisi,
In the distant field of Hiisi!"

Lyylikki then spoke as follows,
Kauppi gave him ready answer:
"Vainly goest thou, Lemminkäinen,
Forth to hunt the elk of Hiisi;
For a piece of rotten timber,
Only will reward your labour."

Little troubled Lemminkäinen,
And he spoke the words which follow: 60
"Make a snowshoe left to run with,

And a right one to kick forward!
I must chase the elk on snowshoes,
In the distant field of Hiisi."

Lyylikki, the smith of snowshoes,
Maker, of the snowshoes,
In the autumn shaped the left one,
In the winter carved the right one,
And he fixed the poles on one day,
Fixed the rings upon another.   70

Now the left was fit to glide with,
And the right for wearing ready,
And the poles were now completed,
And the rings were also fitted.
Poles he bought with skins of otter,
And the rings with ruddy foxskin.

Then he smeared with grease the snowshoes,
Smeared them with the fat of reindeer,
And himself reflected deeply,
And he spoke the words which follow: 80
"Can you, in this youthful frolic,
You, a young and untried hero,
Forward glide upon the left shoe,
And push forward with the right one?"

Said the lively Lemminkäinen,
Answered him the ruddy rascal:
"Yes, upon this youthful frolic
Of a young and untried hero,
I can glide upon the left shoe,
And kick forward with the right one."   90

On his back he bound his quiver,
And his new bow on his shoulder,
In his hands his pole grasped firmly,
On the left shoe glided forward,
And kicked onward with the right one,
And he spoke the words which follow:
"In God's world may there be nothing,
Underneath the arch of heaven,

In the forest to be hunted,
Not a single four-foot runner,
Which may not be overtaken,   100
And can easily be captured
Thus by Kaleva's son with snowshoes,
And with Lemminkäinen hunting."

But the boast was heard by Hiisi,
And by Juutas comprehended;
And an elk was formed by Hiisi,
And a reindeer formed by Juutas,
With a head of rotten timber,
Horns composed of willow-branches,   110
Feet of ropes the swamps which border,
Shins of sticks from out the marshes;
And his back was formed of fence-stakes,
Sinews formed of dryest grass-stalks,
Eyes of water-lily flowers,
Ears of leaves of water-lily,
And his hide was formed of pine-bark,
And his flesh of rotten timber.

Hiisi now the elk instructed,
Thus he spoke unto the reindeer: 120
"Now rush forth thou elk of Hiisi,
On thy legs, O noble creature,
To the breeding-place of reindeer,
Grassy plains of Lapland's children,
Till the snowshoe-men are sweating;
Most of all, this Lemminkäinen!"

Then rushed forth the elk of Hiisi,
Sped away the fleeing reindeer,
Rushing past the barns of Pohja,
To the plains of Lapland's children,   130
In the house the tubs kicked over,
On the fire upset the kettles,
Threw the meat among the ashes,
Spilt the soup among the cinders.

Then arose a great commotion,
On the plains of Lapland's children,

For the Lapland dogs were barking,
And the Lapland children crying,
And the Lapland women laughing,
And the other people grumbling.   140

He, the lively Lemminkäinen,
Chased the elk upon his snowshoes,
Glided o'er the land and marshes,
O'er the open wastes he glided.
Fire was crackling from his snowshoes,
From his staff's end smoke ascending,
But as yet the elk he saw not;
Could not see it; could not hear it.

O'er the hills and dales he glided,
Through the lands beyond the ocean,   150
Over all the wastes of Hiisi,
Over all the heaths of Kalma,
And before the mouth of Surma,
And behind the house of Kalma.
Surma's mouth was quickly opened,
Down was bowed the head of Kalma,
That he thus might seize the hero,
And might swallow Lemminkäinen;
But he tried, and failed to reach him,
Failed completely in his effort.   160

O'er all lands he had not journeyed,
Nor had reached the desert's borders,
In the furthest bounds of Pohja,
In the distant realms of Lapland;
So he journeyed further onward,
Till he reached the desert's borders.

When he reached this distant region,
Then he heard a great commotion,
In the furthest bounds of Pohja,
On the plains of Lapland's children.   170
And he heard the dogs were barking,
And the Lapland children crying,
And the Lapland women laughing,
And the other Lapps were grumbling.

Then the lively Lemminkäinen
Journeyed on in that direction,
Where he heard the dogs were barking
On the plains of Lapland's children;
And he said on his arrival,
And he asked them on his coming: 180
"Wherefore are the women laughing,
Women laughing, children crying,
And the older folks lamenting,
And the grey dogs all are barking?"

"Therefore are the women laughing,
Women laughing, children crying,
And the older folks lamenting,
And the grey dogs all are barking:
Here has charged the elk of Hiisi,
With its hoofs all cleft and polished,   190
In the house the tubs kicked over,
On the fire upset the kettles,
Shaken out the soup within them,
Spilt it all among the ashes."

Thereupon the ruddy rascal,
He the lively Lemminkäinen,
Struck his left shoe in the snowdrift,
Like an adder in the meadow,
Pushed his shoe of pinewood forward,
As it were a living serpent,   200
And he said as he was gliding,
Grasping firm the pole he carried:
"Let the men who live in Lapland,
Help me all to bring the elk home;
And let all the Lapland women
Set to work to wash the kettles;
And let all the Lapland children
Hasten forth to gather splinters;
And let all the Lapland kettles
Help to cook the elk when captured!"   210

Then he poised himself and balanced,
Forward pushed, his strength exerting,
And the first time he shot forward,
From before their eyes he vanished.

Once again he speeded onward,
And they could no longer hear him,
But the third time he rushed onward,
Then he reached the elk of Hiisi.

Then he took a pole of maple,
And he made a birchen collar;   220
Hiisi's elk he tethered with it,
In a pen of oak he placed it:
"Stand thou there, O elk of Hiisi,
Here remain, O nimble reindeer!"

Then upon the back he stroked it,
Patted it upon the belly:
"Would that I awhile might tarry,
And might sleep awhile and rest me,
Here beside a youthful maiden,
With a dove of blooming beauty."   230

This made Hiisi's elk grow furious,
And the reindeer kicked out wildly,
And it spoke the words which follow:
"Lempo's self shall reckon with you,
If you sleep beside a maiden,
And beside a girl should tarry!"

Then it gave a mighty struggle,
And it snapped the birchen collar,
And it broke the pole of maple,
And the pen of oak burst open,   240
And began to hurry forwards,
And the elk rushed wildly onwards,
Over land and over marshes,
Over slopes o'ergrown with bushes,
Till the eyes no more could see it,
And the ears no longer hear it.

Thereupon the ruddy rascal
Grew both sorrowful and angry,
Very vexed and very angry,
And would chase the elk of Hiisi,   250
But as he was rushing forward,
In a hole he broke his left shoe,

Soon both shoes were split to pieces,
In the midst he broke the right one,
Broke the tip from off his snowshoe,
And the poles across the joinings.
While rushed on the elk of Hiisi,
Till its head he saw no longer.

Then the lively Lemminkäinen,
Bowed his head in deep depression,   260
Gazed upon the broken snowshoes,
And he spoke the words which follow:
"Nevermore in all his lifetime
May another hunter venture
Confidently to the forest,
Chasing Hiisi's elk on snowshoes,
Since I went, O me unhappy,
And have spoilt the best of snowshoes,
And the splendid poles have shattered,
And my spearpoint likewise broken!"   270

XIV   Lemminkäinen's death

Lemminkäinen invokes the forest deities, and at length succeeds in capturing the elk, and brings it to Pohjola (1–270). Another task is given him, to bridle the fire-breathing steed of Hiisi. He bridles it and brings it to Pohjola (271–372). A third task is assigned him, to shoot a swan on the river of Tuonela. Lemminkäinen comes to the river, but the despised cowherd, who is lying in wait for him, kills him, and casts his body into the cataract of Tuoni. The son of Tuoni then cuts his body to pieces (373–460).

Then the lively Lemminkäinen
Deeply pondered and reflected,
On the path that he should follow,
Whither he should turn his footsteps:
Should he leave the elk of Hiisi,
And direct his journey homewards,
Should he make another effort,
And pursue the chase on snowshoes,
With the Forest-Queen's permission,
And the favour of the wood-nymphs?   10

Then he spoke the words which follow,
And in words like these expressed him:
"Ukko, thou of Gods the highest,
Gracious Father in the heavens!
Make me now two better snowshoes,
Leather snowshoes fit for sliding,
That I glide upon them swiftly
Over land and over marshes,
Glide throughout the land of Hiisi,
And across the heaths of Pohja,   20
There to chase the elk of Hiisi,
And to catch the nimble reindeer!

In the wood alone I wander,
Toil without another hero,
Through the pathways of Tapiola,
And beside the home of Tapio.
Welcome, wooded slopes and mountains,
Welcome to the rustling pinewoods,
Welcome to the grey head aspens,
And to all who greet me, welcome!   30
Be propitious wood and thicket,
Gracious Tapio, do thou aid me,
Bring the hero to the islands,
To the hills in safety lead him,
Where he can attain the quarry,
Whence he may bring back the booty!

Nyyrikki, O son of Tapio,
Thou the mighty red-capped hero!
Blaze the path across the country,
And erect me wooden guide-posts,   40
That I trace this evil pathway,
And pursue the rightful roadway,
While I seek my destined quarry,
And the booty I am seeking!

Mielikki, the forest's mistress,
Thou the mighty, fair-faced mother!
Let thy gold now wander onward,
And thy silver set in motion,
Right before the man who seeks it,
On the pathway of the seeker!   50

Take the keys of gold, suspended
By the ring that hangs beside thee,
Open thou the stores of Tapio,
And his castle in the forest,
During this my hunting-season,
While I hunt in distant regions!

If thyself thou wilt not trouble,
Strictly charge thy little maidens,
Send thy serving maidens to me,
Give thy orders to thy servants!   60

If thou canst not be my hostess,
Do thou not forbid thy maidens,
For thou hast a hundred maidens,
And a thousand at thy orders,
Those on all thy herds attending,
Likewise all thy game protecting.

Little maiden of the forest,
Tapio's girl, with mouth of honey!
Play upon thy flute of honey,
Whistle through thy pipe of honey,   70
In thy noble mistress' hearing,
Gracious queen of all the forest,
That she soon may hear the music,
And from her repose may rouse her,
For she does not hear at present,
And she but awakens rarely,
Though I supplicate for ever,
With my golden tongue imploring!"

Then the lively Lemminkäinen
Wandered on, but found no booty,   80
Glided through the plains and marshes,
Glided on through the trackless forests,
Where has Jumala his soot-hills,
To the charcoal heaths of Hiisi.

Thus he skated one day, two days,
And at length upon the third day,
Came he to a lofty mountain,
Where he climbed a rock stupendous,
And he turned his eyes to north-west,
To the north across the marshes,   90
And he saw the farms of Tapio,
With the doors all golden shining,
To the north, across the marshes,
On the slope among the thickets.

Then the lively Lemminkäinen
Quickly to the spot approaching,
Pushed his way through all obstructions,
Under Tapio's very windows.

And he looked while stooping forward,
In the sixth among the windows.   100
There were resting game-dispensers,
Matrons of the woods reposing,
All were in their work-day garments,
And with filthy rags were covered.

Said the lively Lemminkäinen,
"Wherefore, Mistress of the Forest,
Dost thou wear thy work-day garments,
Dirty ragged thresher's garments?
You are very black to gaze on,
And your whole appearance dreadful,   110
For your breast is most disgusting,
All your form is very homely.

When before I tracked the forests,
I beheld three castles standing.
One was wooden, one a bone one,
And the third of stone was builded.
There were six bright golden windows
On the sides of every castle,
And if then I gazed within them,
'Neath the wall as I was standing,   120
Saw the lord of Tapio's household,
And the mistress of his household;
Tellervo, the maid of Tapio,
And the rest of Tapio's household,
All in rustling golden garments,
And parading there in silver;
She herself, the Forest-Mistress,
Gracious Mistress of the Forest,
On her wrists were golden bracelets,
Golden rings upon her fingers,   130
On her head a golden head-dress,
And her hair adorned with ducats,
In her ears were golden earrings,
Finest beads her neck encircling.

Gracious Mistress of the Forest,
Of sweet Metsola the matron!
Cast away thy hay-shoes from thee,

And discard thy shoes of birch-bark,
Cast thou off thy threshing garments,
And thy wretched work-day garments,   140
Don thy garments of good fortune,
And thy blouse for game-dispensing,
In the days I track the forest,
Seeking for a hunter's booty!
Long and wearily I wander,
Wearily I track my pathway,
Yet I wander here for nothing,
All the time without a quarry.
If you do not grant me booty,
Nor reward me for my labour,   150
Long and sad will be the evening,
Long the day when game is wanting.

Aged greybeard of the forest,
With thy pine-leaf hat and moss-cloak!
Dress thou now the woods in linen,
And the wilds a cloth throw over.
All the aspens robe in greyness,
And the alders robe in beauty,
Clothe the pine-trees all in silver,
And with gold adorn the fir-trees.   160
Aged pine-trees belt with copper,
Belt the fir-trees all with silver,
Birch-trees with their golden blossoms,
And their trunks with gold adornments.
Make it as in former seasons
Even when thy days were better,
When the fir-shoots shone in moonlight,
And the pine-boughs in the sunlight,
When the wood was sweet with honey,
And the blue wilds flowed with honey,   170
Smelt like malt the heathlands' borders,
From the very swamps ran butter!

Forest-maiden, gracious virgin,
Tuulikki, O Tapio's daughter!
Drive the game in this direction,
Out into the open heathland.
If it runs with heavy footsteps,
Or is lazy in its running,

Take a switch from out the bushes,
Or a birch-twig from the valley,   180
Switch the game upon the haunches,
And upon the flanks, O whip it,
Drive it swiftly on before you,
Make it hasten quickly onward,
To the man who here awaits it,
In the pathway of the hunter!

If the game comes on the footpath,
Drive it forward to the hero,
Do thou put thy hands together,
And on both sides do thou guide it,   190
That the game may not escape me,
Rushing back in wrong direction.
If the game should seek to fly me,
Rushing in the wrong direction,
Seize its ear, and drag it forward
By the horns upon the pathway!

If there's brushwood on the pathway,
Drive it to the pathway's edges;
If a tree should block the pathway,
Then the tree-trunk break asunder!   200

If a fence obstructs the pathway,
Thrust the fence aside before you,
Take five withes to hold it backward,
And seven posts whereon to bind them!

If a river runs before thee,
Or a brook should cross the pathway,
Build thou then a bridge all silken,
With a red cloth for a gateway;
Drive the game by narrow pathways,
And across the quaking marshes,   210
Over Pohjola's wide rivers,
O'er the waterfalls all foaming!

Master of the house of Tapio,
Mistress of the house of Tapio;
Aged greybeard of the forest,

King of all the golden forest;
Mimerkki, the forest's mistress,
Fair dispenser of its treasures,
Blue-robed woman of the bushes,
Mistress of the swamps, red-stockinged!   220
Come, with me thy gold to barter,
Come, with me to change thy silver.
I have gold as old as moonlight,
Silver old as is the sunlight,
Which I won in battle-tumult,
In the contest of the heroes,
Useful in my purse I found it,
Where it jingled in the darkness;
If thy gold thou wilt not barter,
Perhaps thou wilt exchange thy silver."   230

Thus the lively Lemminkäinen
For a week on snowshoes glided,
Sang a song throughout the forest,
There among the depths of jungle,
And appeased the forest's mistress,
And the forest's master likewise,
And delighted all the maidens,
Pleasing thus the girls of Tapio.
Then they hunted and drove onward
From its lair the elk of Hiisi,   240
Past the wooded hills of Tapio,
Past the bounds of Hiisi's mountain,
To the man who waited for it,
To the sorcerer in his ambush.

Then the lively Lemminkäinen
Coiled his lasso, and he threw it
O'er the elk of Hiisi's shoulders,
Round the bull's broad neck he threw it,
That it should not kick in fury,
When upon its back he stroked it.   250

Then the lively Lemminkäinen
Spoke aloud the words which follow:
"Lord of woods, of earth the master,
Fairest creature of the heathlands;

Mielikki, the forest's mistress,
Loveliest of the game-dispensers!
Come to take the gold I promised,
Come ye now to choose the silver,
On the ground lay down your linen,
Spreading out of flax the finest,   260
Underneath the gold that glitters,
Underneath the shining silver,
That upon the ground it fall not,
Nor among the dirt is scattered!"

Then to Pohjola he journeyed,
And he said on his arrival:
"I have chased the elk of Hiisi
On the distant plains of Hiisi.
Give me now, old dame, your daughter.
Give the youthful bride I seek for!"   270

Louhi, Pohjola's old Mistress
Heard his words, and then made answer:
"I will only give my daughter,
Give the youthful bride you seek for,
If you rein the mighty gelding,
He the chestnut steed of Hiisi,
He the foaming foal of Hiisi,
On the bounds of Hiisi's meadow."

Then the lively Lemminkäinen
Took at once a golden bridle,   280
Took a halter all of silver,
And he went to seek the courser,
Went to seek the yellow-maned one,
On the bounds of Hiisi's meadow.

Then he hastened on his journey,
On his way went swiftly forward,
Through the green and open meadows,
To the sacred field beyond them,
And he sought there for the courser,
Seeking for the yellow-maned one.   290
At his belt the bit he carried,
And the harness on his shoulder.

Thus he sought one day, a second,
And at length upon the third day
Came he to a lofty mountain,
And upon a rock he clambered.
And he turned his eyes to eastward,
And he turned his head to sunwards.
On the sand he saw the courser,
'Mid the firs the yellow-maned one.   300
From his hair the flame was flashing,
From his mane the smoke was rising.

Thereupon prayed Lemminkäinen:
"Ukko, thou of Gods the highest,
Ukko, thou of clouds the leader,
Of the scattered clouds conductor!
Open now thy clefts in heaven,
And in all the sky thy windows,
Let the iron hail fall downwards,
Send thou down the frozen masses,   310
On the mane of that good courser,
On the back of Hiisi's courser!"

Ukko then, the great Creator,
Jumala 'mid clouds exalted,
Heard and rent the air asunder,
Clove in twain the vault of heaven,
Scattered ice, and scattered iceblocks,
Scattered down the iron hailstones,
Smaller than a horse's head is,
Larger than a head of man is,   320
On the mane of that good courser,
On the back of Hiisi's courser,

Then the lively Lemminkäinen,
Forward stepped to gaze about him,
And advanced for observation,
And he spoke the words which follow:
"Hiitola's most mighty courser,
Mountain foal, with mane all foam-flecked,
Give me now thy golden muzzle,
Stretch thou forth thy head of silver,   330
Push it in the golden bridle,

With the bit of shining silver!
I will never treat you badly,
And I will not drive you harshly,
And our way is but a short one,
And 'tis but a little journey,
Unto Pohjola's bleak homestead,
To my cruel foster-mother.
With a rope I will not flog you,
With a switch I will not drive you,   340
But with silken cords will lead you,
With a strip of cloth will drive you."

Then the chestnut horse of Hiisi,
Hiisi's horse, with mane all foam-flecked
Forward stretched his golden muzzle,
Forward reached his head of silver,
To receive the golden bridle,
With the bit of shining silver.

Thus did lively Lemminkäinen
Bridle Hiisi's mighty courser,   350
In his mouth the bit adjusted,
On his silver head the bridle,
On his broad back then he mounted,
On the back of that good courser.

O'er the horse his whip he brandished,
With a willow switch he struck him,
And a little way he journeyed
Hasting onward through the mountains,
Through the mountains to the northward,
Over all the snow-clad mountains,   360
Unto Pohjola's bleak homestead.
From the yard the hall he entered,
And he said on his arrival,
Soon as Pohjola he entered:
"I have reined the mighty courser,
Brought the foal of Hiisi bridled,
From the green and open meadows,
And the sacred field beyond them,

And I tracked the elk on snowshoes,
On the distant plains of Hiisi.   370
Give me now, old dame, your daughter,
Give the youthful bride I seek for!"

Louhi, Pohjola's old Mistress,
Answered in the words which follow:
"I will only give my daughter,
Give the youthful bride you seek for,
If the river-swan you shoot me,
Shoot the great bird on the river.
There on Tuoni's murky river,
In the sacred river's whirlpool,   380
Only at a single trial,
Using but a single arrow."

Then the lively Lemminkäinen
He the handsome Kaukomieli,
Went and took his twanging crossbow,
Went away to seek the Long-neck,
Forth to Tuoni's murky river,
Down in Manala's abysses.

On with rapid steps he hastened,
And he went with trampling footsteps,   390
Unto Tuonela's broad river,
To the sacred river's whirlpool,
'Neath his arm a handsome crossbow,
On his back his well-stored quiver.

Märkähattu then, the cowherd,
Pohjola's old sightless greybeard,
There by Tuonela's broad river,
By the sacred river's whirlpool,
Long had lurked, and long had waited,
There for Lemminkäinen's coming.   400

And at length one day it happened,
Came the lively Lemminkäinen
Hastening on, and swift approaching

Unto Tuonela's deep river,
To the cataract most terrific,
To the sacred river's whirlpool.

From the waves he sent a serpent,
Like a reed from out the billows;
Through the hero's heart he hurled it,
And through Lemminkäinen's liver.   410
Through the arm-pit left it smote him,
Through the shoulder right it struck him.

Then the lively Lemminkäinen
Felt himself severely wounded,
And he spoke the words which follow:
"I have acted most unwisely,
That I asked not information
From my mother, she who bore me.
Two words only were sufficient,
Three at most might perhaps be needed,   420
How to act, and live still longer,
After this day's great misfortune.
Charm I cannot water-serpents,
Nor of reeds I know the magic.

O my mother who hast borne me,
And hast nurtured me with labour,
Would that thou might'st know, and hasten
To thy son, who lies in anguish.
Surely thou would'st hasten hither,
To my aid thou then would'st hasten,   430
To thy hapless son's assistance,
At the point of death now lying,
For indeed too young I slumber,
And I die while still so vital."

Then did Pohjola's blind greybeard,
Märkähattu, he the cowherd,
Fling the lively Lemminkäinen,
Casting Kaleva's own offspring
Into Tuoni's murky river,
In the worst of all the whirlpools.   440
Floated lively Lemminkäinen,

Down the cataracts he floated,
Down the rushing stream he floated,
Unto Tuonela's dread dwelling.

Then the bloodstained son of Tuoni
Drew his sword, and smote the hero,
With his gleaming blade he hewed him,   450
While it shed a stream of flashes,
And he hewed him in five fragments,
And in pieces eight he hewed him,
Then in Tuonela's stream cast them,
Where are Manala's abysses.
"Thou may'st toss about for ever,
With thy crossbow and thy arrows,
Shooting swans upon the river,
Water-birds upon its borders!"

Thus did Lemminkäinen perish,
Perished thus the dauntless suitor,
Down in Tuoni's murky river,
Down in Manala's abysses.   460

XV Lemminkäinen's recovery and return home

One day blood begins to trickle from the hair-brush at Lemminkäinen's home, and his mother at once perceives that death has
overtaken her son. She hastens to Pohjola and enquires of Louhi what
has become of him (1–100). The Mistress of Pohjola at length tells
her on what errand she has sent him, and the sun gives her full
information of the manner of Lemminkäinen's death (101–94).
Lemminkäinen's mother goes with a long rake in her hand under the
cataract of Tuoni, and rakes the water till she has found all the
fragments of her son's body, which she joins together, and succeeds in
restoring Lemminkäinen to life by charms and magic salves (195–
554). Lemminkäinen then relates how he perished in the river of
Tuonela, and returns home with his mother (555–650).

Lemminkäinen's tender mother
In her home was always thinking,
"Where has Lemminkäinen wandered,
Whereabouts is Kauko roaming,
For I do not hear him coming
From his world-extended journey?"

Ah, the hapless mother knew not,
Nor the hapless one imagined,
Where her own flesh now was floating,
Where her own blood now was flowing;   10
If he tracked the fir-clad mountains,
Or among the heaths was roaming,
Or upon a lake was floating,
Out upon the foaming billows,
Or in some terrific combat,
In the most tremendous tumult,
With his legs with blood bespattered,
To the knees with blood all crimsoned.

Kyllikki, the lovely housewife,
Wandered round and gazed about her,   20
Through the home of Lemminkäinen,
And through Kaukomieli's homestead;
On the comb she looked at evening,
On the brush she looked at morning,
And at length one day it happened,
In the early morning hours,
Blood from out the comb was oozing,
From the brush was gore distilling.

Kyllikki, the lovely housewife,
Uttered then the words which follow: 30
"Lo, my husband has departed,
And my handsome Kauko wandered
In a country void of houses,
And throughout some trackless desert.
Blood from out the comb is oozing,
Gore is from the brush distilling."

Then did Lemminkäinen's mother
See herself the comb was bleeding,
And began to weep with sorrow:
"O alas, my day is wretched,   40
And my life is most unhappy,
For my son has met misfortune,
And my child all unprotected,
On an evil day was nurtured.
On the poor lad came destruction,
Lost is darling Lemminkäinen.
From the comb the blood is trickling,
And the brush with blood is dripping!"

In her hands her skirt she gathered,
With her arms her dress she lifted,   50
And at once commenced her journey,
Hurried on upon her journey.
Mountains thundered 'neath her footsteps,
Valleys rose and hills were levelled,
And the high ground sank before her,
And the low ground rose before her.

Thus to Pohjola she journeyed,
Asking where her son had wandered,
And she asked in words which follow:
"Tell me, Pohjola's old Mistress,   60
Whither sent you Lemminkäinen,
Whither has my son departed?"

Louhi, Pohjola's old Mistress,
Then replied in words which follow:
"Of your son I know no tidings,
Where he went, or where he vanished.
In his sledge I yoked a stallion,
Chose him out a fiery courser.
Perhaps he sank in ice when rotten,
O'er the frozen lake when driving,   70
Or among the wolves has fallen,
Or some dreadful bear devoured him."

Then said Lemminkäinen's mother,
"This indeed is shameless lying,
For no wolf would touch my offspring,
Not a bear touch Lemminkäinen!
Wolves he'd crush between his fingers,
Bears with naked hands would master.
If you will not truly tell me,
How you treated Lemminkäinen,   80
I the malthouse doors will shatter,
Break the hinges of the Sampo."

Then said Pohjola's old Mistress,
"I have fed the man 'profusely,
And I gave him drink in plenty,
Till he was most fully sated.
In a boat's prow then I placed him,
That he thus should shoot the rapids,
But I really cannot tell you
What befell the wretched creature;   90
In the wildly foaming torrent,
In the tumult of the whirlpool."

Then said Lemminkäinen's mother,
"This indeed is shameless lying!

Tell me now the truth exactly,
Make an end of all your lying,
Whither sent you Lemminkäinen,
Where has Kaleva's son perished?
Or most certain death awaits you,
And you die upon the instant."   100

Then said Pohjola's old Mistress,
"Now at length I'll tell you truly:
Forth to chase the elks I sent him,
And to struggle with the monsters,
And to rein the mighty geldings,
And to put the foals in harness.
Then I sent him forth swan-hunting,
Seeking for the bird so sacred;
But I really cannot tell you
If misfortune came upon him,   110
Or what hindrance he encountered.
Nought I heard of his returning,
For the bride that he demanded,
When he came to woo my daughter."

Then the mother sought the strayed one,
Dreading what mischance had happened,
Like a wolf she tracked the marshes,
Like a bear the wastes she traversed,   120
Like an otter swam the waters,
Badger-like the plains she traversed,
Passed the headlands like a hedgehog,
Like a hare along the lakeshores,
Pushed the rocks from out her pathway,
From the slopes bent down the tree-trunks,
Thrust the shrubs beside her pathway,
From her track she cast the branches.

Long she vainly sought the strayed one,
Long she sought, but found him never;
Of her son the trees she questioned,   130
For the lost one ever seeking.

Said a tree, then sighed a pine-tree,
And an oak made answer wisely:

"I myself have also sorrows,
For your son I cannot trouble,
For my lot's indeed a hard one,
And an evil day awaits me,
For they split me into splinters,
And they chop me into faggots,
In the kiln that I may perish,
Or they fell me in the clearing."   140

Long she vainly sought the strayed one,
Long she sought, but found him never,
And whene'er she crossed a pathway,
Then she bowed herself before it:
"O thou path, whom God created,
Hast thou seen my son pass over;
Hast thou seen my golden apple,
Hast thou seen my staff of silver?"

But the path made answer wisely,
And it spoke and gave her answer: 150
"I myself have also sorrows,
For your son I cannot trouble,
For my lot's indeed a hard one,
And an evil day awaits me.
All the dogs go leaping o'er me,
And the horsemen gallop o'er me,
And the shoes walk heavy on me,
And the heels press hard upon me."

Long she vainly sought the strayed one,
Long she sought, but found him never.   160
Met the moon upon her pathway,
And before the moon she bowed her:
"Golden moon, whom God created,
Hast thou seen my son pass by you;
Hast thou seen my golden apple,
Hast thou seen my staff of silver?"

Then the moon whom God created,
Made a full and prudent answer:

"I myself have many sorrows,
For your son I cannot trouble,   170
For my lot's indeed a hard one,
And an evil day awaits me,
Wandering lonely in the night-time,
In the frost for ever shining,
In the winter keeping vigil,
But in time of summer waning."

Long she vainly sought the strayed one,
Long she sought, but found him never,
Met the sun upon her pathway,
And before the sun she bowed her.   180

"O thou sun, whom God created,
Hast thou seen my son pass by you,
Hast thou seen my golden apple,
Hast thou seen my staff of silver?"

And the sun knew all about it,
And the sun made answer plainly:
"There has gone your son unhappy,
He has fallen and has perished,
Down in Tuoni's murky river,
Manala's primeval river,   190
O'er the surging cataract went he,
With the torrent rushed he downward,
There on Tuonela's dark frontier,
There in Manala's deep valleys."

Then did Lemminkäinen's mother,
Break out suddenly in weeping.
To the craftsman's forge she wended:
"O thou smith, O Ilmarinen,
Thou hast worked before, and yestreen,
On this very day, O forge me,   200
Forge a rake with copper handle,
Let the teeth of steel be fashioned,
Teeth in length a hundred fathoms,
And of fathoms five the handle!"

Then the smith, e'en Ilmarinen,
He the great primeval craftsman,
Forged a rake with copper handle,
And the teeth of steel he fashioned,
Teeth in length a hundred fathoms,
And of fathoms five the handle.   210

Then did Lemminkäinen's mother
Take the mighty rake of iron,
And she rushed to Tuoni's river,
To the sun her prayer addressing:
"O thou sun, whom God created,
Brilliant work of the Creator!
Shine an hour with heat excessive,
Shine again with sultry shimmering,
And again with utmost vigour.
Lull to sleep the race of evil,   220
And in Manala the strong ones,
Weary out the power of Tuoni!"

Then the sun, whom God created,
Shining work of the Creator,
Stooped upon a crooked birch-tree,
Sank upon a crooked alder,
Shone an hour with heat excessive,
Shone again with sultry shimmering,
And again with utmost vigour,
Lulled to sleep the race of evil,   230
And in Manala the strong ones.
Slept the young on sword-hilt resting,
And the old folks staff-supported,
And the spear-men middle-agèd.
Then again he hastened upward,
Sought again the heights of heaven,
Sought again his former station,
To his first abode soared upward.

Then did Lemminkäinen's mother
Take the mighty rake of iron,   240
And to seek her son was raking

All amid the raging whirlpool,
Through the fiercely rushing torrent,
And she raked, yet found she nothing.

Then she went and sought him deeper,
Ever deeper in the river,
Stocking-deep into the water,
Standing waist-deep in the water.

Thus she sought her son by raking
All the length of Tuoni's river,   250
And she raked against the current,
Once and twice she raked the river,
And his shirt at length discovered,
Found the shirt of him unhappy,
And she raked again a third time,
And she found his hat and stockings,
Found his stockings, greatly sorrowing,
Found his hat, with heart-wrung anguish.

Then she waded ever deeper,
Down in Manala's abysses,   260
Raked once more along the river,
Raked again across the river,
And obliquely through the water,
And at length upon the third time,
Up she drew a lifeless carcass,
With the mighty rake of iron.

Yet it was no lifeless carcass,
But the lively Lemminkäinen,
He the handsome Kaukomieli,
Sticking fast upon the rake-prongs,   270
Sticking by his nameless finger,
And the toes upon his left foot.

Thus she fished up Lemminkäinen,
Kaleva's great offspring lifted,
On the rake all shod with copper,
To the light above the water.

Yet were many fragments wanting:
Half his head, a hand was wanting,
Many other little fragments,
And his very life was wanting.   280

As his mother pondered o'er it,
Thus she spoke while sorely weeping:
"Can a man from this be fashioned,
And a hero new created?"

But by chance a raven heard her,
And he answered her in thiswise:
"No man can from this be fashioned,
Not from what you have discovered,
For his eyes the powan's eaten,
And the pike has cleft his shoulders.   290
Cast the man into the water,
Back in Tuonela's deep river,
Perhaps a cod may thence be fashioned,
Or a whale from thence develop."

Lemminkäinen's mother would not
Cast her son into the water,
But again began her raking,
With the mighty rake of copper,
All through Tuonela's deep river,
First along it, then across it,
And his head and hand discovered,   300
And the fragments of his backbone.
Then she found his ribs in pieces,
Likewise many other fragments,
And her son she pieced together,
Shaped the lively Lemminkäinen.

Then the flesh to flesh she fitted,
And the bones together fitted,
And the joints together jointed,
And the veins she pressed together.   310

Then she bound the veins together,
All their ends she knit together,

And with care their threads she counted,
And she spoke the words which follow:
"Fairest goddess of the bloodveins,
Suonetar, O fairest woman,
Lovely weaver of the veinlets,
Working with thy loom so slender,
With the spindle all of copper,
And the wheel composed of iron,   320
Come thou here, where thou art needed,
Hasten hither, where I call thee,
With a lapful of thy veinlets,
And beneath thy arm a bundle,
Thus to bind the veins together,
And to knit their ends together,
Where the wounds are gaping widely,
And where gashes still are open!

If this is not yet sufficient,
In the air there sits a maiden,   330
In a boat adorned with copper,
In a boat with stern of scarlet.
From the air descend, O maiden,
Virgin, from the midst of heaven,
Row thy boat throughout the veinlets,
Through the joints, both forth and backwards,
Through the broken bones, O steer thou,
And throughout the joints when broken!

Bind the veins together firmly
Lay them in the right position,   340
End to end the larger bloodveins,
And the arteries fit together,
Duplicate the smaller bloodveins,
Join the ends of smallest veinlets!

Take thou then thy finest needle,
Thread it next with silken fibre,
Sew thou with the finest needle,
Stitch thou with thy tin-made needle,
Sew the ends of veins together,
Bind them with thy silken fibre!   350

If this is not yet sufficient,
Help me, Jumala, Eternal,
Harness thou thy foal of swiftness,
And equip thy mighty courser,
In thy little sledge then drive thou
Through the bones and joints, O drive thou,
Through the flesh that all is mangled,
Back and forth, throughout the veinlets,
In the flesh the bone then fasten,
Ends of veins knit firm together,   360
'Twixt the bones, O fix thou silver,
Fix the veins with gold together!

Where the skin is rent asunder,
Let the skin be brought together;
Where the veins have snapped asunder,
Let the veins be knit together;
Where through wounds the blood has issued,
Let the blood again be flowing;
Where the bones have broke to splinters,
Let the bones be fixed together;   370
Where the flesh is torn asunder,
Let the flesh be knit together,
Fix it in the right position,
In its right position fix it,
Bone to bone and flesh to flesh fix,
Joint to joint unite thou firmly!"

Thus did Lemminkäinen's mother
Form the man, and shape the hero
To his former life restored him,
To the form he wore aforetime.   380
All the veins had now been counted,
And their ends were knit together,
But as yet the man was speechless,
Nor the child to speak was able.

Then she spoke the words which follow,
And expressed herself in thiswise:
"Whence shall we obtain an ointment,
Whence obtain the drops of honey

That I may anoint the patient
And that I may cure his weakness,   390
That the man his speech recovers,
And again his songs is singing?

O thou bee, thou bird of honey,
King of all the woodland flowerets,
Go thou forth to fetch me honey,
Go thou forth to seek for nectar,
Back from Metsola's fair meadows,
Tapiola, for ever cheerful,
From the cup of many a flower,
And the plumes of grasses many,   400
As an ointment for the patient,
And to quite restore the sick one!."

Then the bee, the bird so active,
Flew away upon his journey,
Forth to Metsola's fair meadows,
Tapiola, for ever cheerful,
Probed the flowers upon the meadows,
With his tongue he sucked the honey
From the tips of six bright flowers,
From the plumes of hundred grasses;   410
Then came buzzing loud and louder,
Rushing on his homeward journey,
With his wings all steeped in honey,
And his plumage soaked with nectar.

Then did Lemminkäinen's mother,
Take from him the magic ointment,
That she might anoint the patient,
And she thus might cure his weakness:
But from this there came no healing,
And as yet the man was speechless.   420

Then she spoke the words which follow:
"O thou bee, my own dear birdling,
Fly thou in a new direction,
Over nine lakes fly thou quickly,
Till thou reach a lovely island,
Where the land abounds with honey,

Where is Tuuri's new-built dwelling,
Palvonen's own roofless dwelling,
There is honey in profusion,
There is ointment in perfection,   430
Fit to bind the veins together,
And to heal the joints completely.
From the meadow bring this ointment,
And the salve from out the meadow,
For upon the wounds I'll spread it,
And anoint the bruises with it!"

Then the bee, that light-winged flier,
Flew again on whirring pinions,
And across nine lakes he travelled,
Half across the tenth he travelled,   440
On he flew one day, a second,
And at length upon the third day,
Never on the reeds reposing,
Nor upon a leaf reposing,
Came he to the lovely island,
Where the land abounds with honey,
Till he reached a furious torrent,
And a holy river's whirlpool.

In this spot was cooked the honey,
And the ointment was made ready   450
In the little earthen vessels,
In the pretty little kettles,
Kettles of a thumb-size only,
And a finger-tip would fill them.

Then the bee, that active worker,
Gathered honey in the meadow,
And a little time passed over,
Very little time passed over,
When he came on whirring pinions,
Coming with his mission finished;   460
In his lap six cups he carried,
Seven upon his back he carried,
Brimming o'er with precious ointment,
With the best of ointment brimming.

Then did Lemminkäinen's mother
Salve him with this precious ointment,
With nine kinds of ointment salved him,
And ten kinds of magic ointment;
Even yet there came no healing,
Still her toil was unavailing.   470

Then she spoke the words which follow,
And expressed herself in thiswise:
"O thou bee, thou bird aërial,
Fly thou forth again the third time,
Fly thou up aloft to heaven,
And through nine heavens fly thou swiftly.
There is honey in abundance,
In the skies as much as needed,
Which was charmed by the Creator,
By pure Jumala was breathed on,   480
When his children he anointed,
Wounded by the powers of evil.
In the honey dip thy pinions,
Soak thy plumage in the nectar,
Bring me honey on thy pinions,
In thy mantle from the forest,
As an ointment for the patient,
And anoint the bruises with it!"

But the bee, the bird of wisdom,
Answered her in words that follow: 490
"How can I perform thy bidding,
I a man so small and helpless?"

"Thou canst rise on high with swiftness,
Fly aloft with easy effort,
O'er the moon, below the daylight,
And amid the stars of heaven,
Flying windlike on the first day
Past the borders of the moon,
On the second day thou soarest
Even to the Great Bear's shoulders,   500
On the third day soaring higher,
O'er the Seven Stars thou risest,

Thence the journey is a short one,
And the distance very trifling,
Unto Jumala's bright dwelling,
And the regions of the blessed."

From the earth the bee rose swiftly,
On his honeyed wings rose whirring,
And he soared on rapid pinions,
On his little wings flew upward.   510
Swiftly past the moon he hurried,
Past the borders of the sunlight,
Rose upon the Great Bear's shoulders,
O'er the Seven Stars' backs rose upward,
Flew to the Creator's cellars,
To the halls of the Almighty.
There the drugs were well concocted,
And the ointment duly tempered
In the pots composed of silver,
Or within the golden kettles.   520
In the midst they boiled the honey,
On the sides was sweetest ointment,
To the southward there was nectar,
To the northward there were ointments.

Then the bee, that bird aërial,
Gathered honey in abundance,
Nectar to his heart's contentment,
And but little time passed over,
Ere the bee again came buzzing,
Humming loudly on his journey,   530
In his lap of horns a hundred,
And a thousand other vessels,
Some of honey, some of liquid,
And the best of all the ointment.

Then did Lemminkäinen's mother
Raise it to her mouth and taste it,
With her tongue the ointment tasted,
With the greatest care she proved it:
"'Tis the ointment that I needed,
And the salve of the Almighty,   540

Used when Jumala the Highest,
The Creator heals all suffering."

Then did she anoint the patient,
That she thus might cure his weakness,
Salved the bones along the fractures,
And between the joints she salved him,
Salved his head and lower portions,
Rubbed him also in the middle,
Then she spoke the words which follow,
And expressed herself in thiswise: 550
"Rise, my son, from out thy slumber,
From thy dreams do thou awaken,
From this place so full of evil,
And a resting-place unholy!"

From his sleep arose the hero,
And from out his dreams awakened,
And at once his speech recovered.
With his tongue these words he uttered:
"Woe's me, long have I been sleeping,
Long have I in pain been lying,   560
And in peaceful sleep reposing,
In the deepest slumber sunken."

Then said Lemminkäinen's mother,
And expressed herself in thiswise:
"Longer yet hadst thou been sleeping,
Longer yet hadst thou been resting,
But for thy unhappy mother,
But for her in pain who bore thee.

Tell me now, my son unhappy,
Tell me that my ears may hear it: 570
Who to Manala has sent thee,
There to drift in Tuoni's river?"

Said the lively Lemminkäinen,
And he answered thus his mother:
"Märkähattu, he the cowherd,
Untamola's blind old rascal,

Down to Manala has sent me,
There to drift in Tuoni's river,
And he raised a water-serpent,
From the waves a serpent lifted,   580
Sent it forth to me unhappy,
But I could not guard against it,
Knowing nought of water-evil,
Nor the evils of the reed-beds."

Then said Lemminkäinen's mother,
"Mighty man of little foresight,
Boasting to enchant the sorcerers,
And to ban the sons of Lapland,
Knowing nought of water-evil,
Nor the evils of the reed-beds!   590

Water-snakes are born in water,
On the waves among the reed-beds,
From the duck's brain springs the serpent,
In the head of the sea-swallow.
Syöjätär spat in the water,
Cast upon the waves the spittle,
And the water stretched it lengthwise,
And the sunlight warmed and softened,
And the wind arose and tossed it,
And the water-breezes rocked it,   600
On the shore the waves they drove it,
And amid the breakers urged it."

Thus did Lemminkäinen's mother
Cause her son with all her efforts,
To resume his old appearance,
And ensured that in the future
He should even be superior,
Yet more handsome than aforetime;
And she asked her son thereafter
Was there anything he needed?   610

Said the lively Lemminkäinen,
"There is something greatly needed,
For my heart is fixed for ever,
And my inclination leads me

To the charming maids of Pohja,
With their lovely locks unbraided;
But the dirty-eared old woman
Has refused to give her daughter,
Till I shoot the duck she asks for,
And the swan shall capture for her,   620
Here in Tuonela's dark river,
In the holy river's whirlpool."

Then spoke Lemminkäinen's mother,
And she answered him in thiswise:
"Leave the poor swans unmolested,
Leave the ducks a peaceful dwelling,
Here on Tuoni's murky river,
Here amid the raging whirlpool!
Best it is to journey homeward
With your most unhappy mother.   630
Praise thou now thy happy future,
And to Jumala give praises,
That he granted his assistance,
And has thus to life awaked thee,
And from Tuoni's paths hath led thee,
And from Mana's realms hath brought thee!
I myself had never conquered,
And alone had nought accomplished,
But for Jumala's compassion,
And the help of the Creator!"   640

Then the lively Lemminkäinen,
Commenced at once his journey homeward,
With his mother, she who loved him,
Homeward with the aged woman.

Here I part awhile with Kauko,
Leave the lively Lemminkäinen,
Long from out my song I leave him,
While I quickly change my subject,
Turn my song in new directions,
And in other furrows labour.   650

XVI Väinämöinen in Tuonela

Väinämöinen orders Sampsa Pellervoinen to seek for wood for boat-building. He makes a boat, but finds himself at a loss for want of three magic words (1–118). As he cannot otherwise obtain them, he goes to Tuonela hoping to procure them there (119–362). Väinämöinen finally escapes from Tuonela, and after his return warns others not to venture there, and describes what a terrible place it is and the horrible abodes in which men dwell there (363–412).

Väinämöinen, old and steadfast,
He the great primeval sorcerer,
Set to work a boat to build him,
And upon a boat to labour,
There upon the cloudy headland,
On the hazy island's summit.
But the workman found no timber,
Boards to build the boat he found not.

Who shall seek for timber for him,
And shall seek an oak-tree for him,   10
For the boat of Väinämöinen,
And a keel to suit the minstrel?

Pellervoinen, earth-begotten,
Sampsa, youth of smallest stature,
He shall seek for timber for him,
And shall seek an oak-tree for him,
For the boat of Väinämöinen,
And a keel to suit the minstrel.

So upon his path he wandered
Through the regions to the north-east,   20
Through one district, then another,
Journeyed after through a third one,
With his gold axe on his shoulder,
With his axe, with copper handle,
Till he found an aspen standing,
Which in height three fathoms measured.

So he went to fell the aspen,
With his axe the tree to sever,
And the aspen spoke and asked him,
With its tongue it spoke in thiswise: 30
"What, O man, desire you from me?
Tell your need, as far as may be."

Youthful Sampsa Pellervoinen,
Answered in the words which follow:
"This is what I wish for from thee,
This I need, and this require I,
'Tis a boat for Väinämöinen;
For the minstrel's boat the timber."

And the aspen said astounded,
Answered with its hundred branches: 40
"As a boat I should be leaking,
And would only sink beneath you,
For my branches they are hollow.
Thrice already in this summer,
Has a grub my heart devoured,
In my roots a worm has nestled."

Youthful Sampsa Pellervoinen
Wandered further on his journey,
And he wandered, deeply pondering,
In the region to the northward.   50

There he found a pine-tree standing,
And its height was full six fathoms,
And he struck it with his hatchet,
On the trunk with axe-blade smote it,
And he spoke the words which follow:

"O thou pine-tree, shall I take thee,
For the boat of Väinämöinen,
And as boatwood for the minstrel?"

But the pine-tree answered quickly,
And it cried in answer loudly,   60
"For a boat you cannot use me,
Nor a six-ribbed boat can fashion;
Full of knots you'll find the pine-tree.
Thrice already in this summer,
In my summit croaked a raven,
Croaked a crow among my branches."

Youthful Sampsa Pellervoinen
Further yet pursued his journey,
And he wandered, deeply pondering,
In the region to the southward,   70
Till he found an oak-tree standing,
Fathoms nine its boughs extended.

And he thus addressed and asked it:
"O thou oak-tree, shall I take thee,
For the keel to make a vessel,
The foundation of a warship?"

And the oak-tree answered wisely,
Answered thus the acorn-bearer:
"Yes, indeed, my wood is suited
For the keel to make a vessel,   80
Neither slender 'tis, nor knotted,
Nor within its substance hollow.
Thrice already in this summer,
In the brightest days of summer,
Through my midst the sunbeams wandered.
On my crown the moon was shining,
In my branches cried the cuckoos,
In my boughs the birds were resting."

Youthful Sampsa Pellervoinen
Took the axe from off his shoulder,   90
With his axe he smote the tree-trunk,

With the blade he smote the oak-tree,
Speedily he felled the oak-tree,
And the beauteous tree had fallen.

First he hewed it through the summit,
All the trunk he cleft in pieces,
After this the keel he fashioned,
Planks so many none could count them,
For the vessel of the minstrel,
For the boat of Väinämöinen.   100

Then the aged Väinämöinen,
He the great primeval sorcerer,
Fashioned then the boat with wisdom,
Built with magic songs the vessel,
From the fragments of an oak-tree,
Fragments of the shattered oak-tree.

With a song the keel he fashioned,
With another, sides he fashioned,
And he sang again a third time,
And the rudder he constructed,   110
Bound the rib-ends firm together,
And the joints he fixed together.

When the boat's ribs were constructed,
And the sides were fixed together,
Still he found three words were wanting,
Which the sides should fix securely,
Fix the prow in right position,
And the stern should likewise finish.

Väinämöinen, old and steadfast,
He the great primeval minstrel,   120
Uttered then the words which follow:
"Woe to me, my life is wretched,
For my boat unlaunched remaineth,
On the waves the new boat floats not!"

So he pondered and reflected
How to find the words he needed,

And obtain the spells of magic,
From among the brains of swallows,
From the heads of flocks of wild swans,
From the shoulders of the goose-flocks.   130

Then he went the words to gather,
And a flock of swans he slaughtered.
And a flock of geese he slaughtered,
And beheaded many swallows,
But the spells he needed found not,
Not a word, not e'en a half one.

So he pondered and reflected:
"I shall find such words by hundreds,
'Neath the tongue of summer reindeer,
In the mouth of whitest squirrel."   140

So he went the words to gather,
That the spells he might discover,
And a field he spread with reindeer,
Loaded benches high with squirrels,
Many words he thus discovered,
But they all were useless to him.

So he pondered and reflected:
"I should find such words by hundreds
In the dark abodes of Tuoni,
In the eternal home of Mana."   150

Then to Tuonela he journeyed,
Sought the words in Mana's kingdom,
And with rapid steps he hastened,
Wandered for a week through bushes,
Through bird-cherry for a second,
And through juniper the third week,
Straight to Manala's dread island,
And the gleaming hills of Tuoni.

Väinämöinen, old and steadfast,
Raised his voice, and shouted loudly   160
There by Tuonela's deep river,

There in Manala's abysses:
"Bring a boat, O Tuoni's daughter,
Row across, O child of Mana,
That the stream I may pass over,
And that I may cross the river!"

Tuoni's short and stunted daughter,
She the dwarfish maid of Mana,
At the time her clothes was washing,
And her clothes she there was beating,
At the river dark of Tuoni,
And in Manala's deep waters.
And she answered him in thiswise,
And she spoke the words which follow:
"Hence a boat shall come to fetch you,
When you shall explain the reason
Why to Manala you travel,
Though disease has not subdued you,
Nor has death thus overcome you,
Nor some other fate o'erwhelmed you."

Väinämöinen, old and steadfast,
Answered in the words which follow:
"It was Tuoni brought me hither,
Mana dragged me from my country."

Tuoni's short and stunted daughter,
She the dwarfish maid of Mana,
Answered in the words which follow:
"Ay, indeed, I know the liar!
If 'twas Tuoni brought you hither,
Mana dragged you from your country,
Then would Tuoni's self be with you,
Manalainen's self conduct you,
Tuoni's hat upon your shoulders,
On your hands the gloves of Mana.
Speak the truth, O Väinämöinen;
What to Manala has brought you?"

Väinämöinen, old and steadfast,
Answered in the words which follow:

"Iron to Manala has brought me,
Steel to Tuonela has dragged me."   200

Tuoni's short and stunted daughter,
She the dwarfish maid of Mana,
Answered in the words which follow:
"Now, indeed, I know the liar!
For if iron to Mana brought you,
Steel to Tuonela had dragged you,
From your clothes the blood would trickle,
And the blood would forth be flowing.
Speak the truth, O Väinämöinen,
For the second time speak truly!"   210

Väinämöinen, old and steadfast,
Answered in the words which follow:
"Water has to Mana brought me,
Waves to Tuonela have brought me."

Tuoni's short and stunted daughter,
She the dwarfish maid of Mana,
Answered in the words which follow:
"Ay, indeed, I know the liar!
If to Mana water brought you,
Waves to Manala had floated,   220
From your clothes would water trickle,
From the borders streaming downward.
Tell me true, without evasion,
What to Manala has brought you?"

Then the aged Väinämöinen,
Gave again a lying answer:
"Fire to Tuonela has brought me,
Flame to Manala conveyed me."

Tuoni's short and stunted daughter,
She the dwarfish maid of Mana,   230
Once again replied in answer:
"Well indeed I know the liar!
Had the fire to Tuoni brought you,
Flame to Manala conveyed you,

Would your hair be singed and frizzled,
And your beard be scorched severely.

O thou aged Väinämöinen,
If you wish the boat to fetch you,
Tell me true, without evasion,
Make an end at last of lying, 240
Why to Manala you travel,
Though disease has not subdued you,
Nor has death thus overcome you,
Nor some other fate o'erwhelmed you."

Said the aged Väinämöinen,
"True it is I lied a little,
And again I spoke a falsehood,
But at length I answer truly:
By my art a boat I fashioned,
By my songs a boat I builded, 250
And I sang one day, a second,
And at length upon the third day,
Broke my sledge as I was singing,
Broke the runner while still singing,
So I came for Tuoni's gimlet,
Sought in Manala a borer,
That my sledge I thus might finish,
And with this might form my song-sledge.
Therefore bring your boat to this side,
Ferry me across the water, 260
And across the straight convey me,
Let me come across the river!"

Tuonetar abused him roundly,
Mana's maiden scolded loudly:
"O thou fool, of all most foolish,
Man devoid of understanding.
Tuonela, thou seekest causeless,
Com'st to Mana free from sickness!
Better surely would you find it
Quickly to regain your country, 270
Many truly wander hither,
Few return to where they come from!"

Said the aged Väinämöinen,
"This might perhaps deter old women,
Not a man, how weak soever,
Not the laziest of heroes!
Bring the boat, O Tuoni's daughter,
Row across, O child of Mana!"

Brought the boat then, Tuoni's daughter,
And the aged Väinämöinen   280
Quickly o'er the straight she ferried,
And across the river rowed him,
And she spoke the words which follow:
"Woe to thee, O Väinämöinen,
For thou com'st to Mana living,
Com'st to Tuonela undying!"

Tuonetar, the noble matron,
Manalatar, aged woman,
Fetched some beer within a tankard,
And in both her hands she held it,   290
And she spoke the words which follow:
"Drink, O aged Väinämöinen!"

Väinämöinen, old and steadfast,
Looked for long within the tankard,
And within it frogs were spawning,
At the sides the worms were wriggling,
And he spoke the words which follow:
"Surely I have not come hither,
Thus to drink from Mana's goblets,
Or to drink from Tuoni's tankards.   300
Those who drink this beer are drunken.
Drinking from such cans they perish."

Then said Tuonela's great mistress,
"O thou aged Väinämöinen,
Why to Manala dost travel,
Why to Tuonela hast ventured,
Though by Tuoni never summoned,
To the land of Mana called not?"

Said the aged Väinämöinen,
"At my boat as I was working,   310
While my new boat I was shaping,
Then I found three words were wanting,
Ere the stern could be completed,
And the prow could be constructed,
But as I could find them nowhere,
In the world where'er I sought them,
Then to Tuonela I travelled,
Journeyed to the land of Mana,
There to find the words I needed,
There the magic words to study."   320

Then said Tuonela's great mistress,
And she spoke the words which follow:
"Ne'er the words will Tuoni give you,
Nor his spells will Mana teach you.
Never shall you leave these regions,
Never while your life remaineth,
Shall you ever journey homeward,
To your country home returning."

Sank the weary man in slumber,
And the traveller lay and slumbered,   330
On the bed prepared by Tuoni,
There outstretched himself in slumber,
And the hero thus was sleeping,
Lay outstretched, his mind awaked.

There's in Tuonela a witch-wife,
Aged crone with crooked chinbone,
And she spins her thread of iron,
And she draws out wire of copper,
And she spun of nets a hundred,
And she wove herself a thousand,   340
In a single night of summer,
On the rock amid the water.

There's in Tuonela a wizard,
And three fingers has the old man,

And he weaves his nets of iron,
And he makes his nets of copper,
And a hundred nets he wove him,
And a thousand nets he plaited,
In the selfsame night of summer,
On the same stone in the water.   350

Tuoni's son with crooked fingers,
Crooked fingers hard as iron,
Took the hundred nets, and spread them
Right across the stream of Tuoni,
Both across and also lengthwise,
And in an oblique direction,
So that Väinö should not 'scape him,
Nor should flee Uvantolainen,
In the course of all his lifetime,
While the golden moon is shining,   360
From the dread abode of Tuoni,
From the eternal home of Mana.

Väinämöinen, old and steadfast,
Uttered then the words which follow:
"May not ruin overtake me,
And an evil fate await me,
Here in Tuonela's dark dwellings,
In the foul abode of Mana?"

Quickly then his shape transforming,
And another shape assuming,   370
To the gloomy lake he hastened,
Like an otter in the reed-beds,
Like an iron snake he wriggled,
Like a little adder hastened
Straight across the stream of Tuoni,
Safely through the nets of Tuoni.

Tuoni's son with crooked fingers,
Crooked fingers, hard as iron,
Wandered early in the morning
To survey the nets extended;   380
Found of salmon-trout a hundred,
Smaller fry he found by thousands,

But he found not Väinämöinen,
Not the old Uvantolainen.

Thus the aged Väinämöinen
Made his way from Tuoni's kingdom,
And he said the words which follow,
And in words like these expressed him:
"Never, Jumala the mighty,
Never let another mortal, 390
Make his way to Mana's country,
Penetrate to Tuoni's kingdom!
Many there indeed have ventured,
Few indeed have wandered homeward,
From the dread abode of Tuoni,
From the eternal home of Mana."

Afterwards these words he added,
And expressed himself in thiswise,
To the rising generation,
And to the courageous people: 400
"Sons of men, O never venture
In the course of all your lifetime,
Wrong to work against the guiltless,
Guilt to work against the sinless,
Lest your just reward is paid you
In the dismal realms of Tuoni!
There's the dwelling of the guilty,
And the resting-place of sinners,
Under stones to redness heated,
Under slabs of stone all glowing, 410
'Neath a coverlet of vipers,
Of the loathsome snakes of Tuoni."

XVII   Väinämöinen and Antero Vipunen

Väinämöinen goes to obtain magic words from Antero Vipunen, and wakes him from his long sleep under the earth (1–98). Vipunen swallows Väinämöinen, and the latter begins to torture him violently in his stomach (99–146). Vipunen tries every means that he can think of to get rid of him by promises, spells, conjurations and exorcisms, but Väinämöinen declares that he will never depart till he has obtained from Vipunen the words which he requires to finish his boat (147–526). Vipunen sings all his wisdom to Väinämöinen, who then leaves his body, returns to his boat-building, and finishes his boat (527–628).

> Väinämöinen, old and steadfast,
> Had not found the words he wanted
> In the dark abode of Tuoni,
> In the eternal realms of Mana,
> And for evermore he pondered,
> In his head reflected ever,
> Where the words he might discover,
> And obtain the charms he needed.   10
>
> Once a shepherd came to meet him,
> And he spoke the words which follow:
> "You can find a hundred phrases,
> And a thousand words discover,
> Known to Antero Vipunen only,
> In his monstrous mouth and body,
> And there is a path which leads there,
> And a cross-road must be traversed,
> Not the best among the pathways,
> Nor the very worst of any.
> Firstly you must leap along it
> O'er the points of women's needles,   20

And another stage must traverse
O'er the points of heroes' sword-blades,
And a third course must be traversed
O'er the blades of heroes' axes."

Väinämöinen, old and steadfast,
Pondered deeply o'er the journey,
To the smithy then he hastened,
And he spoke the words which follow:
"O thou smith, O Ilmarinen,
Forge me straightway shoes of iron,   30
Forge me likewise iron gauntlets,
Make me, too, a shirt of iron,
And a mighty stake of iron,
All of steel, which I will pay for,
Lined within with steel the strongest,
And o'erlaid with softer iron,
For I go some words to seek for,
And to snatch the words of power,
From the giant's mighty body,
Mouth of Vipunen, the wisest."   40

Then the smith, e'en Ilmarinen,
Answered in the words which follow:
"Vipunen has long since perished,
Long has Antero departed
From constructing traps he needed,
And the snares that he had fashioned;
Words from him you cannot hope for;
Half a word you could not look for."

Väinämöinen, old and steadfast,
Started on his way, unheeding,   50
And the first day speeded lightly
O'er the points of women's needles,
And the second day sprang nimbly
O'er the points of heroes' sword-blades,
And upon the third day speeded
O'er the blades of heroes' axes.

Vipunen in songs was famous,
Full of craft the aged hero;

With his songs he lay extended,
Outstretched with his spells of magic.   60
On his shoulders grew an aspen,
From his temples sprang a birch-tree,
On his chin-tip grew an alder,
On his beard a willow-thicket,
On his brow were firs with squirrels,
From his teeth sprang branching pine-trees.
Then at once did Väinämöinen,
Draw his sword and free the iron
From the scabbard formed of leather,
From his belt of lambskin fashioned;   70
Fell the aspen from his shoulders,
Fell the birch-trees from his temples,
From his chin the spreading alders,
From his beard the willow-bushes,
From his brow the firs with squirrels,
From his teeth the branching pine-trees.

Then he thrust his stake of iron
Into Vipunen's mouth he thrust it,
In his gnashing gums he thrust it,
In his clashing jaws he thrust it,   80
And he spoke the words which follow:
"Rouse thyself, O slave of mortals,
Where beneath the earth thou restest,
In a sleep that long has lasted!"

Vipunen, in songs most famous,
Suddenly awoke from slumber,
Feeling he was roughly treated,
And with pain severe tormented.
Then he bit the stake of iron,
Bit the outer softer iron,   90
But the steel he could not sever,
Could not eat the core of iron.

Then the aged Väinämöinen,
Just above his mouth was standing,
And his right foot slipped beneath him,
And his left foot glided onward.

Into Vipunen's mouth he stumbled,
And within his jaws he glided.

Vipunen, in songs most famous,
Opened then his mouth yet wider,   100
And his jaws he wide extended,
Gulped the man with all equipment,
With a shout the hero swallowed,
Him, the aged Väinämöinen.

Vipunen, in songs most famous,
Spoke the very words which follow:
"I have eaten much already,
And on ewes and goats have feasted,
And have barren heifers eaten,
And have also swine devoured,   110
But I ne'er had such a dinner,
Such a morsel never tasted!"

But the aged Väinämöinen,
Uttered then the words which follow:
"Now destruction falls upon me,
And an evil day o'ertakes me,
Prisoned here in Hiisi's stable,
Here in Kalma's narrow dungeon."

So he pondered and reflected
How to live and how to struggle;   120
In his belt a knife had Väinö,
With the haft of curly birchwood,
And from this a boat he fashioned,
And a boat he thus constructed,
And he rowed the boat, and urged it
Back and forth throughout the entrails,
Rowing through the narrow channels,
And exploring every passage.

Vipunen the old musician
Was not thus much incommoded;   130
Then the aged Väinämöinen
As a smith began to labour,
And began to work with iron.

With his shirt he made a smithy,
With his shirt-sleeves made his bellows,
With the fur he made the wind-bag,
With his trousers made the air-pipe,
And the opening with his stockings,
And he used his knee for anvil,
And his elbow for a hammer.   140

Then he quick began to hammer,
Actively he plied his hammer,
Through the livelong night, unresting,
Through the day without cessation
In the stomach of the wise one,
In the entrails of the mighty.

Vipunen, in songs most famous,
Spoke aloud the words which follow:
"Who among mankind can this be,
Who among the roll of heroes?   150
I have gulped a hundred heroes,
And a thousand men devoured,
But his like I never swallowed.
In my mouth the coals are rising,
On my tongue are firebrands resting,
In my throat is slag of iron.

Go thou forth to wander, strange one,
Pest of earth, at once depart thou,
Ere I go to seek thy mother,
Seek thy very aged mother.   160
If I told it to thy mother,
Told the aged one the story,
Great would be thy mother's trouble,
Great the aged woman's sorrow,
That her son should work such evil,
And her child should act so basely.

Still I hardly comprehend it,
Do not comprehend the reason,
How thou, Hiisi, here hast wandered,
Why thou cam'st, thou evil creature,   170
Thus to bite, and thus to torture,

Thus to eat, and thus to gnaw me.
Art thou some disease-created
Death that Jumala ordains me,
Or art thou another creature,
Fashioned and unloosed by others,
Hired beforehand to torment me,
Or hast thou been bribed with money?

If thou art disease-created,
Death by Jumala ordained me,   180
Then I trust in my Creator,
And to Jumala resign me;
For the good the Lord rejects not,
Nor does he destroy the righteous.

If thou art another creature,
And an evil wrought by others,
Then thy race would I discover,
And the place where thou wast nurtured!

Once before have ills assailed me,
Plagues from somewhere have attacked me,   190
From the realms of mighty sorcerers,
From the meadows of the soothsayers,
And the homes of evil spirits,
And the plains where dwell the wizards,
From the dreary heaths of Kalma,
From beneath the firm earth's surface,
From the dwellings of the dead men,
From the realms of the departed,
From the loose earth heaped in hillocks,
From the regions of the landslips,   200
From the loose and gravelly districts,
From the shaking sandy regions,
From the valleys deeply sunken,
From the moss-grown swampy districts,
From the marshes all unfrozen,
From the billows ever tossing,
From the stalls in Hiisi's forest,
From five gorges in the mountains,
From the slopes of copper mountains,
From their summits all of copper,   210

From the ever-rustling pine-trees,
And the rustling of the fir-trees,
From the crowns of rotten pine-trees,
And the tops of rotten fir-trees,
From those spots where yelp the foxes,
Heaths where elk are chased on snowshoes,
From the bear's own rocky caverns,
From the caves where bears are lurking,
From the furthest bounds of Pohja,
From the distant realms of Lapland,   220
From the wastes where grow no bushes,
From the lands unploughed for ever,
From the battle-fields extended,
From the slaughter-place of heroes,
From the fields where grass is rustling,
From the blood that there is smoking,
From the blue seas's watery surface,
From the open sea's broad surface,
From the black mud of the ocean,
From the depth of thousand fathoms,   230
From the fiercely rushing torrents,
From the seething of the whirlpool,
And from Rutja's mighty cataract,
Where the waters rush most wildly,
From the further side of heaven,
Where the rainless clouds stretch furthest,
From the pathway of the spring-wind,
From the cradle of the tempests.

From such regions hast thou journeyed
Thence hast thou proceeded, Torment,   240
To my heart of evil guiltless,
To my belly likewise sinless,
To devour and to torment me,
And to bite me and to tear me?

Pine away, O hound of Hiisi,
Dog of Manala the vilest,
O thou demon, quit my body,
Pest of earth, O quit my liver,
Let my heart be undevoured,
Leave thou, too, my spleen uninjured,   250

Make no stoppage in my belly,
And my lungs forbear to traverse,
Do not pierce me through the navel,
And my loins forbear to injure,
And my backbone do not shatter,
Nor upon my sides torment me!

If my strength as man should fail me,
Then will I invoke a greater,
Which shall rid me of the evil,
And shall drive away the horror.   260

From the earth I call the Earth-Queen,
From the fields, the Lord primeval,
From the earth I call all swordsmen,
From the sands the hero-horsemen,
Call them to my aid and succour,
To my help and aid I call them,
In the tortures that o'erwhelm me,
And amid this dreadful torment.

If you do not heed their presence,
And you will not shrink before them,   270
Come, O forest, with thy people,
Junipers, bring all your army,
Come, O pine-woods, with your household,
And thou pond with all thy children,
With their swords a hundred swordsmen,
And a thousand mail-clad heroes,
That they may assail this Hiisi,
And may overwhelm this Juutas!

If you do not heed their presence,
And you will not shrink before them,   280
Rise thou up, O Water-Mother,
Raise thy blue cap from the billows,
And thy soft robe from the waters,
From the ooze thy form of beauty,
For a powerless hero's rescue,
For a weakly man's protection,
Lest I should be eaten guiltless,
And without disease be slaughtered!

If you will not heed their presence,
And you will not shrink before them,   290
Ancient Daughter of Creation,
Come in all thy golden beauty,
Thou the oldest of all women,
Thou the first of all the mothers,
Come to see the pains that rack me,
And the evil days drive from me,
That thy strength may overcome them,
And perchance may free me from them!

But if this not yet should move you,
And you will not yet draw backwards,   300
Ukko, in the vault of heaven,
On the thundercloud's wide border,
Come thou here, where thou art needed,
Hasten here, where I implore thee,
To dispel the works of evil,
And destroy this vile enchantment,
With thy sword of flame dispel it,
With thy flashing sword-blade smite it!

Go thou horror, forth to wander,
Curse of earth depart thou quickly,   310
Here no more shall be thy dwelling,
And if thou such dwelling needest,
Elsewhere shalt thou seek thy dwelling,
Far from here a home shalt find thee,
In the household of thy master,
In the footsteps of thy mistress!

When you reach your destination,
And your journey you have finished,
In the realms of him who made you,
In the country of your master,   320
Give a signal of your coming,
Let a lightning flash announce it,
Let them hear the roll of thunder,
Let them see the lightning flashing,
And the yard-gate kick to pieces,
Pull a shutter from the window,

Then the house thou soon canst enter,
Rush into the room like whirlwind,
Plant thy foot within it firmly,
And thy heel where space is narrow,   330
Push the men into the corner,
And the women to the doorposts,
Scratch the eyes from out the masters,
Smash the heads of all the women,
Curve thou then to hooks thy fingers,
Twist thou then their heads all crooked!

Or if this is not sufficient,
Fly as cock upon the pathway,
Or as chicken in the farmyard,
With thy breast upon the dunghill,   340
Drive the horses from the stable,
From the stalls the horned cattle,
Push their horns into the dungheap,
On the ground their tails all scatter,
Twist thou then their eyes all crooked,
And their necks in haste then break thou!

Art thou Sickness, tempest-carried,
Tempest-carried, wind-conducted,
And a gift from wind of springtime,
By the frosty air led hither,   350
On the path of air conducted,
On the sledge-way of the spring-wind,
Then upon the trees repose not,
Rest thou not upon the alders,
Hasten to the copper mountain,
Hasten to its copper summit,
Let the wind convey thee thither,
Guarded by the wind of springtide!

But if thou from heaven descended,
From the rainless clouds' broad margins,   360
Then again ascend to heaven,
Once again in air arise thou,
To the clouds where rain is falling,
To the stars that ever twinkle,

That thou there mayst burn like fire,
And that thou mayst shine and sparkle
On the sun's own path of splendour,
And around the moon's bright circle!

If thou art some pest of water,
Hither drifted by the sea-waves,   370
Let the pest return to water,
Journey back amid the sea-waves,
To the walls of muddy castles,
To the crests of waves like mountains,
There amid the waves to welter,
Rocking on the darkling billows!

Cam'st thou from the heaths of Kalma,
From the realms of the departed,
To thy home return thou quickly,
To the dark abodes of Kalma,   380
To the land upheaved in hillocks,
To the land that quakes for ever,
Where the people fall in battle,
And a mighty host has perished!

If thou foolishly hast wandered
From the depths of Hiisi's forest,
From the nest amid the pine-trees,
From thy home among the fir-trees,
Then I drive thee forth and ban thee,
To the depths of Hiisi's forest,   390
To thy home among the fir-trees,
To thy nest among the pine-trees.
There thou mayst remain for ever,
Till the flooring-planks have rotted,
And the wooden walls are mildewed,
And the roof shall fall upon you.

I will drive thee forth and ban thee,
Drive thee forth, O evil creature,
Forth unto the old bear's dwelling,
To the lair of aged she-bear,   400
To the deep and swampy valleys,
To the ever-frozen marshes,

To the swamps for ever quaking,
Quaking underneath the footsteps,
To the ponds where sport no fishes,
Where no perch are ever noticed.

But if there thou find'st no refuge,
Further yet will I then ban thee,
To the furthest bounds of Pohja,
To the distant plains of Lapland,   410
To the barren treeless tundras,
To the country where they plough not,
Where is neither moon nor sunlight,
Where the sun is never shining.
There a charming life awaits thee,
There to roam about at pleasure.
In the woods the elks are lurking.
In the woods men hunt the reindeer,
That a man may still his hunger,
And may satisfy his craving.   420

Even further yet I ban thee,
Banish thee, and drive thee onward,
To the mighty falls of Rutja,
To the fiercely raging whirlpool,
Thither where the trees have fallen,
And the fallen pines are rolling,
Tossing trunks of mighty fir-trees,
Wide-extended crowns of pine-trees.
Swim thou there, thou wicked heathen,
In the cataract's foaming torrent,   430
Round to drive 'mid boundless waters,
Resting in the narrow waters!

But if there you find no refuge,
Further yet will I then ban you,
To the river black of Tuoni,
To the eternal stream of Mana,
Never in thy life escaping,
Never while thy life endureth,
Should I not consent to free thee,
Nor to ransom thee be able,   440
Come with nine sheep thee to ransom,

Which a single ewe has farrowed,
And with bullocks, nine in number,
From a single cow proceeding,
And with stallions, nine in number,
From a single mare proceeding.

Need you horses for your journey,
Or there's aught you need for driving,
Horses I will give in plenty,
Plenty I can give for riding.   450
Hiisi has a horse of beauty,
With a red mane, on the mountain.
Fire is flashing from his muzzle,
And his nostrils brightly shining,
And his hoofs are all of iron,
And of steel are they constructed.
He can climb upon a mountain,
Climb the sloping sides of valleys,
If his rider mounts him boldly,
Urges him to show his mettle.   460

But if this is not sufficient,
Let thee have then Hiisi's snowshoes.
Take the alder-shoes of Lempo,
And the thickest pole of Evil,
Skate thou to the land of Hiisi,
Rushing through the woods of Lempo,
Dashing through the land of Hiisi,
Gliding through the evil country.
If a stone impedes thy pathway,
Crash and scatter it asunder;   470
Lies a branch across thy pathway,
Break the branch in twain when passing;
If a hero bar thy passage,
Drive him boldly from thy pathway!

Go thy way, thou lazy creature,
Go thou forth, thou man of evil,
Now, before the day is dawning,
Or the morning twilight glimmer,
Or as yet the sun has risen,
Or thou yet hast heard the cockcrow!   480

Thou delay'st too long to leave me,
Take thy flight, O evil creature,
Fare thee forth into the moonlight,
Wander forth amid its brightness.

If thou wilt not leave me quickly,
O thou dog without a mother,
I will take the eagles' talons
And the claws of the blood-suckers,
And of birds of prey the talons,
And of hawks the talons likewise,   490
That I thus may seize the demons,
Utterly o'ercome these wretches,
That my head may ache no longer,
Nor my breathing more oppress me.

Once did Lempo's self flee from me,
When he wandered from his mother,
When was aid from Jumala granted,
Gave his aid, the Great Creator.
Wander forth without thy mother,
O thou uncreated creature,   500
Wretched dog without a master,
Forth, O whelp without a mother,
Even while the time is passing,
Even while the moon is waning!"

Väinämöinen, old and steadfast,
Answered in the words which follow:
"Here I find a pleasant dwelling,
Here I dwell in much contentment,
And for bread the liver serves me,
And the fat with drink supplies me,   510
And the lungs are good for cooking,
And the fat is best for eating.

Therefore will I sink my smithy
In thy heart for ever deeper,
And will strike my hammer harder,
Pounding on the tenderest places,
That in all thy life thou never
Freedom from the ill may'st hope for,

If thy spells thou dost not teach me,
All thy magic spells shalt teach me,   520
Till thy spells I learn in fullness,
And a thousand spells have gathered;
Till no spells are hidden from me,
Nor the spells of magic hidden,
That in earth their power is lost not,
Even though the wizards perish."

Vipunen, in songs so famous,
He the sage so old in wisdom,
In whose mouth was mighty magic,
Power unbounded in his bosom,
Opened then his mouth of wisdom,   530
Of his spells the casket opened,
Sang his mighty spells of magic,
Chanted forth of all the greatest,
Magic songs of the Creation,
From the very earliest ages,
Songs that all the children sing not,
Even heroes understand not,
In these dreary days of evil,
In the days that now are passing.   540

Words of origin he chanted,
All his spells he sang in order,
At the will of the Creator,
At behest of the Almighty,
How himself the air he fashioned,
And from air the water parted,
And the earth was formed from water,
And from earth all herbage sprouted.

Then he sang the moon's creation,
Likewise how the sun was fashioned,   550
How the air was raised on pillars,
How the stars were placed in heaven.

Vipunen, in songs the wisest,
Sang in part, and sang in fullness.
Never yet was heard or witnessed,
Never while the world existed,

One who was a better singer,
One who was a wiser wizard.
From his mouth the words were flowing,
And his tongue sent forth his sayings,   560
Quick as legs of foals are moving,
Or the feet of rapid courser.

Through the days he sang unceasing,
Through the nights without cessation.
To his songs the sun gave hearing,
And the golden moon stayed listening,
Waves stood still on ocean's surface,
Billows sank upon its margin,
Rivers halted in their courses,
Rutja's furious cataract halted,   570
Vuoksi's cataract ceased its flowing,
Likewise, too, the river Jordan.

When the aged Väinämöinen
Unto all the spells had listened,
And had learned the charms in fullness,
All the magic spells creative,
He prepared himself to travel
From the wide-spread jaws of Vipunen;
From the belly of the wise one,
From within his mighty body.   580

Said the aged Väinämöinen,
"O thou Antero Vipunen hugest,
Open thou thy mouth gigantic,
And thy jaws extend more widely.
I would quit for earth thy body,
And would take my journey homeward!"

Vipunen then, in songs the wisest,
Answered in the words which follow:
"Much I've drunk, and much have eaten,
And consumed a thousand dainties,   590
But before I never swallowed
Aught like aged Väinämöinen.
Good indeed has been thy coming,
Better'tis when thou departest."

Then did Antero Vipunen open
Wide expanding gums grimacing,
Open wide his mouth gigantic,
And his jaws extended widely,
While the aged Väinämöinen
To his mouth made lengthened journey,   600
From the belly of the wise one,
From within his mighty body.
From his mouth he glided swiftly,
O'er the heath he bounded swiftly,
Very like a golden squirrel,
Or a golden-breasted marten.

Further on his path he journeyed,
Till at length he reached the smithy.
Said the smith, e'en Ilmarinen,
"Have you found the words you wanted,   610
Have you learned the spells creative,
That the boat-sides you can fashion,
Spells to fix the stern together,
And the bows to deftly fashion?"

Väinämöinen, old and steadfast,
Answered in the words which follow:
"Spells a hundred have I gathered,
And a thousand spells of magic,
Secret spells were opened to me,
Hidden charms were all laid open."   620

To his boat he hastened quickly,
And he set to work most wisely,
Set to work the boat to finish,
And he fixed the sides together,
And the stern he fixed together,
And the bows he deftly fashioned,
But the boat he built unhammered,
Nor a chip he severed from it.

XVIII   Väinämöinen and Ilmarinen travel to Pohjola

Väinämöinen sets sail in his new boat to woo the Maiden of Pohja
(1–40). Ilmarinen's sister sees him, calls to him from the shore, learns
the object of his journey, and hastens to warn her brother that a rival
has set forth to Pohjola to claim the bride (41–266). Ilmarinen makes
ready, and rides on horseback to Pohjola along the shore (267–470).
The Mistress of Pohjola sees the suitors approaching, and advises her
daughter to choose Väinämöinen (471–634). But the daughter herself prefers Ilmarinen, the forger of the *Sampo*, and tells Väinämöinen,
who is first to arrive, that she will not marry him (635–706).

Väinämöinen, old and steadfast,
Pondered deeply and reflected
How he best should woo the maiden,
Hasten to the long-haired maiden,
In the gloomy land of Pohja,
Sariola, for ever misty,
She the far-famed Maid of Pohja,
She the peerless Bride of Pohja.

There the hueless boat was lying,
And the boat with red he painted,   10
And adorned the prow with gilding,
And with silver overlaid it;
Then upon the morning after,
Very early in the morning,
Pushed his boat into the water,
In the waves the hundred-boarded,
Pushed it from the barkless rollers,
From the rounded logs of pine-tree.

Then he raised a mast upon it,
On the masts the sails he hoisted,   20
Raised a red sail on the vessel,
And another blue in colour,
Then the boat himself he boarded,
And he walked upon the planking,
And upon the sea he steered it,
O'er the blue and plashing billows.

Then he spoke the words which follow,
And in words like these expressed him:
"Enter, Jumala, my vessel,
Enter here, O thou most gracious,   30
Strengthen thou the hero's weakness,
And the weakling do thou cherish,
On these far-extending waters,
On the wide expanse of billows!

Breathe, O wind, upon the vessel,
Drive, O wave, the boat before thee,
That I need not row with fingers,
Nor may thus disturb the waters,
On the wide expanse of ocean,
Out upon the open ocean!"   40

Annikki, the ever-famous,
Night's fair daughter, maid of twilight.
Long before the day had risen,
Early in the morn had wakened,
And had washed her clothes and spread them,
And had rinsed and wrung the clothing,
Where the red steps reach the furthest,
Where the planking is the broadest,
Out upon the misty headland,
On the hazy island's ending.   50

Then she turned and gazed around her,
In the cloudless air surrounding,
And she gazed aloft to heaven,
And from shore across the water;
Up above the sun was shining,
Down below the waves were gleaming.

O'er the waves her eyes were glancing,
To the south her head was turning,
To the mouth of Suomi's river,
Where the stream of Väinölä opens.   60
On the sea a blotch she sighted,
Something blue among the billows.

Then she spoke the words which follow,
And in terms like these expressed her:
"What's this speck upon the ocean,
What this blue upon the billows?
If it be a flock of wild geese,
Or of other beauteous birdies,
Let them on their rushing pinions
Soar aloft amid the heavens!   70

If it be a shoal of salmon,
Or a shoal of other fishes,
Let them leap as they are swimming,
Plunging then beneath the water!

If it be a rocky island,
Or a stump amid the water,
Billows would then rise above it,
Or the waters drive it forward."

Now the boat came gliding onward,
And the new boat sailed on swiftly   80
Forward to the misty headland,
And the hazy island's ending.

Annikki, the ever-famous,
Saw the vessel fast approaching,
Saw the hundred-boarded passing,
And she spoke the words which follow:
"If thou art my brother's vessel,
Or the vessel of my father,
Then direct thy journey homeward,
To the shore the prow directing,   90
Where the landing-stage is stationed,
While the stern is pointing from it.
If thou art a stranger's vessel,

May'st thou swim at greater distance,
Towards another stage then hasten,
With the stern to this directed!"

'Twas no vessel of her household,
Nor a boat from foreign regions,
But the boat of Väinämöinen,
Built by him, the bard primeval,   100
And the boat approached quite closely,
Onward sailed in hailing distance,
Till a word, and then a second,
And a third were heard distinctly.
Annikki, the ever-famous,
Night's fair daughter, maid of twilight,
Hailed the boat as it approached her:
"Whither goest thou, Väinämöinen,
Whither, hero of the waters,
Wherefore, pride of all the country?"   110

Then the aged Väinämöinen
From the boat made ready answer:
"I am going salmon-fishing,
Where the salmon-trout are spawning,
In the gloomy stream of Tuoni,
On the banks of Death's deep river."

Annikki, the ever-famous,
Answered in the words which follow:
"Tell me not such idle falsehoods!
Well I know the spawning season,   120
For aforetime oft my father
And my grandsire, too, before him,
Often went a salmon-fishing,
And the salmon-trout to capture;
In the boats the nets were lying,
And the boats were full of tackle,
Here lay nets, here lines were resting,
And the beating-poles beside them;
And beneath the seats were tridents,
In the stern, long staves were lying.   130
Whither goest thou, Väinämöinen,
Wherefore, O Uvantolainen?"

Said the aged Väinämöinen,
"Forth in search of geese I wander,
Where the bright-winged birds are sporting,
And the slimy fish are catching,
In the deep sound of the Saxons,
Where the sea is wide and open."

Annikki, the ever-famous,
Answered in the words which follow: 140
"Well I know who speaks me truly,
And can soon detect the liar,
For aforetime oft my father,
And my grandsire, too, before him,
Went abroad the geese to capture,
And to chase the red-beaked quarry,
Then his bow was great, and tight-strung,
And the bow he drew was splendid,
And a black dog leashed securely,
In the stern was tightly tethered,   150
On the strand the hounds were running,
And the whelps across the shingle;
Speak the truth, O Väinämöinen,
Whither do you take your journey?"

Said the aged Väinämöinen,
"Wherefore take I not my journey,
Where a mighty war is raging,
There to fight among my equals,
Where the greaves with blood are spattered,
Even to the knees all crimsoned?"   160

Annikki again insisted,
Loudly cried the tin-adorned one:
"Well I know the ways of battle,
For aforetime went my father
Where a mighty war was raging,
There to fight among his equals,
And a hundred men were rowing,
And a thousand men were standing.
In the prow their bows were lying,
And beneath the seats their sword-blades.   170
Speak the truth, and tell me truly,

Cease to lie, and speak sincerely:
Whither goest thou, Väinämöinen,
Wherefore, O Suvantolainen?"

Then the aged Väinämöinen
Answered in the words which follow:
"Come thou in my boat, O maiden,
In my boat, O maiden seat thee,
And the truth I then will tell thee,
Cease to lie, and speak sincerely!"   180

Annikki, the tin-adorned one,
Cried aloud in indignation:
"May the wind assail thy vessel,
And the east wind fall upon it,
May thy boat capsize beneath thee,
And the prow sink down beneath thee,
If you will not tell me truly
Where you mean to take your journey,
If the truth you will not tell me,
And at last will end your lying!"   190

Then the aged Väinämöinen,
Answered in the words which follow:
"All the truth I now will tell you,
Though at first I lied a little.
Forth I fare to woo a maiden,
Seek the favour of a maiden,
In the gloomy land of Pohja,
Sariola, for ever misty,
In the land where men are eaten,
Where they even drown the heroes."   200

Annikki, the ever-famous,
Night's fair daughter, maid of twilight,
When she knew the truth for certain,
All the truth, without evasion,
Down she threw her veils unwashed,
And unrinsed she left the clothing,
On the pier she left them lying,
Where the red steps had their ending,

In her hand her gown she gathered,
In her hand the folds collected,   210
And began from thence to hasten,
And with rapid pace she hurried,
Till at length she reached the smithy;
To the forge at once she hastened.
There she found smith Ilmarinen,
He the great primeval craftsman.
And he forged a bench of iron,
And adorned it all with silver.
Cubit-high his head was sooted,
On his shoulders ash by fathoms.   220

Annikki the door then entered,
And she spoke the words which follow:
"Smith and brother Ilmarinen,
Thou the great primeval craftsman!
Forge me now a weaver's shuttle,
Pretty rings to deck my fingers,
Golden earrings, two or three pairs,
Five or six linked girdles make me,
For most weighty truth I'll tell you,
All the truth without evasion!"   230

Said the smith, said Ilmarinen,
"If you tell me news important,
Then a shuttle will I forge you,
Pretty rings to deck your fingers,
And a cross upon your bosom,
And the finest head-dress forge you.
If the words you speak are evil,
All your ornaments I'll shatter,
Tear them off to feed the furnace,
And beneath the forge will thrust them."   240

Annikki, the ever-famous,
Answered in the words which follow:
"O thou smith, O Ilmarinen!
Do you still propose to marry
Her, the bride who once was promised,
And as wife was pledged unto you?

While you weld and hammer always,
Ever working with your hammer,
Making horseshoes in the summer,
Iron horseshoes for the winter,   250
Working at your sledge at night-time,
And its frame in daytime shaping,
Forth to journey to your wooing,
And to Pohjola to travel;
One more cunning goes before you,
And another speeds beyond you,
And your own will capture from you,
And your love will ravish from you,
Whom two years ago thou sawest,
Whom two years agone thou wooed'st.   260
Know that Väinämöinen journeys
O'er the blue waves of the ocean,
In a boat with prow all golden,
Steering with his copper rudder,
To the gloomy land of Pohja,
Sariola, for ever misty."

To the smith came grievous trouble,
To the iron-worker sorrow.
From his grasp the tongs slid downward,
From his hand he dropped the hammer.   270

Said the smith, said Ilmarinen:
"Annikki, my little sister,
I will forge you now a shuttle,
Pretty rings to deck your fingers,
Golden earrings, two or three pairs,
Five or six linked girdles make you.
Warm for me the pleasant sauna,
Fill the room with fragrant vapour,
Let the logs you burn be small ones,
And the fire with chips be kindled,   280
And prepare me too some ashes,
And some soap in haste provide me,
That I wash my head and cleanse it,
And I may make white my body
From the coal-dust of the autumn,
From the forge throughout the winter!"

Annikki, whose name was famous,
Heated secretly the sauna,
With the boughs the wind had broken,
And the thunderbolt had shattered.   290
Stones she gathered from the river,
Heated them till they were ready,
Cheerfully she fetched the water,
From the holy well she brought it,
Broke some bath-whisks from the bushes,
Charming bath-whisks from the thickets,
And she warmed the honeyed bath-whisks,
On the honeyed stones she warmed them,
Then with milk she mixed the ashes,
And she made him soap of marrow,   300
And she worked the soap to lather,
Kneaded then the soap to lather,
That his head might cleanse the bridegroom,
And might cleanse himself completely.

Then the smith, e'en Ilmarinen,
He the great primeval craftsman,
Wrought the maiden what she wished for,
And he wrought a splendid head-dress,
While she made the sauna ready,
And she put the bath in order.   310
In her hands he placed the trinkets,
And the maiden thus addressed him:
"Now the sauna's filled with vapour,
And the vapour-bath I've heated,
And have steeped the bath-whisks nicely,
Choosing out the best among them.
Bathe, O brother, at your pleasure,
Pouring water as you need it,
Wash your head to flaxen colour,
Till your eyes shine out like snowflakes."   320

Then the smith, e'en Ilmarinen,
Went to take the bath he needed,
There he bathed himself at pleasure,
And he washed himself to whiteness,
Washed his eyes until they sparkled,
And his temples till they glistened,

And his neck to hen's-egg whiteness,
And his body all was shining.
From the bath the hut he entered,
Changed so much they scarcely knew him,   330
For his face it shone with beauty,
And his cheeks were cleansed and rosy.

Then he spoke the words which follow:
"Annikki, my little sister,
Bring me now a shirt of linen,
And the best of raiment bring me,
That I robe myself completely,
And may deck me like a bridegroom!"

Annikki, the ever-famous,
Brought him then a shirt of linen,   340
For his limbs no longer sweating,
For his body all uncovered.
Then she brought well-fitting trousers,
Which his mother had been sewing,
For his hips, no longer sooty,
And his legs were fully covered.

Then she brought him finest stockings,
Which, as maid, had woven his mother,
And with these his shins he covered,
And his calves were hidden by them.   350
Then she brought him shoes that fitted,
Bext of Saxon boots she brought him,
And with these the stockings covered
Which his mother sewed as maiden;
Then a coat of blue she chose him,
With a liver-coloured lining,
Covering thus the shirt of linen,
Which of finest flax was fashioned,
Then an overcoat of woollen,
Of four kinds of cloth constructed,   360
O'er the coat of bluish colour,
Of the very latest fashion,
And a new fur, thousand-buttoned,
And a hundred-fold more splendid,
O'er the overcoat of woollen,

And the cloth completely hiding;
Round his waist a belt she fastened,
And the belt was gold-embroidered,
Which his mother wrought as maiden,
Wrought it when a fair-haired maiden,   370
Brightly-coloured gloves she brought him,
Gold-embroidered, for his fingers,
Which the Lapland children fashioned;
On his handsome hands he drew them,
Then a high-crowned hat she brought him,
On his golden locks she placed it,
Which his father once had purchased,
When as bridegroom he adorned him.

Thus the smith, e'en Ilmarinen,
Clothed himself, and made him ready,   380
Robed himself, and made him handsome,
And his servant he commanded:
"Yoke me now a rapid courser,
In the sledge adorned so finely,
That I start upon my journey,
And to Pohjola may travel!"

Thereupon the servant answered:
"Horses six are in the stable,
Horses six, on oats that fatten;
Which among them shall I yoke you?"   390

Said the smith, e'en Ilmarinen,
"Take the best of all the stallions,
Put the foal into the harness,
Yoke before the sledge the chestnut,
Then provide me with six cuckoos,
Seven blue birds at once provide me,
That upon the frame they perch them,
And may sing their cheerful music,
That the fair ones may behold them,
And the maidens be delighted.   400
Then provide me with a bearskin,
That I seat myself upon it,
And a second hide of walrus,
That the bright-hued sledge is covered."

Thereupon the skilful servant,
He the servant paid with wages,
Put the colt into the harness,
Yoked before the sledge the chestnut,
And provided six fine cuckoos,
Seven blue birds at once provided,   410
That upon the frame should perch them,
And should sing their cheerful music;
And a bearskin next provided,
That his lord should sit upon it,
And another hide of walrus,
And with this the sledge he covered.

Then the smith, e'en Ilmarinen,
He the great primeval craftsman,
Sent aloft his prayer to Ukko,
And he thus besought the Thunderer: 420
"Scatter forth thy snow, O Ukko,
Let the snowflakes soft be drifted,
That the sledge may glide o'er snowfields,
O'er the snow-drifts gliding swiftly!"

Then the snow did Ukko scatter,
And the snowflakes soft were drifted,
Till the heath-stems all were covered,
On the ground the berry-bushes.

Then the smith, e'en Ilmarinen,
In his sledge of iron sat him,   430
And he spoke the words which follow,
And in words like these expressed him:
"On my reins attend good fortune,
Jumala, my sledge protecting,
That my reins good fortune fail not,
Nor my sledge may break, O Creator!"

In one hand the reins he gathered,
And the whip he grasped with other,
O'er the horse the whip he brandished,
And he spoke the words which follow: 440
"Whitebrow, speed thou quickly onward,
Haste away, O flaxen-maned one!"

On the way the horse sprang forward,
On the water's sandy margin,
By the shores of Sound of Sima,
Past the hills with alders covered.
On the shore the sledge went rattling,
On the beach the shingle clattered.
In his eyes the sand was flying,
To his breast splashed up the water.   450

Thus he drove one day, a second,
Drove upon the third day likewise,
And at length upon the third day,
Overtook old Väinämöinen,
And he spoke the words which follow,
And in words like these expressed him:
"O thou aged Väinämöinen,
Let us make a friendly compact,
That although we both are seeking,
And we both would woo the maiden,   460
Yet by force we will not seize her,
Nor against her will shall wed her!"

Said the aged Väinämöinen,
"I will make a friendly compact,
That we will not seize the maiden,
Nor against her will shall wed her.
Let the maiden now be given
To the husband whom she chooses,
That we nurse not long vexation,
Nor a lasting feud we foster."   470

Further on their way they travelled,
On the path that each had chosen;
Sped the boat, the shore re-echoed,
Ran the horse, the earth resounded.

But a short time passed thereafter,
Very short the time elapsing,
Ere the grey-brown dog was barking,
And the house-dog loudly baying,
In the gloomy land of Pohja,
Sariola, for ever cloudy,   480

Sooner still the dog was growling,
But with less-continued growling,
By the borders of the cornfield,
'Gainst the ground his tail was wagging.

Then exclaimed the Lord of Pohja,
"Go, my daughter, to discover
Why the grey-brown dog is barking,
And the long-eared dog is baying!"

But the daughter made him answer:
"I have not the time, my father,   490
I must clean the largest cowshed,
Tend our herd of many cattle,
Grind the corn between the millstones,
Through the sieve must sift the flour,
Grind the corn to finest flour,
Though the grinder is but feeble."

Gently barked the castle's Hiisi,
And again the dog was growling,
And again said Pohja's Master:
"Go, old dame, and look about you,   500
See why barks the grey-brown house-dog,
Why the castle-dog is growling!"

But the old dame made him answer:
"This is not a time for talking,
For my household cares are heavy,
And I must prepare the dinner.
And must bake a loaf enormous,
And for this the dough be kneading,
Bake the loaf of finest flour,
Though the baker is but feeble."   510

Thereupon said Pohja's Master:
"Women they are always hurried,
And the maidens always busy,
When before the stove they roast them,
When they in their beds are lying;
Son, go you, and look around you!"

Thereupon the son made answer:
"I've no time to look about me;
I must grind the blunted hatchet,
Chop a log of wood to pieces,   520
Chop to bits the largest wood-pile,
And to faggots small reduce it.
Large the pile, and small the faggots,
Though the workman is the weakest."

Still the castle-dog was barking,
And the yard-dog still was barking,
And the furious whelp was baying,
And the island watch-dog howling,
Sitting by the furthest cornfield
And his tail was briskly wagging.   530

Then again said Pohja's Master,
"Not for nought the dog is barking,
Never has he barked for nothing,
Never growls he at the fir-trees."
So he went to reconnoitre,
And he walked across the courtyard,
To the cornfield's furthest borders,
To the path beyond the ploughed land.
Gazed he where the dog's snout pointed,
Where he saw his muzzle pointing,   540
To the hill where winds are blowing,
To the hills where grow the alders,
Then he saw the truth most clearly,
Why the grey-brown dog was barking,
And the pride of earth was baying,
And the woolly-tailed one howling,
For he saw a red boat sailing
Out amid the Bay of Lempi,
And a handsome sledge was driving
On the shore of Sound of Sima.   550

After this the Lord of Pohja
To the house returned directly,
And beneath the roof he hastened,
And he spoke the words which follow:

"There are strangers swiftly sailing
O'er the blue lake's watery surface,
And a gaudy sledge is gliding
On the shore of Sound of Sima;
And a large boat is approaching
To the shore of Bay of Lempi."   560

Then said Pohjola's old Mistress,
"Whence shall we obtain an omen
Why these strangers here are coming?
O my little waiting-maiden,
On the fire lay rowan-faggots,
And the best log in its glowing!
If the log with blood is flowing,
Then the strangers come for battle,
If the log exudes clear water,
Then is peace abiding with us."   570

Then the little maid of Pohja,
She, the modest waiting-maiden,
On the fire laid rowan-faggots,
Placed the best log in its glowing.
From the log no blood was trickling,
Nor did water trickle from it;
From the log there oozed forth honey,
From the log dripped down the nectar.

From the corner spoke Suovakko,
Spoke the old dame 'neath the blankets: 580
"From the log if oozes honey,
From the log if drips the nectar,
Then the strangers who are coming,
May be ranked as noble suitors."

Then did Pohja's aged Mistress,
Pohja's old dame, Pohja's daughter,
To the courtyard fencing hasten,
Hurry quick across the courtyard,
And they gazed across the water,
To the south their heads then turning,   590
And they saw from thence approaching,
Swift a ship of novel fashion,

Of a hundred planks constructed,
Out upon the Bay of Lempi.
Underneath the boat looked bluish,
But the sails of crimson colour.
In the stern there sat a hero,
At the copper rudder's handle,
And they saw a stallion trotting
With a red sledge strange of aspect,   600
And the gaudy sledge was speeding
On the shore of Sound of Sima,
And they saw six golden cuckoos,
Perching on the frame, and calling,
Seven blue birds were likewise perching
On the reins, and these were singing;
And a stalwart hero, sitting
In the sledge, the reins was holding.

Then said Pohjola's old Mistress,
And she spoke the words which follow: 610
"Whom will you accept as husband,
If they really come to woo you,
As a life-companion woo you,
Dove-like in his arms to nestle?

He who in the boat is sailing,
In the red boat fast approaching;
Out upon the Bay of Lempi,
Is the aged Väinämöinen.
In the boat he brings provisions,
And of treasures brings a cargo.   620

He who in the sledge is driving,
In the gaudy sledge is speeding,
On the shore of Sound of Sima,
Is the smith named Ilmarinen.
He with empty hands is coming;
Filled his sledge with spells of magic.

Therefore if the room they enter,
Bring them then the mead in tankard,   630
In the two-eared tankard bring it,
And in his hands place the tankard

Whom thou dost desire to follow;
Choose thou Väinölä's great hero,
He whose boat with wealth is loaded,
And of treasures brings a cargo!"

But the lovely maid of Pohja,
Thus made answer to her mother:
"O my mother, who hast borne me,
O my mother, who hast reared me,
Nothing do I care for riches,
Nor a man profound in wisdom,   640
But a man of lofty forehead,
One whose every limb is handsome.
Never once in former ages,
Gave a maid her life in thiswise.
I, a maid undowered, will follow
Ilmarinen, skilful craftsman,
He it was, who forged the Sampo,
And the coloured cover welded."

Then said Pohja's aged Mistress,
"O indeed, my child, my lambkin,   650
If you go with Ilmarinen,
From whose brow the sweat falls freely,
You must wash the blacksmith's aprons,
And the blacksmith's head wash likewise!"

But the daughter gave her answer,
In the very words which follow:
"Him from Väinölä I choose not,
Nor an aged man will care for,
For an old man is a nuisance,
And an aged man would vex me."   660

Then did aged Väinämöinen
Reach his journey's end the soonest,
And he steered his crimson vessel,
Brought his boat of bluish colour
To the rollers steel-constructed,
To the landing-pier of copper.
After this the house he entered,
Underneath the roof he hastened,

And upon the floor spoke loudly,
Near the door beneath the rafters,   670
And he spoke the words which follow,
And expressed himself in thiswise:
"Wilt thou come with me, O maiden,
Evermore as my companion,
Wife-like on my knees to seat thee,
In my arms as dove to nestle?"

Then the lovely maid of Pohja,
Hastened up to give the answer:
"Have you then the boat constructed,
Built the large and handsome vessel,   680
From the splinters of my spindle,
From the fragments of my shuttle?"

Then the aged Väinämöinen
Answered in the words which follow:
"I have built a noble vessel,
And a splendid boat constructed,
Strongly built to face the tempests,
And the winds its course opposing,
As it cleaves the tossing billows,
O'er the surface of the water,   690
Bladder-like amid the surges,
As a leaf, by current drifted,
Over Pohjola's wide waters,
And across the foaming billows."

Then the lovely maid of Pohja,
Answered in the words which follow:
"Nothing do I reck of seamen,
Heroes boasting of the billows.
Drives the wind their minds to ocean,
And their thoughts the east wind saddens;   700
Therefore thee I cannot follow,
Never pledge myself unto thee,
Evermore as thy companion,
In thy arms as dove to nestle,
Spread the couch whereon thou sleepest,
For thy head arrange the pillows."

XIX   The exploits and betrothal of Ilmarinen

Ilmarinen arrives at the homestead of Pohjola, woos the daughter of the house, and perilous tasks are assigned to him (1–32). Aided by the advice of the Maiden of Pohja he succeeds in performing the tasks successfully. First, he ploughs a field of serpents; secondly, he captures the Bear of Tuoni and the Wolf of Manala; and thirdly, he captures a large and terrible pike in the river of Tuonela (33–344). The Mistress of Pohjola promises and betroths her daughter to Ilmarinen (345–498). Väinämöinen returns from Pohjola in low spirits, and warns every one against going wooing in company with a younger man (499–518).

Then the smith, e'en Ilmarinen,
He the great primeval craftsman,
Came himself into the chamber,
And beneath the roof he hastened.

Brought the maid of mead a beaker,
Placed a can of drink of honey
In the hands of Ilmarinen,
And the smith spoke out as follows:
"Never while my life is left me,
Long as shines the golden moonlight,   10
Will I taste these drinks before me,
Till my own is granted to me,
She for whom so long I waited,
She for whom so long I pined for."

Then said Pohjola's old Mistress,
In the very words which follow:
"Trouble great befalls the suitor,
Comes to her for whom he waiteth;
One shoe still remains unfitted,   20
And unfitted is the other;
But the bride is waiting for you,

And you may indeed receive her,
If you plough the field of vipers,
Where the writhing snakes are swarming,
But without a plough employing,
And without a ploughshare guiding.
Once the field was ploughed by Hiisi,
Lempo seamed it next with furrows,
With the ploughsare formed of copper,
With the plough in furnace smelted;   30
But my own son, most unhappy,
Left the half untilled behind him."

Then the smith, e'en Ilmarinen,
Sought the maiden in her chamber,
And he spoke the words which follow:
"Night's own daughter, twilight maiden,
Do you not the time remember,
When I forged new Sampo for you,
And the brilliant cover welded,
And a binding oath thou sweared'st,   40
By the God whom all men worship,
'Fore the face of Him Almighty,
And you gave a certain promise
Unto me, the mighty hero,
You would be my friend for ever,
Dove-like in my arms to nestle?
Nothing will your mother grant me,
Nor will she her daughter give me,
Till I plough the field of vipers,
Where the writhing snakes are swarming."   50

Then his bride assistance lent him,
And advice the maiden gave him:
"O thou smith, O Ilmarinen,
Thou the great primeval craftsman!
Forge thyself a plough all golden,
Cunningly bedecked with silver!
Then go plough the field of serpents,
Where the writhing snakes are swarming."

Then the smith, e'en Ilmarinen,
Laid the gold upon the anvil,   60

Worked the bellows on the silver,
And he forged the plough he needed,
And he forged him shoes of iron;
Greaves of steel he next constructed,
And with these his feet he covered,
Those upon his shins he fastened;
And he donned an iron mail-coat,
With a belt of steel he girt him,
Took a pair of iron gauntlets,
Gauntlets like to stone for hardness;   70
Then he chose a horse of mettle,
And he yoked the steed so noble,
And he went to plough the acre,
And the open field to furrow.

There he saw the heads all rearing,
Saw the heads that hissed unceasing,
And he spoke the words which follow:
"O thou snake, whom God Created,
You who lift your head so proudly,
Who is friendly and will hearken,   80
Rearing up your head so proudly,
And your neck so proudly lifting;
From my path at once remove you,
Creep, thou wretch, among the stubble,
Creep then down among the bushes,
Or where greenest grass is growing!
If you lift your head from out it,
Ukko then your head shall shatter,
With his sharp and steel-tipped arrows,
With a mighty hail of iron."   90

Then he ploughed the field of vipers,
Furrowed all the land of serpents,
From the furrows raised the vipers,
Drove the serpents all before him,
And he said, returning homeward:
"I have ploughed the field of vipers,
Furrowed all the land of serpents,
Driven before me all the serpents:
Will you give me now your daughter,
And unite me with my darling?"   100

Then did Pohjola's old Mistress,
Answer in the words which follow:
"I will only give the maiden,
And unite you with my daughter,
If you catch the Bear of Tuoni;
Bridle, too, the Wolf of Mana,
Far in Tuonela's great forest,
In the distant realms of Mana.
Hundreds have gone forth to yoke them;
Never one returned in safety."   110

Then the smith, e'en Ilmarinen,
Sought the maiden in her chamber,
And he spoke the words which follow:
"Now the task is laid upon me:
Manala's fierce wolves to bridle,
And to hunt the bears of Tuoni,
Far in Tuonela's great forest,
In the distant realms of Mana."

Then his bride assistance lent him,
And advice the maiden gave him: 120
"O thou smith, O Ilmarinen,
Thou the great primeval craftsman!
Forge thee bits, of steel the hardest,
Forge thee muzzles wrought of iron,
Sitting on a rock in water,
Where the cataracts fall all foaming.
Hunt thou then the Bears of Tuoni,
And the Wolves of Mana bridle."

Then the smith, e'en Ilmarinen,
He the great primeval craftsman,   130
Forged him bits, of steel the hardest,
Forged him muzzles wrought of iron,
Sitting on a rock in water,
Where the three rapids fall all foaming.

Then he went the beasts to fetter,
And he spoke the words which follow:
"Terhenetär, Cloudland's daughter!
With the cloud-sieve sift thou quickly,

And disperse thy mists around me!
Where the beasts I seek are lurking,   140
That they may not hear me moving,
That they may not flee before me!"

Then the Wolf's great jaws he muzzled,
And with iron the Bear he fettered,
On the barren heaths of Tuoni,
In the blue depths of the forest.
And he said, returning homeward:
"Give me now your daughter, old one.
Here I bring the Bear of Tuoni,
And the Wolf of Mana muzzled!"   150

Then did Pohjola's old Mistress
Answer in the words which follow:
"I will give you first the duckling,
And the blue-winged duck will give you,
When the pike, so huge and scaly,
He the fish so plump and floundering,
You shall bring from Tuoni's river,
And from Manala's abysses;
But without a net to lift it,
Using not a hand to grasp it.   160
Hundreds have gone forth to seek it,
Never one returned in safety."

Then there came distress upon him,
And affliction overwhelmed him,
As he sought the maiden's chamber,
And he spoke the words which follow:
"Now a task is laid upon me,
Greater still than all the former;
For the pike, so huge and scaly,
He the fish so plump and floundering,   170
I must bring from Tuoni's river,
From the eternal stream of Mana,
But with neither snare nor drag-net,
Nor with help of other tackle."

Then his bride assistance lent him,
And advice the maiden gave him:

"O thou smith, O Ilmarinen,
Do thou not be so despondent!
Forge thee now a fiery eagle,
Forge a bird of fire all flaming!   180
This the mighty pike shall capture,
Drag the fish so plump and floundering,
From the murky stream of Tuoni,
And from Manala's abysses."

Then the smith, e'en Ilmarinen,
Deathless artist of the smithy,
Forged himself a fiery eagle,
Forged a bird of fire all flaming,
And of iron he forged the talons,
Forged the claws of steel the hardest,   190
Wings like sides of boat constructed;
Then upon the wings he mounted,
On the eagle's back he sat him,
On the wing-bones of the eagle.

Then he spoke unto the eagle,
And the mighty bird instructed:
"O my eagle, bird I fashioned,
Fly thou forth, where I shall order,
To the turbid stream of Tuoni,
And to Manala's abysses: 200
Seize the pike, so huge and scaly,
He the fish so plump and floundering!"

Then the bird, that noble eagle,
Took his flight, and upward soaring,
Forth he flew the pike to capture,
Fish with teeth of size terrific,
In the river-depths of Tuoni,
Down in Manala's abysses:
To the water stretched a pinion,
And the other touched the heavens;   210
In the sea he dipped his talons,
On the cliffs his beak he whetted.

Thus the smith, e'en Ilmarinen,
Journeyed forth to seek his booty

In the depths of Tuoni's river,
While the eagle watched beside him.

From the water rose a kelpie
And it clutched at Ilmarinen,
By the neck the eagle seized it,
And the kelpie's head he twisted.   220
To the bottom down he forced it,
To the black mud at the bottom.

Then came forth the pike of Tuoni,
And the water-dog came onward.
Not a small pike of the smallest,
Nor a large pike of the largest;
Long his tongue as twain of axe-shafts,
Long his teeth as rake-shaft measures,
Wide his gorge as three great rivers,
Seven boats' length his back extended,   230
And the smith he sought to seize on,
And to swallow Ilmarinen.

But the eagle rushed against him,
And the bird of air attacked him;
Not an eagle of the small ones,
Nor an eagle of the large ones:
Long his beak as hundred fathoms,
Wide his gorge as six great rivers,
Six spears' length his tongue extended,
Five scythes' length his talons measured;   240
And he saw the pike so scaly,
Saw the fish so plump and floundering.
Fiercely on the fish he darted,
Rushed against the fish so scaly.

Then the pike so large and scaly,
He the fish so plump and floundering,
Tried to drag the eagle's pinions
Underneath the sparkling waters,
But the eagle swift ascended,
Up into the air he raised him,   250
From the grimy ooze he raised him,
To the sparkling water o'er it.

Back and forth the eagle hovered,
And again he made an effort,
And he struck one talon fiercely
In the pike's terrific shoulders,
In the water-dog's great backbone,
And he fixed the other talon
Firmly in the steel-hard mountain,
In the rocks as hard as iron.   260
From the stone slipped off the talon,
Slipped from off the rocky mountain,
And the pike again dived downward,
In the water slid the monster,
Slipped from off the eagle's talons,
From the great bird's claws terrific,
But his sides were scored most deeply,
And his shoulders cleft asunder.

Once again, with iron talons,
Swooped again the furious eagle,   270
With his wings all fiery glowing,
And his eyes like flame that sparkled,
Seized the pike with mighty talons,
Grasped the water-dog securely,
Dragged the huge and scaly monster,
Raised him from the tossing water,
From the depths beneath the billows,
To the water's sparkling surface.

Then the bird with claws of iron,
Made a third and final effort,   280
Brought the mighty pike of Tuoni,
He the fish so plump and floundering,
From the river dark of Tuoni,
And from Manala's abysses.
Scarce like water flowed the water
From the great pike's scales stupendous;
Nor like air the air extended
When the great bird flapped his pinions.

Thus the iron-taloned eagle
Bore the pike so huge and scaly,   290
To the branches of an oak-tree,

To a pine-tree's crown, wide spreading.
There he feasted on the booty,
Open ripped the fish's belly,
Tore away the fish's breastbone,
And the head and neck he sundered.

Said the smith, said Ilmarinen:
"O thou wicked, wretched eagle,
What a faithless bird I find you,
You have seized upon the quarry,   300
And have feasted on the booty,
Open ripped the fish's belly,
Torn away the fish's breastbone,
And the head and neck have sundered!"

But the iron-taloned eagle
Rose and soared away in fury,
High aloft in air he raised him,
To the borders of the cloudland;
Fled the clouds, the heavens were thundering
And the props of air bowed downward: 310
Ukko's bow in twain was broken,
In the moon the horns sharp-pointed.

Then the smith, e'en Ilmarinen,
Took the pike's head, which he carried,
To the old crone as a present,
And he spoke the words which follow:
"Make of this a chair for ever,
In the halls of lofty Pohja."

Then he spoke the words which follow,
And in words like these expressed him: 320
"I have ploughed the field of serpents,
Furrowed all the land of serpents;
Bridled, too, the wolves of Mana,
And have chained the bears of Tuoni;
Brought the pike so huge and scaly,
He the fish so plump and floundering,
From the river deep of Tuoni,
And from Manala's abysses.

Will you give me now the maiden,
And bestow your daughter on me?"   330

Then said Pohjola's old Mistress,
"Badly have you done your errand,
Thus the head in twain to sever,
Open rip the fish's belly,
Tear away the fish's breastbone,
Feasting thus upon the booty."

Then the smith, e'en Ilmarinen,
Answered in the words that follow:
"Never can you bring, undamaged,
Quarry from the best of regions.   340
This is brought from Tuoni's river,
And from Manala's abysses.
Is not yet the maiden ready,
She for whom I longed and laboured?"

Then did Pohjola's old Mistress
Answer in the words which follow:
"Yes, the maiden now is ready,
She for whom you longed and laboured.
I will give my tender duckling,
And prepare the duck I cherished,   350
For the smith, for Ilmarinen,
At his side to sit for ever,
On his knee as wife to seat her,
Dove-like in his arms to nestle."

On the floor a child was sitting,
On the floor a child was singing:
"To our room there came already,
Came a bird into our castle;
From the north-east flew an eagle,
Through the sky a hawk came flying,   360
In the air one wing was flapping,
On the sea the other rested,
With his tail he swept the ocean,
And to heaven his head he lifted;
And he gazed around, and turned him,

Back and forth the eagle hovered,
Perched upon the heroes' castle,
And his beak he whetted on it,
But the roof was formed of iron,
And he could not pierce within it.   370

So he gazed around and turned him,
Back and forth the eagle hovered,
Perched upon the women's castle,
And his beak he whetted on it,
But the roof was formed of copper,
And he could not pierce within it.

So he gazed around and turned him,
Back and forth the eagle hovered,
Perched upon the maidens' castle,
And his beak he whetted on it,   380
And the roof was formed of linen,
And he forced his way within it.

Then he perched upon the chimney,
Then upon the floor descended,
Pushed aside the castle's shutter,
Sat him at the castle window,
Near the wall, all green his feathers,
In the room, his plumes a hundred.

Then he scanned the braidless maidens,
Gazing on the long-haired maiden,   390
On the best of all the maidens,
Fairest maid with hair unbraided,
And her head with beads was shining,
And her head with beauteous blossoms.

In his claws the eagle seized her,
And the hawk with talons grasped her,
Seized the best of all the party,
Of the flock of ducks the fairest,
She the sweetest-voiced and tenderest,
She the rosiest and the whitest,   400
She the bird of air selected,
In his talons far he bore her,

She who held her head the highest,
And her form of all the shapeliest,
And her feathers of the finest,
And her plumage of the softest."

Then did Pohjola's old Mistress
Answer in the words that follow:
"Wherefore dost thou know, my darling,
Or hast heard, my golden apple,   410
How the maiden grew amongst us,
And her flaxen hair waved round her?
Perhaps the maiden shone with silver,
Or the maiden's gold was famous.
Has our sun been shining on you,
Or the moon afar been shining?"

From the floor the child made answer,
And the growing child responded:
"Therefore did your darling know it,
And your fostling learned to know it.   420
In the far-famed maidens' dwelling,
In the home where dwells the fair one;
Good report rejoiced the father,
When he launched his largest vessel;
But rejoices more the mother,
When the largest loaf is baking,
And the wheaten bread is baking,
That the guests may feast profusely.

Thus it was your darling knew it,
Far around the strangers knew it,   430
How the young maid grew in stature,
And how tall grew up the maiden:
Once I went into the courtyard,
And I wandered to the storehouse,
Very early in the morning,
In the earliest morning hours,
And the soot in streaks ascended,
And the smoke in clouds rose upward,
From the far-famed maiden's dwelling,
From the blooming maiden's homestead,   440
And the maid herself was grinding,

Busy working at the handmill;
Rung the mill like call of cuckoo,
And the pestle quacked like wild geese,
And the sieve like bird was singing,
And the stones like beads were rattling.

Forth a second time I wandered,
And into the field I wandered,
In the meadow was the maiden,
Stooping o'er the yellow heather;   450
Working at the red-stained dye-pots,
Boiling up the yellow kettles.

When I wandered forth a third time
Sat the maid beneath the window;
There I heard the maiden weaving,
In her hands the comb was sounding,
And I heard the shuttle flying,
As in cleft of rock the ermine,
And the comb-teeth heard I sounding,
As the wooden shaft was moving,   460
And the weaver's beam was turning,
Like a squirrel in the tree-tops."

Then did Pohjola's old Mistress
Answer in the words which follow:
"There, O there, dearest maiden!
Have I not for ever told thee,
Not to sing among the pine-trees,
Not to sing amid the valleys,
Not to arch thy neck too proudly,
Nor thy white arms leave uncovered,   470
Nor thy young and beauteous bosom,
Nor thy shape so round and graceful?

I have warned thee all the autumn,
And besought thee all the summer,
Likewise in the spring have cautioned,
At the second springtide sowing,
To construct a secret dwelling,
With the windows small and hidden,
Where the maids may do their weaving,

And may work their looms in safety,   480
All unheard by Suomi's gallants,
Suomi's gallants, far-famed suitors."

From the floor the child made answer,
And the fortnight-old responded:
"Easily a horse is hidden,
In the stall, with fine-tailed horses;
Hard it is to hide a maiden,
And to keep her long locks hidden.
Though you build of stone a castle,
And amid the sea shall rear it,   490
Though you keep your maidens in it,
And should rear your darlings in it,
Still the girls cannot be hidden,
Nor attain their perfect stature,
Undisturbed by lusty gallants,
Lusty gallants, choicest suitors.
Mighty men, with lofty helmets,
Men who shoe with steel their horses."

Then the aged Väinämöinen
Head bowed down, and deeply grieving: 500
Wandered on his journey homeward,
And he spoke the words which follow:
"Woe is me, a wretched creature,
That I did not learn it sooner,
That in youthful days one weddeth,
And must choose a life-companion!
All thing else a man may grieve for,
Save indeed an early marriage,
When in youth already children,
And a household he must care for."   510

Thus did warn old Väinämöinen,
Cautioned thus Suvantolainen,
That old men against the younger,
Should not struggle for a fair one:
Warned them not to swim too proudly,
Neither try to race in rowing,
Nor to seek to woo a maiden,
With a younger man contending.

XX   The great ox, and the brewing of the ale

An enormous ox is slaughtered in Pohjola (1–118). They brew ale and prepare a feast (119–516). They dispatch messengers to invite the heroes to the wedding, but Lemminkäinen is expressly passed over (517–614).

How shall we our song continue,
And what legends shall we tell you?
Thus will we pursue our story;
These the legends we will tell you:
How in Pohjola they feasted,
How the drinking-bout was godlike.

Long prepared they for the wedding,
For the feast provided all things,
In the household famed of Pohja,
Halls of Sariola the misty.   10

What provisions were provided,
What did they collect together,
For a lengthy feast at Pohja,
For the multitude of drinkers,
For the feasting of the people,
For the multitude of feasters?

In Carelia grew a bullock,
Fat an ox they reared in Finland,
Not a large one, not a small one,
But a calf of middle stature: 20

While he switched his tail in Häme,
Stooped his head to Kemi's river,
Long his horns one hundred fathoms,
Muzzle broad as half a hundred,
For a week there ran an ermine
All along the yoke he carried,
All day long there flew a swallow
'Twixt the mighty ox's horn-tips,
Striving through the space to hasten,
Nor found resting-place between them;   30
Month-long ran a summer-squirrel
From his neck unto his tail-end,
Nor did he attain the tail-tip,
Till a month had quite passed over.

'Twas this calf of size stupendous,
'Twas this mighty bull of Finland,
Whom they led forth from Carelia
Till they reached the fields of Pohja.
By his horns, a hundred led him,
And a thousand dragged his muzzle,   40
And they led the ox still further,
Till to Pohjola they brought him.

On his road the ox proceeded
By the Sound of Sariola strayed;
Browsed the grass in marshy places,
While his back the clouds were touching;
But they could not find a butcher,
Who could fell the country's marvel
On the list of Pohja's children,
'Mid the mighty host of people,   50
Not among the youthful people,
Nor among the very aged.

From afar an old man journeyed,
Virokannas from Carelia;
And he spoke the words which follow:
"Wait thou, wait, thou ox unhappy,
While I go and fetch my mallet.
If I strike you with my mallet
On the skull, unhappy creature,

Never in another summer,   60
Would you turn about your muzzle,
Or your tail would jerk around you,
Here among the fields of Pohja,
By the Sound of Sariola strayed."

Then the old man went to strike him,
Virokannas moved against him,
Went to slay the ox unhappy;
But his head the ox was turning,
And his black eyes he was blinking.
To a pine-tree sprang the old man,   70
Virokannas in the bushes,
In the scrubby willow-thicket.

After this they sought a butcher,
Who the mighty ox could slaughter,
From Carelia's lovely country,
From the vast expanse of Suomi,
From the gentle land of Russia,
From the hardy land of Sweden,
From the regions wide of Lapland,
From the mighty land of Turja,   80
And they sought through Tuoni's regions,
In the depths of Mana's kingdom,
And they sought, but no one found they,
Long they searched, but vainly searched they.

Yet again they sought a butcher,
Sought again to find a slaughterer,
On the ocean's shining surface,
On the wide-extending billows.

From the dark sea rose a hero,
Rose a hero from the sea-swell,   90
From the shining surface rising,
From the wide expanse of water.
He was not among the greatest,
But in nowise of the smallest:
In a bowl would he lie sleeping,
And beneath a sieve stand upright.

'Twas an old man, iron-fisted,
Iron-coloured, too, to gaze on;
On his head a stony helmet;
Shoes of stone his feet protected;   100
In his hand a knife, gold-bladed,
And the haft o'erlaid with copper.

Thus the people found a butcher,
And at length they found a slaughterer,
Who should fell the bull of Finland,
And should fell the country's marvel.

Scarce had he beheld the quarry,
Than at once his neck he shattered,
On his knees he forced the bullock,
And upon his side he threw him.   110

Did he yield them much provisions?
Not so very much he yielded:
Of his flesh a hundred barrels,
And a hundred fathoms sausage;
Seven boat-loads of blood they gathered,
Six large casks with fat were loaded,
All for Pohjola's great banquet,
Feast of Sariola the misty.

Then they built a house in Pohja,
Built a house with hall enormous,   120
Fathoms nine its sides extended,
And the breadth thereof was seven.
If a cock crowed at the smoke-hole,
Underneath they could not hear it,
If a dog at end was barking,
At the door they did not hear it.

Then did Pohjola's old Mistress
Walk across the flooring's planking,
To the middle of the chamber,
And she pondered and reflected: 130
"How shall I get ale sufficient,
And shall brew the beer most wisely,

To prepare it for the wedding,
When the beer will much be needed?
How to brew the beer I know not,
Nor how ale was first concocted."

By the stove there sat an old man,
From the stove spoke up the old man:
"Ale of barley is concocted,
And the drink with hops is flavoured,   140
Yet they brew not save with water,
And the aid of furious fire.

Hop is called the son of Revel;
Planted in the ground when little,
With a plough they ploughed the region,
Like an ant, away they cast him
Close to Kaleva's great well-spring,
There where Osmo's field is sloping;
There the tender plant sprang upward,
And the green shoot mounted quickly.   150
Up a little tree it mounted,
Rising to the leafy summit.
Sowed, by chance, an old man barley,
In the fresh-ploughed field of Osmo,
And the barley sprouted bravely,
And it grew and flourished greatly,
On the new-ploughed field of Osmo,
Kaleva's descendant's cornland.

But a little time passed over,
When the hops exclaimed from tree-top,   160
And upon the field the barley,
And in Kaleva's well-water:
'When shall we be yoked together,
Each with other be united?
Life in solitude is weary;
Better two or three together.'

Osmotar, the ale-constructer
She, the maid who beer concocted,
Took, on this, the grains of barley,

Gathered six of grains of barley,   170
Seven hop-tassels next she gathered,
And eight ladles took of water,
Then upon the fire she placed it,
And allowed it there to simmer,
And she boiled the ale of barley
Through the fleeting days of summer,
Out upon the cloudy headland,
Cape upon the shady island;
Poured it then in wooden barrels,
And in tubs of birchwood stored it.   180

Thus she brewed the ale and stored it,
But the ale was not fermented;
And she pondered and reflected,
And she spoke the words which follow:
'What must now be added to it,
What is needful to provide for,
That the ale may be fermented,
And the beer be brought to foaming?'

Kalevatar, beauteous maiden,
She the maid with slender fingers,   190
Which she ever moves so deftly,
She whose feet are shod so lightly,
Felt about the seams of staving,
Groping all about the bottom,
Trying one and then the other,
In the midst of both the kettles;
Found a splinter at the bottom,
From the bottom took a splinter.

Then she turned it and reflected:
'What might perhaps be fashioned from it,   200
In the hands of lovely maiden,
In the noble damsel's fingers,
Brought into the hands of maiden,
To the noble damsel's fingers?'

In her hands the maiden took it,
In the noble damsel's fingers,

And she clapped her hands together,
Both her hands she rubbed together,
Rubbed them on her thighs together,
And a squirrel white created.   210

Then she gave her son directions,
And instructed thus the squirrel:
O thou squirrel, gold of woodlands,
Flower of woodlands, charm of country,
Speed thou forth where I shall bid thee,
Where I bid thee and direct thee:
Forth to Metsola's bright regions,
And to Tapiola's great wisdom.
There a little tree climb upward,
Heedful to the leafy summit,   220
That the eagle may not seize thee,
Nor the bird of air may grasp thee.
From the pine-tree bring me pine-cones,
From the fir bring shoots of fir-tree,
Bring them to the hands of maiden,
For the beer of Osmo's daughter!'

Knew the squirrel now his pathway,
Trailed his bushy tail behind him,
And his journey soon accomplished,
Quickly through the open spaces,   230
Past one wood, and then a second,
And a third he crossed obliquely,
Into Metsola's bright regions,
And to Tapiola's great wisdom.

There he saw three lofty spruce-trees,
There he saw four slender pine-trees,
Climbed a spruce-tree in the valley,
On the heath he climbed a pine-tree,
And the eagle did not seize him,
Nor the bird of air did grasp him.   240

From the spruce he broke the spruce-cones,
From the pine the leafy tassels,
In his claws he hid the pine-cones,
And within his paws he rolled them,

To the maiden's hands he brought them,
To the noble damsel's fingers.

In the beer the maiden laid them,
In the ale she placed them likewise,
But the ale was not fermented,
Nor the fresh drink yet was working.   250

Osmotar, the ale-preparer,
She, the maid who beer concocted,
Pondered yet again the matter.
'What must now be added to it,
That the ale shall be fermented,
And the beer be brought to foaming?'

Kalevatar, beauteous maiden,
She, the maid with slender fingers,
Which she ever moves so deftly,
She whose feet are shod so lightly,   260
Felt about the seams of staving,
Groping all about the bottom,
Trying one, and then the other,
In the midst of both the kettles,
Found a chip upon the bottom,
Took the chip from off the bottom.

Then she turned it and reflected,
'What might perhaps be fashioned from it,
In the hands of lovely maiden,
In the noble damsel's fingers,   270
Brought into the hands of maiden,
To the noble damsel's fingers?'

In her hands the maiden took it
In the noble damsel's fingers,
And she clapped her hands together,
Both her hands she rubbed together,
Rubbed them on her thighs together:
And she made a gold-breast marten.

Thus the marten she instructed,
Thus the orphan child directed: 280

'O my marten, O my birdling,
O my fair one, beauteous-hided!
Thither go, where I shall bid thee,
Where I bid thee, and direct thee:
To the Bear's own rocky cavern,
Where the forest bears are prowling,
Where the bears are always fighting,
Where they lurk in all their fierceness.
With thy hands scrape foam together,
In thy paws the yeast then carry,   290
To the maiden's hands convey it,
And to Osmo's daughter's shoulders!'

Understood the way the marten,
Forth the golden-breasted hastened,
And his journey soon accomplished,
Quickly through the open spaces,
Past one stream, and then a second,
And a third he crossed obliquely,
To the Bear's own rocky cavern,
To the caverns bear-frequented,   300
Where the bears are always fighting,
Where they lurk in all their fierceness,
In the rocks as hard as iron,
And among the steel-hard mountains.

From the bears' mouths foam was dropping,
From their furious jaws exuding;
In his hands the foam he gathered,
With his paws the foam collected,
To the maiden's hands he brought it,
To the noble damsel's fingers.   310

In the ale the maiden poured it,
In the beer she poured it likewise,
But the ale was not fermented,
Nor the drink of men foamed over.

Osmotar, the ale-preparer,
She the maid who beer concocted,
Pondered yet again the matter:
'What must now be added to it,

That the ale shall be fermented,
And the beer be brought to foaming?'   320

Kalevatar, beauteous maiden,
She the maid with slender fingers,
Which she ever moves so deftly,
She whose feet are shod so lightly
Felt about the seams of staving,
Groping all about the bottom,
Trying one and then the other,
Then the space between the kettles,
On the ground a pea pod saw she;
And from the ground the pod she lifted.   330

Then she turned it, and surveyed it:
'What might perhaps be fashioned from it,
In the hands of lovely maiden,
In the noble damsel's fingers,
Brought into the hands of maiden,
To the noble damsel's fingers?'

In her hands the maiden took it,
In the noble damsel's fingers,
And she clapped her hands together,
Both her hands she rubbed together,   340
Rubbed them on her thighs together,
And a bee she thus created.

And the bee she thus instructed,
And the bee she thus directed:
'O thou bee, thou bird so nimble,
King of all the flowery meadows,
Thither fly, where I shall bid thee,
Where I bid thee and direct thee:
To an isle on ocean's surface,
Where the reefs arise from ocean.   350
There a maiden lies in slumber,
With her belt of copper loosened;
By her side springs sweetest herbage,
On her lap rest honey grasses.
On thy wings bring sweetest honey,
Bring thou honey on thy clothing,

From the fairest of the herbage,
From the bloom of golden flowerets,
To the maiden's hands convey it,
And to Osmo's daughter's shoulders!'   360

Then the bee, that bird so nimble,
Flew away, and hastened onward,
And his journey soon accomplished,
Speeding o'er the open spaces,
First across the sea, along it,
Then in an oblique direction,
To an isle on ocean's surface,
Where the reefs arise from ocean.
There he saw the maiden sleeping,
With a tin brooch on her bosom,   370
Resting in an unmowed meadow,
All among the fields of honey;
By her side grew golden grasses,
At her belt sprang silver grasses.

Then he soaked his wings with honey,
Plunged his plumes in liquid honey,
From the brightest of the herbage,
From the tips of golden flowerets;
To the maiden's hands he brought it,
To the noble damsel's fingers.   380

In the ale the maiden cast it,
In the beer she poured it likewise,
And the beer at length fermented,
And the fresh drink now foamed upward,
From within the new-made barrels,
From within the tubs of birchwood,
Foaming upward to the handles,
Rushing over all the edges;
To the ground it wished to trickle,
And upon the floor ran downward.   390

But a little time passed over,
Very little time passed over,
When the heroes flocked to drink it,
Chief among them Lemminkäinen.

Drunk was Ahti, drunk was Kauko,
Drunken was the ruddy rascal,
With the ale of Osmo's daughter,
And the beer of Kalevatar.

Osmotar, the ale-preparer,
She, the maid who beer concocted,
Uttered then the words which follow: 400
'Woe is me, my day is wretched,
For I brewed the ale so badly
And the beer so ill concocted,
That from out the tubs 'tis flowing,
And upon the floor is gushing!'

From a tree there sang a bullfinch.
From the roof-tree sang a throstle:
'No, the ale is not so worthless;
'Tis the best of ale for drinking;   410
If into the casks you pour it,
And should store it in the cellar,
Store it in the casks of oakwood,
And within the hoops of copper.'

Thus was ale at first created,
Beer of Kaleva concocted,
Therefore is it praised so highly,
Therefore held in greatest honour,
For the ale is of the finest,
Best of drinks for prudent people;   420
Women soon it brings to laughter,
Men it warms into good humour,
And it makes the prudent merry,
But it brings the fools to raving."

Then did Pohjola's old Mistress,
When she heard how ale was fashioned,
Water pour in tubs the largest,
Half she filled the new-made barrels,
Adding barley as 'twas needed,
Shoots of hop enough she added,   430
And the ale began she brewing,
And the beer began its working,

In the new tubs that contained it,
And within the tubs of birchwood.

'Twas for months the stones were glowing,
And for summers water boiling,
Trees were burning on the islands,
Water from the wells was carried.
Bare of trees they left the islands,
And the lakes were greatly shrunken,   440
For the ale was in the barrels,
And the beer was stored securely
For the mighty feast of Pohja,
For carousing at the mansion.

From the island smoke was rising,
On the headland fire was glowing;
Thick the clouds of smoke were rising,
In the air there rose the vapour.
For the fire was burning fiercely,
And the fire was brightly glowing,   450
Half it filled the land of Pohja,
Over all Carelia spreading.
All the people gazed upon it,
Gazed, and then they asked each other:
"Wherefore is the smoke arising,
In the air the vapour rising?
'Tis too small for smoke of battle,
'Tis too large for herdsman's bonfire."

Then rose Lemminkäinen's mother,
At the earliest dawn of morning,   460
And she went to fetch some water.
Clouds of smoke she saw arising,
Up from Pohjola's dominions,
And she spoke the words which follow:
"Perhaps it is the smoke of combat,
Perhaps it is the fire of battle."

Ahti, dweller on the island,
He the handsome Kaukomieli,
Wandered round and gazed about him,
And he pondered and reflected: 470

"I must go and look upon it,
From a nearer spot examine,
Whence the smoke is thus ascending,
Filling all the air with vapour,
If it be the smoke of combat,
If it be the fire of battle."

Kauko went to gaze about him,
And to learn whence smoke was rising,
But it was not fire of battle,
Neither was it fire of combat,   480
But 'twas fire where ale was brewing,
Likewise where the beer was brewing,
Near where Sound of Sariola spreads,
Out upon the jutting headland.

Then did Kauko gaze around him,
And one eye he rolled obliquely,
And he squinted with the other,
And his mouth he pursed up slowly,
And at last he spoke, while gazing,
And across the sound he shouted:,   490
"O my dearest foster-mother,
Pohjola's most gracious Mistress!
Brew thou ale of extra goodness,
Brew thou beer the best of any,
For carousing at the mansion,
Specially for Lemminkäinen,
At my wedding, now preparing,
With thy young and lovely daughter!"

Now the ale was quite fermented,
And the drink of men was ripened,   500
And the red ale stored they safely,
And the good beer stored securely.
Underneath the ground they stored it,
Stored it in the rocky cellars,
In the casks of oak constructed,
And behind the taps of copper.

Then did Pohjola's old Mistress
All the food provide for feasting,

And the kettles all were singing,
And the stewpans all were hissing,   510
And large loaves of bread were baking,
And she stirred great pots of porridge,
Thus to feed the crowds of people,
At the banquet at the mansion,
At the mighty feast of Pohja,
The carouse at Sariola dim.

Now the bread they baked was ready,
And were stirred the pots of porridge,
And a little time passed over,
Very little time passed over,   520
When the ale worked in the barrels,
And the beer foamed in the cellars:
"Now must some one come to drink me,
Now must some one come to taste me,
That my fame may be reported,
And that they may sing my praises!"

Then they went to seek a minstrel,
Went to seek a famous singer,
One whose voice was of the strongest,
One who knew the finest legends.   530
First to sing they tried a salmon,
If the voice of trout was strongest;
Singing is not work for salmon,
And the pike recites no legends;
Crooked are the jaws of salmon,
And the teeth of pike spread widely.

Yet again they sought a singer,
Went to seek a famous singer,
One whose voice was of the strongest,
One who knew the finest legends,   540
And they took a child for singer,
Thought a boy might sing the strongest.
Singing is not work for children,
Nor are splutterers fit for shouting;
Crooked are the tongues of children,
And the roots thereof are crooked.

Then the red ale grew indignant,
And the fresh drink fell to cursing,
Pent within the oaken barrels,
And behind the taps of copper: 550
"If you do not find a minstrel,
Do not find a famous singer,
One whose voice is of the strongest,
One who knows the finest legends,
Then the hoops I'll burst asunder,
And among the dust will trickle!"

Then did Pohjola's old Mistress
Send the guests their invitations,
Sent her messengers to journey,
And she spoke the words which follow: 560
"O my maid, of all the smallest,
O my waiting-maid obedient,
Call the people all together,
To the great carouse invite them,
Call the poor, and call the needy,
Call the blind, and call the wretched,
Call the lame, and call the cripples;
In the boat row thou the blind men;
Bring the lame ones here on horseback,
And in sledges bring the cripples!   570

Ask thou all the folk of Pohja,
And of Kaleva the people:
Ask the aged Väinämöinen,
Greatest he of all the minstrels,
Only ask not Lemminkäinen,
Ask not Ahti Saarelainen!"

Then the maid, of all the smallest,
Answered in the words which follow:
"Wherefore ask not Lemminkäinen,
Only Ahti Saarelainen?"   580

Then did Pohjola's old Mistress,
In these very words make answer:
"Therefore ask not Kaukomieli,

Not the reckless Lemminkäinen.
He is always quick to quarrel,
And to fight is always ready.
And at weddings works he mischief,
And at banquets grievous scandal,
Brings to shame the modest maidens,
Clad in all their festive garments."   590

Then the maid, of all the smallest,
Answered in the words which follow:
"How shall I know Kaukomieli
That I leave him uninvited?
For I know not Ahti's dwelling,
Nor the house of Kaukomieli."

Then did Pohjola's old Mistress,
Answer in the words which follow:
"Easy may you hear of Kauko,
Learn of Ahti Saarelainen.   600
Ahti dwells upon an island,
Dwells the rascal near the water,
Where the bay outspreads the broadest,
At the curve of Kauko's headland."

Then the maid, of all the smallest,
She the handmaid hired for money,
Bid the guests from six directions,
And in eight the news she carried;
All she asked of Pohja's people,
And of Kaleva the people,   610
Of the householders the poorest,
And the poorest clad amongst them,
Only not the youth named Ahti,
For she left him uninvited.

XXI   The wedding feast of Pohjola

The bridegroom and his party are received at Pohjola (1–226). The guests are hospitably entertained with abundance of food and drink (227–52). Väinämöinen sings and praises the people of the house (253–438).

Then did Pohjola's old Mistress,
Crone of Sariola the misty,
Sometimes out of doors employ her,
Sometimes in the house was busied;
And she heard how whips were cracking,
On the shore heard sledges rattling,
And her eyes she turned to northward,
Towards the sun her head then turning,
And she pondered and reflected:
"Wherefore are these people coming   10
On my shore, to me unhappy?
Is it perhaps a hostile army?"

So she went to gaze around her,
And observe the portent nearer;
It was not a hostile army,
But of guests a great assembly,
And her son-in-law amid them,
With a mighty host of people.

Then did Pohjola's old Mistress,
Crone of Sariola the misty,   20
When she saw the bridegroom's party,
Speak aloud the words which follow:
"As I thought, the wind was blowing
And a faggot-stack o'erthrowing,
On the beach the billows breaking,
On the strand the shingle rattling.
So I went to gaze around me,

And observe the portent nearer;
But I found no wind was blowing,
Nor the faggot-stack was falling, 30
On the beach no waves were breaking,
On the strand no shingle rattling.
'Twas my son-in-law's assemblage,
Twice a hundred men in number.

How shall I detect the bridegroom
In the concourse of the people?
He is known among the people,
As in clumps of trees the cherry,
Like an oak-tree in the thickets,
Or the moon, 'mid stars in heaven. 40

Black the steed that he is driving,
Which a ravenous wolf resembles,
Or a raven, keen for quarry,
Or a lark, with fluttering pinions.
Six there are of golden song-birds,
On his shafts all sweetly singing,
And of blue birds, seven are singing
Sitting on the sledge's traces."

From the road was heard a clatter,
Past the well the runners rattled, 50
In the court arrived the bridegroom,
In the yard the people with him,
In the midst appeared the bridegroom,
With the greatest of the party,
He was not the first among them,
But by no means last among them.

"Off, ye youths, and out ye heroes,
To the court, O ye who loiter,
That ye may remove the breastbands,
And the traces ye may loosen, 60
That the shafts may quick be lowered;
Lead into the house the bridegroom!"

Then the bridegroom's horse sped onward
And the bright-hued sledge drew forward

Through the courtyard of the Master,
When said Pohjola's old Mistress:

"O my slave, whom I have hired,
Best among the village servants,
Take the horse that brought the bridegroom,
With the white mark on his frontlet,   70
From the copper-plated harness,
From the tin-decked breastband likewise,
From the best of reins of leather,
And from harness of the finest.
Lead the courser of the bridegroom,
And with greatest care conduct him
By the reins, of silken fabric,
By the bridle, decked with silver,
To the softest place for rolling,
Where the meadow is the smoothest,   80
Where the drifted snow is finest,
And the land of milky whiteness!

Lead the bridegroom's horse to water,
To the spring that flows the nearest,
Where the water all unfrozen,
Gushes forth, like milk the sweetest,
'Neath the roots of golden fir-trees,
Underneath the bushy pine-trees.

Fodder thou the bridegroom's courser,
From the golden bowl of fodder,   90
From the bowl adorned with copper,
With the choicest meal of barley,
And with well-boiled wheat of summer,
And with pounded rye of summer!

Then conduct the bridegroom's courser
To the best of all the stables,
To the best of resting-places,
To the hindmost of the stables.
Tether there the bridegroom's courser,
To the ring of gold constructed,   100
To the smaller ring of iron,
To the post of curling birchwood,
Place before the bridegroom's courser,

Next a tray with oats o'erloaded,
And with softest hay another,
And a third with chaff the finest!

Curry then the bridegroom's courser,
With the comb of bones of walrus,
That the hair remain unbroken,
Nor his handsome tail be twisted;   110
Cover then the bridegroom's courser
With a cloth of silver fabric,
And a mat of golden texture,
And a horse-wrap decked with copper!

Now my little village laddies,
To the house conduct the bridegroom,
Gently lift his hat from off him,
From his hands his gloves take likewise!

I would fain see if the bridegroom,
Presently the house can enter,   120
Ere the doors are lifted from it,
And they have removed the doorposts,
And have lifted up the crossbars,
And the threshold has been sunken,
And the nearer walls are broken,
And the floor-planks have been shifted!

But the house suits not the bridegroom,
Nor the great gift suits the dwelling,
Till the doors are lifted from it,
And they have removed the doorposts,   130
And have lifted up the crossbars,
And the threshold has been sunken,
And the nearer walls been broken,
And the flooring-planks been shifted,
For the bridegroom's head is longer,
And the bridegroom's ears are higher.

Let the crossbars then be lifted,
That his head the roof may touch not,
Let the threshold now be sunken,
That his footsoles may not touch it,   140

Let them now set back the doorposts,
That the doors may open widely,
When at length the bridegroom enters,
When the noble youth approaches!

Praise, O Jumala most gracious,
For the bridegroom now has entered!
I would now the house examine,
Cast my gaze around within it,
See that washed are all the tables,
And the benches swabbed with water,   150
Scoured the smooth planks of the boarding,
And the flooring swept and polished!

Now that I the house examine,
'Tis so changed I scarcely know it,
From what wood the room was fashioned,
How the roof has been constructed,
And the walls have been erected,
And the flooring been constructed.

Side-walls are of bones of hedgehog,
Hinder-walls of bones of reindeer,   160
Front-walls of the bones of glutton,
And of bones of lamb the crossbar.
All the beams are wood of apple,
And the posts of curling birchwood,
Round the stove rest water-lilies,
Scales of bream compose the ceiling.

And one bench is formed of iron,
Others made from Saxon timber,
Gold-inlaid are all the tables;
Floor o'erspread with silken carpets.   170

And the stove is bright with copper,
And the stove-bench stone-constructed,
And the hearth composed of boulders,
And with Kaleva's tree is boarded."

Then the house the bridegroom entered,
Hastened on beneath the roof-tree,

And he spoke the words which follow:
"Grant, O Jumala, thy blessing
Underneath this noble roof-tree,
Underneath this roof so splendid!"   180

Then said Pohjola's old Mistress,
"Hail, all hail, to thee, who enters
In this room of small dimensions,
In this very lowly cottage,
In this wretched house of firwood,
In this house of pine constructed!

O my little waiting-maiden,
Thou the village maid I hired!
Bring a piece of lighted birchbark,
To a tarry torch apply it,   190
That I may behold the bridegroom,
And the bridegroom's eyes examine,
Whether they are blue or reddish;
Whether they are white as linen!"

Then the little waiting-maiden,
She, the little village maiden,
Brought a piece of lighted birchbark,
To a tarry torch applied it.

"From the bark the flame springs spluttering,
From the tar black smoke's ascending,   200
So his eyes might perhaps be sooted,
And his handsome face be blackened,
Therefore bring a torch all flaming,
Of the whitest wax constructed!"

Then the little waiting-maiden,
She the little village maiden,
Lit a torch, and brought it flaming,
Of the whitest wax constructed.

White like wax the smoke was rising,
And the flame ascended brightly,   210
And the bridegroom's eyes were shining,
And his face was all illumined.

"Now the bridegroom's eyes I gaze on!
They are neither blue nor reddish,
Neither are they white like linen,
But his eyes they shine like sea-foam,
Like the sea-reed are they brownish,
And as lovely as the bulrush.

Now my little village laddies,
Hasten to conduct the bridegroom   220
To a seat among the highest,
To a place the most distinguished,
With his back towards the blue wall,
With his face towards the red board,
There among the guests invited,
Facing all the shouting people."

Then did Pohjola's old Mistress,
Feast her guests in noble fashion,
Feast them on the best of butter,
And with cream-cakes in abundance;   230
Thus she served the guests invited,
And among them first the bridegroom.

On the plates was placed the salmon,
At the sides the pork was stationed,
Dishes filled to overflowing,
Laden to the very utmost,
Thus to feast the guests invited;
And among them first the bridegroom.

Then said Pohjola's old Mistress,
"O my little waiting-maiden,   240
Bring me now the ale in measures,
Bring it in the jugs two-handled,
For the guests we have invited,
And the bridegroom chief among them!"

Then the little waiting-maiden,
She, the servant hired for money,
Brought the measures as directed,
Handed round the five-hooped tankards,
Till, with ale from hops concocted,

All the beards with foam were whitened;   250
All the beards of guests invited;
And among them most the bridegroom's.

What about the ale was spoken,
Of the ale in five-hooped tankards,
When at length it reached the minstrel,
Reached the greatest of the singers,
He the aged Väinämöinen,
First and oldest of the singers,
He the minstrel most illustrious,
He the greatest of the Sages?   260

First of all the ale he lifted,
Then he spoke the words which follow:
"O thou ale, thou drink delicious,
Let the drinkers be not moody!
Urge the people on to singing,
Let them shout, with mouth all golden,
Till our lords shall wonder at it,
And our ladies ponder o'er it,
For the songs already falter,
And the joyous tongues are silenced.   270
When the ale is ill-concocted,
And bad drink is set before us,
Then the minstrels fail in singing,
And the best of songs they sing not,
And our cherished guests are silent,
And the cuckoos call no longer.

Therefore who shall chant unto us,
And whose tongue shall sing unto us,
At the wedding feast of Pohja,
This carouse at Sariola held?   280
Benches will not sing unto us,
Save when people sit upon them,
Nor will floors hold cheerful converse,
Save when people walk upon them,
Neither are the windows joyful,
If the lords should gaze not from them,
Nor resound the table's edges,
If men sit not round the tables,

Neither do the smoke-holes echo,
If men sit not 'neath the smoke-holes".   290

On the floor a child was sitting,
On the stove-bench sat a milkbeard,
From the floor exclaimed the infant,
And the boy spoke from the stove-bench:
"I am not in years a father,
Undeveloped yet my body,
But however small I may be,
If the other big ones sing not,
And the stouter men will shout not,
And the ruddy cheeked will sing not,   300
Then I'll sing, although a lean boy,
Though a thin boy, I will whistle,
I will sing, though weak and meagre,
Though my stomach is not rounded,
That the evening may be cheerful,
And the day may be more honoured."

By the stove there sat an old man,
And he spoke the words which follow:
"That the children sing befits not,
Nor these feeble folk should carol.   310
Children's songs are only falsehoods,
And the songs of girls are foolish.
Let the wisest sing among us,
Who upon the bench is seated!"

Then the aged Väinämöinen,
Answered in the words which follow:
"Are there any who are youthful,
Of the noblest of the people,
Who will clasp their hands together,
Hook their hands in one another,   320
And begin to speak unto us,
Swaying back and forth in singing,
That the day may be more joyful,
And the evening be more blessed?"

From the stove there spoke the old man,
"Never was it heard among us,

Never heard or seen among us,
Nor so long as time existed,
That there lived a better minstrel,
One more skilled in all enchantment,   330
Than myself when I was warbling,
As a child when I was singing,
Singing sweetly by the water,
Making all the heath re-echo,
Chanting loudly in the firwood,
Talking likewise in the forest.

Then my voice was loud and tuneful,
And its tones were most melodious,
Like the flowing of a river,
Or the murmur of a streamlet,   340
Gliding as o'er snow the snowshoes,
Like a yacht across the billows;
But 'tis hard for me to tell you
How my wisdom has departed:
How my voice so strong has failed me,
And its sweetness has departed.
Now it flows no more like river,
Rising like the tossing billows,
But it halts like rake in stubble,
Like the hoe among the pine-roots,   350
Like a sledge in sand embedded,
Or a boat on rocks when stranded."

Then the aged Väinämöinen,
In such words as these expressed him:
"If no other bard comes forward
To accompany my singing,
Then alone my songs I'll carol,
And will now commence my singing,
For to sing was I created,
As an orator was fashioned;   360
How, I ask not in the village,
Nor I learn my songs from strangers."

Then the aged Väinämöinen,
Of the song the lifelong pillar,
Set him to the pleasant labour,

Girt him for the toil of singing,
Loud he sang his songs so pleasing,
Loud he spoke his words of wisdom.

Sang the aged Väinämöinen,
Sang by turns, and spoke his wisdom,   370
Nor did words that suited fail him,
Neither were his songs exhausted,
Sooner stones in rocks were missing,
Or a pond lacked water-lilies.

Therefore thus sang Väinämöinen
Through the evening for their pleasure,
And the women all were laughing,
And the men in high good-humour,
While they listened and they wondered
At the chants of Väinämöinen,   380
For amazement filled the hearers,
Wonder those who heard him singing.

Said the aged Väinämöinen,
When at length his song he ended,
"This is what I have accomplished
As a singer and magician,
Little can I thus accomplish,
And my efforts lead me nowhere;
But, if sang the great Creator,
Speaking with his mouth of sweetness,   390
He would sing his songs unto you,
As a singer and magician.

"He would sing the sea to honey,
And to peas would sing the gravel,
And to malt would sing the seasand,
And to salt would sing the gravel,
Forest broad would sing to cornland,
And the wastes would sing to wheatfields,
Into cakes would sing the mountains,
And to hens' eggs change the mountains.   400

"As a singer and magician,
He would speak, and he would order,

And would sing unto this homestead,
Cowsheds ever filled with cattle,
Lanes o'erfilled with beauteous blossoms,
And the plains o'erfilled with milch-kine,
Full a hundred horned cattle,
And with udders full, a thousand.

As a singer and magician,
He would speak and he would order   410
For our host a coat of lynxskin,
For our mistress cloth-wrought dresses,
For her daughters boots with laces,
And her sons with red shirts furnish.

Grant, O Jumala, thy blessing,
Evermore, O great Creator,
Unto those we see around us,
And again in all their doings,
Here, at Pohjola's great banquet,
This carouse at Sariola held,   420
That the ale may stream in rivers,
And the mead may flow in torrents,
Here in Pohjola's great household,
In the halls at Sariola built,
That by day we may be singing,
And may still rejoice at evening
Long as our good host is living,
In the lifetime of our hostess!

Jumala, do thou grant thy blessing,
O Creator, shed thy blessing,   430
On our host at head of table,
On our hostess in her storehouse,
On their sons, the nets when casting,
On their daughters at their weaving.
May they have no cause for trouble,
Nor lament the year that follows,
After their protracted banquet,
This carousal at the mansion!"

XXII   The tormenting of the bride

The bride is prepared for her journey and is reminded of her past life and of the altered life than now lies before her (1–124). She becomes very sorrowful (125–84). They bring her to weeping (185–382). She weeps (383–448). They comfort her (449–522).

When the drinking-bout was ended,
And the feast at length was over,
At the festival at Pohja,
Bridal feast held at Pimentola,
Then said Pohjola's old Mistress,
To the bridegroom, Ilmarinen,
"Wherefore sit'st thou, highly-born one,
Waitest thou, O pride of country?
Sit'st thou here to please the father,
Or for love of mother waitest,   10
Or our dwelling to illumine,
Or the wedding guests to honour?

Not for father's pleasure wait'st thou,
Nor for love thou bear'st the mother,
Nor the dwelling to illumine,
Nor the wedding guests to honour;
Here thou sit'st for maiden's pleasure,
For a young girl's love delaying,
For the fair one whom thou long'st for,
Fair one with unbraided tresses.   20

Bridegroom, dearest of my brothers,
Wait for a week, and yet another;
For thy loved one is not ready,
And her toilet is not finished:
Only half her hair is plaited,
And a half is still unplaited.

Bridegroom, dearest of my brothers,
Wait a week, and yet another,
For thy loved one is not ready,
And her toilet is not finished: 30
One sleeve only is adjusted,
And unfitted still the other.

Bridegroom, dearest of my brothers,
Wait a week, and yet another,
For thy loved one is not ready,
And her toilet is not finished:
For one foot is shod already,
But unshod remains the other.

Bridegroom, dearest of my brothers,
Wait a week, and yet another,   40
For thy loved one is not ready,
And her toilet is not finished.
For one hand is gloved already,
And ungloved is still the other.

Bridegroom, dearest of my brothers,
Thou hast waited long unwearied;
For thy love at length is ready,
And thy duck has made her toilet.

Go thou forth, O plighted maiden,
Follow thou, O dove new-purchased!   50
Near to thee is now thy union,
Nearer still is thy departure,
He who leads thee forth is with thee,
At the door is thy conductor,
And his horse the bit is champing,
And his sledge awaits the maiden.
Thou wast fond of bridegroom's money,
Reaching forth thy hands most greedy,
Glad to take the chain he offered,
And to fit the rings upon thee.   60
Now the longed-for sledge is ready,
Eager mount the sledge so gaudy,
Travel quickly to the village,
Quickly speeding on thy journey!

Hast thou never, youthful maiden,
On both sides surveyed the question,
Looked beyond the present moment,
When the bargain was concluded?
All thy life must thou be weeping,
And for many years lamenting,   70
How thou left'st thy father's household,
And thy native land abandoned,
From beside thy tender mother,
From the home of she who bore thee.

O the happy life thou leddest,
In this household of thy father!
Like a wayside flower thou grewest,
Or upon the heath a strawberry,
Waking up to feast on butter,
Milk, when from thy bed arising,   80
Wheaten-bread, from couch upstanding,
From thy straw, the fresh-made butter,
Or, if thou could eat no butter,
Strips of pork thou then could'st cut thee.

Never yet wast thou in trouble,
Never hadst thou cause to worry;
To the fir-trees tossed thou trouble,
Worry to the stumps abandoned,
Care to pine-trees in the marshlands,
And upon the heaths the birch-trees.   90
Like a leaflet thou wast fluttering,
As a butterfly wast fluttering,
Berry-like in native soil,
Or on open ground a raspberry.

But thy home thou now art leaving,
To another home thou goest,
To another mother's orders,
To the household of a stranger.
Different there from here thou'lt find it
In another house 'tis different: 100
Other tunes the horns are blowing,
Other doors thou hearest jarring,
Other gates thou hearest creaking,

Other voices at the hinges.
There the doors thou hardly findest,
Strange unto thee are the gateways,
Not like household daughter art thou,
May not dare to blow the fire,
Nor the stove canst rightly heaten,
So that thou canst please the master.   110

"Didst thou think, O youthful maiden,
Didst thou think, or didst imagine,
Only for a night to wander,
In the morn again returning?
'Tis not for one night thou goest,
Not for one night, not for two nights,
For a longer time thou goest.
Thou for months and days hast vanished,
Lifelong from thy father's dwelling,
For the lifetime of thy mother,   120
And the yard will then be longer,
And the threshold lifted higher,
If again thou ever comest,
To thy former home returning."

Now the hapless girl was sighing,
Piteously she sighed and panted,
And her heart was filled with trouble,
In her eyes the tears were standing,
And at length she spoke as follows:
"Thus I thought, and thus imagined,   130
And throughout my life imagined,
Said throughout my years of childhood:
Thou art not as maid a lady
In the wardship of thy parents,
In the meadows of thy father,
In thy aged mother's dwelling.
Thou wilt only be a lady
When thy husband's home thou seekest,
Resting one foot on the threshold,
In his sledge the other placing,   140
Then thy head thou liftest higher,
And thy ears thou liftest higher.

"This throughout my life I wished for,
All my youthful days I hoped for,
And throughout the year I wished it,
Like the coming of the summer.
Now my hope has found fulfilment,
Near the time of my departure;
One foot resting on the threshold,
In my husband's sledge the other,   150
But I do not yet know rightly,
If my mind has not been altered:
Not with joyful thoughts I wander
Nor do I depart with pleasure
From the golden home beloved,
Where I passed my life in childhood,
Where I passed my days of girlhood,
Where my father lived before me.
Sadly I depart in sorrow,
Forth I go, most sadly longing,   160
As into the night of autumn,
As on slippery ice in springtime,
When on ice no track remaineth,
On its smoothness rests no footprint.

What may be the thoughts of others,
And of other brides the feelings?
Do not other brides encounter,
Bear within their hearts the trouble,
Such as I, unhappy, carry?
Blackest trouble rests upon me,   170
Black as coal my heart within me,
Coal-black trouble weighs upon me.

Such the feelings of the blessed,
Such the thinking of the happy;
As the spring day at its dawning,
Or the sunny spring-day morning;
But what thoughts do now torment me,
And what thoughts arise within me?
Like unto a pond's flat margin,
Or of clouds the murky border;   180
Like the gloomy nights of autumn,

Or the dusky day of winter,
Or, as I might better say it,
Darker than the nights of autumn!"

Then an old crone of the household,
In the house for long abiding,
Answered in the words which follow:
"There you see now, youthful maiden!
Dost remember: how I told thee,
And a hundred times repeated,   190
Take no pleasure in a lover,
In a lover's mouth rejoice not,
Do not let his eyes bewitch thee,
Nor his handsome feet admire?
Though his mouth speaks charming converse,
And his eyes are fair to gaze on,
Yet upon his chin is Lempo;
In his mouth there lurks destruction.

Thus I always counsel maidens,
And to all their kind I counsel;   200
Though great people come as suitors,
Mighty men should come as wooers,
Yet return them all this answer;
And on thy side speak unto them,
In such words as these address them,
And in thiswise speak unto them:
'Not the least would it beseem me,
Not beseem me, or become me,
As a daughter-in-law to yield me,
As a slave to yield my freedom.   210
Such a pretty girl as I am,
Suits it not to live as slave-girl,
To depart consent I never,
To submit to rule of others.
If another word you utter,
I will give you two in answer,
If you by my hair would pull me,
And you by my locks would drag me,
From my hair I'd quickly shake you,
From my locks dishevelled drive you.'   220

But to this thou hast not hearkened,
To my words thou hast not listened,
Wilfully thou sought'st the fire,
In the boiling tar hast cast thee.
Now the fox's sledge awaits thee,
To the bear's hug art thou going,
And the fox's sledge will take thee,
Far away the bear convey thee,
Ever slave to other masters,
Ever slave of husband's mother.   230

From thy home to school thou goest,
From thy father's house to suffering.
Hard the school to which thou goest:
Long the pain to which thou goest,
Reins for thee are brought already,
Iron fetters all in order,
Not for others are they destined,
But alas, for thee, unhappy.

Shortly wilt thou feel their harshness,
Helpless feel, and unprotected,   240
For the father's chin is wagging,
And the mother's tongue is stormy;
And the brother's words are coldness,
And the sister's harsh reproaches.

Hear, O maiden, what I tell thee,
What I speak, and what I tell thee,
In thy home thou wast a floweret,
And the joy of father's household,
And thy father called thee Moonlight,
And thy mother called thee Sunshine,   250
And thy brother Sparkling Water,
And thy sister called thee Blue-Cloth.
To another home thou goest,
There to find a stranger mother.
Never is a stranger mother
Like the mother who has borne thee:
Seldom does she give good counsel,

Seldom gives the right instructions.
Sprig the father shouts against thee,
Slut the mother calls unto thee,   260
And the brother calls thee Doorstep,
And the sister, Nasty Creature.

Now the best that could await thee,
Best the fate that could await thee,
If as fog thou wert dispersing,
From the house like smoke departing,
Blown like leaf away that flutters,
As a spark away is drifted.

But a bird that flies thou art not,
Nor a leaf away that flutters,   270
Nor a spark in drafts that's drifting,
Nor the smoke from house ascending.

Lack-a-day, O maid, my sister!
Changed hast thou, and what art changing!
Thou hast changed thy much-loved father
For a father-in-law, a bad one;
Thou hast changed thy tender mother
For a mother-in-law most stringent;
Thou hast changed thy noble brother
For a brother-in-law so crook-necked;   280
And exchanged thy gentle sister
For a sister-in-law all cross-eyed;
And hast changed thy couch of linen
For a sooty hearth to rest on;
And exchanged the clearest water
For the muddy margin-water;
And the sandy shore hast bartered
For the black mud at the bottom;
And thy pleasant meadow bartered
For a dreary waste of heathland;   290
And thy hills of berries bartered
For the hard stumps of a clearing.

Didst thou think, O youthful maiden,
Think, O dove, full-fledged at present,
Care would end and toil be lessened,
With the party of this evening,

When to rest thou shalt betake thee,
And to sleep thou art conducted?

But to rest they will not lead thee,
Nor to sleep will they conduct thee;   300
Nought awaits thee now but watching,
Nought awaits thee now save trouble,
Heavy thoughts will come upon thee,
Saddened thoughts will overwhelm thee.
Long as thou didst wear no head-dress,
Wert thou also free from trouble;
When no linen veil waved round thee,
Thou wast also free from sorrow.
Now the head-dress brings thee trouble,
Heavy thoughts the linen fabric,   310
And the linen veil brings sorrow,
And the flax brings endless trouble.

How may live at home a maiden?
Maid in father's house abiding;
Like a monarch in his palace,
Only that the sword is wanting!
But a son's wife's fate is dismal!
With her husband she is living
As a prisoner lives in Russia,
Only that the jailor's wanting.   320

Work she must in working season,
And her shoulders stoop with weakness,
And her body faints with weakness,
And with sweat her face is shining.
Then there comes another hour
When there's need to make the fire,
And to put the hearth in order,
She must force her hands to do it.

Long must seek, this girl unhappy,
Long the hapless one must seek for.   330
Salmon's mind, and tongue of perchling,
And her thoughts from perch in fishpond,
Mouth of bream, of chub the belly,
And from water-hen learn wisdom.

'Tis beyond my comprehension,
Nine times can I not imagine,
To the mother's much-loved daughters,
Best beloved of all her treasures,
Whence should come to them the spoiler,
Where the greedy one was nurtured,   340
Eating flesh, and bones devouring,
To the wind their hair abandoning,
And their tresses wildly tossing,
To the wind of springtime gives them.

Weep thou, weep thou, youthful maiden,
When thou weepest, weep thou sorely!
Weep thyself of tears a handful,
Fill thy fists with tears of longing,
Drop them in thy father's dwelling,
Pools of tears upon the flooring,   350
Till the room itself is flooded,
And above the floor in billows!
If thou weepest yet not freely
Thou shalt weep when thou returnest,
When to father's house thou comest,
And shalt find thy aged father
Suffocated in the sauna,
'Neath his arm a dried-up bath-whisk.

Weep thou, weep thou, youthful maiden,
When thou weepest, weep thou sorely;   360
If thou weepest not yet freely,
Thou shalt weep when thou returnest,
When to mother's house thou comest,
And thou find'st thy aged mother
Suffocated in the cowshed,
In her dying lap a straw-sheaf.

Weep thou, weep thou, youthful maiden,
When thou weepest, weep thou sorely.
If thou weepest yet not freely,
Thou shalt weep when thou returnest,   370
When to this same house thou comest,
And thou find'st thy rosy brother

Fallen in the porch before it,
In the courtyard helpless fallen.

Weep thou, weep thou, youthful maiden,
When thou weepest, weep thou sorely.
If thou weepest yet not freely,
Thou shalt weep when thou returnest,
When to this same house thou comest,
And thou find'st thy modest sister   380
Fallen down upon the pathway,
And beneath her arm a mallet."

Then the poor girl broke out sobbing,
And a while she sobbed and panted,
And she soon commenced her weeping,
Pouring forth her tears in torrents.

Then she wept of tears a handful,
Filled her fists with tears of longing,
Wet she wept her father's dwelling,
Pools of tears upon the flooring,   390
And she spoke the words which follow,
And expressed herself in thiswise:
"O my sisters, dearest to me,
Of my life the dear companions,
All companions of my childhood,
Listen now to what I tell you!
'Tis beyond my comprehension
Why I feel such deep oppression,
Making now my life so heavy,
Why this trouble weighs upon me,   400
Why this darkness rests upon me;
How I should express my sorrow.

Otherwise I thought and fancied,
Wished it different, all my lifetime,
Thought to go as goes the cuckoo,
Crying 'Cuckoo' from the hill-tops,
Now the day I have attained to,
Come the time that I had wished for;
But I go not like the cuckoo,

Crying 'Cuckoo' from the hill-tops,   410
More as duck amid the billows,
On the wide bay's open waters,
Swimming in the freezing water,
Shivering in the icy water.

Woe, my father and my mother,
Woe, alas, my aged parents!
Whither would you now dismiss me,
Drive a wretched maid to sorrow,
Make me thus to weep for sorrow,
Overburdened thus with trouble,   420
With distress so heavy-burdened,
And with care so overloaded?

Better, O unhappy mother,
Better, dearest who hast borne me,
O thou dear one, who hast suckled,
Nurtured me throughout my lifetime,
Hadst thou swaddled up a tree-stump,
And hadst bathed a little pebble,
Rather than have washed thy daughter,
And have swaddled up thy darling,   430
For this time of great affliction,
And of this so grievous sorrow!

Many speak unto me elsewise,
Many counsel me in thiswise:
'Do not, fool, give way to sorrow,
Let not gloomy thoughts oppress thee.'
Do not, O ye noble people,
Do not speak to me in thiswise!
Far more troubles weigh upon me,
Than in a cascade are pebbles,   440
Than in swampy ground the willows,
Or the heath upon the marshland.
Never can a horse pull forward,
And a shod horse struggle onward,
And the sledge sway not behind him,
And the collar shall not tremble.
Even thus I feel my trouble,
And oppressed by dark forebodings."

From the floor there sang an infant,
From the hearth a growing infant: 450
"Wherefore dost thou weep, O maiden,
Yielding to such grievous sorrow?
Cast thy troubles to the horses,
Sorrow to the sable gelding.
Leave complaints to mouths of iron,
Lamentations to the thick-heads;
Better heads indeed have horses,
Better heads, and bones much harder,
For their arching necks are firmer,
All their frame is greatly stronger.   460

No, thou hast no cause for weeping,
Nor to yield to grievous sorrow;
To the marsh they do not lead thee,
Push thee not into the ditches.
Leavest thou these fertile cornfields,
Yet to richer fields thou goest,
Though they take thee from the brewery,
'Tis to where the ale's abundant.

If around thee now thou gazest,
Just beside thee where thou standest,   470
There thy bridegroom stands to guard thee,
By thy side thy ruddy husband.
Good thy husband, good his horses,
All things needful fill his cellars,
And the grouse are loudly chirping,
On the sledge, as glides it onwards,
And the thrushes make rejoicing,
As they sing upon the traces,
And six golden cuckoos likewise
Flutter on the horse's collar,   480
Seven blue birds are also perching,
On the sledge's frame, and singing.

Do not yield thee thus to trouble,
O thou darling of thy mother!
For no evil fate awaits thee,
But in better case thou comest,
Sitting by thy farmer husband,

Underneath the ploughman's mantle,
'Neath the chin of the bread-winner,
In the arms of skilful fisher,   490
Warm from chasing elk on snowshoes,
And from bathing after bear-hunt!

Thou hast found the best of husbands,
And hast won a mighty hero:
For his bow is never idle,
Neither on the pegs his quivers;
And the dogs in house he leaves not,
Nor in hay lets rest the puppies.

Three times in this spring already,
In the earliest hours of morning,   500
Has he stood before the fire,
Rising from his couch of bushes;
Three times in this spring already
On his eyes the dew has fallen,
And the shoots of pine-trees combed him,
And the branches brushed against him.

All his people he exhorted,
To increase his flocks in number,
For indeed the bridegroom owneth
Flocks that wander through the birchwoods,   510
Tramp their way among the sand-hills,
Seek for pasture in the valleys;
Hundreds of the horned cattle,
Thousands with their well-filled udders;
On the plains are stacks in plenty,
In the valley crops abundant,
Alder-woods for cornland suited,
Meadows where the barley's springing,
Stony land for oats that's suited,
Watered regions, fit for wheatfields.
All rich gifts in peace await thee,   520
Pennies plentiful as pebbles."

XXIII   The instructing of the bride

The bride is instructed and directed how to conduct herself in her husband's house (1–478). An old vagrant woman relates the experiences of her life as a daughter, as a wife, and after her separation from her husband (479–850).

Now the girl must be instructed,
And the bride be taught her duty;
Who shall now instruct the maiden,
And shall teach the girl her duty?
Osmotar, experienced woman,
Kaleva's most beauteous maiden;
She shall give the maid instruction,
And shall teach the unprotected
How to bear herself with prudence,
And with wisdom to conduct her,   10
In her husband's house with prudence,
To his mother most obedient.

So she spoke the words which follow,
And in terms like these addressed her:
"O thou bride, my dearest sister,
Thou my darling, best-beloved,
Listen now to what I tell thee,
For a second time repeated!
Now thou goest, a flower transplanted,
Like a strawberry forward creeping,   20
Whisked, like shred of cloth, to distance,
Satin-robed, to distance hurried,
From thy home, renowned so greatly,
From thy dwelling-place so beauteous.

To another home thou comest,
To a stranger household goest;
In another house 'tis different,
Otherwise in strangers' houses.
Walk thou there with circumspection,
And prepare thy duties wisely   30
Not as on thy father's acres,
Or the lands of thine own mother.
Where they sing among the valleys,
And upon the pathways shouting.

When from out this house thou goest,
All thy doings must be different;
Three things leave at home behind thee:
Sleep indulged in through the daytime,
Counsels of thy dearest mother,
And fresh butter from the barrels!   40

All thy thoughts must now be altered;
Leave thy sleepiness behind thee,
Leave it for the household maiden,
By the stove so idly sitting.
To the bench-end cast thy singing,
Joyous carols to the windows,
Girlish ways unto the bath-whisks,
And thy pranks to blanket-edges,
Naughtiness to the stove-bench,
On the floor thy lazy habits,   50
Or renounce them to thy bridesmaid,
And into her arms unload them,
That she take them to the bushes,
Out upon the heath convey them!

Other habits wait thy learning,
And the old must be forgotten.
Father's love thou leave behind thee;
Learn to love thy husband's father.
Deeper now must thou incline thee,
Fitting language must thou utter!   60

Other habits wait thy learning,
And the old must be forgotten.

Mother's love thou leav'st behind thee;
Learn to love thy husband's mother.
Deeper now must thou incline thee,
Fitting language must thou utter!

Other habits wait thy learning,
And the old must be forgotten.
Brother's love thou leav'st behind thee;
Learn to love thy husband's brother.   70
Deeper now must thou incline thee,
Fitting language must thou utter!

Other habits wait thy learning,
And the old must be forgotten.
Sister's love thou leav'st behind thee;
Learn to love thy husband's sister.
Deeper now must thou incline thee,
Fitting language must thou utter!

Never may'st thou in thy lifetime,
While the golden moon is shining,   80
Seek a house of doubtful morals,
With the worthless men consorting,
For a house must needs be moral,
And a house must needs be noble,
And for sense a husband wishes,
And desires the best behaviour.
Heedfulness will much be needed,
In a house of doubtful morals;
Steadiness will much be wanting
If a man's of doubtful morals.   90

Is the old man a wolf in corner,
By the hearth the crone a she-bear,
Brother-in-law on step a viper,
In the yard like nail the sister,
Equal honour must thou give them,
Deeper must thou then incline thee,
Than thou bowed before thy mother,
In the house of thine own father,
Than thou bowed before thy father,
Or before thy dearest mother!   100

Thou wilt always need in future
Ready wit and clear perception,
And thy thoughts must all be prudent,
Firmly fixed thy understanding,
Eyes of keenness in the evening,
That the fire is always brilliant,
Ears of sharpness in the morning,
Thus to listen for the cockcrow.
If the cockcrow once has sounded,
Though the second has not sounded,   110
It becomes the young to rouse them,
Though the old folk still are resting.

If the cock should not be crowing,
Nor the master's bird be crying,
Let the moon for cockcrow serve thee,
Take the Great Bear for thy guidance.
Often thou should'st seek the open,
Often go the moon to gaze on,
From the Great Bear seek instruction,
And the distant stars to gaze on.   120

If you see the Great Bear clearly,
With his front to south directed,
And his tail extending northward,
Then 'tis time for thee to rouse thee
From the side of thy young husband,
Leaving him asleep and ruddy,
Fire to seek among the ashes
Seeking for a spark in firebox,
Blowing then the fire discreetly,
That from carelessness it spread not.   130

If no fire is in the ashes,
And no spark is in the firebox,
Coax thou then thy dearest husband,
And cajole thy handsome husband:
'Light me now the fire, my dearest,
Just a spark, my darling berry!'

If you have a flint, a small one,
And a little piece of tinder,

Strike a light as quick as may be,
Light the pine-chip in the holder,   140
Then go out to clear the cowshed,
And the cattle do thou fodder,
For the mother's cow is lowing,
And the father's horse is neighing,
And her chain the son's cow rattles,
And the daughter's calf is lowing,
That the soft hay should be thrown them,
And the clover laid before them.

Go thou stooping on the pathway,
Bend thou down among the cattle,   150
Gently give the cows their fodder,
Give the sheep their food in quiet,
Spread it straight before the cattle,
Drink unto the calves so helpless,
To the foals give straw well-chosen,
To the lambkins hay the softest,
See that on the swine thou tread'st not,
Nor the hogs with foot thou spurnest,
Take thou to the swine the food-trough,
Set before the hogs the food-tray!   160

Do not rest thee in the cowshed,
Do not loiter with the sheep-flock;
When thou'st visited the cowshed,
And hast looked to all the cattle,
Do thou quickly hasten homeward,
Home returning like a blizzard,
For the baby there is crying,
Crying underneath the blanket,
And the poor child still is speechless,
And its tongue no words can utter,   170
Whether it is cold or hungry,
Or if something else annoys it,
Ere its well-known friend is coming,
And the mother's voice it heareth.

When into the room thou comest,
Come thou fourth into the chamber;
In thy hand a water-bucket,

Underneath thy arm a besom,
And between thy teeth a pine-chip;
Thou art then the fourth among them!   180

Sweep thou then the floor to cleanness,
Sweep thou carefully the planking,
And upon the floor pour water,
Not upon the heads of babies.
If you see a child there lying,
Though thy sister-in-law's the infant,
Up upon the bench then lift it,
Wash its eyes, and smooth its hair down,
Put some bread into its handies,
And upon the bread spread butter,   190
But if bread perchance be wanting,
Put a chip into its handies!

Then the tables must be scoured,
At the week-end at the latest;
Wash them, and the sides remember,
Let the legs be not forgotten;
Then the benches wash with water,
Sweep thou too the walls to cleanness,
And the boards of all the benches,
And the walls with all their corners!   200

If there's dust upon the tables,
Or there's dust upon the windows,
Dust them carefully with feathers,
Wipe them with a wetted duster,
That the dust should not be scattered,
Nor should settle on the ceiling.

From the stove scrape all the crust off,
From the ceiling wipe the soot off,
And the ceiling-props remember,
Nor should'st thou forget the rafters,   210
That the house be all in order,
And a fitting place to live in!

Hear, O maiden, what I tell thee,
What I say, and what I tell thee,

Do not go without thy clothing,
Nor without thy shift disport thee,
Move about without thy linen,
Or without thy shoes go shuffling:
Greatly shocked would be thy bridegroom,
And thy youthful husband grumble!   220

In the yard there grows a rowan,
Thou with reverent care should'st tend it,
Holy is the tree there growing,
Holy likewise are its branches,
On its boughs the leaves are holy,
And its berries yet more holy,
For a damsel may discover,
And an orphan thence learn teaching,
How to please her youthful husband,
To her bridegroom's heart draw nearer.   230

Let thy ears be keen as mouse-ears,
Let thy feet as hare's be rapid,
And thy young neck proudly arching,
And thy fair neck proudly bending,
Like the juniper uprising,
Or the cherry's verdant summit!
Likewise hold thyself discreetly,
Always ponder and consider;
Never venture thou to rest thee
On the bench at length extended,   240
Nor upon thy bed to rest thee,
There to yield thee to thy slumbers!

Comes the brother from his ploughing,
Or the father from the storehouse,
Or thy husband from his labour,
He, thy fair one, from the clearing:
Haste to fetch the water-basin,
Hasten thou to bring a towel,
Bowing with respect before them,
Speaking words of fond affection!   250

Comes the mother from the storehouse,
In her arms the flour-filled basket,

Run across the yard to meet her,
Bowing with respect before her,
Take thou from her hands the basket,
Quickly to the house to bear it!

If you do not know your duty,
Do not comprehend it fully,
What the work that waits the doing,
Where you should begin your labours,   260
Ask the old crone then in thiswise:
'O my mother-in-law beloved,
How is this work to be managed,
And arranged these household matters?'

And the old crone thus will answer,
And your mother-in-law will tell you:
'Thus this work is to be managed,
And arranged these household matters,
Pounding thus, and grinding thiswise,
And the handmill quickly turning.   270
Likewise do thou fetch the water,
That the dough be fitly kneaded,
Carry logs into the bakehouse,
And the oven heat thou fully,
Set thou then the loaves for baking,
And the large cakes bake thou likewise,
Wash thou then the plates and dishes,
Likewise washing clean the meal-tubs.'

When thy work she thus has told thee,
And thy mother-in-law has taught thee,   280
From the stones the parched corn taking,
Hasten to the room for grinding;
But when you at length have reached it,
And the room for grinding entered,
Do not carol as thou goest,
Do not shout thy very loudest,
Leave it to the stones to carol,
Talking through the handmill's opening,
Neither do thou groan too loudly,
Let the handmill groan unto thee;   290

Lest thy father-in-law should fancy
Or thy mother-in-law imagine
That with discontent thou groanest,
And art sighing from vexation!
Lift the meal, and sift it quickly,
To the room in dish convey it,
Bake thou there the loaves with pleasure,
After thou with care hast kneaded,
That the flour becomes not lumpy,
But throughout is mixed most smoothly!   300

If you see the bucket leaning,
Take the bucket on your shoulder,
On your arm the water-bucket.
Go thou then to fetch the water.
Carry thou the bucket nicely,
On the yoke-end do thou fix it,
Like the wind returning quickly,
Like the wind of springtime rushing,
By the water do not linger,
By the well forbear to rest thee,   310
Lest thy father-in-law should fancy,
Or thy mother-in-law imagine
That you wished to see your likeness,
And your beauty to admire,
Rosy cheeks in water painted,
In the well your charms reflected!

When you wander to the wood-pile,
Wander there to fetch the faggots,
Do not split them up at random,
Take some faggots of the aspen,   320
Lift thou up the faggots gently,
Make as little noise as may be,
Lest thy father-in-law should fancy,
Or thy mother-in-law imagine,
That you pitch them down in crossness,
And in temper make them clatter!

When you wander to the storehouse,
Thither go to fetch the flour,

Do not linger in the storehouse,
Do not long remain within it,   330
Lest thy father-in-law should fancy,
Or thy mother-in-law imagine,
You were doling out the flour,
Sharing with the village women.

When you go to wash the dishes,
And the pots and pans to scour,
Wash the jugs and wash the handles,
And the rims of mugs for drinking,
Sides of cups with circumspection,
Handles of the spoons remembering!   340
Mind thou, too, the spoons and count them,
Look thou to the dishes also,
Lest the dogs should steal them from you,
Or the cats should take them from you,
Or the birds away should take them,
Or the children should upset them:
For the village swarms with children,
Many little heads thou findest,
Who might carry off the dishes,
And the spoons about might scatter.   350

When the evening bath is wanted,
Fetch the water and the bath-whisks,
Have the bath-whisks warm and ready,
Air thou well of smoke the sauna.
Do not take too long about it,
Do not loiter in the sauna,
Lest thy father-in-làw should fancy,
Or thy mother-in-law imagine,
You were lying on the bath-boards,
On the bench your head reclining!   360

When the room again you enter,
Then announce the bath is ready:
'O my father-in-law beloved,
Now the bath is fully ready:
Water brought, and likewise bath-whisks,
All the boards are cleanly scoured.
Go and bathe thee at thy pleasure,

Wash thou there as it shall please thee,
I myself will mind the steaming,
Standing underneath the boarding!'   370

When the time has come for spinning,
And the time has come for weaving,
In the village seek not counsel,
Do not cross the ditch for teaching,
Seek it not in other households,
Nor the weaver's comb from strangers

Spin thyself the yarn thou needest,
With thy fingers do thou spin it,
Let the yarn be loosely twisted,
But the flaxen thread more closely.   380
Closely in a ball then wind it,
On the winch securely twist it,
Fix it then upon the warp-beam,
And upon the loom secure it,
Then the shuttle fling thou sharply,
But the yarn do thou draw gently.
Weave the thickest woollen garments,
Woollen gowns construct thou likewise,
From a single fleece prepare them,
From a winter fleece construct them,   390
From the wool of lamb of springtime,
And the fleece of ewe of summer!

Listen now to what I tell thee,
And to what again I tell thee:
Thou must brew the ale of barley,
From the malt the sweet drink fashion,
From a single grain of barley,
And by burning half a tree-trunk!

When the malt begins to sweeten,
Take thou up the malt and taste it.   400
With the rake disturb it never,
Do not use a stick to turn it,
Always use your hands to stir it,
And your open hands to turn it.
Go thou often to the malthouse,

Do not let the sprout be injured,
Let the cat not sit upon it,
Or the tomcat sleep upon it.
Of the wolves have thou no terror,
Fear thou not the forest monsters,   410
When thou goest to the sauna,
Or at midnight forth must wander!

When a stranger pays a visit,
Be not angry with the stranger,
For a well-appointed household,
Always has for guests provision:
Scraps of meat that are not needed,
Cakes of bread the very nicest.
Ask the guest to sit and rest him,
With the guest converse in friendship,   420
With thy talk amuse the stranger,
Till the dinner shall be ready!

When the house the stranger's leaving,
And he's taking his departure,
Do not thou go with the stranger
Any further than the housedoor,
Lest the husband should be angry,
And thy darling should be gloomy!

If you e'er feel inclination
To the village forth to wander,   430
Ask permission ere thou goest,
There to gossip with the strangers.
In the time that you are absent,
Speak thy words with heedful caution,
Do not grumble at your household,
Nor thy mother-in-law abuse thou!

If the village girls should ask you,
Any of the village women,
'Does your mother-in-law give butter,
As at home your mother gave you?'   440
Never do thou make the answer,
'No, she does not give me butter!'
Tell thou always that she gives it,

Gives it to you by the spoonful,
Though 'twas only once in summer,
And 'twas old and nearly rancid!

List again to what I tell thee,
And again impress upon thee:
When at length this house thou leavest,
And thou comest to the other,   450
Do thou not forget thy mother,
Or despise thy dearest mother,
For it was thy mother reared thee,
And her beauteous breasts that nursed thee,
From her own delightful body,
From her form of perfect whiteness.
Many nights has she lain sleepless,
Many meals has she forgotten,
While she rocked thee in thy cradle,
Watching fondly o'er her infant.   460

She who should forget her mother,
Or despise her dearest mother,
Ne'er to Manala should travel,
Nor to Tuonela go cheerful:
There in Manala is anguish,
Hard in Tuonela the reckoning,
If she has forgot her mother,
Or despised her dearest mother.
Tuoni's daughters come reproaching,
Mana's maidens all come mocking: 470
'Why hast thou forgot thy mother,
Or despised thy dearest mother?
Great the sufferings of thy mother,
Great her sufferings when she bore thee,
Lying groaning in the sauna,
On a couch of straw extended,
When she gave thee thy existence,
Giving birth to thee, the vile one!"

On the ground there sat an old crone,
Sat an old dame 'neath her mantle,   480
Wanderer o'er the village threshold,
Left to tramp the country's footpaths,

And she spoke the words which follow,
And in words like these expressed her:
"To his mate the cock was singing,
Sang the hen's child to his fair one,
And in March the crow was croaking,
And in days of spring was chattering;
It is I should now be singing,
Let them rather check their chanting,   490
They at home have all their dear ones,
Always near to ones who love them;
But no love nor house is left me,
And all love departed from me.

Hear, O sister, what I tell thee!
When thy husband's house thou seekest,
Follow not thy husband's notions,
As was done by me unhappy.
Larks have tongues, and husbands notions;
Follow not the lover's utterance!   500

I was as a flower that flourished,
As a wild rose in the thicket,
And I grew as grows a sapling,
Grew into a slender maiden.
I was beauteous as a berry,
Rustling in its golden beauty;
In my father's yard a duckling,
On my mother's floor a gosling,
Water-bird unto my brother,
And a goldfinch to my sister.   510
Flowerlike walked I on the pathway,
As upon the plain the raspberry,
Skipping on the sandy lakeshore,
Dancing on the flower-clad hillocks,
Singing loud in every valley,
Carolling on every hill-top,
Sporting in the leafy forests,
In the charming woods rejoicing.

As the trap the fox-mouth seizes,
And the tongue entraps the ermine,   520
Towards a man inclines a maiden,

And the ways of other households.
So created is the maiden,
That the daughter's inclination
Leads her married, as step-daughter,
As the slave of husband's mother.

As a berry grows in marshland,
And in other waters, cherry.
Like a cranberry sought I sorrow,
Like a strawberry exhortation.　　　　　530
Every tree appeared to bite me,
Every alder seemed to tear me,
Every birch appeared to scold me,
Every aspen to devour me.

As my husband's bride they brought me,
To my mother-in-law they led me.
Here there were, as they had told me,
Waiting for the wedded maiden,
Six large rooms of pine constructed,
And of bedrooms twice as many.　　　　　540
Barns along the forest-borders,
By the roadside flowery gardens,
By the ditches fields of barley,
And along the heaths were oatfields,
Chests of corn threshed out already,
Other chests awaiting threshing,
Hundred coins received already,
And a hundred more expected.

Foolishly had I gone thither,
Recklessly my hand had given:　　　　　550
For six props the house supported,
Seven small poles the house supported,
And the woods were filled with harshness,
And with lovelessness the forests,
By the roadsides dreary deserts,
In the woodlands thoughts of evil,
Chests containing spoilt provisions,
Other chests beside them spoiling;
And a hundred words reproachful,
And a hundred more to look for.　　　　　560

But I let it not distress me,
Hoping there to live in quiet,
Wishing there to dwell in honour,
And a peaceful life to live there;
But when first the room I entered,
Over chips of wood I stumbled,
On the door I knocked my forehead,
And my head against the doorposts.
At the door were eyes of strangers:
Darksome eyes were at the entrance,　　　　　570
Squinting eyes in midst of chamber,
In the background eyes most evil.
From the mouths the fire was flashing,
From beneath the tongues shot firebrands,
From the old man's mouth malicious,
From beneath his tongue unfriendly.
But I let it not distress me,
In the house I dwelt unheeding,
Hoping still to live in favour,
And I bore myself with meekness,　　　　　580
And with legs of hare went skipping,
With the step of ermine hurried,
Very late to rest retired,
Very early rose to suffering.
But, unhappy, won no honour,
Mildness brought me only sorrow,
Had I tossed away the torrents,
Or the rocks in twain had cloven.

Vainly did I grind coarse flour,
And with pain I crushed its hardness,　　　　　590
That my mother-in-law should eat it,
And her ravenous throat devour it,
At the table-end while sitting,
From a dish with golden borders.
But I ate, unhappy daughter,
Flour scraped up, to handmill cleaving,
With my ladle from the hearthstone,
With my spoon from off the pestle.

Oft I brought, O me unhappy,
I, the son's wife, to his dwelling,　　　　　600

Mosses from the swampy places,
And as bread for me I baked it.
Water from the well I carried,
And I drank it up in mouthfuls.
Fish I ate, O me unhappy,
Smelts I ate, O me unhappy,
As above the net I leaned me,
In the boat as I was swaying,
For no fish received I ever
From my mother-in-law neglectful,   610
Neither in a day of plenty,
Nor a day of double plenty.

Fodder gathered I in summer,
Winter worked I with the pitchfork,
Even as a labourer toiling,
Even as a hired servant,
And my mother-in-law for ever,
Evermore for me selected,
Worst of all the flails for threshing,
Heaviest mallet from the grainloft,   620
From the beach the heaviest mallet,
In the stall the largest pitchfork.
Never did they think me weary,
Nor my weakness e'er considered,
Though the toils had wearied heroes,
Or the strength of foals exhausted.
Thus did I, a girl unhappy,
Work at proper time for working,
And my shoulders stooped with weakness;
And at other times they ordered   630
That the fire should now be kindled,
With my hands that I should stir it.

To their hearts' desire they scolded,
With their tongues they heaped reproaches
On my spotless reputation,
On my character, though stainless.
Evil words they heaped upon me,
And abuse they showered upon me,
Like the sparks from furious fire,
Or a very hail of iron.   640

Until then despaired I never,
And had spent my life as erstwhile
There to aid the harsh old woman,
To her fiery tongue submitting:
But 'twas this that brought me evil,
This that caused me greatest anguish,
When to wolf was changed my husband,
To a growling bear converted,
Turned his side to me when eating,
Turned his back asleep or working.   650

I myself broke out in weeping,
And I pondered in the storehouse,
And my former life remembering,
And my life in former seasons,
In the homestead of my father,
In my sweetest mother's dwelling.

Then in words I spoke my feelings,
And I spoke the words which follow:
'Well indeed my dearest mother
Understood to rear her apple,   660
And the tender shoot to cherish,
But she knew not where to plant it:
For the tender shoot is planted
In a very evil station,
In a very bad position,
'Mid the hard roots of a birch-tree,
There to weep while life remaineth,
And to spend the months lamenting.

Surely, surely, I am worthy
Of a home than this much better,   670
Worthy of a larger homestead,
And a floor more wide-extended,
Worthy of a better partner,
And a husband far more handsome.
But I'm bound to hulking husband,
Held fast by a podgy master,
Like a very crow's his body,
With a beak like any raven,

And his mouth like wolf's is greedy,
And his form a bear resembles. 680

Such a one I might have found me,
If I'd wandered to the mountains,
Picked from off the road a pine-stump,
From the wood a stump of alder,
Laid as snout a turf of grasses,
Made his beard of moss from tree-trunks,
Head of clay, and mouth all stony,
And his eyes from coals of fire,
Knobs of birch his ears then fashioned,
And his legs from forking willows.' 690

While my song I thus was singing,
Sighing in my grievous trouble,
He, my husband, chanced to hear it,
At the wall as he was standing.
When I heard him then approaching,
At the storehouse gate when standing,
I was conscious of his coming,
For I recognized his footstep.
And his hair in wind was tossing,
And his hair was all disordered, 700
And his gums with rage were grinning,
And his eyes with fury staring,
In his hand a stick of cherry,
'Neath his arm a club he carried,
And he hurried to attack me,
And upon the head he struck me.

When the evening came thereafter,
And there came the time for sleeping,
At his side a rod he carried,
Took from nail a whip of leather, 710
Not designed to flay another,
But alas, for me, unhappy.

Then when I myself retired,
To my resting-place at evening,
By my husband's side I stretched me,

By my side my husband rested,
When he seized me by the elbows,
With his wicked hands he grasped me,
And with willow rods he beat me,
And the haft of bone of walrus.   720

From his cold side then I raised me,
And I left the bed of coldness,
But behind me ran my husband,
From the door came wildly rushing.
In my hair his hands he twisted,
Grasping it in all his fury,
In the wind my hair he scattered,
To the winds of spring abandoned.

What advice should now be followed,
Where had I to look for counsel?   730
Shoes of steel I put upon me,
Bands of copper put upon me,
As I stood beyond the house-wall.
In the lane for long I listened,
Till the wretch should calm his fury,
And his passion had subsided,
But his anger never slumbered,
Neither for a time abated!

At the last the cold o'ercame me,
In my hiding-place so dismal,   740
Where I stood beyond the house-wall,
And behind the door I waited,
And I pondered and reflected:
'This I cannot bear for ever,
Nor can bear their hatred longer,
Longer can I not endure it,
In this dreadful house of Lempo,
In this lair of evil demons.'

From the handsome house I turned me,
And my pleasant home abandoned,   750
And commenced my weary wanderings,
Through the swamps and through the lowlands,
Past the open sheets of water,

Past the cornfields of my brother;
There the dry pines all were rustling,
And the crowns of fir-trees singing,
All the crows were croaking loudly,
And the magpies all were chattering:

'Here for thee no home remaineth,
In the house thy birth which witnessed.'   760

But I let it not distress me,
As I neared my brother's homestead,
But the gates themselves addressed me,
And the cornfields all lamented:
'Wherefore hast thou thus come homeward,
What sad news to hear, O wretched?
Long ago has died thy father,
Perished has thy sweetest mother,
All estranged is now thy brother,
And his wife is like a Russian.'   770

But I let it not distress me,
And at once the house I entered,
At the door I grasped the handle,
Cold within my hand I felt it.

After, when the room I entered,
In the doorway I was standing,
And the mistress stood there proudly,
But she did not come to meet me,
Nor to me her hand she offered.
I myself was proud as she was,   780
And I would not go to meet her,
And my hand I would not offer.
On the stove my hand I rested.
Cold I felt the very hearthstones,
To the burning coals I reached it;
In the stove the coals were frozen.

On the bench there lay my brother,
Lazy on the bench extended,
On his shoulders soot by fathoms,
And by spans upon his body,   790

On his head glowed coals a yard high,
And of hard-caked soot a quartful.

Asked my brother of the stranger,
Of the guest he thus inquired:
'Stranger, why hast crossed the water?'

And on this I gave him answer:
'Dost thou then not know thy sister,
Once the daughter of thy mother?
We are children of one mother,
Of one bird are we the nestlings: 800
By one goose have we been nurtured,
In one grouse's nest been fostered.'

Then my brother broke out weeping,
From his eyes the tears were falling.

To his wife then said my brother,
And he whispered to his darling:
'Bring some food to give my sister!'
But with mocking eyes she brought me
Cabbage-stalks from out the kitchen,
Whence the whelp the fat had eaten,   810
And the dog had licked the salt from,
And the black dog had his meal of.

To his wife then said my brother,
And he whispered to his darling:
'Fetch some ale to give the stranger!'
But with mocking eyes she carried
Water only for the stranger,
But, instead of drinking water,
Water she had washed her face in,
And her sister washed her hands in.   820

From my brother's house I wandered,
Left the house that I was born in,
Hurried forth, O me unhappy,
Wandered on, O me unhappy,
Wretched on the shores to wander,
Toiling on, for ever wretched,

Always to the doors of strangers,
Always to the gates of strangers,
On the beach, with poorest children,
Sufferers of the village poorhouse.   830

There were many of the people,
Many were there who abused me,
And with evil words attacked me,
And with sharpest words repulsed me.
Few there are among the people
Who have spoken to me kindly,
And with kindly words received me,
And before the stove who led me,
When I came from out the rainstorm,
Or from out the cold came shrinking,   840
With my dress with rime all covered,
While the snow my fur cloak covered.

In my youthful days I never,
I could never have believed it,
Though a hundred told me of it,
And a thousand tongues repeated
Such distress should fall upon me,
Such distress should overwhelm me,
As upon my head has fallen,
Laid upon my hands such burdens."   850

XXIV   The departure of the bride and bridegroom

The bridegroom is instructed how he should behave towards his bride, and is cautioned not to treat her badly (1–264). An old beggar relates how he once brought his wife to reason (265–96). The bride remembers with tears that she is now quitting her dear birthplace for the rest of her life, and says farewell to all (297–462). Ilmarinen lifts his bride into the sledge and reaches his home on the evening of the third day (463–528).

Now the girl had well been lectured,
And the bride had been instructed;
Let me now address my brother,
Let me lecture now the bridegroom:
"Bridegroom, dearest of my brothers,
Thou the best of all my brothers,
Dearest of my mother's children,
Gentlest of my father's children,
Listen now to what I tell thee,
What I speak and what I tell thee,   10
Of thy linnet who awaits thee,
And the dove that thou hast captured!

Bridegroom, bless thy happy fortune,
For the fair one granted to thee;
When thou praisest, praise thou loudly,
Loudly praise the good that's granted,
Loudly praise thou thy Creator,
For the gracious gift He granted!
And her father praise thou also,
Even more her mother praise thou,   20
They who reared their lovely daughter
To the charming bride beside thee!

Stainless sits the maid beside thee!
Maiden bright to thee united,
Pledged to thee in all her beauty,
Fair one under thy protection,
Charming girl upon thy bosom,
At thy side so sweetly blushing,
Girl with strength to help in threshing,
Or to help thee in the hayfield,   30
Skilful, too, to do the washing,
Quick to bleach the clothes to whiteness,
Skilful, too, the thread in spinning,
Rapid, too, the cloth when weaving.

And I hear her loom resounding,
As upon the hill the cuckoo,
And I see her shuttle darting,
As the ermine through a thicket,
And the reel she twists as quickly
As the squirrel's mouth a fir-cone.   40
Never sound has slept the village,
Nor the country people slumbered,
For her loom's incessant clatter,
And the whizzing of the shuttle.

O thou loved and youthful bridegroom,
Handsomest of all the people!
Forge thou now a scythe of sharpness,
Fix the best of handles on it,
Carve it, sitting in the doorway,
Hammer it upon a tree-stump.   50
When there comes the time of sunshine,
Take thy young wife to the meadow,
Look thou where the grass is rustling,
And the harder grass is crackling,
And the reeds are gently murmuring,
And the sorrel gently rustling,
Also note where stand the hillocks,
And the shoots from stumps arising!

When another day is dawning,
Let her have a weaver's shuttle,   60

And a batten that shall suit it,
And a loom of best construction,
And a treadle of the finest.
Make the weaver's chair all ready,
For the damsel fix the treadle,
Lay her hand upon the batten.
Soon the shuttle shall be singing,
And the treadle shall be thumping,
Till the rattling fills the village,
And the noise is heard beyond it: 70
And the crones will all perceive it,
And the village women question:
'Who is this we hear a-weaving?'
And you thus must make them answer:
"Tis my own, my darling, weaving,
'Tis my loved one makes the clatter,
Shall she loosen now the fabric,
And the shuttle cease from throwing?'

'Let her not the fabric loosen,
Nor the shuttle cease from throwing.   80
Thus may weave the Moon's fair daughters,
Thus may spin the Sun's fair daughters,
Even thus the Great Bear's daughters.
Of the lovely stars the daughters.'

O thou loved and youthful bridegroom,
Handsomest of all the people,
Set thou forth upon thy journey,
Hasten to commence thy journey,
Bear away thy youthful maiden,
Bear away thy dove so lovely.   90
From thy finch depart thou never,
Nor desert thy darling linnet;
In the ditches do not drive her,
Nor against the hedge-stakes drive her,
Nor upset her on the tree-stumps,
Nor in stony places cast her!

In her father's house she never,
In her dearest mother's homestead,

In the ditches has been driven,
Nor against the hedge-stakes driven,   100
Nor upset upon the tree-stumps,
Nor upset in stony places.

O thou loved and youthful bridegroom,
Handsomest of all the people!
Never may'st thou send the damsel,
Never may'st thou push the fair one
In the corner there to loiter,
Or to rummage in the corner.
In her father's house she never,
Never in her mother's household,   110
Went to loiter in the corner,
Or to rummage in the corner.
Always sat she at the window,
In the room she sat, and rocked her,
As her father's joy at evening,
And her mother's love at morning.

Never may'st thou, luckless husband,
Never may'st thou lead thy dovekin,
Where with arum-roots the mortar,
Stands, the rind to pound from off them,   120
Or her bread from straw prepare her,
Neither from the skin of pine-trees!
In her father's house she never,
In her tender mother's household,
Needed thus to use the mortar,
Pounding thus the rind from marsh-roots,
Nor from straw her bread prepare her,
Neither from the skin of pine-tree.

May'st thou always lead this dovekin
To a slope with corn abundant,   130
Or to help her from the rye-bins,
From the barley-bins to gather,
Whence large loaves of bread to bake her,
And the best of ale to brew her,
Loaves of wheaten-bread to bake her,
Kneaded dough for cakes prepare her!

Bridegroom, dearest of my brothers,
Never may'st thou make this dovekin,
Nor may'st cause our tender gosling,
Down to sit, and weep in sadness.   140
If there comes an hour of evil,
And the damsel should be dreary
Yoke thou in the sledge the chestnut,
Or the white horse do thou harness,
Drive her to her father's dwelling,
To her mother's home familiar!

Never may'st thou treat this dovekin,
Never may this darling linnet,
Ever be like slave-girl treated,
Neither like a hired servant,   150
Neither be forbid the cellar,
Nor the storehouse closed against her!
Never in her father's dwelling,
In her tender mother's household,
Was she treated like a slave-girl,
Neither like a hired servant,
Neither was forbid the cellar,
Nor the storehouse closed against her.
Always did she cut the wheatbread,
And the hens' eggs also looked to,   160
And she looked to all the milk-tubs,
Looked within the ale-casks likewise,
In the morn the storehouse opened,
Locked it also in the evening.

O thou loved and youthful bridegroom,
Handsomest of all the people,
If thou treatest well the damsel,
Thou wilt meet a good reception
When thou seek'st her father's dwelling,
Visiting her much loved mother.   170
Thou thyself wilt well be feasted,
Food and drink be set before thee,
And thy horse will be unharnessed,
And be led into the stable,
Drink and fodder set before him,
And a bowl of oats provided.

Never, surely, may our damsel,
May our well-beloved linnet,
Be in hissing tones upbraided,
That from no high race she springeth!   180
For in very truth our damsel
Comes of great and famous lineage.
If of beans you sow a measure
One bean each, it yields her kinsfolk;
If of flax you sow a measure,
But a thread it yields to each one.

Never may'st thou, luckless husband,
Badly treat this beauteous damsel,
Nor chastise her with the slave-whip,
Weeping 'neath the thongs of leather,   190
'Neath the five-lashed whip lamenting,
Out beyond the barn lamenting!
Never was the maid aforetime,
Never in her father's dwelling,
With the slave-whip e'er corrected,
Weeping 'neath the thongs of leather,
'Neath the five-lashed whip lamenting,
Out beyond the barn lamenting.

Stand thou like a wall before her,
Stand before her like a doorpost: 200
Do not let thy mother beat her,
Do not let thy father scold her,
Do not let the guests abuse her,
Do not let the neighbours blame her.
Drive the mob away with whipping,
Beat thou other people only,
Do thou not oppress thy darling,
Nor chastise thy heart's beloved,
Whom for three long years thou wait'st for,
She whom thou alone hast longed for!   210

Bridegroom, give thy bride instruction,
And do thou instruct thy apple,
In the bed do thou instruct her,
And behind the door advise her,
For a whole year thus instruct her,

Thus by word of mouth advise her,
With thine eyes the next year teach her,
And the third year teach by stamping!

If to this she pays no heeding,
Nor concerns herself about it,   220
Choose a reed where reeds are growing,
From the heath fetch thou some horse-tail,
And with these correct the damsel,
In the fourth year thus correct her,
With the stalks then whip her lightly,
With the rough edge of the sedges,
But with whip-lash do not strike her,
Neither with the rod correct her!

If to this she pays no heeding,
Nor concerns herself about it,   230
Bring a switch from out the thicket,
In the dell select a birch-rod,
Underneath thy fur cloak hide it,
That the neighbours may not know it,
Let the damsel only see it;
Threaten her, but do not touch her!

If to this she pays no heeding,
Nor concerns herself about it,
With the switch correct the damsel,
With the birch-rod do thou teach her,   240
But within the room four-cornered,
Or within the hut moss-covered.
Do not beat her in the meadow,
Do not whip her in the cornfield,
Lest the noise should reach the village,
And to other homes the quarrel,
Neighbours' wives should hear the crying,
And the uproar in the forest!

Always strike her on the shoulders,
On her buttocks do thou strike her,   250
On her eyes forbear to strike her,
On her ears forbear to touch her;
Lumps would rise upon her temples,

And her eyes with blue be bordered,
And the brother-in-law would question,
And the father-in-law perceive it,
And the village ploughmen see it,
And would laugh the village women:
'Has she been among the spear-thrusts,
Has she marched into a battle,   260
Or the mouth of wolf attacked her,
Or the forest bear has mauled her,
Or was perhaps the wolf her husband,
Was the bear perchance her consort?'"

By the stove there lay an old man,
By the hearth there sat a beggar;
From the stove there spoke the old man,
From the hearth there spoke the beggar:
"Never may'st thou, luckless husband,
Listen to thy wife's opinion,   270
Tongue of lark, and whim of women,
Like myself, a youth unhappy!
For both bread and meat I bought her,
Bought her butter, ale I bought her,
Every sort of fish I bought her,
Bought her all sorts of provisions,
Home-brewed ale the best I bought her,
Likewise wheat from foreign countries.

But she let it not content her,
Nor did it improve her temper,   280
For one day the room she entered,
And she grasped my hair, and tore it,
And her face was quite distorted,
And her eyes were wildly rolling,
Always scolding in her fury,
To her heart's contentment scolding,
Heaping foul abuse upon me,
Roaring at me as a sluggard.

But I knew another method,
Knew another way to tame her,   290
So I peeled myself a birch-shoot,
When she came, and called me birdie;

But when juniper I gathered,
Then she stooped, and called me darling;
When I lifted rods of willow,
On my neck she fell embracing."

Now the hapless girl was sighing,
Sighing much, and sobbing sadly;
Presently she broke out weeping,
And she spoke the words which follow: 300
"Soon must now depart the others,
And the time is fast approaching,
But my own departure's nearer,
Swiftly comes my time for parting.
Mournful is indeed my going,
Sad the hour of my departure,
From this far-renowned village,
And this ever-charming homestead,
Where my face was ever joyful,
And I grew to perfect stature,   310
All the days that I was growing,
While my childhood's years were passing.
Until now I never pondered,
Nor believed in all my lifetime,
Never thought on my departure,
Realized my separation,
From the precincts of this castle,
From the hill where it is builded.
Now I feel I am departing,
And I know that I am going.   320
Empty are the parting goblets,
And the ale of parting finished,
And the sledges all are waiting,
Front to fields, and back to homestead,
With one side towards the stables,
And the other to the cowhouse.

Whence comes now my separation,
Whence my sadness at departure,
How my mother's milk repay her.
Or the goodness of my father,   330
Or my brother's love repay him,
Or my sister's fond affection?

Thanks to thee, my dearest father,
For my former life so joyful,
For the food of days passed over,
For the best of all the dainties.

Thanks to thee, my dearest mother,
For my childhood's cradle-rocking,
For thy tending of the infant,
Whom thou at thy breast hast nurtured.   340

Also thanks, my dearest brother,
Dearest brother, dearest sister,
Happiness to all the household,
All companions of my childhood,
Those with whom I lived and sported,
And who grew from childhood with me.

May thou not, O noble father,
May thou not, O tender mother,
Or my other noble kindred,
Or my race, the most illustrious,   350
Ever fall into affliction,
Be oppressed by grievous trouble,
That I thus desert my country,
That I wander to a distance!
Shines the sun of the Creator,
Beams the moon of the Creator,
And the stars of heaven are shining,
And the Great Bear is extended
Ever in the distant heavens,
Evermore in other regions,   360
Not alone at father's homestead,
In the home where passed my childhood.

Truly must I now be parted
From the home I loved so dearly,
From my father's halls be carried,
From among my mother's cellars;
Leave the swamps and fields behind me,
Leave behind me all the meadows,
Leave behind the sparkling waters,
Leave the sandy shore behind me,   370

Where the village women bathe them,
And the shepherd-boys are splashing.

I must leave the quaking marshes,
And the wide-extending lowlands,
And the peaceful alder-thickets,
And the tramping through the heather,
And the strolling past the hedgerows,
And the loitering on the pathways,
And my dancing through the farmyards,
And my standing by the house-walls,   380
And the cleaning of the planking,
And the scrubbing of the flooring,
Leave the fields where leap the reindeer,
And the woods where run the lynxes,
And the wastes where flock the wild geese,
And the woods where birds are perching.

Now indeed I am departing,
And my dear one parts now with me,
In the folds of nights of autumn,
On the thin ice of the springtime,   390
On the ice I leave no traces,
On the slippery ice no footprints,
From my dress no thread upon it,
Nor in snow my skirt's impression.

If I should return in future,
And again my home revisit,
Mother hears my voice no longer,
Nor my father heeds my weeping,
Though I'm sobbing in the corner,
Or above their heads am speaking,   400
For the young grass springs already
And the juniper is sprouting
O'er the sweet face of my mother,
And the cheeks of her who bore me.

If I should return in future
To the wide-extended homestead,
I shall be no more remembered,
Only by two little objects;

At the lowest hedge are hedge-bands,
At the furthest field are hedge-stakes,   410
These I fixed when I was little,
As a girl with twigs I bound them.

But my mother's barren heifer,
Unto which I carried water,
And which as a calf I tended,
She will low to greet my coming,
From the dunghill of the farmyard,
Or the wintry fields around it;
She will know me, when returning,
As the daughter of the household.   420

Then my father's splendid stallion,
Which I fed when I was little,
Which as girl I often foddered,
He will neigh to greet my coming,
From the dunghill of the farmyard,
Or the wintry fields around it;
He will know me, when returning,
As the daughter of the household.

Then the dog, my brother's favourite
Which as child I fed so often,   430
Which I trained when in my girlhood,
He will bark to greet my coming,
From the dunghill of the farmyard,
Or the wintry fields around it;
He will know me, when returning,
As the daughter of the household.

But the others will not know me,
To my former home returning,
Though my boats are still the old ones,
As when here I lived aforetime,   440
By the shores where swim the powans,
And the nets are spread as usual.

Now farewell, thou room beloved,
Thou my room, with roof of boarding;
Good it were for me returning,

That I once again should scrub thee!
Now farewell, thou hall beloved,
Thou my hall, with floor of boarding;
Good it were for me returning,
That I once again should scrub thee!   450

Now farewell, thou yard beloved,
With my lovely mountain-ashtrees;
Good it were for me returning,
Once again to wander round thee!

Now farewell to all things round me,
Berry-bearing fields and forests,
And the flower-bearing roadsides,
And the heaths o'ergrown with heather,
And the lakes with hundred islands,
And the depths where swim the powans,   460
And the fair hills with the fir-trees,
And the swampy ground with birch-trees."

Then the smith, e'en Ilmarinen,
In the sledge the maiden lifted,
With his whip he lashed the coursers,
And he spoke the words which follow:
"Now farewell to all the lakeshores,
Shores of lakes, and slopes of meadows,
All the pine-trees on the hill-sides,
And the tall trees in the firwoods,   470
And behind the house the alders,
And the junipers by well-sides,
In the plains, all berry-bushes,
Berry-bushes, stalks of grasses,
Willow-bushes, stumps of fir-trees,
Alder-leaves, and bark of birch-trees!"

Thus at length, smith Ilmarinen
Forth from Pohjola departed,
With the children farewells singing,
And they sang the words which follow: 480
"Hither flew a bird of blackness,
Through the wood he speeded swiftly,
Well he knew to lure our duckling,

And entice from us our berry,
And he took from us our apple,
Drew the fish from out the water,
Lured her with a little money,
And enticed her with his silver.
Who will fetch us now the water,
Who will take us to the river?   490

Now remain the buckets standing,
And the yoke is idly rattling,
And the floor unswept remaineth,
And unswept remains the planking,
Empty now are all the pitchers,
And the jugs two-handled dirty!"

But the smith, e'en Ilmarinen,
With the young girl hastened homeward,
Driving rattling on his journey,
From the magic coast of Pohja,   500
By the shores of Sound of Sima.
On he drove across the sandhills,
Shingle crashed, and sand was shaking,
Swayed the sledge, the pathway rattled,
Loudly rang the iron runners,
And the frame of birch resounded,
And the curving laths were rattling,
Shaking was the cherry collar,
And the whiplash whistling loudly,
And the rings of copper shaking,   510
As the noble horse sprang forward,
As the White-front galloped onward.

Drove the smith one day, a second,
Driving likewise on the third day;
With one hand the horse he guided,
And with one embraced the damsel,
One foot on the sledge-side rested,
Underneath the rug the other.
Quick they sped, and fast they journeyed,
Days passed by, the road grew shorter,
And at length upon the third day,   520
Just about the time of sunset,

Hove in sight the smith's fair dwelling
And they came to Ilma's homestead,
And the smoke in streaks ascended,
And the smoke rose thickly upward,
From the house in wreaths arising,
Up amid the clouds ascending.

XXV The homecoming of the bride and bridegroom

The bride, the bridegroom and their company are received at the home of Ilmarinen (1–382). The company are hospitably entertained with food and drink: and Väinämöinen sings the praises of the host, the hostess, the inviter, the bridesmaid, and the other wedding-guests (383–672). On the way back Väinämöinen's sledge breaks down, but he repairs it, and drives home (673–738).

Long already 'twas expected,
Long expected and awaited,
That the new bride soon would enter
The abode of Ilmarinen;
And the eyes with rheum were dripping
Of the old folks at the windows,
And the young folks' knees were failing
As about the door they waited,
And the children's feet were freezing,
By the wall as they were standing,   10
Mid-aged folks their shoes were spoiling,
As upon the beach they wandered.

And at length upon a morning,
Just about the time of sunrise,
From the wood they heard a rattling,
As the sledge came rushing onward.

Lokka, then the kindest hostess,
Kaleva's most handsome matron,
Uttered then the words which follow:
"'Tis my son's sledge now approaching,   20
As from Pohjola he cometh,
And he brings the youthful damsel!
Straight he journeys to this country,
To the homestead hastens onward,
To the house his father gave him,
Which his parents had constructed."

Therefore thus did Ilmarinen
Hasten forward to the homestead,
To the house his father gave him,
Which his parents had constructed.   30
Hazel-grouse were twittering blithely
On the collar formed of saplings,
And the cuckoos all were calling,
On the sledge's sides while sitting,
And the squirrels leaped and frolicked
On the shafts of maple fashioned.

Lokka, then the kindest hostess,
Kaleva's most beauteous matron,
Uttered then the words which follow,
And in words like these expressed her: 40
"For the new moon waits the village,
And the young await the sunrise,
Children search where grow the berries,
And the water waits the tarred boat;
For no half-moon have I waited,
Nor the sun have I awaited,
But waited for my brother,
For my brother and step-daughter,
Gazed at morning, gazed at evening,
Knew not what had happened to them,   50
If a child he had been rearing,
Or a lean one he had fattened,
That he came not any sooner,
Though he faithfully had promised
Soon to turn his footsteps homeward,
Ere defaced had been his footprints.

Ever gazed I forth at morning,
And throughout the day I pondered,
If my brother was not coming,
Nor his sledge was speeding onward   60
Swiftly to his little homestead,
To this very narrow dwelling.
Though the horse were but a straw one,
And the sledge were but two runners,
Yet a sledge I still would call it,
And a sledge would still esteem it,

If it homeward brought my brother,
And another fair one with him.

Thus throughout my life I wished it,
This throughout the day I looked for, 70
Till my head bowed down with gazing,
And my hair bulged up in ridges,
And my bright eyes were contracted,
Hoping for my brother's coming
Swiftly to this little household,
To this very narrow dwelling,
And at length my son is coming,
And in truth is coming swiftly,
With a lovely form beside him,
And a rose-cheeked girl beside him! 80

Bridegroom, O my dearest brother,
Now the white-front horse unharness,
Do thou lead the noble courser
To his own familiar pasture,
To the oats but lately garnered;
Then bestow thy greetings on us,
Greet us here, and greet the others,
All the people of the village!

When thou hast bestowed thy greetings,
Thou must tell us all thy story. 90
Did thy journey lack adventures,
Hadst thou health upon thy journey,
To thy mother-in-law when faring,
To thy father-in-law's dear homestead,
There to woo and win the maiden,
Beating down the gates of battle,
And the maiden's castle storming,
Breaking down the walls uplifted,
Stepping on her mother's threshold,
Sitting at her father's table? 100

But I see without my asking,
And perceive without inquiry,
He has prospered on his journey,
With his journey well contented.

He has wooed and won the gosling,
Beaten down the gates of battle,
Broken down the boarded castle,
And the walls of linden shattered,
When her mother's house he entered,   110
And her father's home he entered.
In his care is now the duckling,
In his arms behold the dovekin,
At his side the modest damsel,
Shining in her radiant beauty.

Who has brought the lie unto us,
And the ill report invented,
That the bridegroom came back lonely,
And his horse had sped for nothing?   120
For the bridegroom comes not lonely
Nor his horse has sped for nothing;
Perhaps the horse has brought back something
For his white mane he is shaking,
For the noble horse is sweating,
And the foal with foam is whitened,
From his journey with the dovekin,
When he drew the blushing damsel.

In the sledge stand up, O fair one,
On its floor, O gift most noble,
Do thou raise thyself unaided,
And do thou arise unlifted,   130
If the young man tries to lift thee,
And the proud one seeks to raise thee.

From the sledge do thou upraise thee,
From the sledge do thou release thee,
Walk upon this flowery pathway,
On the path of liver-colour,
Which the swine have trod quite even,
And the hogs have trampled level,
Over which have passed the lambkins,
And the horses' manes swept over!   140

Step thou with the step of gosling,
Strut thou with the feet of duckling,

In the yard that's washed so cleanly,
On the smooth and level grassplot,
Where the father rules the household,
And the mother holds dominion,
To the workplace of the brother,
And the sister's blue-flowered meadow.
Set thy foot upon the threshold,
Then upon the porch's flooring,   150
On the honeyed floor advance thou,
Next the inner rooms to enter,
Underneath these famous rafters,
Underneath this roof so lovely!

It was in this very winter,
In the summer just passed over,
Sang the floor composed of duckbones,
That thyself should stand upon it,
And the golden roof resounded
That thou soon should'st walk beneath it,   160
And the windows were rejoicing,
For thy sitting at the windows.

It was in this very winter,
In the summer just passed over,
Often rattled the door handles,
For the ringed hands that should close them,
And the stairs were likewise creaking
For the fair one robed so grandly,
And the doors stood always open,
And their opener thus awaited.   170

It was in this very winter,
In the summer just passed over,
That the room around has turned it,
Unto those the room who dusted,
And the hall has made it ready
For the sweepers, when they swept it,
And the very barns were chirping
To the sweepers as they swept them.

It was in this very winter,
In the summer just passed over,   180

That the yard in secret turned it
To the gatherer of the splinters,
And the storehouses bowed downward,
For the wanderer who should enter,
Rafters bowed, and beams bent downward
To receive the young wife's wardrobe.

It was in this very winter,
In the summer just passed over,
That the pathways had been sighing
For the sweeper of the pathways,   190
And the cowsheds nearer drawing
To the cleanser of the cowsheds;
Songs and dances were abandoned,
Till should sing and dance our duckling.

On this very day already,
And upon the day before it,
Early has the cow been lowing,
And her morning hay expecting,
And the foal has loud been neighing
That his truss of hay be cast him,   200
And the lamb of spring has bleated,
That its food its mistress bring it.

On this very day already,
And upon the day before it,
Sat the old folks at the windows,
On the beach there ran the children,
By the wall there stood the women,
In the porch-door youths were waiting,
Waiting for the youthful mistress,
And the bride they all awaited.   210

Hail to all within the household,
Likewise hail to all the heroes,
Hail, O barn, and all within thee,
Barn, and all the guests within thee,
Hail, O hall, and all within thee,
Birchbark roof, and all thy people,
Hail, O room, and all within thee,
Hundred-boards, with all thy children!

Hail, O moon, to thee, O monarch,
And the bridal train so youthful!   220
Never was there here aforetime,
Never yesterday nor ever,
Was a bridal train so splendid:
Never were such handsome people.

Bridegroom, O my dearest brother,
Let the red cloths now be loosened,
Laid aside the veils all silken;
Let us see thy cherished marten,
Whom for five long years thou wooed'st,
And for eight years thou hast longed for!   230

Hast thou brought whom thou hast wished for,
Hast thou brought with thee the cuckoo,
From the land a fair one chosen,
Or a rosy water-maiden?

But I see without my asking,
Comprehend without inquiry,
Thou has really brought the cuckoo,
Hast the blue duck in thy keeping;
Greenest of the topmost branches,
Thou hast brought from out the greenwood,   240
Freshest of the cherry-branches,
From the freshest cherry-thickets."

On the floor there sat an infant,
From the floor spoke out the infant:
"O my brother, what thou bringest,
Is a tar-stump void of beauty,
Half as long as a tar-barrel,
Tall as is a winding frame.

Shame, O shame, unhappy bridegroom,
All thy life thou hast desired,   250
Vowed to choose from hundred maidens,
And among a thousand maidens,
Bring the noblest of the hundred,
From a thousand unattractive;
From the swamp you bring a lapwing,

From the hedge you bring a magpie,
From the field you bring a scarecrow,
From the fallow field a blackbird.

What has she as yet accomplished,
In the summer just passed over,   260
If the mitts she was not knitting,
Nor begun to make the stockings?
Empty to the house she cometh,
To our household brings no presents,
Mice are squeaking in the baskets,
Long-eared mice are in the coppers."

Lokka, most accomplished hostess,
Kaleva's most handsome matron,
Heard these wondrous observations,
And replied in words which follow: 270
"Wretched child, what art thou saying?
To thy own disgrace thou speakest!
Thou may'st wonders hear of others,
Others may'st perchance disparage,
But thou may'st not shame this damsel,
Nor the people of this household!

Bad the words that thou hast uttered,
Bad the words that thou hast spoken,
With the mouth of calf of night-time,
With the head of day-old puppy;   280
Handsome is this noble damsel,
Noblest she of all the country,
Even like a ripening cranberry,
Or a strawberry on the mountain,
Like the cuckoo in the tree-top,
Little bird in mountain-ashtree,
In the birch a feathered songster,
White-breast bird upon the maple.

Ne'er from Saxony came ever,
Nor in Viro could they fashion   290
Such a girl of perfect beauty,
Such a duck without an equal,
With a countenance so lovely,

And so noble in her stature,
And with arms of such a whiteness,
And with slender neck so graceful.

Neither comes the damsel dowerless,
Furs enough she brought us hither,
Blankets, too, as gifts she brought us,
Cloths as well she carried with her.   300

Much already has this damsel
Wrought by working with her spindle,
On her own reel has she wound it,
With her fingers much has finished.
Cloths of very brilliant lustre
Has she folded up in winter,
In the spring days has she bleached them,
In the summer months has dried them;
Splendid sheets the beds to spread on,
Cushions soft for heads to rest on,   310
Silken neckcloths of the finest,
Woollen mantles of the brightest.

Noble damsel, fairest damsel,
With thy beautiful complexion,
In the house wilt thou be honoured,
As in father's house the daughter,
All thy life shalt thou be honoured,
As in husband's house the mistress!

Never will we cause thee trouble,
Never trouble bring upon thee.   320
To the swamp thou wast not carried,
Nor on ditch-side were you taken,
From the cornfields rich they brought thee,
But to better fields they led thee,
And they took thee from the ale-house,
To a home where ale is better.

Noble girl, and fairest damsel,
One thing only will I ask thee:
Didst thou notice on thy journey
Shocks of corn that stood uplifted,   330

Ears of rye in shocks uplifted,
All belonging to this homestead,
From the ploughing of thy husband?
He has ploughed and he has sown it.

Dearest girl, and youthful damsel,
That is what I now will tell thee,
Thou hast willed our house to enter:
Be contented with the household.
Here 'tis good to be the mistress,
Good to be a fair-faced daughter,   340
Sitting here among the milk-pans,
Butter dishes at thy service.
This is pleasant for a damsel,
Pleasant for a fair-faced dovekin.
Broad the planking of the sauna,
Broad within the rooms the benches,
Here the master's like thy father,
And the mistress like thy mother,
And the sons are like thy brothers,
And the daughters like thy sisters.   350

If the longing e'er should seize thee,
And the wish should overtake thee,
For the fish thy father captured,
Or for grouse to ask thy brother,
From thy brother-in-law ask nothing,
From thy father-in-law ask nothing;
Best it is to ask thy husband,
Ask him to obtain them for thee.
There are not within the forest
Any four-legged beasts that wander,   360
Neither birds in air that flutter
Two-winged birds with rushing pinions,
Neither in the shining waters
Swarm the best of all the fishes,
Which thy husband cannot capture;
He can catch and bring them to thee.

Here 'tis good to be a damsel,
Here to be a fair-faced dovekin;
Need is none to work the stone-mill;

Need is none to work the mortar;   370
Here the wheat is ground by water,
And the rye by foaming torrents,
And the stream cleans all utensils,
And the lake-foam cleanses all things.

O thou lovely little village,
Fairest spot in all the country!
Grass below, and cornfields over,
In the midst between the village.
Fair the shore below the village,
By the shore is gleaming water,   380
Where the ducks delight in swimming,
And the water-fowl are sporting."

Drink they gave the bridal party,
Food and drink they gave in plenty,
Meat provided in abundance,
Loaves provided of the finest,
And they gave them ale of barley,
Spicy drink, from wheat concocted.
Roast they gave them in abundance,
Food and drink in all abundance,   390
In the dishes red they brought it,
In the handsomest of dishes.
Cakes were there, in pieces broken,
Likewise there were lumps of butter,
Powans too, to be divided,
Salmon too, to cut to pieces,
With the knives composed of silver,
And with smaller knives all golden.

Ale unpurchased there was flowing,
Mead for which you could not bargain;   400
Ale flowed from the ends of rafters,
Honey from the taps was oozing,
Ale around the lips was foaming,
Mead the mood of all enlivened.

Who among them should be cuckoo,
Who should sing a strain most fitting?

Väinämöinen, old and steadfast,
He the great primeval minstrel,
He himself commenced his singing,
Set about composing verses,   410
And he spoke the words which follow,
And expressed himself in thiswise:
"O my own beloved brethren,
O most eloquent companions,
O my comrades, ready talkers,
Listen now to what I tell you!
Rarely kiss the geese each other,
Rarely sisters gaze on sisters,
Rarely side by side stand brothers,
Side by side stand mother's children,   420
In these desert lands so barren,
In the wretched northern regions.

Shall we give ourselves to singing,
Set about composing verses?
None can sing except the singer,
None can call save vernal cuckoo,
None can dye, except Sinetär,
None can weave save Kankahatar.

Lapland's children, they are singing,
And the hay-shod ones are chanting,   430
As the elk's rare flesh they feast on,
Or the meat of smaller reindeer,
Wherefore then should I not carol,
Wherefore should our children sing not,
While upon the ryebread feasting,
Or when eating is concluded?

Lapland's children, they are singing,
And the hay-shod ones are chanting,
As they drink from water-pitchers,
While the bark bread they are chewing.   440
Wherefore then should I not carol,
Wherefore should our children sing not,
While the juice of corn we're drinking,
And the best-brewed ale of barley?

Lapland's children they are singing,
And the hay-shod ones are chanting,
Even by the sooty fire,
As they lay the coals upon it.
Wherefore then should I not carol,
Wherefore should our children sing not,   450
Underneath these famous rafters,
Underneath a roof so splendid?

Good it is for men to dwell here,
Good for women to reside here,
All among the barrels ale-filled,
Standing close beside the mead-tubs,
Near the sound where swarm the powans,
Near the place for netting salmon,
Where the food is never failing,
And the drink is never stinted.   460

Good it is for men to dwell here,
Good for women to reside here,
Here to eat by care untroubled,
Here to live without affliction,
Here to eat unvexed by trouble,
And to live without a sorrow,
Long as lives our host among us,
All the lifetime of our hostess.

Which shall I first praise in singing,
Shall it be the host or hostess?   470
Always first they praise the heroes,
Therefore first I praise the Master,
He who first prepared the marshland,
And along the shore who wandered,
And he brought great stumps of fir-trees,
And he trimmed the crowns of fir-trees,
Took them to a good position,
Firmly built them all together,
For his race a great house builded,
And he built a splendid homestead: 480
Walls constructed from the forest,

Rafters from the fearful mountains,
Laths from out of the woods provided,
Beams from berry-bearing heathlands,
Bark from cherry-bearing uplands,
Moss from off the quaking marshes.

And the house is well-constructed,
And the roof securely fastened.
Here a hundred men were gathered,
On the house-roof stood a thousand,   490
When this house was first constructed,
And the flooring duly fitted.

Be assured our host so worthy,
In the building of this homestead,
Oft his hair exposed to tempest,
And his hair was much disordered.
Often has our host so noble,
On the rocks his gloves left lying,
Lost his hat among the fir-trees,
In the marsh has sunk his stockings.   500

Often has our host so noble
In the early morning hours,
When no others had arisen,
And unheard by all the village,
Left the cheerful fire behind him,
Watched for birds in wattled wigwam,
And the thorns his head were combing,
Dew his handsome eyes was washing.

Thus receives our host so noble,
In his home his friends around him;   510
Filled the benches are with singers,
And with joyous guests the windows,
And the floor with talking people,
Porches, too, with people shouting,
Near the walls with people standing,
Near the fence with people walking,
Through the yard are folks parading,
Children on the ground are creeping.

Now I first have praised the master,
I will praise our gracious hostess,   520
She who has prepared the banquet,
And has filled the table for us.

Large the loaves that she has baked us,
And she stirred us up thick porridge,
With her hands that move so quickly,
With her soft and tenfold fingers,
And she let the bread rise slowly,
And the guests with speed she feasted;
Pork she gave them in abundance,
Gave them cakes piled up in dishes,   530
And the knives were duly sharpened,
And the pointed blades pressed downward,
As the salmon were divided,
And the pike were split asunder.
Often has our noble mistress,
She the most accomplished housewife,
Risen up before the cockcrow,
And before the hen's son hastened,
That she might prepare the needful,
That the work might all be finished,   540
That the beer might be concocted,
And the ale be ready for us.

Well indeed our noble hostess,
And this most accomplished housewife,
Best of ale for us concocted,
And the finest drink set flowing.
'Tis composed of malted barley,
And of malt the very sweetest,
And with wood she has not turned it,
With a stake she has not moved it,   550
Only with her hands has raised it,
Only with her arms has turned it,
In the sauna filled with vapour,
On the boarding, scoured so cleanly.

Nor did she, our noble hostess,
And this most accomplished mistress,

Let the germs mature them fully,
While on ground the malt was lying.
Oft she went into the sauna,
Went alone, at dead of midnight,
Fearing not the wolf should harm her,   560
Nor the wild beasts of the forest.

Now that we have praised the hostess,
Let us also praise the inviter;
Who was chosen as inviter,
And upon the road to guide us?
Best inviter of the village,
Best of guides in all the village.

There we look on our inviter,
Clad in coat from foreign countries;   570
Round his arms 'tis tightly fitted,
Neatly round his waist 'tis fitted.
There we look on our inviter,
In a narrow cloak attired;
On the sand the skirts are sweeping,
On the ground the train is sweeping.

Of his shirt we see a little,
Only see a very little,
As if Kuutar's self had wove it,
And the tin-adorned one wrought it.   580

Here we look on our inviter,
Belted with a belt of woollen,
Woven by the Sun's fair daughter,
By her beauteous fingers broidered,
In the times ere fire existed,
And when all unknown was fire.

Here we look on our inviter,
With his feet in silken stockings,
And with silk are bound his stockings,
And his garters are of satin,   590
And with gold are all embroidered,
And are all adorned with silver.

Here we look on our inviter,
Best of Saxon shoes he's wearing,
Like the swans upon the river,
Or the ducks that swim beside them,
Or the geese among the thickets,
Birds of passage in the forests.

Here we look on our inviter,
With his golden locks all curling,   600
And his golden beard is plaited,
On his head a lofty helmet:
Up among the clouds it rises,
Through the forest's glancing summit;
Such a one you could not purchase
For a hundred marks or thousand.

Now that I have praised the inviter,
I will also praise the bridesmaid!
Whence has come to us the bridesmaid,
Whence was she, the happiest, chosen?   610

Thence has come to us the bridesmaid,
Thence was she, the happiest, chosen,
Where is Tanikka's strong fortress,
From without the new-built castle.

No, she came from other regions,
Not at all from such a region;
Thence has come to us the bridesmaid,
Thence was she, the happiest, chosen,
Brought to us across the water,
And across the open ocean.   620

No, she came from other regions,
Not at all from such a region,
Grew like strawberry in the country,
On the heaths where cranberries flourish,
On the field of beauteous herbage,
On the heath of golden flowerets,
Thence has come to us the bridesmaid,
Thence was she, the happiest, chosen.

And the bridesmaid's mouth is pretty,
As the spindle used in Suomi,   630
And the bridesmaid's eyes are sparkling,
As the stars that shine in heaven,
Gleaming are the damsel's temples,
As upon the lake the moonlight.

Here we look upon our bridesmaid;
Round her neck a chain all golden,
On her head a golden head-dress,
On her hands are golden bracelets,
Golden rings upon her fingers,
In her ears are golden earrings,   640
Loops of gold upon her temples,
And her brows are bead-adorned.

And I thought the moon was shining,
When her golden clasp was gleaming,
And I thought the sun was shining,
When I saw her collar gleaming,
And I thought a ship was sailing,
When I saw her head-dress moving.

Now that I have praised the bridesmaid,
I will glance at all the people;   650
Very handsome are the people,
Stately are the aged people,
And the younger people pretty,
All the group is stout and handsome.

I have gazed at all the people,
Yet I knew them all already;
But before it never happened,
Nor in future times will happen,
That we meet so fine a household,
Or we meet such handsome people,   660
Where the old folks are so stately,
And the younger people pretty.
Clothed in white are all the people,
Like the forest in the hoarfrost,
Under like the golden dawning:
Over like the morning twilight,

Easy to obtain was silver,
Gold among the guests was scattered,
In the grass were littered purses,
In the lanes were bags of money,   670
For the guests who were invited,
For the guests most greatly honoured."

Väinämöinen, old and steadfast,
Of the song the mighty pillar,
After this his sledge ascended,
Homeward drove upon his journey,
And he sang his songs for ever,
Sang, and chanted spells of magic,
Sang a song, and sang a second,
But, as he the third was singing,   680
Clashed against a rock the runners,
Crashed the shafts against a tree-stump,
And the sledge broke off his chanting,
And the runners stopped his singing,
And the shafts in fragments shattered,
And the boards broke all asunder.

Spoke the aged Väinämöinen,
In the very words which follow:
"Are there none among the youthful,
Of the rising generation,   690
Or perchance among the aged,
Of the sinking generation,
Who to Tuonela can wander,
And can go to Mana's country,
Thence to fetch me Tuoni's auger,
Bring me Mana's mighty auger,
That a new sledge I may fashion,
Or repair my sledge that's broken?"

But said all the younger people,
And the aged people answered: 700
"There are none among the youthful,
None at all among the aged,
None of race so highly noble,
None is such a mighty hero,
As to Tuonela to travel,

Journey to the land of Mana,
Thence to bring you Tuoni's auger,
And from Mana's home to bring it,
That a new sledge you may fashion,
Or repair the sledge that's broken."   710

Then the aged Väinämöinen,
He the great primeval minstrel,
Went again to Tuoni's country,
Journeyed to the home of Mana,
Fetched from Tuonela the auger,
Brought from Mana's home the auger.

Then the aged Väinämöinen
Sang a blue wood up before him;
In the forest rose an oak-tree,
And a splendid mountain-ashtree,   720
And from these a sledge he fashioned,
And he shaped his runners from them,
And for shafts prepared them likewise,
And the frame he thus constructed,
Made a sledge to suit his purpose,
And a new sledge he constructed.
In the shafts the horse he harnessed,
Yoked before the sledge the chestnut,
In the sledge himself he seated,
And upon the seat he sat him,   730
And without the whip the courser,
Sped, by beaded whip unharassed,
To his long-accustomed fodder,
To the food that waited for him,
And he brought old Väinämöinen,
He the great primeval minstrel,
To his own door, widely open,
To the threshold brought him safely.

XXVI Lemminkäinen's journey to Pohjola

Lemminkäinen, greatly offended that he was not invited to the wedding, resolves to go to Pohjola, although his mother dissuades him from it, and warns him of the many dangers that he will have to encounter (1–382). He sets forth and succeeds in passing all the dangerous places by his skill in magic (383–776).

Ahti dwelt upon an island,
By the bay near Kauko's headland,
And his fields he tilled industrious,
And the fields he trenched with ploughing,
And his ears were of the finest,
And his hearing of the keenest.

Heard he shouting in the village,
From the lake came sounds of hammering,
On the ice the sound of footsteps,
On the heath a sledge was rattling,   10
Therefore in his mind he fancied,
In his brain the notion entered,
That at Pohjola was wedding,
And a drinking-bout in secret!

Mouth and head awry then twisting,
And his black beard all disordered,
In his rage the blood departed
From the cheeks of him unhappy,
And at once he left his ploughing,
'Mid the field he left the ploughshare,   20
On the spot his horse he mounted,
And he rode directly homeward,
To his dearest mother's dwelling,
To his dear and aged mother.

And he said as he approached her,
And he called, as he was coming:
"O my mother, aged woman,
Bring thou food, and bring it quickly,
That the hungry man may eat it,
And the moody man devour it,   30
While they warm the sauna for me,
And the bath-house set in order,
That the man may wash and cleanse him,
And adorn him like a hero!"

Then did Lemminkäinen's mother,
Bring him food, and bring it quickly,
That the hungry man might eat it,
And the moody man devour it,
While they put the bath in order,
And arranged the sauna for him.   40

Then the lively Lemminkäinen
Quickly ate the food she gave him,
Hurried then into the sauna,
Hastened quickly to the bath-house,
There it was the finch now washed him,
There the bullfinch washed and cleansed him,
Washed his head to flaxen whiteness,
And his throat to shining whiteness.

From the bath the room he entered,
And he spoke the words which follow: 50
"O my mother, aged woman,
Seek the storehouse on the mountain,
Bring me thence my shirt, the fine one,
Likewise bring the finest clothing,
That I now may put it on me,
And may fitly clothe me in it!"

But his mother asked him quickly,
Asked him thus, the aged woman:
"Whither goes my son, my dearest,
Dost thou go to hunt the lynxes,   60
Or to chase the elk on snowshoes,
Or perchance to shoot a squirrel?"

Answered lively Lemminkäinen,
Said the handsome Kaukomieli:
"O my mother who hast borne me,
Not to hunt the lynx I wander,
Nor to chase the elk on snowshoes,
Neither go I squirrel shooting;
But I seek the feast at Pohja,
And the secret drinking-party, 70
Therefore fetch my shirt, the fine one,
Bring me, too, the finest clothing,
That I hasten to the wedding,
And may wander to the banquet!"

But his mother would forbid him,
Vainly would his wife dissuade him,
Two, whose like were not created,
And three daughters of Creation,
Sought to hold back Lemminkäinen
Back from Pohjola's great banquet. 80

To her son then said the mother,
And her child advised the old one:
"Do not go, my son, my dearest,
O my dearest son, my Kauko,
Go not to the feast at Pohja,
To that mansion's drinking-party!
For indeed they did not ask you,
And 'tis plain they do not want you!"

Then the lively Lemminkäinen
Answered in the words which follow: 90
"Only bad men go for asking;
Uninvited good men dance there.
There are always invitations,
Always a sufficient summons,
In the sword with blade of sharpness,
And the edge so brightly flashing."

Still did Lemminkäinen's mother
Do her utmost to restrain him:
"Go not, son, to sure destruction,
Unto Pohjola's great banquet! 100

Full of terrors is thy journey,
On thy way are mighty wonders,
Thrice indeed doth death await thee;
Thrice the man with death is threatened."

Answered lively Lemminkäinen,
Said the handsome Kaukomieli,
"Death is only for the women,
Everywhere they see destruction;
But a hero need not fear it,
Nor need take extreme precautions.   110
But let this be as it may be,
Tell me that my ears may hear it,
Tell me the first death that waits me,
Tell the first and tell the last one."

Then said Lemminkäinen's mother,
Answered then, the aged woman:
"I will tell the deaths that wait you,
Not as you would have me tell them;
Of the first death I will tell you,
And this death is first among them.   120

When a little way you've travelled
On the first day of your journey,
You will reach a fiery river,
Flaming right across your pathway,
In the stream a cataract fiery,
In the fall a fiery island,
On the isle a peak all fiery,
On the peak a fiery eagle,
One who whets his beak at night-time,
And his claws in daytime sharpens,   130
For the strangers who are coming,
And the people who approach him."

Answered lively Lemminkäinen,
Said the handsome Kaukomieli,
"This is perhaps a death for women,
But 'tis not a death for heroes.
For I know a plan already,

And a splendid scheme to follow:
I'll create, by songs of magic,
Both a man and horse of alder.   140
They shall walk along beside me,
And shall wander on before me,
While I like a duck am diving,
Like a scoter duck am diving,
'Neath the soaring eagle's talons,
Talons of the mighty eagle.
O my mother, who hast borne me,
Tell me now of death the second!"

Then said Lemminkäinen's mother,
"Such the second death that waits you: 150
When a little way you've journeyed,
On the second day of travel,
You will reach a trench of fire,
Right across the path extending,
Ever to the east extending,
North-west endlessly extending,
Full of stones to redness heated,
Full of blocks of stone all glowing,
And a hundred there have ventured,
And a thousand there have perished,   160
Hundreds with their swords have perished,
And a thousand steel-clad heroes."

Answered lively Lemminkäinen,
Said the handsome Kaukomieli,
"Such a death no man will perish,
Nor is this a death for heroes,   170
For I know a trick already,
Know a trick, and see a refuge;
And a man of snow I'll sing me,
Make of frozen snow a hero,
Push him in the raging fire,
Push him in the glowing torment,
Bathe him in the glowing sauna,
With a bath-whisk made of copper,
I myself behind him pressing,
Pushing through the fire a pathway,

That my beard unburnt remaineth,
And my locks escape a singeing.
O my mother who hast borne me,
Of the third death tell me truly!"   180

Then said Lemminkäinen's mother,
"Such the third death that awaits you:
When you've gone a little further,
And another day have travelled,
Unto Pohjola's dread gateway,
Where the pathway is the narrowest,
Then a wolf will rush upon you,
And a bear for his companion,
There in Pohjola's dread gateway,
Where the pathway is the narrowest.   190
Hundreds have been there devoured,
Heroes have by thousands perished;
Wherefore should they not devour thee,
Kill thee likewise, unprotected?"

Answered lively Lemminkäinen,
Said the handsome Kaukomieli,
"Perhaps a young ewe might be eaten,
Or a lamb be torn to pieces,
Not a man, how weak soever,
Not the sleepiest of the heroes!   200
With a hero's belt I'm girded,
And I wear a hero's armour,
Fixed with buckles of a hero,
So be sure I shall not hasten,
Unto Untamo's dread wolf's jaws,
In the throat of that curst creature.

'Gainst the wolf I know a refuge,
'Gainst the bear I know a method;
For the wolf's mouth sing a muzzle,
For the bear sing iron fetters,   210
Or to very chaff will chop them,
Or to merest dust will sift them;
Thus I'll clear the path before me,
Reach the ending of my journey."

Then said Lemminkäinen's mother,
"Even yet your goal you reach not,
There are still upon your pathway,
On your road tremendous marvels!
Three terrific dangers wait you,
Three more deaths await the hero;   220
And there even yet await you,
On the spot the worst of marvels;
When a little way you've travelled,
Up to Pohjola's enclosure,
There a fence is reared of iron,
And a fence of steel erected,
From the ground to heaven ascending,
From the heavens to earth descending.
Spears they are which form the hedgestakes
And for wattles, creeping serpents,   230
Thus the fence with snakes is wattled,
And among them there are lizards,
And their tails are always waving,
And their thick heads always swelling,
And their round heads always hissing,
Heads turned out, and tails turned inwards.
On the ground are other serpents,
On the path are snakes and adders,
And above, their tongues are hissing,
And below, their tails are waving.   240
One of all the most terrific
Lies before the gate across it,
Longer is he than a roof-tree,
Than the gate-posts is he thicker,
And above, his tongue is hissing,
And above, his mouth is hissing,
Lifted not against another,
Threatening thee, O luckless hero!"

Answered lively Lemminkäinen,
Said the handsome Kaukomieli: 250
"Such a death is perhaps for children;
But 'tis not a death for heroes,
For I can enchant the fire,
And can quench a glowing furnace,

And can ban away the serpents,
Twist the snakes between my fingers.
Only yesterday it happened
That I ploughed a field of adders;
On the ground the snakes were twisting,
And my hands were all uncovered.   260
With my nails I seized the vipers,
In my hands I took the serpents,
Ten I killed among the vipers,
And the serpents black by hundreds.
Still my nails are stained with snake-blood,
And my hands with slime of serpents.
Therefore will I not permit me,
And by no means will I journey
As a mouthful for the serpents,
To the sharp fangs of the adders.   270
I myself will crush the monsters,
Crush the nasty things to pieces,
And will sing away the vipers,
Drive the serpents from my pathway,
Enter then the yard of Pohja,
And into the house will force me."

Then said Lemminkäinen's mother,
"O my son, forbear to venture,
Into Pohjola's dread castle,
House of Sariola all timbered;   280
For the men with swords are girded,
Heroes all equipped for battle,
Men with drink of hops excited,
Very furious from their drinking.
They will sing thee, most unhappy,
To the swords of all the keenest;
Better men their songs have vanquished,
Mighty ones been overpowered."

Answered lively Lemminkäinen,
Said the handsome Kaukomieli: 290
"Well, but I have dwelt already
There in Pohjola's dread fortress.
Not a Lapp with spells shall chain me,
Forth no son of Turja drive me.

I'll enchant the Lapp by singing,
Drive away the son of Turja,
And in twain will sing his shoulders,
From his chin his speech I'll sever,
Tear his shirt apart by singing,
And I'll break in two his breastbone."   300

Then said Lemminkäinen's mother,
"O alas, my son unhappy,
Dost thou think of former exploits,
Brag'st thou of thy former journey?
True it is thou hast resided
There in Pohjola's dread fortress,
But they sent thee all a-swimming,
Floating overgrown with pond-weed,
O'er the raging cataract driven,
Down the stream in rushing waters.   310
Thou hast known the Falls of Tuoni,
Manala's dread stream hast measured,
There would'st thou to-day be swimming,
But for thine unhappy mother!

Listen now to what I tell thee.
When to Pohjola thou comest,
All the slope with stakes is bristling,
And the yard with poles is bristling,
All with heads of men surmounted,
And one stake alone is vacant,   320
And to fill the stake remaining,
Will they cut thy head from off thee."

Answered lively Lemminkäinen,
Said the handsome Kaukomieli:
"Let a weakling ponder o'er it,
Let the worthless find such ending!
After five or six years' warfare,
Seven long summers spent in battle,
Not a hero would concern him,
Nor retire a step before it.   330
Therefore bring me now my mail-shirt,
And my well-tried battle armour!
I my father's sword will fetch me,

And my father's sword-blade look to.
In the cold it long was lying,
In a dark place long was hidden;
There has it been ever weeping,
For a hero who should wield it."

Thereupon he took his mail-shirt,
Took his well-tried battle armour,   340
And his father's trusty weapon,
Sword his father always wielded,
And against the ground he thrust it,
On the floor the point he rested,
With his hand the sword he bended
Like the fresh crown of the cherry,
Or the juniper when growing.
Said the lively Lemminkäinen,
"Hard 'twill be in Pohja's castle,
Rooms of Sariola the misty,   350
Such a sword as this to gaze on,
Such a sword-blade to encounter."

From the wall his bow he lifted,
From the peg he took a strong bow,
And he spoke the words which follow,
And expressed himself in thiswise:
"I would hold the man deserving,
And regard him as a hero,
Who to bend this bow was able,
And could bend it and could string it,   360
There in Pohjola's great castle,
Rooms of Sariola the misty."

Then the lively Lemminkäinen,
He the handsome Kaukomieli,
Put his shirt of mail upon him,
Clad himself in arms of battle,
And his slave he thus commanded,
And he spoke the words which follow:
"O my servant, bought with money,
Workman, whom I got for money!   370
Harness now my horse of battle,
Harness me my fiery war-horse,

That unto the feast I journey,
Drinking-bout at house of Lempo!"

Then the prudent slave, obedient,
Hastened quickly to the courtyard,
And the foal at once he harnessed,
And prepared the fiery red one,
And he said on his returning,
"I have done what you commanded,   380
And the horse have harnessed for you,
And the best of foals have harnessed."

Then the lively Lemminkäinen
Thought him ready for his journey,
Right hand urging, left restraining,
And his sinewy fingers smarting,
Now would start, and then reflected,
Started then in reckless fashion.

Then her son his mother counselled,
Warned her child, the aged woman,   390
At the door, beneath the rafters,
At the place where stand the kettles:
"O my only son, my dearest,
O my child, of all the strongest,
When thou com'st to the carousal,
And thou comest where thou wishest,
Drink thou half a goblet only,
Drink the measure to the middle,
And the other half return thou;
Give the worst half to a worse one.   400
In the goblet rests a serpent,
And a worm within the measure!"

Yet again her son she cautioned,
To her child again gave warning,
At the last field's furthest limit,
At the last of all the gateways:
"When thou com'st to the carousal,
And thou comest where thou wishest,
Sit upon a half-seat only,
Step thou with a half-step only,   410

And the other half return thou;
Give the worst half to a worse one,
Thus wilt thou a man be reckoned,
And a most illustrious hero,
And through armies push thy pathway,
And will crush them down beneath thee,
In the press of mighty heroes,
In the throng of men of valour!"

Then departed Lemminkäinen,
When the horse in sledge was harnessed.   420
With his ready whip he struck him,
With his beaded whip he smote him,
And the fiery steed sprang forward,
Onward sped the rapid courser.

When a short way he had journeyed,
For about an hour had travelled,
There he saw a flock of blackfowl;
In the air the grouse flew upward,
And the flock ascended rushing
From before the speeding courser.   430

On the ice there lay some feathers
Cast by grouse upon the roadway;
These collected Lemminkäinen,
And he put them in his pocket,
For he knew not what might happen,
Or might chance upon his journey.
In a house are all things useful,
Can at need be turned to something.

Then he drove a little further,
On his road a little further,   440
When to neigh began the courser,
Pricked his long ears up in terror.

Then the lively Lemminkäinen,
He the handsome Kaukomieli,
In the sledge at once leaned forward,
Bending down to gaze about him.
There he saw, as said his mother,

As his own old mother warned him,
How there flowed a fiery river,
Right across the horse's pathway, 450
In the stream a cataract fiery,
In the fall a fiery island,
On the isle a peak all fiery,
On the peak a fiery eagle.
In his throat the fire was seething,
And his mouth with flame was glowing,
And his plumage fire was flashing,
And the sparks around were scattering.

Kauko from afar he noticed,
From afar saw Lemminkäinen: 460
"Whither wilt thou go, O Kauko,
Whither goes the son of Lempi?"

Answered lively Lemminkäinen,
Said the handsome Kaukomieli,
"Unto Pohja's feast I journey,
The carousal held in secret.
Turn thee on one side a little,
From the youth's path do thou turn thee,
Let the traveller make his journey,
Do not hinder Lemminkäinen, 470
Therefore move aside a little,
Let him now pursue his journey!"

Thereupon the eagle answered,
Hissing from his throat of fire:
"I will let the traveller pass me,
Will not hinder Lemminkäinen,
Through my mouth will let him hasten
Let him thus pursue his journey.
Thither shall thy path direct thee,
Fortunate shall be thy journey, 480
To the banquet thou art seeking,
Where thou all thy life may'st rest thee."

Little troubled Lemminkäinen,
And he let it not concern him,
But he felt into his pocket,

And his pouch he opened quickly,
Took the feathers of the blackfowl,
Leisurely he rubbed the feathers,
And between his palms he rubbed them,
'Twixt his fingers ten in number,   490
And a flock of grouse created,
And a flock of capercailzies,
In the eagle's beak he thrust them,
To his greedy throat he gave them,
To the eagle's throat all fiery,
In the fire-bird's beak he thrust them;
Thus he freed himself from danger,
And escaped the first day's danger.

With his whip he struck the courser,
With the beaded whip he struck him,   500
And the horse sped quickly onward,
And the steed sprang lightly forward.
Then he drove a little further,
But a little way had travelled,
When the horse again was shying,
And again the steed was neighing.

From the sledge again he raised him,
And he strove to gaze around him,
And he saw, as said his mother,
As his aged mother warned him,   510
Right in front a trench of fire,
Right across the path extending,
Ever to the east extending,
North-west endlessly extending,
Full of stones to redness heated,
Full of blocks of stone all glowing,

Little troubled Lemminkäinen,
But he raised a prayer to Ukko:
"Ukko, thou, of Gods the highest,
Ukko, thou, our Heavenly Father!   520
Send thou now a cloud from north-west,
Send thou from the west a second,
And a third to east establish.
In the north-east let them gather,

Push their borders all together,
Drive them edge to edge together,
Let the snow fall staff-deep round me,
Deep as is the length of spear-shaft,
On these stones to redness heated,
Blocks of stone all fiery glowing!"   530

Ukko, then, of Gods the highest,
He the aged Heavenly Father,
Sent a cloud from out the north-west,
From the west he sent a second,
In the east a cloud let gather,
Let them gather in the north-east;
And he heaped them all together,
And he closed the gaps between them,
Let the snow fall staff-deep downward,
Deep as is the length of spear-shaft,   540
On the stones to redness heated,
Blocks of stone all fiery glowing.
From the snow a pond was fashioned,
And a lake with icy waters.

Then the lively Lemminkäinen
Sang a bridge of ice together,
Stretching right across the snow-pond,
From the one bank to the other,
O'er the fiery trench passed safely,
Passed the second day in safety.   550

With his whip he urged the courser,
Cracked the whip all bead-embroidered,
And began to travel quickly,
As the courser trotted onward.

Quick he ran a verst, a second,
For a short space well proceeded,
When he suddenly stopped standing,
Would not stir from his position.

Then the lively Lemminkäinen
Started up to gaze around him.   560
In the gate the wolf was standing,

And the bear before the passage,
There in Pohjola's dread gateway,
At the end of a long passage.

Then the lively Lemminkäinen,
He the handsome Kaukomieli,
Quickly felt into his pocket,
What his pouch contained exploring,
And he took some ewe's wool from it,
And until 'twas soft he rubbed it,   570
And between his palms he rubbed it,
'Twixt his fingers ten in number.

On his palms then gently breathing,
Ewes ran bleating forth between them,
Quite a flock of sheep he fashioned,
And a flock of lambs among them,
And the wolf rushed straight upon them,
And the bear rushed after likewise,
While the lively Lemminkäinen,
Further drove upon his journey.   580

Yet a little space he journeyed,
Unto Pohjola's enclosure.
There a fence was raised of iron,
Fenced with steel the whole enclosure,
In the ground a hundred fathoms,
In the sky a thousand fathoms,
Spears they stood around like hedgestakes,
And for wattles creeping serpents;
Thus the fence with snakes was wattled
And among them there were lizards,   590
And their tails were always waving,
And their thick heads always swelling,
Rows of heads erected always,
Heads turned out and tails turned inwards.

Then the lively Lemminkäinen
Gave himself to his reflections:
"This is what my mother told me,
This is what my mother dreaded;
Here I find a fence tremendous

Reared aloft from earth to heaven,   600
Down below there creeps a viper,
Deeper yet the fence is sunken,
Up aloft a bird is flying,
But the fence is builded higher."

Natheless was not Lemminkäinen
Greatly troubled or uneasy;
From the sheath he drew his knife out,
From the sheath an iron weapon,
And he hewed the fence to pieces,
And in twain he clove the hedgestakes;   610
Thus he breached the fence of iron,
And he drove away the serpents
From the space between five hedgestakes,
Likewise from the space 'twixt seven,
And himself pursued his journey,
On to Pohjola's dark portal.
In the path a snake was twisting,
Just in front across the doorway,
Even longer than the roof-tree,
Thicker than the hall's great pillars,   620
And the snake had eyes a hundred,
And the snake had tongues a thousand,
And his eyes than sieves were larger,
And his tongues were long as spear-shafts,
And his fangs were like rake-handles;
Seven boats' length his back extended.

Then the lively Lemminkäinen
Would not instantly move onward
To the snake with eyes a hundred,
And the snake with tongues a thousand.   630

Spoke the lively Lemminkäinen,
Said the handsome Kaukomieli:
"Serpent black and subterranean,
Worm whose hue is that of Tuoni,
Thou amidst the grass who lurkest,
At the roots of Lempo's foliage,
Gliding all among the hillocks,

Creeping all among the tree-roots!
Who has brought thee from the stubble,
From the grass-roots has aroused thee,   640
Creeping here on ground all open,
Creeping there upon the pathway?
Who has sent thee from thy nettles,
Who has ordered and provoked thee
That thy head thou liftest threatening,
And thy neck thou stiffly raisest?
Was't thy father or thy mother,
Or the eldest of thy brothers,
Or the youngest of thy sisters,
Or some other near relation?   650

Close thy mouth, thy head conceal thou,
Hide thou quick thy tongue within it,
Coil thyself together tightly,
Roll thyself into a circle,
Give me way, though but a half-way,
Let the traveller make his journey,
Or begone from out the pathway.
Creep, thou vile one, in the bushes,
In the holes among the heathland,
And among the moss conceal thee,   660
Glide away, like ball of worsted,
Like a withered stick of aspen!
Hide thy head among the grass-roots,
Hide thyself among the hillocks,
'Neath the turf thy mouth conceal thou,
Make thy dwelling in a hillock.
If you lift your head from out it,
Ukko surely will destroy it,
With his nails, all steely-pointed,
With a mighty hail of iron!"   670

Thus was Lemminkäinen talking,
But the serpent heeded nothing,
And continued always hissing,
Darting out its tongue for ever,
And its mouth was always hissing
At the head of Lemminkäinen.

Then the lively Lemminkäinen
Of an ancient spell bethought him,
Which the old crone had advised him,
Which his mother once had taught him. 680

Said the lively Lemminkäinen,
Spoke the handsome Kaukomieli,
"If you do not heed my singing,
And it is not quite sufficient,
Still you will swell up with anguish
When an ill day comes upon you.
Thou wilt burst in two, O vile one,
O thou toad, in three will burst thou,
If I should seek out your mother,
And should search for your ancestress. 690
Well I know thy birth, vile creature,
Whence thou comest, earthly horror:
Ogress Syöjätär's your mother,
And the sea-fiend was your parent;.

Syöjätär she spat in water,
In the waves she left the spittle,
By the wind 'twas rocked thereafter,
Tossed upon the water-current;
Thus for six years it was shaken,
Thus for seven whole summers drifted, 700
On the ocean's shining surface,
And upon the swelling billows.
Thus for long the water stretched it,
By the sun 'twas warmed and softened,
To the land the billows drove it,
On the beach a wave upcast it.

Walked three Daughters of Creation
On the beach of stormy ocean,
On the beach, the waves that bounded,
On the beach they saw the spittle, 710
And they spoke the words which follow:
'What might perhaps of this be fashioned,
If a life by the Creator,
And if eyes were granted to it?'

This was heard by the Creator,
And he spoke the words which follow:
'Evil only comes from evil,
And a toad from toad's foul vomit,
If I gave a life unto it,
And if eyes were granted to it.'   720

But the words were heard by Hiisi,
One for mischief always ready,
And he set about creating;
Hiisi gave a life unto it,
Of the slime of toad disgusting,
From Syöjätär's filthy spittle,
Formed from this a twisting serpent,
To a black snake he transformed it.

Whence the life he gave unto it?   730
Life he brought from Hiisi's coal-heap.
Whence was then its heart created?
Out of Syöjätär's own heartstrings.
Whence the brains for this foul creature?
From a mighty torrent's foaming.
Whence its sense obtained the monster?
From a furious cataract's foaming.
Whence a head, this foul enchantment?
From the bean, a bean all rotten.

Whence were then its eyes created?   740
From a seed of flax of Lempo.
Whence were the toad's ears created?
From the leaves of Lempo's birch-tree.
Whence was then its mouth constructed?
Syöjätär's own mouth supplied it.
Whence the tongue in mouth so evil?
From the spear of Keitolainen.
Teeth for such an evil creature?
From the awns of Tuoni's barley.
Whence its filthy gums created?
From the gums of Kalma's maiden.   750
Whence was then its back constructed?
Of the coals of Hiisi's fire.

Whence its wriggling tail constructed?
From the plaits of self the Evil.
Whence its entails were constructed?
These were drawn from Death's own girdle.

This thy origin, O serpent,
This thy honour, as reported!
Black snake from the world infernal,
Serpent of the hue of Tuoni,   760
Hue of earth, and hue of heather,
All the colours of the rainbow.
Go from out the wanderer's pathway,
From before the travelling hero,
Yield the pathway to the traveller,
Make a way for Lemminkäinen
To the feast at Pohja holden,
Where they hold the great carousal!"

Then the snake obeyed his orders,
And the hundred-eyed drew backward,   770
And the great snake twisted sideways,
Turning in a new direction,
Giving thus the traveller pathway,
Making way for Lemminkäinen
To the feast at Pohja holden,
And the secret-held carousal.

XXVII The duel at Pohjola

Lemminkäinen comes to Pohjola and behaves with the greatest inso-
lence (1–204). The Lord of Pohjola grows angry, and as he can do
nothing against Lemminkäinen by magic, he challenges him to a duel
(205–82). In the course of the duel Lemminkäinen strikes off the head
of the Lord of Pohjola, and to avenge this, the Mistress of Pohjola
raises an army against him (283–420).

Now that I have brought my Kauko,
Carried Ahto Saarelainen,
Often past Death's jaw expanded,
Past the very tongue of Kalma,
To the banquet held at Pohja,
And to the concealed carousal,
Now must I relate in detail,
And my tongue relate in fulness,
How the lively Lemminkäinen,
He the handsome Kaukomieli,   10
To the homestead came of Pohja,
Halls of Sariola the misty,
Uninvited to the banquet,
To the drinking-bout unbidden.

Thus the lively Lemminkäinen,
Ruddy youth, and arrant scoundrel,
In the room at once came forward,
Walking to the very middle;
'Neath him swayed the floor of linden,
And the room of firwood rattled.   20

Spoke the lively Lemminkäinen,
And he said the words which follow:
"Greetings to ye on my coming,
Greetings also to the greeter!
Hearken, Pohjola's great Master,

Have you here within this dwelling,
Barley for the horse's fodder,
Beer to offer to the hero?"

There sat Pohjola's great Master,
At the end of the long table,   30
And from thence he made his answer,
In the very words which follow:
"Perhaps there is within this dwelling,
Standing room for your fine courser,
Nor would I indeed forbid you
In the room a quiet corner,
Or to stand within the doorway,
In the doorway, 'neath the rafters,
In the space between two kettles,
There where three large hooks are hanging."   40

Then the lively Lemminkäinen
Tore his black beard in his anger,
'Twas the colour of a kettle,
And he spoke the words which follow:
"Lempo might perchance be willing,
Thus to stand within the doorway,
Where he might with soot be dirtied,
While the soot falls all around him!
But at no time did my father,   50
Never did my aged father
Ever stand in such a station,
In the doorway, 'neath the rafters!
There was always room sufficient
For his horse within the stable,
And a clean room for the hero,
And a place to put his gloves in,
Pegs whereon to hang his mittens,
Walls where swords may rest in order.
Why should I not also find it,
As my father always found it?"   60

After this he strode on further,
To the end of the long table,
At the bench-end then he sat him,
At the end of bench of firwood,

And the bench it cracked beneath him,
And the bench of firwood tottered.

Said the lively Lemminkäinen,
"Seems to me that I'm unwelcome,
As no ale is offered to me,
To the guest who just has entered."   70

Ilpotar, the noble Mistress,
Answered in the words which follow:
"O thou boy, O Lemminkäinen,
Not as guest thou com'st among us,
But upon my head to trample,
And to make it bow before you,
For our ale is still in barley,
Still in malt the drink delicious,
And the wheatbread still unbaken,
And unboiled the meat remaineth.   80
Yesternight you should have entered,
Or perchance have come to-morrow."

Then the lively Lemminkäinen,
Twisted mouth and turned his head round,
Tore his black beard in his anger,
And he spoke the words which follow:
"Eaten is the feast already,
Finished feast, and drunk the bride-ale,
And the ale has been divided,
To the men the mead been given,   90
And the cans away been carried,
And the pint-pots laid in storage!

Pohjola's illustrious Mistress,
Long-toothed Mistress of Pimentola!
Thou hast held the wedding badly,
And in doggish fashion held it,
Baked the bread in loaves enormous,
Thou hast brewed the beer of barley,
Six times sent thy invitations,
Nine times hast thou sent a summons,   100
Thou hast asked the poor, the wretched,
Asked the scum, and asked the wastrels,

Asked the leanest of the loafers,
Labourers with one garment only;
All folks else thou hast invited,
Me rejected, uninvited.

Wherefore should I thus be treated,
When I sent myself the barley?
Others brought it by the spoonful,
Others poured it out by dishfuls,   110
But I poured it out in bushels,
By the half-ton out I poured it,
Of my own, the best of barley,
Corn which I had sown aforetime.

'Tis not now that Lemminkäinen,
Is a guest of great distinction,
For no ale is offered to me,
Nor the pot set on the fire.
In the pot is nothing cooking,
Not a pound of pork you give me,   120
Neither food nor drink you give me,
Now my weary journey's ended."

Ilpotar, the noble Mistress,
Uttered then the words which follow:
"O my little waiting-maiden,
O my ever-ready servant,
Put into the pot some dinner,
Bring some ale to give the stranger!"

Then the girl, the child so wretched,
Washed the worst of all the dishes,   130
And the spoons she then was wiping,
And the ladles she was scouring,
Then into the pot put dinner:
Bones of meat, and heads of fishes,
Very ancient stalks of turnips,
Crusts of bread of stony hardness,
And a pint of ale she brought him,
And a can of filthy victuals,
Gave it lively Lemminkäinen,
That he should drink out the refuse,   140

And she spoke the words which follow:
"If you are indeed a hero,
Can you drink the ale I bring you,
Nor upset the can that holds it?"

Lemminkäinen, youth so lively,
Looked at once into the pint-pot,
And below a worm was creeping,
In the midst there crept a serpent,
On the edge were serpents creeping,
Lizards also there were gliding.   150

Said the lively Lemminkäinen,
Loudly grumbled Kaukomieli,
"Off to Tuonela the bearer,
Quick to Manala the handmaid,
Ere the moon again has risen,
Or this very day is ended!"
Afterwards these words he added,
"O thou beer, thou drink so nasty,
In an evil hour concocted,
Evil only lurks within thee!   160
Notwithstanding I will drink it,
On the ground will cast the refuse,
With my nameless finger lift it,
With my left thumb will I lift it."

Then he felt into his pocket,
And within his pouch was searching,
Took an angle from his pocket,
Iron hooks from out his satchel,
Dropped it down into the pint-pot,
In the ale began to angle: 170
Hooked the snakes upon his fish-hooks,
On his hooks the evil vipers,
Up he drew of toads a hundred,
And of dusky snakes a thousand.
Down upon the ground he threw them,
Threw them all upon the planking;
Thereupon a sharp knife taking,
From the sheath he quickly drew it,

Cut the heads from off the serpents,
Broke the necks of all the serpents.   180
Then he drank the ale with gusto,
Drank the black mead with enjoyment,
And he spoke the words which follow:
"As a guest I am not honoured,
Since no ale was brought unto me
Which was better worth my drinking,
Offered me by hands more careful,
In a larger vessel brought me;
Since no ram was slaughtered for me,
No gigantic steer was slaughtered,   190
In the hall no ox they brought me,
From the house of hoofed cattle."

Then did Pohjola's great Master,
Answer in the words which follow:
"Wherefore have you then come hither,
Who invited you among us?"

Answered lively Lemminkäinen,
Said the handsome Kaukomieli:
"Good is perhaps the guest invited,
Better still if uninvited.   200
Hearken then, thou son of Pohja,
Pohjola's illustrious Master,
Give me ale for cash directly,
Reach me here some drink for money!"

Then did Pohjola's great Master,
Angry grow and greatly furious,
Very furious and indignant,
Sang a pond upon the flooring,
In the front of Lemminkäinen,
And he said the words which follow: 210
"Here's a river you may drink of,
Here's a pond that you may splash in."

Little troubled Lemminkäinen,
And he spoke the words which follow:

"I'm no calf by women driven,
Nor a bull with tail behind me,
That I drink of river-water,
Or from filthy ponds the water."

Then himself began to conjure,
And himself commenced his singing,   220
Sang upon the floor a bullock,
Mighty ox with horns all golden,
And he soon drank up the puddle,
Drank the river up with pleasure.

But the mighty son of Pohja,
By his spells a wolf created,
And upon the floor he sang him,
To devour the fleshy bullock.

Lemminkäinen, youth so lively,
Sang a white hare to his presence,   230
And upon the floor 'twas leaping,
Near the wolf jaws widely opened.

But the mighty son of Pohja,
Sang a dog with pointed muzzle;
And the dog the hare devoured,
Rent the Squint-eye into fragments.

Lemminkäinen, youth so lively,
On the rafters sang a squirrel,
And it frolicked on the rafters,
And the dog was barking at it.   240

But the mighty son of Pohja,
Sang a golden-breasted marten,
And the marten seized the squirrel,
On the rafter's end while sitting.

Lemminkäinen, youth so lively,
Sang a fox of ruddy colour,
And it killed the gold-breast marten,
And destroyed the handsome-haired one.

But the mighty son of Pohja
By his spells a hen created, 250
And upon the ground 'twas walking,
Just before the fox's muzzle.

Lemminkäinen, youth so lively,
Thereupon a hawk created,
Quickly with its claws it seized it,
And it tore the hen to pieces.

Then said Pohjola's great Master,
In the very words which follow:
"Better will not be the banquet,
Nor the guest-provision lessened. 260
House for work, the road for strangers,
Unrefreshed from the carousal!
Quit this place, O scamp of Hiisi,
Haste away from all folks' knowledge,
To thy home, O toad the basest,
Forth, O scoundrel, to thy country!"

Answered lively Lemminkäinen,
Said the handsome Kaukomieli,
"None would let himself be banished,
Not a man, how bad soever, 270
From this place be ever driven,
Forced to fly from such a station."

Then did Pohjola's great Master,
Snatch his sword from wall where hanging,
Grasp in haste the sharpened weapon,
And he spoke the words which follow:
"O thou Ahti Saarelainen,
O thou handsome Kaukomieli!
Let us match our swords together,
Match the glitter of the sword-blades, 280
Whether my sword is the better,
Or is Ahti Saarelainen's!"

Said the lively Lemminkäinen,
"Little of my sword is left me,

For on bones it has been shattered,
And on skulls completely broken!
But let this be as it may be,
If no better feast is ready,
Let us struggle, and determine
Which of our two swords is favoured!   290
Ne'er in former times my father
In a duel had been worsted,
Why should then his son be different,
Or his child be like a baby?"

Sword he took, and bared his sword blade,
And he drew his sharp-edged weapon,
Drew it from the leather scabbard,
Hanging at his belt of lambskin.
Then they measured and inspected
Which of their two swords was longer,   300
And a very little longer,
Was the sword of Pohja's Master,
As upon the nail of blackness,
Or a half-joint of a finger.

Spoke then Ahti Saarelainen,
Said the handsome Kaukomieli,
"As your sword is rather longer,
Let the first attack be yours."

Then did Pohjola's great Master,
Aim a blow, and tried to strike him,   310
Aimed his sword, but never struck it,
On the head of Lemminkäinen.
Once indeed he struck the rafters,
And the beams resounded loudly,
And across the beam was shattered,
And the arch in twain was broken.

Then spoke Ahti Saarelainen,
Said the handsome Kaukomieli:
"Well, what mischief did the rafters,
And what harm the beam effected,   320
That you thus attack the rafters,
And have made the arch to rattle?

Hear me, son of Pohja's country,
Pohjola's illustrious Master!
Awkward 'tis in room to combat,
Trouble would it give the women,
If the clean room should be damaged,
And with blood defiled the flooring.
Let us go into the courtyard,
In the field outside to battle,   330
On the grass outside to combat.
In the yard the blood looks better,
In the yard it looks more lovely,
On the snow it looks more fitting."

Out into the yard they wandered,
And they found therein a cowhide,
And they spread it in the courtyard,
And they took their stand upon it.
Then said Ahti Saarelainen,
"Hearken, O thou son of Pohja!   340
As your sword is rather longer,
And your sword is more terrific,
Perhaps indeed you need to use it,
Just before your own departure,
Or before your neck is broken.
Strike away, O son of Pohja!"

Fenced away the son of Pohja,
Struck a blow, and struck a second,
And he struck a third blow after,
But he could not strike him fairly,   350
Could not scratch the flesh upon him,
From his skin a single bristle.

Then spoke Ahti Saarelainen,
Said the handsome Kaukomieli,
"Give me leave to try a little,
For at last my time is coming!"

Natheless Pohjola's great Master,
Did not pay the least attention,
Striking on, without reflection,

Ever striking, never hitting.   360
From his sword-blade flashed red fire,
And its edge was always gleaming
In the hands of Lemminkäinen,
And the sheen extended further,
As against the neck he turned it
Of the mighty son of Pohja.

Said the handsome Lemminkäinen,
"Hearken, Pohjola's great Master,
True it is, thy neck so wretched,
Is as red as dawn of morning.   370

Thereupon the son of Pohja,
He, the mighty lord of Pohja,
Bent his eyes that he might witness
How his own neck has been reddened.
Then the lively Lemminkäinen,
Hurriedly a stroke delivered,
With his sword he struck the hero,
Quickly with the sword he struck him.

Full and fair he struck the hero,
Struck his head from off his shoulders,   380
And the skull from neck he severed,
As from off the stalk a turnip,
Or an ear of corn is severed,
From a fish a fin divided.
In the yard the head went rolling,
And the skull in the enclosure,
As when it is struck by arrow
Falls the capercail from tree-top.

In the ground stood stakes a hundred,
In the yard there stood a thousand,   390
On the stakes were heads a hundred,
Only one stake still was headless.
Then the lively Lemminkäinen
Took the head of the poor fellow;
From the ground the skull he lifted,
And upon the stake he set it.

Then did Ahti Saarelainen,
He the handsome Kaukomieli,
Once again the house re-enter,
And he spoke the words which follow: 400
"Wicked maid, now bring me water,
That I wash my hands and cleanse them,
From the blood of wicked Master,
From the gore of man of evil!"

Furious was the Crone of Pohja,
Wild with wrath and indignation,
And at once she sang up swordsmen,
Heroes well equipped for battle.
Up she sang a hundred swordsmen,
Sang a thousand weapon-bearers,   410
Lemminkäinen's head to capture,
From the neck of Kaukomieli.

Now the time seemed really coming,
Fitting time for his departure,
Terror came at length upon him,
And too hard the task before him;
From the house the youthful Ahti
Lemminkäinen quick departed,
From the feast prepared at Pohja,
From the unannounced carousal.   420

XXVIII Lemminkäinen and his mother

Lemminkäinen escapes with all speed from Pohjola, comes home and asks his mother where he can hide himself from the people of Pohjola, who will soon attack him in his home, a hundred to one (1–164). His mother reproaches him for his expedition to Pohjola, suggests various places of concealment, and at length advises him to go far across the lakes to a distant island, where his father once lived in peace during a year of great war (165–294).

Then did Ahti Saarelainen,
He the lively Lemminkäinen,
Haste to reach a place for hiding,
Hasten quickly to remove him
From the dreary land of Pohja,
From the gloomy house of Sara.
From the room he rushed like blizzard,
To the yard like snake he hurried,
That he might escape the evil,
From the crime he had committed.   10
When he came into the courtyard,
Then he gazed around and pondered,
Seeking for the horse he left there,
But he nowhere saw him standing;
In the field a stone was standing,
On the waste a clump of willows.

Who will come to give him counsel,
Who will now advise and help him,
That his head come not in danger,
And his hair remain uninjured,   20
Nor his handsome hair be draggled
In the courtyard foul of Pohja?
In the village heard he shouting,
Uproar too from other homesteads,
Lights were shining in the village,
Eyes were at the open windows.

Then must lively Lemminkäinen,
Then must Ahti Saarelainen,
Alter now his shape completely,
And transform without delaying,   30
And must soar aloft as eagle,
Up to heaven to soar attempting;
But the sun his face was scorching,
And the moon shone on his temples.

Then the lively Lemminkäinen,
Sent aloft a prayer to Ukko:
"Ukko, Jumala most gracious,
Thou the wisest in the heavens,
Of the thunderclouds the leader,
Of the scattered clouds the ruler!   40
Let it now be gloomy weather,
And a little cloudlet give me,
So that under its protection
I may hasten homeward quickly,
Homeward to my dearest mother,
Unto the revered old woman!"

As he flew upon his journey,
As he chanced to look behind him,
There he saw a hawk, a grey one,
And its eyes were fiery-glowing,   50
As it were the son of Pohja,
Like the former lord of Pohja.

And the grey hawk called unto him,
"Ahti, O my dearest brother,
Think you on our former combat,
Head to head in equal contest?"

Then said Ahti Saarelainen,
Said the handsome Kaukomieli,
"O my hawk, my bird so charming,
Turn thyself and hasten homeward,   60
To the place from which you started,
To the gloomy land of Pohja.
Hard it is to catch the eagle,
Clutch the strong-winged bird with talons."

Then he hurried quickly homeward,
Homeward to his dearest mother,
And his face was full of trouble,
And his heart with care o'erladen.

Then his mother came to meet him,
As along the path he hurried,   70
As he past the fence was walking,
And his mother first bespoke him:
"O my son, my son, my youngest,
Thou the strongest of my children!
Why returnest thou so sadly,
Home from Pohjola's dark regions?
Hast thou harmed thyself by drinking
At the drinking-bout of Pohja?
If the goblet made thee suffer,
Here a better one awaits thee,   80
Which thy father won in battle,
Which he fought for in the contest."

Said the lively Lemminkäinen,
"O my mother who hast borne me!
If the goblet made me suffer,
I would overcome the masters,
Overcome a hundred heroes,
And would face a thousand heroes."

Then said Lemminkäinen's mother,
"Wherefore art thou then in trouble?   90
If the horse has overcome you,
Wherefore let the horse annoy you?
If the horse has overcome you,
You should buy yourself a better,
With your father's lifelong savings,
Which the aged man provided!"

Said the lively Lemminkäinen,
"O my mother who hast borne me!
If I quarrelled with the courser,
Or the foal had over-reached me,   100
I myself have shamed the masters,
Overcome the horses' drivers,

Foals and drivers I have vanquished,
And the heroes with their coursers."

Then said Lemminkäinen's mother,
"Wherefore art thou then in trouble,
Wherefore is thy heart so troubled,
As from Pohjola thou comest?
Have the women laughed about you,
Or the maidens ridiculed you?   110
If the women laughed about you,
Or the maidens ridiculed you,
There are maidens to be jeered at,
Other women to be laughed at."

Said the lively Lemminkäinen,
"O my mother who hast borne me,
If the women laughed about me,
Or the maidens ridiculed me,
I would laugh at all their menfolk,
And would wink at all the maidens;   120
I would shame a hundred women,
And a thousand brides would make them."

Then said Lemminkäinen's mother,
"What has chanced, my son, my darling,
Hast thou perhaps encountered something
As to Pohjola thou wentest?
Have you eaten perhaps too freely,
Eaten much, too much have drunken,
Or at night perchance when resting
Have you seen a dream of evil?"   130

Then the lively Lemminkäinen,
Answered in the words which follow:
"Perhaps old women may remember,
What in sleep they saw in vision!
Though my nightly dreams I think on,
Yet are those of daytime better.
O my mother, aged woman,
Fill my bag with fresh provisions,
With a good supply of flour,
And a lump of salt add likewise,   140

For thy son must travel further,
Journey to another country,
Journey from this house beloved,
Journey from this lovely dwelling,
For the men their swords are whetting,
And the lance-tips they are sharpening."

Then his mother interrupted,
Asking him his cause of trouble:
"Wherefore whet the men their sword-blades,
Wherefore sharpen they the lance-tips?"   150

Answered lively Lemminkäinen,
Said the handsome Kaukomieli,
"Therefore do they whet their sword-blades,
Therefore they the lance-tips sharpen:
On the head of me unhappy,
On my neck to bring destruction.
From a quarrel rose a duel,
There in Pohjola's enclosure;
I have slain the son of Pohja,
Slain the very lord of Pohja,   160
Then rose Pohjola to battle,
Close behind me comes the tumult,
Raging all for my destruction,
To surround a single warrior."

Then his mother gave him answer,
To her child the old crone answered:
"I myself already told you,
And I had already warned you,
And forbidden you most strictly
Not to Pohjola to venture.   170
Had you stayed at home in quiet,
Living in your mother's dwelling,
Safely in your parent's homestead,
In the home of her who bore thee,
Then no war had ever risen,
Nor appeared a cause of contest.
Whither now, my son unhappy,
Canst thou flee, unhappy creature,
Go to hide thee from destruction,

Flying from thy wicked action,   180
Lest thy wretched head be captured,
And thy handsome neck be severed,
That thy hair remain uninjured,
Nor thy glossy hair downtrodden?"

Said the lively Lemminkäinen,
"No such refuge do I know of,
Where a safe retreat awaits me,
Where I from my crime can hide me.
O my mother who hast borne me,
Where do you advise my hiding?"   190

Answered Lemminkäinen's mother,
And she spoke the words which follow:
"No, I know not where to hide you,
Where to hide you or to send you.
As a pine upon the mountain,
Juniper in distant places,
There might still misfortune find thee,
Evil fate might rise against thee:
Often is the mountain pine-tree
Cut to pieces into torches,   200
And the juniper on heathland,
Into posts is often cloven.
As a birch-tree in the valley,
Or an alder in the greenwood,
There might still misfortune find thee:
Evil fate might rise against thee:
Often is the valley birch-tree
Chopped to pieces into faggots,
Often is the alder-thicket
Cut away to make a clearing.   210

As a berry on the mountain,
Or upon the heath a cranberry,
Or upon the plain a strawberry,
Or in other spots a bilberry,
There might still misfortune find thee,
Evil fate might rise against thee:
For the girls might come to pluck thee,
Tin-adorned ones might uproot thee.

In the lake as pike when hiding,
Powan in slow-flowing river,   220
There misfortune still might find thee:
And at last destruction reach thee:
If there came a youthful fisher,
He might cast his net in water,
And the young in net might take thee,
And the old with net might capture.

Didst thou roam as wolf in forest,
Or a bear in rugged country,
There might still misfortune find thee,
Evil fate might rise against thee: 230
If a sooty tramp was passing,
He perchance might spear the growler,
Or the wolves bring to destruction,
And the forest bears might slaughter."

Then the lively Lemminkäinen
Answered in the words which follow:
"I myself know evil places,
Worst of all do I esteem them,
There where any death might seize me,
And at last destruction reach me.   240
O my mother who hast reared me,
Mother who thy milk hast given!
Whither would'st thou bid me hide me,
Whither should I now conceal me?
Death's wide jaws are just before me,
At my beard destruction's standing,
Every day for me it waiteth,
Till my ruin is accomplished."

Then said Lemminkäinen's mother,
And she spoke the words which follow: 250
"I can tell the best of places,
Tell you one the best of any,
Where to hide yourself completely,
And your crime conceal for ever,
For I know a little country,
Know a very little refuge,
Wasted not, and safe from battle,

And untrodden by the swordsmen.
Swear me now by oaths eternal,
Binding, free from all deception,   260
In the course of six, ten summers,
Nevermore to go to battle,
Neither for the love of silver,
Nor perchance if gold was needed."

Then said lively Lemminkäinen,
"Now I swear by oaths the strongest,
Never in the first of summers,
Nor in any other summer,
Mix myself in mighty battles,
In the clashing of the sword-blades.   270
Wounds are still upon my shoulders,
In my breast deep wounds still rankle,
From my former battle-pleasures,
In the midst of all the tumult,
In the midst of mighty battles,
Where the heroes all contended."

Then did Lemminkäinen's mother
Answer in the words which follow:
"Take the boat your father left you,
And betake yourself to hiding.   280
Traverse nine lakes in succession,
Half the tenth one must thou traverse,
To an island on its surface,
Where the cliffs arise from water.
There in former times your father
Hid, and kept himself in safety,
In the furious fights of summer,
In the hardest years of battle.
There you'll find a pleasant dwelling,
And a charming place to linger.   290
Hide thyself a year, a second,
In the third year come thou homeward,
To your father's well-known homestead,
To the dwelling of your parents."

XXIX   Lemminkäinen's adventures on the island

Lemminkäinen sails across the lakes in his boat and comes safely to the island (1–180). There he lives pleasantly among the girls and women till the return of the men from warfare, who conspire against him (181–290). Lemminkäinen flies from the island, much to the grief both of the girls and himself (291–402). His boat is wrecked in a violent storm, but he escapes by swimming to land, makes a new boat, and arrives safely on the shores of his own country (403–52). He finds his old house burned, and the whole surroundings laid waste, when he begins to weep and lament, especially for the loss of his mother (453–514). His mother, however, is still alive, having taken refuge in a thick forest where Lemminkäinen finds her to his great joy (515–46). She relates how the army of Pohjola came and burned down the house. Lemminkäinen promises to build a finer house after he has revenged himself upon the people of Pohjola, and describes his pleasant life in the island of refuge (547–602).

Lemminkäinen, youth so lively,
He the handsome Kaukomieli,
Took provisions in his satchel,
In his wallet summer-butter,
Butter for a year to last him,
For another, pork sufficient,
Then he travelled off to hide him,
Started in the greatest hurry,
And he said the words which follow:
"Now I go, and I'm escaping,   10
For the space of three whole summers,
And for five years in succession.
Be the land to snakes abandoned,
Let the lynxes snarl in greenwood,
In the fields the reindeer wander,
In the brakes the geese conceal them.

Fare thee well, my dearest mother!
If the people come from Pohja,
From Pimentola the army,
And about my head they ask you,   20
Say that I have fled before them,
And have taken my departure,
And I have laid waste my clearing,
That which I had reaped so lately!"

Then he pushed his boat in water,
On the waves he launched his vessel,
From the rollers steel he launched it,
From the haven lined with copper.
On the mast the sails he hoisted,
And he spread the sails of linen,   30
At the stern himself he seated,
And prepared him for his journey,
Sitting by his birchwood rudder,
With the stern-oar deftly steering.

Then he spoke the words which follow,
And in words like these expressed him:
"Wind, inflate the sails above me,
Wind of spring, drive on the vessel,
Drive with speed the wooden vessel,
Onward drive the boat of pinewood   40
Forward to the nameless island,
And the nameless promontory!"

So the wind the bark rocked onward,
O'er the foaming lake 'twas driven,
O'er the bright expanse of water,
Speeding o'er the open water,
Rocking while two moons were changing,
Till a third was near its ending.

At the cape were maidens sitting,
There upon the blue sea's margin   50
They were gazing, and were casting
Glances o'er the azure billows.
One was waiting for her brother,
And another for her father,

But the others all were waiting,
Waiting each one for a lover.

In the distance spied they Kauko,
Sooner still the boat of Kauko,
Like a little cloud in distance,
Just between the sky and water.   60

And the island-maids reflected,
Said the maidens of the island:
"What's this strange thing in the water,
What this wonder on the billows?
If a boat of our relations,
Sailing vessel of our island,
Hasten then, and speed thee homeward,
To the harbour of the island,
That we hear the tidings quickly,
Hear the news from foreign countries,   70
If there's peace among the shore-folks,
Or if war is waged among them."

Still the wind the sail inflated,
And the billows drove the vessel.
Soon the lively Lemminkäinen
Guided to the isle the vessel,
To the island's point he drove it,
Where it ends in jutting headland.

And he said on his arrival,
To the cape as he was coming,   80
"Is there room upon this island,
On the surface of this island,
Where the boat may land upon it,
And to dry land I may bring it?"

Said the girls upon the island,
And the island-maidens answered:
"There is room upon this island,
On the surface of the island,
Where the boat may land upon it,
And to dry land you may bring it.   90
There are havens for the vessel,

On the beach sufficient rollers,
To receive a hundred vessels,
Though the boats should come by thousands."

Then the lively Lemminkäinen
On the land drew up his vessel,
On the wooden rollers laid it,
And he spoke the words which follow:
"Is there room upon this island,
On the surface of the island,   100
Where a little man may hide him,
And a weak man may take refuge

From the din of furious battle,
And the clash of steely sword-blades?"
Said the girls upon the island,
And the island-maidens answered:
"There is room upon this island,
On the surface of the island,
Where a little man may hide him:
And a weak man may conceal him.   110
Here are very many castles,
Stately mansions to reside in,
Though there came a hundred heroes,
And a thousand men of valour."

Said the lively Lemminkäinen,
And he spoke the words which follow:
"Is there room upon this island,
On the surface of the island,
Where there stands a birch-tree forest,
And a stretch of other country,   120
Where I perhaps may make a clearing,
Cultivate my goodly clearing?"

Said the girls upon the island,
And the island-maidens answered:
"There is not upon this island,
On the surface of the island,
Not the space your back could rest on,
Land not of a bushel's measure,
Where you perhaps might make a clearing,

Cultivate your goodly clearing.   130
All the land is now divided,
And the fields in plots are measured,
And allotted are the fallows,
Grassland managed by the commune."

Said the lively Lemminkäinen,
Asked the handsome Kaukomieli,
"Is there room upon this island,
On the surface of the island,
Space where I my songs may carol,
Space where I may sing my ballads?   140
Words within my mouth are melting,
And between my gums are sprouting."

Said the girls upon the island,
And the island-maidens answered:
"There is room upon this island,
On the surface of the island,
Space where you may sing your ballads,
And intone your splendid verses,
While you sport amid the greenwood,
While you dance among the meadows."   150

Then the lively Lemminkäinen
Hastened to commence his singing.
In the courts sang mountain-ashtrees,
In the farmyards oaks grew upward.
On the oaks were equal branches,
And on every branch an acrorn,
Golden globes within the acorns,
And upon the globes were cuckoos.
When the cuckoos all were calling,
From their mouths was gold distilling,   160
From their beaks was copper flowing,
Likewise silver pouring onward
To the hills all golden-shining,
And among the silver mountains.

Once again sang Lemminkäinen,
Once again he sang and chanted,
Gravel sang to pearls of beauty,

All the stones to gleaming lustre,
All the stones to glowing redness,
And the flowers to golden glory.   170

Then again sang Lemminkäinen;
In the yard a well created,
O'er the well a golden cover,
And on this a golden bucket,
That the lads might drink the water,
And their sisters wash their faces.

Ponds he sang upon the meadows,
In the ponds blue ducks were floating,
Temples golden, heads of silver,
And their webs were all of copper.   180

Then the island maidens wondered,
And the girls were all astounded
At the songs of Lemminkäinen,
And the craft of this great hero.

Said the lively Lemminkäinen,
Spoke the handsome Kaukomieli,
"I have sung a song most splendid,
But perchance might sing a better,
If beneath a roof I sang it,   190
At the end of the deal table.
If a house you cannot give me,
There to rest upon the planking,
I will hum my tunes in forest,
Toss my songs among the bushes."

Said the maidens of the island,
Answered after full reflection:
"There are houses you may enter,
Handsome halls that you may dwell in,
Safe from cold to sing your verses,
In the open speak your magic."   200

Then the lively Lemminkäinen,
Entered in a house directly,
Where he sang a row of pint-pots,
At the end of the long table.

All the pots with ale were brimming,
And the cans with mead the finest,
Filled as full as one could fill them,
Dishes filled to overflowing.
In the pots was beer in plenty,
And the mead in covered tankards,   210
Butter too, in great abundance,
Pork was likewise there in plenty,
For the feast of Lemminkäinen,
And for Kaukomieli's pleasure.

Kauko was of finest manners,
Nor to eat was he accustomed,
Only with a knife of silver,
Fitted with a golden handle.
So he sang a knife of silver,
And a golden-hafted knife-blade,   220
And he ate till he was sated,
Drank the ale in full contentment.

Then the lively Lemminkäinen,
Roamed about through every village,
For the island-maidens' pleasure,
To delight the braidless damsels,
And where'er his head was turning,
There he found a mouth for kissing,
Wheresoe'er his hand was outstretched,
There he found a hand to clasp it.   230

And at night he went to rest him,
Hiding in the darkest corner;
There was not a single village
Where he did not find ten homesteads,
There was not a single homestead
Where he did not find ten daughters,
There was none among the daughters,
None among the mother's children,
By whose side he did not stretch him,
On whose arm he did not rest him.   240

Thus a thousand brides he found there,
Rested by a hundred widows;

Two in half-a-score remained not,
Three in a completed hundred,
Whom he left untouched as maidens,
Or as widows unmolested.

Thus the lively Lemminkäinen
Lived a life of great enjoyment,
For the course of three whole summers
In the island's pleasant hamlets,　　　　　　250
To the island-maidens' rapture,
The content of all the widows;
One alone he did not trouble:
'Twas a poor and aged maiden,
At the furthest promontory,
In the tenth among the hamlets.

As he pondered on his journey,
And resolved to wend him homeward,
Came the poor and aged maiden,
And she spoke the words which follow:　　260
"Handsome hero, wretched Kauko,
If you will not think upon me,
Then I wish that as you travel,
May your boat on rocks be stranded."

Rose he not before the cockcrow,
Nor before the hen's child rose he,
From his sporting with the maiden,
Laughing with the wretched woman.

Then upon a day it happened,
And upon a certain evening,　　　　　　　270
He resolved to rise and wander,
Waiting not for morn or cockcrow.

Long before the time he rose up,
Sooner than the time intended,
And he went around to wander,
And to wander through the village,
For his sporting with that damsel,
To amuse the wretched woman.

As alone by night he wandered,
Through the villages he sauntered   280
To the isle's extremest headland,
To the tenth among the hamlets,
He beheld not any homestead
Where three rooms he did not notice,
There was not a room among them
Where he did not see three heroes,
And he saw not any hero,
With a sword-blade left unwhetted,
Sharpened thus to bring destruction
On the head of Lemminkäinen.   290

Then the lively Lemminkäinen
Spoke aloud the words which follow:
"Woe to me, the day is dawning,
And the pleasant sun is rising
O'er a youth, of all most wretched,
O'er the neck of me unhappy!
Lempo may perchance a hero
With his shirt protect and cover,
Perhaps will cover with his mantle,
Cast it round him for protection   300
Though a hundred men attack him,
And a thousand press upon him!"

Unembraced he left the maidens,
And he left them unmolested,
And he turned him to his vessel,
Luckless to his boat he hurried:
But he found it burned to ashes,
Utterly consumed to ashes!

Mischief now he saw approaching,
O'er his head ill days were brooding,   310
So began to build a vessel,
And a new boat to construct him.

Wood was failing to the craftsman,
Boards with which a boat to fashion,
But he found of wood a little,
Begged some wretched bits of boarding:

Five small splinters of a spindle,
And six fragments of a bobbin.

So from these a boat he fashioned,
And a new boat he constructed,   320
By his magic art he made it,
With his secret knowledge made it,
Hammered once, one side he fashioned,
Hammered twice, called up the other,
Hammered then a third time only,
And the boat was quite completed.

Then he pushed the boat in water,
On the waves he launched the vessel,
And he spoke the words which follow,
And expressed himself in thiswise: 330
"Float like bladder on the water,
On the waves like water-lily!
Eagle, give me now three feathers,
Eagle, three, and two from raven,
For the wretched boat's protection,
For the wretched vessel's bulwarks!"

Then he stepped upon the planking,
At the stern he took his station,
Head bowed down, in deep depression,
With his head all sadly drooping,   340
Since by night he dare not tarry,
Nor by day could linger longer,
For the island-maidens' pleasure,
Sporting with the braided damsels.

Spoke the lively Lemminkäinen,
Said the handsome Kaukomieli:
"Now the youth must take departure,
And must travel from these dwellings,
Joyless leave behind these damsels,
Dance no longer with the fair ones.   350
Surely when I have departed,
And have left this land behind me,
Never will rejoice these damsels,
Nor the braided girls be jesting,

In their homes so full of sadness,
In the courtyards now so dreary."

Wept the island girls already,
Damsels at the cape lamented:
"Wherefore goest thou, Lemminkäinen,
And departest, hero-bridegroom?   360
Dost thou go for maidens' coyness,
Or for scarcity of women?"

Spoke the lively Lemminkäinen,
Said the handsome Kaukomieli,
"'Tis not for the maidens' coyness,
Nor the scarcity of women.
I have had a hundred women,
And embraced a thousand maidens;
Thus departeth Lemminkäinen,
Quits you thus your hero-bridegroom,   370
Since the great desire has seized me,
Longing for my native country,
Longing for my own land's strawberries,
For the slopes where grow the raspberries,
For the maidens on the headland,
And the fair ones of my mansion."

Then the lively Lemminkäinen
Pushed into the waves the vessel,
Blew the wind, and then it blustered;
Rising waves drove on the vessel   380
O'er the surface of the blue sea,
And across the open water.
On the beach there stood the sad ones,
On the shingles the unhappy,
And the island girls were weeping,
And the golden maids lamenting.

Wept for long the island-maidens,
Damsels on the cape lamented,
Long as they could see the masthead,
And the ironwork was gleaming,   390
But they wept not for the masthead,
Nor bewailed the iron fittings,

By the mast they wept the steersman,
He who wrought the iron fittings.

Lemminkäinen too was weeping,
Long he wept, and long was saddened,
Long as he could see the island,
Or the outline of its mountains;
But he wept not for the island,
Nor lamented for the mountains, 400
But he wept the island-damsels,
For the mountain geese lamented.

Then the lively Lemminkäinen
O'er the blue sea took his journey,
And he voyaged one day, a second,
And at length upon the third day
Rose a furious wind against him,
And the whole horizon thundered.
Rose a great wind from the north-west,
And a strong wind from the north-east, 410
Struck one side and then the other,
Thus the vessel overturning.

Then the lively Lemminkäinen
Plunged his hands into the water,
Rowing forward with his fingers,
While his feet he used for steering.

Thus he swam by night and daytime
And with greatest skill he steered him,
And a little cloud perceived he,
In the west a cloud projecting, 420
Which to solid land was changing,
And became a promontory.

On the cape he found a homestead,
Where he found the mistress baking,
And her daughters dough were kneading:
"O thou very gracious mistress,
If you but perceived my hunger,
Thought upon my sad condition,.
You would hurry to the storehouse,

To the alehouse like a snowstorm,   430
And a can of ale would fetch me,
And a strip of pork would fetch me,
In the pan would broil it for me,
And would pour some butter on it,
That the weary man might eat it,
And the fainting hero drink it.
Nights and days have I been swimming
Out upon the ocean's billows,
With the wind as my protector.
At the mercy of the sea-waves."   440

Thereupon the gracious mistress
Hastened to the mountain storehouse,
Sliced some butter in the storehouse,
And a slice of pork provided,
In the pan thereafter broiled it,
That the hungry man might eat it.
Then she fetched of ale a canful,
For the fainting hero's drinking,
And she gave him a new vessel,
And a boat completely finished,   450
Which to other lands should take him,
And convey him to his birthplace.

Then the lively Lemminkäinen
Started on his homeward journey,
Saw the lands and saw the beaches,
Here the islands, there the channels,
Saw the ancient landing-stages,
Saw the former dwelling-places,
And he saw the pine-clad mountains,
All the hills with fir-trees covered,   460
But he found no more his homestead,
And the walls he found not standing;
Where the house before was standing,
Rustled now a cherry-thicket,
On the mound were pine-trees growing,
Juniper beside the well-spring.

Spoke the lively Lemminkäinen,
Said the handsome Kaukomieli,

"I have roamed among these forests,
O'er the stones, and plunged in river,   470
And have played about the meadows,
And have wandered through the cornfields.
Who has spoiled my well-known homestead,
And destroyed my charming dwelling?
They have burned the house to ashes,
And the wind's dispersed the ashes!"

Thereupon he fell to weeping,
And he wept one day, a second,
But he wept not for the homestead,
Nor lamented for the storehouse,   480
But he wept the house's treasure,
Dearer to him than the storehouse.

Then he saw a bird was flying,
And a golden eagle hovering,
And he then began to ask it:
"O my dearest golden eagle,
Can you not perchance inform me,
What has happened to my mother,
To the fair one who has borne me,
To my dear and much-loved mother?"   490

Nothing knew the eagle of her,
Nor the stupid bird could tell him,
Only knew that she had perished;
Said a raven she had fallen,
And had died beneath the sword-blades,
'Neath the battle-axes fallen.

Answered lively Lemminkäinen,
Said the handsome Kaukomieli:
"O my fair one who hast borne me,
O my dear and much-loved mother!   500
Hast thou perished, who hast borne me,
Hast thou gone, O tender mother?
Now thy flesh in earth has rotted,
Fir-trees o'er thy head are growing,
Juniper upon thy ankles,
On thy finger-tips are willows!

Thus my wretched doom has found me,
And an ill reward has reached me,
That my sword I dared to measure,
And I dared to raise my weapons   510
There in Pohjola's great castle,
In the fields of Pimentola.
But my own race now has perished,
Perished now is she who bore me!"

Then he looked, and turned on all sides,
And he saw a trace of footsteps,
Where the grass was lightly trampled,
And the heath was slightly broken.
Then he went the way they led him,
And he found a little pathway;   520
To the forest led the pathway,
And he went in that direction.

Thus he walked a verst, a second,
Hurried through a stretch of country,
And in darkest shades of forest,
In the most concealed recesses,
There he saw a hidden sauna,
Saw a little cottage hidden,
In a cleft two rocks protected,
In a nook between three fir-trees;   530
There he saw his tender mother,
There beheld the aged woman.

Then the lively Lemminkäinen,
Felt rejoiced beyond all measure,
And he spoke the words which follow,
And in words like these expressed him:
"O my very dearest mother,
O my mother, who hast nursed me,
Thou art living still, O mother,
Watchful still, my aged mother!   540
Yet I thought that thou had'st perished,
And wast lost to me for ever,
Perished underneath the sword-blades,
Or beneath the spears had'st fallen,

And I wept my pretty eyes out,
And my handsome cheeks were ruined."

Then said Lemminkäinen's mother,
"True it is that I am living,
But was forced to fly my dwelling,
And to seek a place of hiding   550
In this dark and gloomy forest,
In the most concealed recesses,
When came Pohjola to battle,
Murderous hosts from distant countries,
Seeking but for thee, unhappy,
And our home they laid in ruins,
And they burned the house to ashes,
And they wasted all the holding."

Said the lively Lemminkäinen:
"O my mother, who hast borne me,   560
Do not give thyself to sadness,
Be not sad, and be not troubled!
We will now erect fresh buildings,
Better buildings than the others,
And will wage a war with Pohja,
Overthrowing Lempo's people."

Then did Lemminkäinen's mother
Answer in the words which follow:
"Long hast thou, my son, been absent,
Long, my Kauko, hast been living   570
In a distant foreign country,
Always in the doors of strangers,
On a nameless promontory,
And upon an unknown island."

Answered lively Lemminkäinen,
Said the handsome Kaukomieli:
"There to dwell was very pleasant,
Charming was it there to wander.
There the trees are crimson-shining,
Red the trees, and blue the country,   580
And the pine-boughs shine like silver,

And the flowers of heath all golden,
And the mountains are of honey,
And the rocks are made of hens' eggs,
Flows the mead from withered pine-trees,
Milk flows from the barren fir-trees,
Butter flows from corner-fences,
From the posts the ale is flowing.

There to dwell was very pleasant,
Lovely was it to reside there;   590
Afterwards 'twas bad to live there,
And unfit for me to live there:
They were anxious for the maidens,
And suspicious of the women,
Lest the miserable wenches,
And the fat and wicked creatures,
Might by me be badly treated,
Visited too much at night time.
But I hid me from the maidens,
And the women's daughters guarded,   600
Just as hides the wolf from porkers,
Or the hawks from village poultry."

XXX Lemminkäinen and Tiera

Lemminkäinen goes to ask his former comrade-in-arms, Tiera, to join him in an expedition against Pohjola (1–122). The Mistress of Pohjola sends the Frost against them, who freezes the boat in the sea, and almost freezes the heroes themselves in the boat, but Lemminkäinen restrains it by powerful charms and invocations (123–316). Lemminkäinen and his companions walk across the ice to the shore, wander about in the waste for a long time in a miserable plight, and at last make their way home (317–500).

Ahti, youth without compare,
Lemminkäinen young and lively,
Very early in the morning,
In the very earliest morning,
Sauntered downward to the boathouse,
To the landing-stage he wandered.

There a wooden boat was weeping,
Boat with iron rowlocks grieving:
"Here am I, for sailing ready,
But, O wretched one, rejected.   10
Ahti rows not forth to battle,
For the space of six, ten summers,
Neither for the lust of silver,
Or if need of gold should drive him."

Then the lively Lemminkäinen
Struck his glove upon the vessel,
With embroidered mitten struck it,
And he said the words which follow:
"Care thou not, O deck of pinewood,
Nor lament, O timber-sided.   20
Thou once more shalt go to battle,

And shalt mingle in the combat,
Shalt again be filled with warriors,
Ere to-morrow shall be ended."

Then he went to seek his mother,
And he said the words which follow:
"Do not weep for me, O mother,
Nor lament, thou aged woman,
If I once again must wander,
And again must go to battle;   30
For my mind resolve has taken,
And a plan my brain has seized on,
To destroy the folk of Pohja,
And revenge me on the scoundrels."

To restrain him sought his mother,
And the aged woman warned him:
"Do not go, my son, my dearest,
Thus 'gainst Pohjola to combat!
There perchance might death o'ercome thee,
And destruction fall upon thee."   40

Little troubled Lemminkäinen,
But he thought on his departure,
And he started on his journey,
And he spoke the words which follow:
"Can I find another hero,
Find a man, and find a swordsman,
Who will join in Ahti's battle,
And with all his strength will aid me?

Well is Tiera known unto me,
Well with Kuura I'm acquainted,   50
He will be a second hero,
He's a hero and a swordsman,
He will join in Ahti's battle,
And with all his strength will aid me."

Through the villages he wandered,
Found his way to Tiera's homestead,
And he said on his arrival,
Spoke the object of his coming:

"O my Tiera, faithful comrade,
Of my friends most loved and dearest!   60
Thinkest thou on days departed,
On the life we lived aforetime,
When we wandered forth together,
To the fields of mighty battles?
There was not a single village
Where ten houses were not numbered,
There was none among the houses,
Where ten heroes were not living,
There was none among the heroes,
Not a man, however valiant,   70
None who did not fall before us,
By us twain who was not slaughtered."

At the window worked the father,
And a spear-shaft he was carving;
By the threshold stood the mother,
Busy as she churned the butter;
At the door the ruddy brothers,
And they wrought a sledge's framework;
At the bridge-end stood the sisters,
And the clothes they there were wringing.   80

From the window spoke the father,
And the mother from the threshold,
From the door the ruddy brothers,
From the bridge-end spoke the sisters:
"Tiera cannot go to battle,
Nor may strike with spear in warfare.
Other duties call for Tiera,
He has made a lifelong compact;
For a young wife has he taken,
As the mistress of his household,   90
But untouched is she at present,
Uncaressed is still her bosom."

By the stove was Tiera resting,
By the stove-side Kuura rested,
At the stove one foot he booted,
And the other at the stove-bench,
At the gate his belt he tightened,

In the open girt it round him;
Then did Tiera grasp his spear-shaft,
Not the largest of the largest,   100
Nor the smallest of the smallest,
But a spear of mid dimensions.
On the blade a steed was standing,
On the side a foal was trotting,
At the joint a wolf was howling,
At the haft a bear was growling.

Thus his spear did Tiera brandish,
And he brandished it to whirring,
Hurled it then to fathom-deepness
In the stiff clay of the cornfield,   110
In a bare spot of the meadow,
In a flat spot free from hillocks.

Then his spear was placed by Tiera
With the other spears of Ahti,
And he went and made him ready,
Swift to join in Ahti's battle.

Then did Ahti Saarelainen
Push his boat into the water,
Like a snake in grass when creeping,
Even like a living serpent,   120
And he sailed away to north-west,
On the sea that borders Pohja.

Then did Pohjola's old Mistress
Call the wicked Frost to aid her,
On the sea that borders Pohja,
On the deep and open water,
And she said the words which follow,
Thus she spoke and thus commanded:
"O my Frost, my boy so little,
O thou foster-child I nurtured!   130
Go thou forth where I shall bid thee,
Where I bid thee, and I send thee.
Freeze the boat of that great scoundrel,
Boat of lively Lemminkäinen,
On the ocean's open surface,

On the endless waste of waters!
Freeze thou too the master in it,
Freeze thou in the boat the rascal,
That he nevermore escape thee,
In the course of all his lifetime, 140
If myself I do not loose him,
If myself I do not free him!"

Then the Frost, that wicked fellow,
And a youth the most malicious,
Went upon the sea to freeze it,
And upon the waves he brooded.
Forth he went, as he was ordered,
And upon the land he wandered,
Bit the leaves from off the branches,
Grass from off the flowerless meadows. 150

Then he came upon his journey
To the sea that borders Pohja,
To the endless waste of water,
And upon the first night only
Froze the bays and froze the lakelets,
Hurried forward on the seashore,
But the sea was still unfrozen,
And the waves were still unstiffened.
If a small finch skimmed the water,
On the waves a water-wagtail, 160
Still its claws remained unfrozen,
And its little head unstiffened.

On the second night, however,
He began to work more strongly,
Growing insolent extremely,
And he now grew most terrific,
Then the ice on ice he loaded,
And the great Frost still was freezing,
And with ice he clothed the mountains,
Scattered snow to height of spear-shaft, 170
Froze the boat upon the water,
Ahti's vessel on the billows.

Then he would have frozen Ahti,

And in ice his feet would fasten,
And he seized upon his fingers,
And beneath his toes attacked him.
Angry then was Lemminkäinen,
Very angry and indignant;
Pushed the Frost into the fire,
Pushed him in an iron furnace.   180

With his hands the Frost then seized he,
Grasped him in his fists securely,
And he spoke the words which follow,
And in words like these expressed him:
"Frost O thou, Puhuri's offspring,
Thou, the son of cold of winter,
Do not make my fingers frozen,
Nor my little toes thus stiffen.
Let my ears remain unhandled,
Do not freeze my head upon me!   190

There's enough that may be frozen,
Much is left you for your freezing,
Though the skins of men you freeze not,
Nor the forms of mother's children:
Be the plains and marshes frozen,
Freeze the stones to frozen coldness,
Freeze the willows near the water,
Grasp the aspen till it murmurs,
Peel the bark from off the birch-tree,
And the pine-trees break to pieces,   200
But the men you shall not trouble,
Nor the hair of mother's children!

If this is not yet sufficient,
Other things remain for freezing.
Thou may'st freeze the stones when heated,
And the slabs of stone when glowing,
Thou may'st freeze the iron mountains,
And the rocks of steely hardness,
And the mighty river Vuoksi,
Or the Imatra terrific,   210
Stop the course of raging whirlpool,
Foaming in its utmost fury!

Shall I tell you of your lineage,
And shall I make known your honours?
Surely do I know thy lineage,
All I know of thine uprearing;
For the Frost was born 'mid willows,
Nurtured in the sharpest weather,
Near to Pohjola's great homestead,
Near the hall of Pimentola,   220
Sprung from father, ever crime-stained,
And from a most wicked mother.

Who was it the Frost who suckled,
Bathed him in the glowing weather?
Milkless wholly was his mother,
And his mother wholly breastless.

Adders 'twas the Frost who suckled,
Adders suckled, serpents fed him,
Suckled with their pointless nipples,
Suckled with their dried-up udders,   230
And the Northwind rocked his cradle,
And to rest the cold air soothed him,
In the wretched willow-thicket,
In the midst of quaking marshes.

And the boy was reared up vicious,
Led an evil life destructive,
But as yet no name was given,
To a boy so wholly worthless;
When at length a name was given,
Frost it was they called the scoundrel.   240

Then he wandered by the hedges,
Always dancing in the bushes,
Wading through the swamps in summer
On the broadest of the marshes,
Roaring through the pines in winter,
Crying out among the fir-trees,
Crashing through the woods of birch-trees,
Sweeping through the alder-thickets,
Freezing all the trees and grasses,
Making level all the meadows.   250

From the trees he bit the foliage,
From the heather bit the blossoms,
Cracked the bark from off the pine-trees,
And the twigs from off the fir-trees.

Now that thou hast grown to greatness,
And attained thy fullest stature,
Dar'st thou me with cold to threaten,
And to seize my ears attemptest,
To attack my feet beneath me,
And my finger-tips attacking?   260
But I shall not let you freeze me.
Not to miserably chill me;
Fire I'll thrust into my stockings,
In my boots thrust burning firebrands,
In the seams thrust glowing embers,
Fire I'll thrust beneath my shoestrings,
That the Frost may never freeze me,
Nor the sharpest weather harm me.

Thither will I now condemn thee,
To the furthest bounds of Pohja,   270
To the place from whence thou camest,
To the home from whence thou camest.
Freeze upon the fire the kettles,
And the coals upon the hearthstone,
In the dough the hands of women,
And the boy in young wife's bosom,
In the ewes the milk congeal thou,
And in mares let foals be frozen!

If to this thou pay'st no heeding,
Then indeed will I condemn thee   280
To the midst of coals of Hiisi,
Even to the hearth of Lempo,
Thrust thee there into the furnace,
Lay thee down upon the anvil,
Unprotected from the hammer,
From the pounding of the hammer,
That the hammer beat thee helpless,
And the hammer beat thee sorely.

If this will not overcome thee,
And my spells are insufficient, 290
Still I know another station,
Know a fitting station for thee:
I will lead thy mouth to summer,
And thy tongue to home of summer,
Whence thou never canst release thee,
In the course of all thy lifetime,
If I do not give thee freedom,
And should not myself release thee!"

Then the Frost, the son of Northwind,
Felt that he was near destruction, 300
Whereupon he prayed for mercy,
And he spoke the words which follow:
"Let us understand each other,
Nor the one the other injure,
In the course of all our lifetime,
While the golden moon is shining.

Should'st thou hear that I would freeze you,
Or again should misbehave me,
Thrust me then into the furnace,
Sink me in the blazing fire, 310
In the smith's coals do thou sink me,
Under Ilmarinen's anvil,
Or my mouth to summer turn thou,
And my tongue to home of summer,
Never more release to hope for,
In the course of all my lifetime!"

Then the lively Lemminkäinen
Left his vessel in the ice-floes,
Left his captured ship of battle,
And proceeded on his journey; 320
Tiera too, the other hero,
Followed in his comrade's footsteps.

O'er the level ice they wandered,
'Neath their feet the smooth ice crunching,
And they walked one day, a second,

Runo XXX

And at length upon the third day,
Then they saw the Cape of Hunger,
And afar the wretched village.

'Neath the cape there stood a castle,
And they spoke the words which follow: 330
"Is there meat within the castle,
Is there fish within the household,
For the worn and weary heroes,
And the men who faint with hunger?"
Meat was none within the castle,
Nor was fish within the household.

Spoke the lively Lemminkäinen,
Said the handsome Kaukomieli:
"Fire consume this wretched mansion,
Water sweep away such castles!"   340
He himself pursued his journey,
Pushing onward through the forest,
On a path with houses nowhere,
On a pathway that he knew not.

Then the lively Lemminkäinen,
He the handsome Kaukomieli,
Shore the wool from stones in passing,
From the rocks the hair he gathered,
And he wove it into stockings,
Into mittens quickly wrought it,   350
In the mighty cold's dominion,
Where the Frost was freezing all things.

On he went to seek a pathway,
Searching for the right direction.
Through the wood the pathway led him,
Led him in the right direction.

Spoke the lively Lemminkäinen,
Said the handsome Kaukomieli:
"O my dearest brother Tiera!
Now at length we're coming somewhere,   360

Now that days and months we've wandered,
In the open air for ever."

Then did Tiera make him answer,
And he spoke the words which follow:
"We unhappy sought for vengeance,
Recklessly we sought for vengeance,
Rushing forth to mighty conflict
In the gloomy land of Pohja,
There our lives to bring in danger,
Rushing to our own destruction,   370
In this miserable country,
On a pathway that we knew not.

Never is it known unto us,
Never known and never guessed at,
What the pathway is that leads us,
Or the road that may conduct us
To our death at edge of forest,
Or on heath to meet destruction,
Here in the abode of ravens,
In the fields by crows frequented.   380

And the ravens here are flocking,
And the evil birds are croaking,
And the flesh the birds are tearing,
And with blood the crows are sated,
And the ravens' beaks are moistened
In the wounds of us, the wretched;
To the rocks our bones they carry,
And upon the stones they cast them.

Ah, my hapless mother knows not,
Never she, with pain who bore me,   390
Where her flesh may now be carried,
And her blood may now be flowing,
Whether in the furious battle,
In the equal strife of foemen,
Or upon a lake's broad surface,
On the far-extending billows,

Or on hills with pine-cones loaded,
Wandering 'mid the fallen branches.

And my mother can know nothing
Of her son, the most unhappy,   400
Only know that he has perished,
Only know that he has fallen;
And my mother thus will weep me,
Thus lament, the aged woman:
'Thus my hapless son has perished,
And the wretched one has fallen;
He has sown the seed of Tuoni,
Harrows now in Kalma's country.
Perhaps the son I love so dearly,
Perhaps my son, O me unhappy,   410
Leaves his bows untouched for ever,
Leaves his handsome bows to stiffen.
Now the birds may live securely,
In the leaves the grouse may flutter,
Bears may live their lives of rapine,
In the fields the reindeer roll them.' "

Answered lively Lemminkäinen,
Said the handsome Kaukomieli:
"Thus it is, unhappy mother,
Thou unhappy, who hast borne me!   420
Thou a flight of doves hast nurtured,
Quite a flock of swans hast nurtured,
Rose the wind, and all were scattered,
Lempo came, and he dispersed them,
One in one place, one in other,
And a third in yet another.

I remember times aforetime,
And the better days remember,
How like flowers we gathered round thee,
In one homeland, just like berries.   430
Many gazed upon our figures,
And admired our forms so handsome,
Otherwise than in the present,
In this time so full of evil.
Once the wind was our acquaintance,

And the sun was gazing on us;
Now the clouds are gathering round us,
And the rain has overwhelmed us;
But we let not trouble vex us,
Even in our greatest sorrow,   440
Though the girls were living happy,
And the braidless maids were jesting,
And the women all were laughing,
And the brides were sweet as honey,
Tearless, spite of all vexation,
And unshaken when in trouble.

Yet we are not here enchanted,
Not bewitched, and not enchanted,
Here upon the paths to perish,
Sinking down upon our journey,   450
In our youth to sadly perish,
In our bloom to meet destruction.

Let those whom the sorcerers harassed,
And bewitched with eyes of evil,
Let them make their journey homeward,
And regain their native country.
Be the sorcerers' selves enchanted,
And with songs bewitched their children;
Let their race for ever perish,
And their race be brought to ruin!   460

Ne'er in former times my father,
Never has my aged father
Yielded to a sorcerer's orders,
Or the wiles of Lapland's wizards.
Thus my father spoke aforetime,
And I now repeat his sayings:
'Guard me, O thou kind Creator,
Guard me, Jumala most gracious,
Aid me with thy hand of mercy,
With thy mighty power protect me,   470
From the plots of men of evil,
And the thoughts of aged women,
And the curses of the bearded,
And the curses of the beardless!

Grant us now thy aid eternal,
Be our ever-faithful guardian,
That no child be taken from us,
And no mother's child shall wander
From the path of the Creator,
Which by Jumala was fashioned!"   480

Then the lively Lemminkäinen,
He the handsome Kaukomieli,
From his care constructed horses,
Coursers black composed from trouble,
Reins from evil days he fashioned,
Saddles from his secret sorrows;
Then his horse's back he mounted,
On his white-front courser mounted,
And he rode upon his journey,
At his side his faithful Tiera,   490
And along the shores he journeyed,
On the sandy shores proceeded,
Till he reached his tender mother,
Reached the very aged woman.

Now will I abandon Kauko,
Long from out my song will leave him;
But I'll show the way to Tiera,
Send him on his homeward journey.
Now my song aside will wander,
While I turn to other matters.   500

XXXI   Untamo and Kullervo

Untamo wages war against his brother Kalervo, overthrows Kalervo
and his army, sparing only a single pregnant woman of the whole
clan. She is carried away to Untamo's people, and gives birth to her
son Kullervo (1–82). Kullervo resolves in his cradle to take revenge
on Untamo, and Untamo attempts several times to put him to death,
but without success (83–202). When Kullervo grows up, he spoils all
his work, and therefore Untamo sells him as a slave to Ilmarinen
(203–374).

'Twas a mother reared her chickens,
Large the flock of swans she nurtured;
By the hedge she placed the chickens,
Sent the swans into the river,
And an eagle came and scared them,
And a hawk that came dispersed them,
And a flying bird dispersed them.
One he carried to Carelia,
Into Russia bore the second,
In its home he left the third one.   10

Whom the bird to Russia carried
Soon grew up into a merchant;
Whom he carried to Carelia,
Kalervo was called by others,
While the third at home remaining,
Bore the name of Untamoinen,
For his father's lifelong anguish,
And his mother's deep affliction.

Untamoinen laid his netting
Down in Kalervo's fish-waters;   20
Kalervoinen saw the netting,
In his bag he put the fishes.

Untamo of hasty temper
Then became both vexed and angry,
And his fingers turned to battle,
With his open palms he urged it,
Making strife for fishes' entrails,
And for perch-fry made a quarrel.

Thus they fought and thus contended,
Neither overcame the other,   30
And though one might smite the other,
He himself again was smitten.

At another time it happened,
On the next and third day after,
Kalervoinen oats was sowing,
Back of Untamoinen's dwelling.

Sheep of Untamo most reckless
Browsed the oats of Kalervoinen,
Whereupon his dog ferocious
Tore the sheep of Untamoinen.   40

Untamo began to threaten
Kalervo, his very brother;
Kalervo's race vowed to slaughter,
Smite the great, and smite the little,
And to fall on all the people,
And their houses burn to ashes.

Men with swords in belt he mustered,
Weapons for their hands provided,
Little boys with spikes in girdle,
Handsome youths who shouldered axes,   50
And he marched to furious battle,
Thus to fight his very brother.

Kalervoinen's son's fair consort
Then was sitting near the window,
And she looked from out the window,
And she spoke the words which follow:
"Is it smoke I see arising,
Or a gloomy cloud that rises,

On the borders of the cornfields,
Just beyond the new-made pathway?"   60

But no dark cloud there was rising,
Nor was smoke ascending thickly,
But 'twas Untamo's assemblage
Marching onward to the battle.

On came Untamo's assemblage,
In their belts their swords were hanging,
Kalervo's folk overwhelming,
And his mighty race they slaughtered,
And they burned his house to ashes,
Like a level field they made it.   70

Left of Kalervo's folk only
But one girl, and she was pregnant;
Then did Untamo's assemblage
Lead her homeward on their journey,
That she there might sweep the chamber,
And the floor might sweep from litter.

But a little time passed over,
When a little boy was born her,
From a most unhappy mother,
So by what name should they call him?   80
Kullervo his mother called him,
Untamo, the Battle-hero.

Then the little boy they swaddled,
And the orphan child they rested
In the cradle made for rocking,
That it might be rocked to lull him.

So they rocked the child in cradle,
Rocked it till his hair was tossing,
Rocked him for one day, a second,
Rocked him on the third day likewise,   90
When the boy began his kicking,
And he kicked and pushed about him,
Tore his swaddling bands to pieces,
Freed himself from all his clothing,

Then he broke the lime-wood cradle,
All his rags he tore from off him.

And it seemed that he would prosper,
And become a man of mettle.
Untamola thought already
That when he was grown to manhood,   100
He would grow both wise and mighty,
And become a famous hero,
As a servant worth a hundred,
Equal to a thousand servants.

Thus he grew for two and three months,
But already in the third month,
When a boy no more than knee-high,
He began to speak in thiswise:
"Presently when I am bigger,
And my body shall be stronger,   110
I'll avenge my father's slaughter,
And my mother's tears atone for."

This was heard by Untamoinen,
And he spoke the words which follow:
"He will bring my race to ruin,
Kalervo reborn is in him!"

Thereupon the heroes pondered
And the old crones all considered
How to bring the boy to ruin,
So that death might come upon him.   120
Then they put him in a barrel,
In a barrel did they thrust him,
And they pushed it to the water,
Pushed it out upon the billows.

Then they went to look about them,
After two nights, after three nights,
If the boy had sunk in water,
Or had perished in the barrel.

In the waves he was not sunken,
Nor had perished in the barrel,   130

He had 'scaped from out the barrel,
And upon the waves was sitting,
In his hand a rod of copper,
At the end a line all silken,
And for sea-fish he was fishing,
As he floated on the water.
There was water in the ocean,
Which perchance might fill two ladles,
Or if more exactly measured,
Partly was a third filled also.   140

Untamo again reflected,
"How can we o'ercome the infant,
That destruction come upon him,
And that death may overtake him?"

Then he bade his servants gather
First a large supply of birch-trees,
Pine-trees with their hundred needles,
Trees from which the pitch was oozing,
For the burning of the infant,
And for Kullervo's destruction.   150

So they gathered and collected
First a large supply of birch-trees,
Pine-trees with their hundred needles,
Trees from which the pitch was oozing,
And of bark a thousand sledgefuls,
Ash-trees, long a hundred fathoms.
Fire beneath the wood they kindled,
And the pyre began to crackle,
And the boy they cast upon it,
'Mid the glowing fire they cast him.   160

Burned the fire a day, a second,
Burning likewise on the third day,
When they went to look about them;
Knee-deep sat the boy in ashes,
In the embers to his elbows.
In his hand he held the coal-rake,
And was stirring up the fire,
And he raked the coals together.

Not a hair was singed upon him,
Not a lock was even tangled.   170

Then did Untamo grow angry:
"Where then can I place the infant,
That we bring him to destruction,
And that death may overtake him?"
So upon a tree they hanged him,
Strung him up upon an oak-tree.

Two nights and a third passed over,
And upon the dawn thereafter,
Untamo again reflected:
"Time it is to look around us,   180
Whether Kullervo has fallen,
Or is dead upon the gallows."

Then he sent a servant forward,
Back he came, and thus reported:
"Kullervo not yet has perished,
Nor has died upon the gallows.
Pictures on the tree he's carving,
In his hands he holds a graver.
All the tree is filled with pictures,
All the oak-tree filled with carvings;   190
Here are men, and here are sword-blades,
And the spears are leaning by them."

Where should Untamo seek aidance,
'Gainst this boy, the most unhappy?
Whatsoever deaths he planned him,
Or he planned for his destruction,
In the jaws of death he fell not,
Nor could he be brought to ruin.

And at length he grew full weary
Of his efforts to destroy him,   200
So he reared up Kullervoinen
As a slave beneath his orders.

Thereupon said Untamoinen,
And he spoke the words which follow:

"If you live as it is fitting,
Always acting as is proper,
In my house I will retain you,
And the work of servants give you.
I will pay you wages for it,
As I think that you deserve it,   210
For your waist a pretty girdle,
Or upon your ear a buffet."

So when Kullervo was taller,
And had grown about a span-length,
Then he found some work to give him,
That he should prepare to labour.
'Twas to rock a little infant,
Rock a child with little fingers:
"Watch with every care the infant,
Give it food, and eat some also,   220
With his napkins in the river,
Wash his little clothes and cleanse them!"

So he watched one day, a second,
Broke his hand, and gouged his eyes out,
And at length upon the third day,
Let the infant die of sickness,
Cast the napkins in the river,
And he burned the baby's cradle,

Untamo thereon reflected:
"Such a one is quite unfitted
To attend to little children,   230
Rock the babes with little fingers.
Now I know not where to send him,
Nor what work I ought to give him.
Perhaps he ought to clear the forest?"
So he went to clear the forest.

Kullervo, Kalervo's offspring,
Answered in the words which follow:
"Now I first a man can deem me,
When my hands the axe are wielding.   240
I am handsomer to gaze on,
Far more noble than aforetime,

Five men's strength I feel within me
And I equal six in valour."

Then he went into the smithy,
And he spoke the words which follow:
"O thou smith, my dearest brother,
Forge me now a little hatchet,
Such an axe as fits a hero,
Iron tool for skilful workman,   250
For I go to clear the forest,
And to fell the slender birch-trees."

So the smith forged what he needed,
And an axe he forged him quickly;
Such an axe as fits a hero,
Iron tool for skilful workman.

Kullervo, Kalervo's offspring,
Set to work the axe to sharpen,
And he ground it in the daytime,
And at evening made a handle.   260

Then he went into the forest,
High upon the wooded mountains,
There to seek the best of planking,
And to seek the best of timber.

With his axe he smote the tree-trunks,
With the blade of steel he felled them,
At a stroke the best he severed,
And the bad ones at a half-stroke.

In a rage large trees were struck down,
Eight in all he felled before him,   270
And he spoke the words which follow,
And in words like these expressed him:
"Lempo may the work accomplish,
Hiisi now may shape the timber!"

In a stump he struck his axe-blade,
And began to shout full loudly,
And he piped, and then he whistled,
And he said the words which follow:

"Let the wood be felled around me,
Overthrown the slender birch-trees,   280
Far as sounds my voice resounding,
Far as I can send my whistle!

Let no sapling here be growing,
Let no blade of grass be standing,
Never while the earth endureth,
Or the golden moon is shining,
Here in Kalervo's son's forest,
Here upon the good man's clearing!
If the seed on earth has fallen,
And the young corn should shoot upward,   290
If the sprout should be developed,
And the stalk should form upon it,
May it never come to earing,
Or the sta'k-end be developed!"

Then the mighty Untamoinen,
Wandered forth to gaze about him,
Learn how Kalervo's son cleared it,
And the new slave made a clearing:
But he found not any work done,
And the young man had not cleared it.   300

Untamo thereon reflected,
"For such labour he's unsuited,
He has spoiled the best of timber,
And has felled the best for planking!
Now I know not where to send him,
Nor what work I ought to give him.
Should I let him make a fencing?"
So he went to make a fencing.

Kullervo, Kalervo's offspring,
Set himself to make a fencing,   310
And for this he took whole pine-trees,
And he used them for the fence-stakes,
Took whole fir-trees from the forest,
Wattled them to make the fencing,
Bound the branches fast together
With the largest mountain-ashtrees;

But he made the fence continuous,
And he made no gateway through it,
And he spoke the words which follow,
And in words like these expressed him: 320
"He who cannot raise him birdlike,
Nor upon two wings can hover,
Never may he pass across it,
Over Kalervo's son's fencing!"

Then did Untamo determine
Forth to go and gaze around him,
Viewing Kalervo's son's fencing
By the slave of war constructed.
Stood the fence without an opening
Neither gap nor crevice through it,   330
On the solid earth it rested,
Up among the clouds it towered.

Then he spoke the words which follow:
"For such labour he's unsuited.
Here's the fence without an opening,
And without a gateway through it.
Up to heaven the fence is builded,
To the very clouds uprising;
None can ever pass across it,
Pass within through any opening.   340
Now I know not where to send him,
Nor what work I ought to give him.
There is rye for threshing ready."
So he sent him to the threshing.

Kullervo, Kalervo's offspring,
Set himself to do the threshing,
And the rye to chaff he pounded,
Into very chaff he threshed it.

Soon thereafter came the master,
Strolling forth to gaze around him,   350
See how Kalervo's son threshed it,
And how Kullervoinen pounded:
All the rye to chaff was pounded,
Into very chaff he'd threshed it.

Untamoinen then was angry:
"As a labourer he is useless.
Whatsoever work I give him,
All his work he spoils from malice.
Shall I take him into Russia,
Shall I sell him in Carelia,   360
To the smith named Ilmarinen,
That he there may wield the hammer?"

Kalervo's son took he with him,
And he sold him in Carelia,
To the smith named Ilmarinen,
Skilful wielder of the hammer.

What then gave the smith in payment?
Great the payment that he made him;
For he gave two worn-out kettles,
And three halves of hooks he gave him,   370
And five worn-out scythes he gave him,
And six worn-out rakes he gave him,
For a man the most unskilful,
For a slave completely worthless.

XXXII Kullervo and the wife of Ilmarinen

The wife of Ilmarinen makes Kullervo her herdsman and maliciously bakes him a stone in his lunch (1–32). She then sends him out with the cattle, after using the usual prayers and charms for their protection from bears in the pasture (33–548).

Kullervo, Kalervo's offspring,
Old man's son, with blue-dyed stockings,
Finest locks of yellow colour,
And with shoes of best of leather,
To the smith's house went directly,
Asked for work that very evening,
Asked the master in the evening,
And the mistress in the morning:
"Give me something now to work at,
Give me work that I may do it,   10
Set me something now to work at,
Give some work to me the wretched!"

Then the wife of Ilmarinen,
Pondered deeply on the matter,
What the new slave could accomplish,
What the new-bought wretch could work at,
And she took him as her herdsman,
Who should herd her flocks extensive.

Then the most malicious mistress,
She, the smith's wife, old and jeering,   20
Baked a loaf to give the herdsman,
And a great cake did she bake him,
Oats below and wheat above it,
And between, a stone inserted.

Then she spread the cake with butter,
And upon the crust laid bacon,
Gave it as the slave's allowance,
As provision for the herdsman.
She herself the slave instructed,
And she spoke the words which follow: 30
"Do not eat the food I give you,
Till in wood the herd is driven."

Then did Ilmarinen's housewife
Send the herd away to pasture,
And she spoke the words which follow,
And in words like these expressed her:
"Send the cows among the bushes,
And the milkers in the meadow:
Those with wide horns to the aspens,
Those with curved horns to the birches,   40
That they thus may fatten on them,
And may load themselves with tallow,
There upon the open meadows,
And among the wide-spread borders,
From the lofty birchen forest,
And the lower growing aspens,
From among the golden fir-woods,
From among the silver woodlands.

Watch them, Jumala most gracious,
Guard them, O thou kind Creator,   50
Guard from harm upon the pathway,
And protect them from all evil!
That they come not into danger,
Nor may fall in any evil.

As beneath a shelter watch them,
Keep them under thy protection,
Watch them also in the open,
When beyond the fold protect them,
That the herd may grow more handsome,
And the mistress' cattle prosper,   60
To the wish of our well-wishers,
'Gainst the wish of our ill-wishers!

If my herdsman is a bad one,
Or the milkmaids should be timid,
Make the willow then a herdsman,
Let the alder watch the cattle,
Let the mountain-ash protect them,
And the cherry lead them homeward,
That the mistress need not seek them,
Nor need other folks be anxious!   70

If the willow will not herd them,
Nor the mountain-ash protect them,
Nor the alder watch the cattle,
Nor the cherry lead them homeward,
Send thou then thy better servants,
Send the Daughters of Creation,
That they may protect my cattle,
And the whole herd may look after!
Very many are thy maidens,
Hundreds are beneath thy orders,   80
Dwelling underneath the heavens,
Noble Daughters of Creation.

Suvetar, the best of women,
Etelätär, Nature's old one,
Hongatar, the noble mistress,
Katajatar, maiden fairest,
Pihlajatar, little damsel,
Tuometar, of Tapio daughter,
Mielikki, the wood's step-daughter,
Tellervo, the maid of Tapio!   90
May ye all protect my cattle,
And protect the best among them,
Through the beauty of the summer,
In the pleasant time of leafage,
While the leaves on trees are moving,
Grass upon the ground is waving!

Suvetar, the best of women,
Etelätär, Nature's old one,
Spread thou out thy robe of softness,
And do thou spread out thy apron,   100

As a covering for my cattle,
For the hiding of the small ones,
That no ill winds blow upon them,
Nor an evil rain fall on them!

Do thou guard my flock from evil,
Guard from harm upon the pathways,
And upon the quaking marshes,
Where the surface all is shifting,
Where the marsh is always moving,
And the depths below are shaking,   110
That they come not into danger,
Nor may fall in any evil,
That no hoof in swamp is twisted,
Nor may slip among the marshes,
Save when Jumala perceives it,
'Gainst the will of him, the Holy!

Fetch the cow-horn from a distance,
Fetch it from the midst of heaven,
Bring the mead-horn down from heaven,
Let the honey-horn be sounded.   120
Blow into the horn then strongly,
And repeat the tunes resounding,
Blow then flowers upon the hummocks,
Blow then fair the heathland's borders,
Make the meadow's borders lovely,
And the forest borders charming,
Borders of the marshes fertile,
Of the springs the borders rolling!

Then give fodder to my cattle,
Give the cattle food sufficient,   130
Give them food of honey-sweetness,
Give them drink as sweet as honey,
Feed them now with hay all golden,
And the heads of silvery grasses,
From the springs of all the sweetest,
From the streams that flow most swiftly,
From the swiftly-rushing torrents,
From the swiftly-running rivers,
From the hills all golden-shining,
And from out the silvery meadows!   140

Dig them also wells all golden
Upon both sides of the pastures,
That the herd may drink the water,
And the sweet juice then may trickle
Down into their teeming udders,
Down into their swelling udders,
That the veins may all be moving,
And the milk may flow in rivers,
And the streams of milk be loosened,
And may foam the milky torrents,   150
And the milk-streams may be singing,
And the milk-streams may be oozing,
And the milk be always flowing,
And the stream be always dropping,
Over all the spiteful malice,
Slip through all the evil forces,
May no milk flow down to Mana,
Envy rob the yield from livestock!

There are many who are wicked,
And who send the milk to Mana,   160
And whose envy rots the cow's milk,
Give the cattle's yield to others.
They are few, but they are skilful
Who can bring the milk from Mana,
Sour milk from village storage,
And the fresh from other quarters.

Never has indeed my mother
Sought for counsel in the village,
Brought it from another household,
But she fetched her milk from Mana,   170
Sour milk from those who stored it,
And fresh milk obtained from others;
Had the milk from distance carried,
Had it fetched from distant regions,
Fetched the milk from realms of Tuoni,
'Neath the earth from Mana's kingdom.
Secretly at night they brought it,
And in murky places hid it,
That the wicked should not hear it,

Nor the worthless ones should know it,   180
Nor the evil ones should harm it,
Nor the envious ones desire.

Thus my mother always told me
In the very words which follow:
'Where has gone the yield of cattle,
Whither has the milk now vanished?
Has it been conveyed to strangers,
Carried to the village storehouse,
In the laps of beggar-wenches,
In the arms of those who envy,   190
Or among the trees been carried,
And been lost amid the forest,
And been scattered in the woodlands,
Or been lost upon the heathlands?

'But no milk shall go to Mana,
Nor the yield of cows to strangers,
In the laps of beggar-wenches,
In the arms of those who envy,
Nor among the trees be carried,
Nor be lost amid the forest,   200
Nor be scattered in the woodlands
Nor be lost upon the heathlands.
In the house the milk is useful,
And at all times it is needed:
In the house there waits the mistress,
In her hand the wooden milk-pail.'

Suvetar, the best of women,
Etelätär, Nature's old one!
Go and fodder my Syötikki,
Give thou drink to my Juotikki,   210
Milk confer upon Hermikki,
And fresh fodder give Tuorikki,
Give thou milk unto Mairikki,
Put fresh milk into the cowhouse,
From the heads of brightest herbage,
And the reeds of all the forest,
From the lovely earth up-springing,

From the hillocks rich in honey,
From the sweetest meadow-grasses,
And the berry-bearing regions,   220
From the goddess of the heather,
And the nymph who tends the grasses,
And the milkmaid of the cloudlets,
And the maid in midst of heaven.
Give the cows their milk-filled udders
Always filled to overflowing,
To be milked by little woman,
That a little girl may milk them!

Rise, O virgin, from the valley,
From the mire, in gorgeous raiment,   230
From the spring, O maiden, rise thou,
From the ooze arise, O fairest!
From the spring take thou some water,
Sprinkle thou my cattle with it,
That the cattle may be finer,
And the mistress' cattle prosper,
Ere the coming of the mistress,
Ere the milkmaid look upon them,
She, the most unskilful mistress,
And the very timid milkmaid.   240

Mielikki, the forest's mistress,
Of the herds the bounteous mother,
Send the tallest of thy handmaids,
And the best among thy servants,
That they may protect my cattle,
And my herd be watched and tended
Through the finest of the summers,
In the good Creator's summer,
Under Jumala's protection,
And protected by his favour!   250

Tellervo, O maid of Tapio,
Little daughter of the forest,
Clad in soft and beauteous garments,
With thy yellow hair so lovely,
Be the guardian of the cattle,
Do thou guard the mistress' cattle

All through Metsola so lovely,
And through Tapiola's bright regions
Do thou guard the herd securely,
Do thou watch the herd unsleeping!   260

With thy lovely hands protect them,
With thy slender fingers stroke them,
Till they shine like skins of lynxes,
Like the finest fins of fishes,
Like the hue of the lake creatures,
Like the wool of ewe of meadow.
Come at evening and night's darkness,
When the twilight round is closing,
Then do thou lead home my cattle,
Lead them to their noble mistress,   270
On their backs the water pouring,
Lakes of milk upon their cruppers!

When the sun to rest has sunken,
And the bird of eve is singing,
Then I say unto my cattle,
Speak unto my horned creatures:
'Come ye home, ye curve-horned cattle,
Milk-dispensers to the household,
In the house 'tis very pleasant,
Where the floor is nice for resting.   280
On the waste 'tis bad to wander,
Or upon the shore to bellow,
Therefore you should hasten homeward,
And the women fire will kindle,
In the field of honeyed grasses,
On the ground o'ergrown with berries.'

Nyyrikki, O son of Tapio,
Blue-coat offspring of the forest!
Take the stumps of tallest pine-trees,
And the lofty crowns of fir-trees,   290
For a bridge in miry places,
Where the ground is bad for walking,
Deep morass, and swampy moorland,
And the treacherous pools of water!
Let the curve-horned cattle wander,

And the split-hoofed cattle gallop,
Unto where the smoke is rising,
Free from harm, and free from danger,
Sinking not into the marshes,
Nor embogged in miry places!   300

If the cattle pay no heeding,
Nor will home return at nightfall,
Pihlajatar, little damsel,
Katajatar, fairest maiden,
Quickly cut a branch of birch-tree,
Take a rod from out the bushes,
Likewise take a whip of cherry,
And of juniper to scourge them,
From the back of Tapio's castle,
From among the slopes of alder.   310
Drive the herd towards the household,
At the time for sauna-heating;
Homeward drive the household cattle,
Cows from Metsola's great forest!

Otso, apple of the forest,
With thy honey-paws so curving,
Let us make a peace between us,
Haste to make a peace between us,
So that always and for ever
In the days that we are living,   320
Thou wilt fell no hooféd cattle,
Nor wilt overthrow the milch-kine,
Through the finest of the summer,
In the good Creator's summer!

When thou hear'st the cow-bells ringing,
Or thou hear'st the cow-horn sounding,
Cast thee down among the hillocks,
Sleep thou there among the meadow,
Thrust thine ears into the stubble,
Hide thy head among the hillocks,   330
Or conceal thee in the thickets,
To thy mossy lair retreat thou,

Go thou forth to other districts,
Flee away to other hillocks,
That thou mayst not hear the cow-bells,
Nor the talking of the herdsmen!

O my Otso, O my darling,
Handsome one, with paws of honey,
I forbid thee to approach them,
Or molest the herd of cattle,   340
Neither with thy tongue to touch them,
Nor with ugly mouth to seize them,
With thy teeth to tear to pieces,
Neither with thy claws to scratch them.

Go thou slouching through the meadow,
Go in secret through the pasture,
Slinking off when bells are ringing,
Shun the talking of the shepherds!
If the herd is on the heathland,
Then into the swamps retreat thou;   350
If the herd is in the marshes,
Then conceal thee in the thickets;
If the herd should climb the mountain,
Quickly then descend the mountain;
If the herd should wander downward,
Wander then along the mountain;
If they wander in the bushes,
To the thicker woods retreat thou;
If the thicker wood they enter,
Wander then into the bushes!   360
Wander like the golden cuckoo,
Like the dove of silver colour,
Move aside as moves the powan,
Glide away like fish in water,
As a flock of wool drifts sideways,
Or a roll of flax the lightest,
In thy fur thy claws conceal thou,
In thy gums thy teeth conceal thou,
That the herd thou dost not frighten,
Nor the little calves be injured!   370

Let the cattle rest in quiet,
Leave in peace the hooféd cattle,
Let the herd securely wander,
Let them march in perfect order
Through the swamps and through the open,
Through the tangle of the forest,
Never do thou dare to touch them,
Nor to wickedly molest them!

Keep the former oath thou sworest,
There by Tuonela's deep river,   380
By the raging fall of water,
At the knees of the Creator.
Thou hast been indeed permitted,
Three times in the course of summer,
To approach the bells when ringing,
And the tinkling of the cow-bells,
But 'tis not permitted to thee,
Nor permission has been given,
To commence a work of evil,
Or a deed of shame accomplish.   390

Should thy frenzy come upon thee,
And thy teeth be seized with longing!
Cast thy frenzy in the bushes,
On the heath thy evil longing!
Then attack the trees all rotten,
Overthrow the rotten birch-trees,
Turn to trees in water standing,
Growl in berry-bearing districts!

If the need for food should seize thee,
Or for food the wish thou feelest,   400
Eat the fungi in the forest,
And do thou break down the ant-hills,
And the red roots do thou delve for;
These are Metsola's sweet dainties.
Eat no grass reserved for fodder,
Neither do thou hurt my pasture!

When in Metsola the honey
Is fermenting and is working,

On the hills of golden colour,
And upon the plains of silver,   410
There is food for those who hunger,
There is drink for all the thirsty,
There is food to eat that fails not,
There is drink that never lessens.

Let us make a league eternal,
Make an endless peace between us,
That we live in perfect quiet
And in comfort all the summer,
And to us the lands are common,
And our provender delicious.   420

If thou dost desire a combat,
And wouldst live in hopes of battle,
Let us combat in the winter,
And contend in time of snowfall!
When the marshes thaw in summer,
And the pools are all unfrozen,
Never venture to approach thou,
Where the golden herd is living!

When thou comest to this country,
And thou movest in this forest,   430
We at any time will shoot you,
Though the gunners should be absent.
There are very skilful women,
All of them accomplished housewives,
And they will destroy your pathway,
On your journey bring destruction,
Lest you might work any evil,
Or indulge in any mischief,
Ill by Jumala not sanctioned,
And against his blessed orders.   440

Ukko, thou, of Gods the highest!
Shouldst thou hear that he is coming,
Then do thou transform my cattle,
Suddenly transform my cattle,
Into stones convert my own ones,
Change my fair ones into tree-trunks,

When the monster roams the district,
And the big one wanders through it!

If I were myself a Bruin,
Roamed about a honey-pawed one,   450
Never would I dare to venture
To the feet of aged women.
There are many other regions,
There are many other penfolds,
Where a man may go to wander,
Roaming aimless at his pleasure.
Therefore move thy paws across them,
Do thou move thy paws across them,
In the blue wood's deep recesses,
In the depths of murmuring forest.   460

On the heath o'er pine-cones wander,
Tramp thou through the sandy districts,
Go thou where the way is level,
Do thou bound along the lakeshore,
To the furthest bounds of Pohja,
To the distant plains of Lapland.
There indeed mayst thou be happy,
Good it is for thee to dwell there,
Wandering shoeless in the summer,
Wandering sockless in the autumn,   470
Through the wide expanse of marshland,
And across the wide morasses.

But if thou should not go thither,
If thou canst not find the pathway,
Hasten then to distant regions,
Do thou wander, on thy pathway
Unto Tuonela's great forest,
Or across the heaths of Kalma!
There are marshes to be traversed,
There are heaths that thou mayst traverse,   480
There is Kirjos, there is Karjos,
There are many other bullocks,
Fitted with their iron neck-chains,
Ten among them altogether;

There the lean kine quickly fatten,
And their bones are soon flesh-covered.

Be propitious, wood and forest,
Be thou gracious, O thou blue wood,
Give thou peace unto the cattle,
And protection to the hoofed ones,   490
Through the whole length of the summer,
Of the Lord the loveliest season!

Kuippana, thou king of woodland,
Active greybeard of the forest,
Hold thy dogs in careful keeping,
Watch thou well thy dogs and guard them;
Thrust some fungus in one nostril,
In the other thrust an apple,
That they may not smell the cattle,
And they may not scent their odour!   500
Bind their eyes with silken ribands,
Likewise bind their ears with linen,
That they may not hear them moving,
And they may not see them walking!

If this is not yet sufficient,
And they do not much regard it,
Then do thou forbid thy children,
Do thou drive away thy offspring.
Lead them forth from out this forest,
From this lakeshore do thou drive them,   510
From the lands where roam the cattle,
From among the spreading willows,
Do thou hide thy dogs in caverns,
Nor neglect to bind them firmly,
Bind them with the golden fetters,
With the slender silver fetters,
That they may commit no evil,
And be guilty of no outrage!

If this is not yet sufficient,
And they do not much regard it,   520
Ukko, then, O golden monarch,

Ukko, O thou silver guardian,
Hearken to my words so golden,
Listen to my lovely sayings!
Take a snaffle made of rowan,
Fix it on their stumpy muzzles;
Or if rowan will not hold them,
Cast thou then a copper muzzle;
If too weak is found the copper,
Forge thou then an iron muzzle;   530
If they break the iron muzzle,
And it should itself be shattered,
Drive thou then a stake all golden,
Through the chin and through the jawbone,
Do thou close their jaws securely,
Fix them that they cannot move them,
That they cannot move their jawbones,
And their teeth can scarcely open,
If the iron is not opened,
If the steel should not be loosened,   540
If with knife it is not severed,
If with hatchet 'tis not broken!"

Then did Ilmarinen's housewife,
Of the smith the wife so artful,
Drive from out their stalls the cattle,
Send the cattle forth to pasture,
After them she sent the shepherd,
That the slave should drive the cattle.

XXXIII   The death of Ilmarinen's wife

While Kullervo is in the pasture in the afternoon he tries to cut the
cake with his knife which he completely spoils, and this goes to his
heart the more because the knife was the only remembrance left to
him of his family (1–98). To revenge himself on the mistress, he drives
the cattle into the marshes to be devoured by beasts of the forest, and
gathers together a herd of wolves and bears, which he drives home in
the evening (99–184). When the mistress goes to milk them she is
torn to pieces by the wild beasts (185–296).

Kullervo, Kalervo's offspring,
Put the loaf into his wallet,
Drove the cows along the marshes,
While across the heath he wandered,
And he spoke as he was going,
And repeated on his journey:
"Woe to me, a youth unhappy,
And a youth of wretched fortune!
Wheresoe'er I turn my footsteps,
Nought but idleness awaits me;   10
I must watch the tails of oxen,
And must watch the calves I follow,
Always tramping through the marshes,
Through the worst of level country!"

Upon a hillock then he rested,
On a sunny slope he sat him,
And he then composed these verses,
And expressed himself in singing:
"Sun of Jumala, O shine thou,
Of the Lord, thou wheel, shine warmly,   20
On the warder of the smith's herd,
And upon the wretched shepherd,
Not on Ilmarinen's household,

Least of all upon the mistress,
For the mistress lives luxurious,
And the wheaten-bread she slices,
And the finest cakes devours,
And she spreads them o'er with butter,
Gives the wretched shepherd dry bread,
Dry crusts only for his chewing,   30
Only oaten-cake she gives me,
Even this with chaff she mixes,
Even straw she scatters through it,
Gives for food the bark of pine-tree,
Water in a cup of birch-bark,
Upscooped 'mid the grassy hillocks.

March, O sun, thou wheat, O wander,
Sink, O Jumala's own season,
Hasten, sun, among the pine-trees,
Wander, wheat, into the bushes,   40
'Mid the junipers, O hasten,
Fly thou to the plains of alder,
Lead thou then the herdsman homeward,
Give him butter from the barrel,
Let him eat the freshest butter,
Over all the cakes extending!"

But the wife of Ilmarinen
While the shepherd was lamenting,
And while Kullervo was singing,
Ate the butter from the barrel,   50
And she ate the freshest butter,
And upon the cakes she spread it,
But cold soup had she made ready,
And for Kullervo cold cabbage,
Whence the dog the fat had eaten,
And the black dog made a meal from,
And the spotted dog been sated,
And the brown dog had sufficient.

From the branch there sang a birdling,
Sang a small bird from the bushes: 60
"Time 'tis for the servant's supper,
O thou orphan boy, 'tis evening."

Kullervo, Kalervo's offspring,
Looked, and saw the sun was sinking,
And he said the words which follow:
"Now the time has come for eating,
Yes, the time has come for drinking,
Time it is to take refreshment."

So to rest he drove the cattle,
On the heath he drove the cattle,   70
And he sat him on a hillock,
And upon a green hill sat him.
From his back he took his wallet,
Took the cake from out the wallet,
And he turned it round and eyed it,
And he spoke the words which follow:
"Many a cake is outside handsome,
And the crust looks smooth from outside,
But within is only fir-bark,
Only chaff beneath the surface."   80

From the sheath he took his knife out,
And to cut the cake attempted:
On the stone the knife struck sharply,
And against the stone was broken.
From the knife the blade was broken;
And in two the knife was broken.

Kullervo, Kalervo's offspring,
Looked, and saw the knife was broken,
And at length he burst out weeping,
And he said the words which follow: 90
"Save this knife I'd no companion,
Nought to love except this iron,
'Twas an heirloom from my father,
And the aged man had used it.
Now against a stone 'tis broken,
'Gainst a piece of rock 'tis shattered
In the cake of that vile mistress,
Baked there by that wicked woman!

How shall I for this reward her,
Woman's prank, and damsel's mockery,   100

And destroy the base old woman,
And that wicked wench, the bakeress?"

Then a crow cawed from the bushes,
Cawed the crow, and croaked the raven:
"O thou wretched golden buckle,
Kalervo's surviving offspring!
Wherefore art thou so unhappy,
Wherefore is thy heart so troubled?
Take a switch from out the bushes,
And a birch from forest-valley,   110
Drive the foul beasts in the marshes,
Chase the cows to the morasses,
Half to largest wolves deliver,
Half to bears amid the forest!

Call thou all the wolves together,
All the bears do thou assemble,
Change the wolves to little cattle,
Make the bears the larger cattle,
Lead them then like cattle homeward,
Lead them home like brindled cattle;   120
Thus repay the woman's jesting,
And the wicked woman's insult!"

Kullervo, Kalervo's offspring,
Uttered then the words which follow:
"Wait thou, wait thou, whore of Hiisi!
For my father's knife I'm weeping,
Soon wilt thou thyself be weeping,
And be weeping for thy milchkine."

From the bush a switch he gathered,
Juniper as whip for cattle,   130
Drove the cows into the marshes,
And the oxen in the thickets:
Half of these the wolves devoured,
To the bears he gave the others;
And he sang the wolves to cattle,
And he changed the bears to oxen,

Made the first the little cattle,
Made the last the larger cattle.

In the south the sun was sinking,
In the west the sun descended,   140
Bending down towards the pine-trees
At the time of cattle-milking.
Then the dusty wicked herd-boy,
Kullervo, Kalervo's offspring,
Homeward drove the bears before him,
And the wolf-flock to the farmyard,
And the bears he thus commanded,
And the wolves he thus instructed:
"Tear the mistress' thighs asunder,
See that through her calves you bite her,   150
When she comes to look around her,
And she bends her down to milk you!"

Then he made a pipe of cow-bone,
And a whistle made of ox-horn,
From Tuomikki's leg a cow-horn,
And a flute from heel of Kirjo;
Then upon the horn blew loudly,
And upon his pipe made music.
Thrice upon the hill he blew it,
Six times at the pathway's opening.   160

Then did Ilmarinen's housewife,
Wife of smith, an active woman,
Who for milk had long been waiting,
And expecting summer butter,
Hear the music on the marshes,
And upon the heath the cattle,
And she spoke the words which follow,
And expressed herself in thiswise:
"Praise to Jumala be given,
Sounds the pipe, the herd is coming!   170
Whence obtained the slave the cow-horn,
That he made a horn to blow on?
Wherefore does he thus come playing,

Blowing tunes upon the cow-horn,
Blowing till he bursts the eardrums,
And he gives me quite a headache?"

Kullervo, Kalervo's offspring,
Answered in the words which follow:
"In the swamp the horn was lying,
From the sand I brought the cow-horn;   180
To the lane I brought your cattle,
In the shed the cows are standing;
Make thick smoke for milking-time,
And come out to milk the cattle."

Then did Ilmarinen's housewife
Bid the mother milk the cattle:
"Mother, go and milk the cattle,
Do thou go to tend the cattle,
For I think I cannot finish
Kneading dough as I would have it."   190

Kullervo, Kalervo's offspring,
Answered in the words which follow:
"Ever do the thrifty housewives,
Ever do the careful housewives
Go the first to milk the cattle,
Set themselves to milk the cattle."

Then did Ilmarinen's housewife
Hasten forth to smoke the cattle,
And she went to milk the cattle,
And surveyed the herd before her,   200
Gazed upon the horned cattle,
And she spoke the words which follow:
"Beauteous is the herd to gaze on,
Very sleek the horned cattle,
Hairs been brushed to look like lynx-skin,
Like the wool of sheep of forest,
Well-filled, too, are all their udders,
Dugs expanded with their fulness."

So she stooped her down to milk them,
And she sat her down for milking,   210

Pulled a first time and a second,
And attempted it a third time;
Then a wolf sprang fiercely at her,
And a bear came fiercely after.
At her mouth the wolf was tearing,
And the bear tore through her tendons,
Halfway through her calves they bit her,
And they broke across her shinbones.

Kullervo, Kalervo's offspring
Thus repaid the damsel's jesting,   220
Damsel's jesting, woman's mocking,
Thus repaid the wicked woman.

Ilmarinen's wife illustrious
Then herself was brought to weeping,
And she spoke the words which follow:
"Ill thou dost, O wicked herdsman,
Driving bears unto the homestead,
To the yard these wolves gigantic!"

Kullervo, Kalervo's offspring
Heard, and thus he made her answer: 230
"Ill I did, a wicked herd-boy,
Not so great as wicked mistress:
In my loaf a stone she baked me,
Baked a lump of rock within it,
On the stone my knife struck sharply,
'Gainst the rock my knife was shattered;
'Twas the knife of mine own father,
Of our race a cherished heirloom!"

Then said Ilmarinen's housewife,
"O thou herd-boy, dearest herd-boy!   240
Wilt thou alter thy intention,
And recall thy words of magic,
And release me from the wolf's jaws,
From the bear's claws now release me?
Better shirts will I then give you,
And will give you handsome trousers,
Give you wheaten-bread, and butter,
And the sweetest milk for drinking,

For a year no work will give you,
Give you light work in the second.   250

If you haste not to release me,
Come not quickly to my rescue,
Death will quickly fall upon me,
And to earth shall I be altered."

Kullervo, Kalervo's offspring,
Answered in the words which follow:
"If you die, so may you perish,
If you perish, may you perish!
Room there is in earth to hold you,
Room in Kalma's home for lost ones,   260
For the mightiest there to slumber,
For the proudest to repose them."

Then said Ilmarinen's housewife,
"Ukko, thou, of Gods the highest!
Haste to bend thy mighty crossbow,
Of thy bows the best select thou,
Take thou then a bolt of copper,
And adjust it to the crossbow,
Shoot thou then a flaming arrow,
Shoot thou forth the bolt of copper,   270
Shoot it quickly through the arm-pits ,
Shoot it that it split the shoulders.
Thus let Kalervo's son perish,
Shoot thou dead this wicked creature,
Shoot him with the steel-tipped arrow,
Shoot him with thy bolt of copper!"

Kullervo, Kalervo's offspring,
Uttered then the words which follow:
"Ukko, thou, of Gods the highest,
Shoot me not as she has prayed thee,   280
Shoot the wife of Ilmarinen,
Do thou kill this wicked woman,
Ere from off this spot she riseth,
Or can move herself from off it!"

Then did Ilmarinen's housewife,
Wife of that most skilful craftsman,
On the spot at once fall dying,
Fell, as falls the soot from kettle,
In the yard before her homestead,
In the narrow yard she perished.   290

Thus it was the young wife perished,
Thus the fairest housewife perished,
Whom the smith so long had yearned for,
And for six long years was sought for,
As the joy of Ilmarinen,
Pride of him, the smith so famous.

XXXIV Kullervo and his parents

Kullervo escapes from the homestead of Ilmarinen, and wanders
sorrowfully through the forest, where he meets with the Old Woman
of the Forest, who informs him that his father, mother, brothers and
sisters are still living (1–128). Following her directions he finds them
on the borders of Lapland (129–88). His mother tells him that she
had long supposed him to be dead, and also that her elder daughter
had been lost when gathering berries (189–246).

Kullervo, Kalervo's offspring,
He, the youth with blue-dyed stockings,
And with yellow hair the finest,
And with shoes of finest leather,
Hurried quickly on his journey
From the home of Ilmarinen,
Ere report could reach the master
Of the death his wife had suffered,
And might harm him in his anger,
And he might at once destroy him.   10

From the smith he hurried piping,
Joyful left the lands of Ilma,
On the heath his horn blew loudly,
Shouted loudly in the clearing,
And he dashed through plains and marshes,
While the heath re-echoed loudly,
And his horn kept loudly blowing,
And made horrible rejoicing.

In the smithy did they hear it,
At the forge the smith was standing,   20
To the lane he went to listen,
To the yard to look around him,
Who was playing in the forest,
And upon the heath was piping.

Then he saw what just had happened,
Saw the truth without deception:
There he saw his wife was resting,
Saw the fair one who had perished,
Where she in the yard had fallen,
On the grass where she was lying.   30

Even while the smith was standing,
All his heart was dark with sorrow;
Many nights he spent in weeping,
Many weeks his tears were flowing,
And his soul like tar was darkened,
And his heart than soot no lighter.

Kullervo still wandered onwards,
Aimlessly he hurried forward,
For a day through thickest forest,
Through the timber-grounds of Hiisi,   40
And at evening, when it darkened,
Down upon the ground he threw him.

There the orphan boy was sitting,
And the friendless one reflected:
"Wherefore have I been created,
Who has made me, and has doomed me,
Thus 'neath moon and sun to wander
'Neath the open sky for ever?

Others to their homes may journey,
And may travel to their dwellings,   50
But my home is in the forest,
And upon the heath my homestead.
In the wind I find my fire-place,
In the rain I find my sauna.

Never, Jumala most gracious,
Never in the course of ages,
Form a child thus mis-created,
Doomed to be for ever friendless,
Fatherless beneath the heavens,
From the first without a mother,   60
As thou, Jumala, hast made me,

And has formed me to be wretched,
Formed me like a wandering seagull,
Like a seagull on the sea-cliffs.
Shines the sun upon the swallow,
Brightly shines upon the sparrow,
In the air the birds are joyous,
I myself am never happy,
On my life the sun shines never,
And my life is always joyless.   70

Now I know not who has nursed me,
And I know not who has borne me,
For, as water-hens are used to,
Or as ducks among the marshes,
Like the teal on shore she left me,
Or in hollow stone, merganser.

I was small, and lost my father,
I was weak, and lost my mother,
Dead is father, dead is mother,
All my mighty race has perished;   80
Shoes of ice to wear they left me,
Filled with snow they left my stockings,
On the ice they left me lying,
Rolling on the platform left me,
Thus I fell into the marshes,
And amid the mud was swallowed.

But in all my life I never,
Never in my life I hastened,
Through the swamp to make a platform,
Or a bridge in marshy places;   90
But I sank not in the marshes,
For I had two hands to help me,
And I had five nimble fingers,
And ten nails to lift me from it."

Then into his mind it entered,
In his brain he fixed the notion
Unto Untamo to journey,
There his father's wrongs avenging,
Father's wrongs, and tears of mother,
And the wrongs himself had suffered.   100

Then he spoke the words which follow:
"Wait thou, wait thou, Untamoinen,
Watch thou, of my race destroyer!
If I seek thee out in battle,
I will quickly burn thy dwelling,
And thy farms to flame deliver."

Then an old dame came to meet him,
Blue-robed Lady of the Forest;
And she spoke the words which follow,
And in words like these expressed her: 110
"'Whither goeth Kullervoinen,
Where will Kalervo's son hasten?"

Kullervo, Kalervo's offspring,
Answered in the words which follow:
"In my mind the thought has entered,
In my brain has fixed the notion
Hence to other lands to wander,
Unto Untamo's own village,
There my father's death avenging,
Father's wrongs, and tears of mother,   120
There with fire to burn the houses,
And to burn them up completely."

But the old wife made him answer,
And she spoke the words which follow:
"No, your race has not yet perished,
Nor has Kalervo been murdered;
For your father still is living,
And on earth in health your mother."

"O my dearest of old women!
Tell me, O my dear old woman,   130
Where I yet may find my father,
Where the fair one who has borne me?"

"Thither is thy father living,
There the fair one who has borne thee,
Far away on Lapland's borders,
On the borders of a fishpond."

O my dearest of old women!
Tell me, O my dear old woman,
How I best can journey to them,
And the road I may discover?"   140

"Easy 'tis for thee to journey,
Though to thee unknown the pathway.
Through the forest must thou journey,
By the river thou must travel,
Thou must march one day, a second,
And must march upon the third day,
Then must turn thee to the north-west,
Till you reach a wooded mountain,
Then march on beneath the mountain,
Go the left side of the mountain,   150
Till thou comest to a river,
On the right side thou wilt find it,
By the riverside go further,
Till three waterfalls rush foaming,
When thou comest to a headland
With a narrow tongue projecting,
And a house at point of headland
And beyond a hut for fishing.
There thy father still is living,
There the fair one who has borne thee,   160
There thou'lt also find thy sisters,
Two among the fairest maidens."

Kullervo, Kalervo's offspring,
Started then upon his journey,
And he marched one day, a second,
Likewise marched upon the third day,
Then he turned him to the north-west,
Till he reached a wooded mountain;
Then he marched halfway below it,
Turning westward from the mountain,   170
Till at length he found the river,
And he marched along the river,
On the west bank of the river,
Past three water-falls he journeyed,
Till at length he reached a headland
With a narrow tongue projecting,

And a house at point of headland,
And beyond, a hut for fishing.

Thereupon the house he entered,
In the room they did not know him: 180
"From what lake has come the stranger,
From what country is the wanderer?"

"Is your son then all forgotten,
Know you not your child, your offspring,
Who by Untamo's marauders,
With them to their home was carried,
Greater not than span of father,
Longer not than mother's spindle?"

Then his mother interrupted,
And exclaimed the aged woman: 190
"O my son, my son unhappy,
O my golden brooch so wretched!
Hast thou then, with eyes yet living,
Wandered through these countries hither,
When as dead I long had mourned thee,
Long had wept for thy destruction?

I had two sons in the past days,
And two daughters of the fairest,
And among them two have vanished,
Two are lost among the elder: 200
First my son in furious battle,
Then my daughter, how, I know not.
Though my son has reached the homestead,
Never has returned my daughter."

Kullervo, Kalervo's offspring,
In his turn began to question:
"How then has your daughter vanished,
What has happened to my sister?"

Then his mother gave him answer,
And she spoke the words which follow: 210
"Thus has disappeared my daughter,
Thus it happened to your sister.

To the wood she went for berries,
Sought for raspberries 'neath the mountain,
There it is the dove has vanished,
There it is the bird has perished,
Thus she died without our knowledge,
How she died we cannot tell you.

Who is longing for the maiden?
Save her mother, no one missed her!   220
First her mother went to seek her,
And her mother sought, who missed her,
Forth I went, unhappy mother,
Forth I went to seek my daughter,
Through the wood like bear I hurried,
Speeding through the wastes like otter;
Thus I sought one day, a second,
Sought her also on the third day.
When the third day had passed over,
For a long time yet I wandered,   230
Till I reached a mighty mountain,
And a peak of all the highest,
Calling ever on my daughter,
Ever grieving for the lost one:
'Where is now my dearest daughter?
O my daughter, come thou homeward!'

Thus I shouted to my daughter,
Grieving ever for the lost one;
And the mountains made me answer,
And the heaths again re-echoed: 240
'Call no more upon thy daughter,
Call no more, and shout no longer!
Never will she come back living,
Nor return unto her household,
Never to her mother's dwelling,
To her aged father's boathouse.' "

XXXV Kullervo and his sister

Kullervo attempts to do different kinds of work for his parents, but only succeeds in spoiling everything, so his father sends him to pay the land-dues (1–68). On his way home he meets his sister who was lost gathering berries, whom he drags into his sledge (69–188). Afterwards, when his sister learns who he is, she throws herself into a torrent, but Kullervo hurries home, relates his sister's terrible fate to his mother, and proposes to put an end to his own life (189–344). His mother dissuades him from suicide and advises him to retire to some retreat where he may be able to recover from his remorse. But Kullervo resolves before all things to avenge himself on Untamo (345–72).

Kullervo, Kalervo's offspring,
With the very bluest stockings,
After this continued living,
In the shelter of his parents,
But he comprehended nothing,
Nor attained to manly wisdom,
For his rearing had been crooked,
And the child was rocked all wrongly,
By perversest foster-father,
And a foolish foster-mother.   10

Then to work the boy attempted,
Many things he tried his hand at,
And he went the fish to capture,
And to lay the largest drag-net,
And he spoke the words which follow,
Pondered as he grasped the oar:
"Shall I pull with all my efforts,
Row, exerting all my vigour;
Shall I row with common efforts,
Row no stronger than is needful?"   20

And the steersman gave him answer,
And he spoke the words which follow:
"Pull away with all your efforts,
Row, exerting all your vigour,
Row the boat in twain you cannot,
Neither break it into fragments."

Kullervo, Kalervo's offspring,
Pulled thereat with all his efforts,
Rowed, exerting all his vigour,
Rowed in twain the wooden rowlocks,   30
Ribs of juniper he shattered,
And he smashed the boat of aspen.

Kalervo came forth to see it,
And he spoke the words which follow:
"No, you understand not rowing,
You have split the wooden rowlocks,
Ribs of juniper have shattered,
Shattered quite the boat of aspen.
Thresh the fish into the drag-net,
Perhaps you'll thresh the water better."   40

Kullervo, Kalervo's offspring,
Then went forth to thresh the water,
And as he the pole was lifting,
Uttered he the words which follow:
"Shall I thresh with all my efforts,
Putting forth my manly efforts;
Shall I thresh with common efforts,
As the threshing-pole is able?"
Answered thereupon the net-man,
"Would you call it proper threshing,   50
If with all your strength you threshed not,
Putting forth your manly efforts?"

Kullervo, Kalervo's offspring,
Threshed away with all his efforts,
Putting forth his manly efforts.
Into soup he churned the water,
Into tow he threshed the drag-net,
Into slime he crushed the fishes.

Kalervo came forth to see it,
And he spoke the words which follow: 60
"No, you understand not threshing,
Into tow is threshed the drag-net,
And the floats to chaff are beaten,
And the meshes torn to fragments;
Therefore go and pay the taxes,
Therefore go and pay the land-dues!
Best it is for you to travel,
Learning wisdom on the journey."

Kullervo, Kalervo's offspring,
With the very bluest stockings,   70
And with yellow hair the finest,
And with shoes of finest leather,
Went his way to pay the taxes,
And he went to pay the land-dues.
When he now had paid the taxes,
And had also paid the land-dues,
In his sledge he quickly bounded,
And upon the sleigh he mounted,
And began to journey homeward,
And to travel to his country.   80

And he drove, and rattled onward,
And he travelled on his journey,
Traversing the heath of Väinö,
Clearings made so long aforetime.

And by chance a maiden met him,
With her yellow hair all flowing,
There upon the heath of Väinö,
Clearings made so long aforetime.

Kullervo, Kalervo's offspring,
Checked the sledge upon the instant,   90
And began a conversation,
And began to talk and wheedle:
"Come into my sledge, O maiden,
Rest upon the furs within it!"

From her snowshoes said the maiden,
And she answered, while still gliding:
"In thy sledge may Death now enter,
On thy furs be Sickness seated!"

Kullervo, Kalervo's offspring,
With the very bluest stockings,   100
With his whip then struck his courser,
With his beaded whip he lashed him.
Sprang the horse upon the journey,
Rocked the sledge, the road was traversed,
And he drove and rattled onward,
And he travelled on his journey,
On the sea's extended surface,
And across the open water,
And by chance a maiden met him,
Walking on, with shoes of leather,   110
O'er the sea's extended surface,
And across the open water.

Kullervo, Kalervo's offspring,
Checked his horse upon the instant,
And his mouth at once he opened,
And began to speak as follows:
"Come into my sledge, O fair one,
Pride of earth, and journey with me!"

But the maiden gave him answer,
And the well-shod maiden answered: 120
"On thy sledge may Tuoni seek thee,
Manalainen journey with thee!"

Kullervo, Kalervo's offspring,
With the very bluest stockings,
With the whip then struck his courser,
With his beaded whip he lashed him.
Sprang the horse upon his journey,
Rocked the sledge, the way was shortened,
And he rattled on his journey,
And he sped upon his pathway,   130
Straight across the heaths of Pohja,
And the borders wide of Lapland.

And by chance a maiden met him,
Wearing a tin brooch, and singing,
Out upon the heaths of Pohja,
And the borders wide of Lapland.

Kullervo, Kalervo's offspring,
Checked his horse upon the instant,
And his mouth at once he opened,
And began to speak as follows: 140
"Come into my sledge, O maiden,
Underneath my rug, my dearest,
And you there shall eat my apples,
And shall crack my nuts in comfort!"

But the maiden gave him answer,
And the tin-adorned one shouted:
"At your sledge I spit, O villain,
Even at your sledge, O scoundrel!
Underneath your rug is coldness,
And within your sledge is darkness."   150

Kullervo, Kalervo's offspring,
With the very bluest stockings,
Dragged into his sledge the maiden,
And into the sledge he pulled her,
And upon the furs he laid her,
Underneath the rug he rolled her.

And the maiden spoke unto him,
Thus spoke out the tin-adorned one:
"From the sledge at once release me,
Leave the child in perfect freedom,   160
That I hear of nothing evil,
Neither foul nor filthy language,
Or upon the ground I'll throw me,
And will break the sledge to splinters,
And will smash your sledge to atoms,
Break the wretched sledge to pieces!"

Kullervo, Kalervo's offspring,
With the very bluest stockings,
Opened then his hide-bound coffer,

Clanging raised the pictured cover,   170
And he showed her all his silver,
Out he spread the choicest fabrics,
Stockings too, all gold-embroidered,
Girdles all adorned with silver.

Soon the fabrics turned her dizzy,
To a bride the money changed her,
And the silver it destroyed her,
And the shining gold deluded.

Kullervo, Kalervo's offspring,
With the very bluest stockings,   180
Thereupon the maiden flattered,
And he wheedled and caressed her,
With one hand the horse controlling,
On the maiden's breast the other.

Then he sported with the maiden,
Wearied out the tin-adorned one,
'Neath the rug all copper-tinselled,
And upon the furs all spotted.

Then when Jumala brought morning,
On the second day thereafter,   190
Then the damsel spoke unto him,
And she asked, and spoke as follows:
"Tell me now of your relations,
What the brave race that you spring from,
From a mighty race it seems me,
Offspring of a mighty father."

Kullervo, Kalervo's offspring,
Answered in the words which follow:
"No, my race is not a great one,
Not a great one, not a small one,   200
I am just of middle station,
Kalervo's unhappy offspring,
Stupid boy, and very foolish,
Worthless child, and good for nothing.
Tell me now about your people,
And the brave race that you spring from,

Perhaps from mighty race descended,
Offspring of a mighty father."

And the girl made answer quickly,
And she spoke the words which follow: 210
"No, my race is not a great one,
Not a great one, not a small one,
I am just of middle station,
Kalervo's unhappy daughter,
Stupid girl, and very foolish,
Worthless child, and good for nothing.

When I was a little infant,
Living with my tender mother,
To the wood I went for berries,
'Neath the mountain sought for raspberries.   220
On the plains I gathered strawberries,
Underneath the mountain, raspberries,
Plucked by day, at night I rested,
Plucked for one day and a second,
And upon the third day likewise,
But the pathway home I found not;
In the woods the pathways led me,
And the footpath to the forest.

There I stood, and burst out weeping,
Wept for one day and a second,   230
And at length upon the third day,
Then I climbed a mighty mountain,
To the peak of all the highest.
On the peak I called and shouted,
And the woods made answer to me,
While the heaths re-echoed likewise:
'Do not call, O girl so senseless,
Shout not, void of understanding!
There is no one who can hear you,
None at home to hear your shouting!'   240

Then upon the third and fourth days,
Lastly on the fifth and sixth days,
I to take my life attempted,
Tried to hurl me to destruction,

But by no means did I perish,
Nor could I, the wretched, perish!

Would that I, poor wretch, had perished,
Hapless one, had met destruction,
That the second year thereafter,
Or the third among the summers,   250
I had shone forth as a grass-blade,
As a lovely flower existed,
On the ground a beauteous berry,
Even as a scarlet cranberry,
Then I had not heard these horrors,
Would not now have known these terrors."

Soon as she had finished speaking,
And her speech had scarce completed,
Quickly from the sledge she darted,
And she rushed into the river,   260
In the furious foaming cataract,
And amid the raging whirlpool,
There she found the death she sought for,
There at length did death o'ertake her,
Found in Tuonela a refuge,
In the waves she found compassion.

Kullervo, Kalervo's offspring,
From his sledge at once descended,
And began to weep full loudly,
With a piteous lamentation: 270
"Woe my day, O me unhappy,
Woe to me, and all my household,
For indeed my very sister,
I my mother's child have outraged!
Woe my father, woe my mother,
Woe to you, my aged parents,
To what purpose have you reared me,
Reared me up to be so wretched!
Far more happy were my fortune,
Had I ne'er been born or nurtured,   280
Never in the air been strengthened,
Never in this world had entered.

Wrongly I by death was treated,
Nor disease has acted wisely,
That they did not fall upon me,
And when two nights old destroy me."

With his knife he loosed the collar,
From the sledge the chains he severed,
On the horse's back he vaulted,
On the whitefront steed he galloped,   290
But a little way he galloped,
But a little course had traversed,
When he reached his father's dwelling,
Reached the grass-plot of his father.

In the yard he found his mother:
"O my mother, who hast borne me,
O that thou, my dearest mother,
E'en as soon as thou hadst borne me,
In the sauna smoke hadst laid me,
And the sauna doors had bolted,   300
That amid the smoke I smothered,
And when two nights old had perished,
Smothered me among the blankets,
With the curtain thou hadst choked me,
Thrust the cradle in the fire,
Pushed it in the burning embers!
If the village folk had asked thee:
'Why is in the room no cradle?
Wherefore have you locked the sauna?'
Then might this have been the answer: 310
'In the fire I burned the cradle,
Where on hearth the fire is glowing,
While I made the malt in sauna,
While the malt was fully sweetened.' "

Then his mother asked him quickly,
Asked him thus, the aged woman:
"O my son, what happened to thee,
What's the dreadful news thou bringest?
Seems from Tuonela thou comest;
As from Manala thou comest."   320

Kullervo, Kalervo's offspring,
Answered in the words which follow:
"Horrors now must be reported,
And most horrible misfortunes.
I have wronged my very sister,
And my mother's child dishonoured!

First I went and paid the taxes,
And I also paid the land-dues,
And by chance there came a maiden,
And I sported with the maiden,   330
And she was my very sister,
And the child of mine own mother!

Thereupon to death she cast her,
Plunged herself into destruction,
In the furious foaming cataract,
And amid the raging whirlpool.
But I cannot now determine
Not decide and not imagine
How myself to death should cast me,
I the hapless one, should slay me,   340
In the mouths of wolves all howling,
In the throats of bears all growling,
In the whale's vast belly perish,
Or between the teeth of lake-pike?"

But his mother made him answer:
"Do not go, my son, my dearest,
To the mouths of wolves all howling,
Nor to throats of bears all growling,
Neither to the whale's vast belly,
Neither to the teeth of lake-pike!   350
Large enough the Cape of Suomi,
Wide enough are Savo's borders,
For a man to hide from evil,
And a criminal conceal him.
Hide thee there for five years, six years,
There for nine long years conceal thee,
Till a time of peace has reached thee,
And the years have calmed thine anguish."

Kullervo, Kalervo's offspring,
Answered in the words which follow: 360
"Nay, I will not go in hiding,
Fly not forth, a wicked outcast,
To the mouth of Death I wander,
To the gate of Kalma's courtyard,
To the place of furious fighting,
To the battle-field of heroes.
Upright still is standing Unto,
And the wicked man unfallen;
Unavenged my father's sufferings,
Unavenged my mother's tear-drops,   370
Counting not my bitter sufferings,
Wrongs that I myself have suffered."

XXXVI The death of Kullervo

Kullervo prepares for war and leaves home joyfully, for no one but his mother is sorry that he is going to his death (1–154). He comes to Untamola, lays waste the whole district, and burns the homestead (155–250). On returning home he finds his home deserted, and no living thing about the place but an old black dog, with which he goes into the forest to shoot game for food (251–96). While traversing the forest he arrives at the place where he met his sister, and ends his remorse by killing himself with his own sword (297–360).

> Kullervo, Kalervo's offspring,
> With the very bluest stockings,
> Now prepared himself for battle,
> And prepared himself for warfare.
> For an hour his sword he sharpened,
> Sharpened spear-point a while longer.
>
> Then his mother spoke unto him:
> "Do not go, my son unhappy,
> Go not to this mighty battle,
> Go not where the swords are clashing!   10
> He who goes for nought to battle,
> He who wilful seeks the combat,
> In the fight shall find his death-wound,
> And shall perish in the conflict;
> By the sword-blades shall he perish,
> Thus shall fall, and thus shall perish,
>
> If against a goat thou fightest,
> And wouldst meet in fight a he-goat,
> Then the goat will overcome thee,
> In the mud the he-goat cast thee,   20
> That like dog thou home returnest,
> Like a frog returnest homeward."

Kullervo, Kalervo's offspring,
Answered in the words which follow:
"In the swamps I shall not sink me,
Nor upon the heath will stumble,
In the dwelling-place of ravens,
In the fields where crows are croaking.
If I perish in the battle,
Sinking on the field of battle,   30
Noble 'tis to fall in battle,
Fine 'mid clash of swords to perish!
Exquisite the battle-fever,
Quickly hence a youth it hurries,
Takes him quickly forth from evil,
There he falls no more to hunger."

Then his mother spoke and answered:
"If you perish in the battle,
Who shall cater for your father,
And shall tend the old man daily?"   40

Kullervo, Kalervo's offspring,
Answered in the words that follow:
"Let him perish on the dust-heap,
Leave him in the yard to perish!"

"Who shall cater for your mother,
And shall tend the old dame daily?"

"Let her die upon a haycock,
In the cowshed let her stifle!"

"Who shall cater for thy brother,
Tend him day by day in future?"   50

"Let him perish in the forest,
Let him faint upon the meadow!"

"Who shall cater for thy sister,
Tend her day by day in future?"

"Let her fall in well, and perish,
Let her fall into the wash-tub!"

Kullervo, Kalervo's offspring,
Just as he his home was leaving,
Spoke these words unto his father:
"Now farewell, O noble father!   60
Shall you perhaps be weeping sorely,
If you hear that I have perished,
And have vanished from the people,
And have perished in the battle?"

Then his father gave him answer:
"Not for thee shall I be weeping,
If I hear that you have perished,
For another son I'll rear me,
And a better son will rear me,
And a son by far more clever."   70

Kullervo, Kalervo's offspring,
Answered in the words which follow:
"Nor for you shall I be weeping,
If I hear that you have perished.
I will make me such a father:
Mouth of clay, and head of stonework,
Eyes of cranberries from the marshes,
And a beard of withered stubble,
Legs of willow-twigs will make him,
Flesh of rotten trees will make him."   80

Then he spoke unto his brother:
"Now farewell, my dearest brother!
Shall you weep for my destruction,
If you hear that I have perished,
And have vanished from the people,
And have fallen in the battle?"

But his brother gave him answer:
"Not for you shall I be weeping,
If I hear that you have perished.
I will find myself a brother,
Better brother far than thou art,   90
And a brother twice as handsome."

Kullervo, Kalervo's offspring,
Answered in the words which follow:
"Nor for you shall I be weeping,
If I hear that you have perished.
I will make me such a brother:
Head of stone, and mouth of sallow,
Eyes of cranberries I will make him,
Make him hair of withered stubble,   100
Legs of willow-twigs will make him,
Flesh of rotten trees will make him."

Then he spoke unto his sister:
"Now farewell, my dearest sister!
Shall you weep for my destruction,
If you hear that I have perished,
And have vanished from the people,
And have perished in the battle?"

But his sister gave him answer:
"Not for you shall I be weeping,   110
If I hear that you have perished.
I will find myself a brother,
Better brother far than thou art,
And a brother far more clever."

Kullervo, Kalervo's offspring,
Answered in the words which follow:
"Nor for you shall I be weeping,
If I hear that you have perished.
I will make me such a sister:
Head of stone and mouth of sallow,   120
Eyes of cranberries I will make her,
Make her hair of withered stubble,
Ears of water-lily make her,
And of maple make her body."

Then he said unto his mother:
"O my mother, O my dearest,
Thou the fair one who hast borne me,
Thou the golden one who nursed me,

Shalt thou weep for my destruction,
Shouldst thou hear that I have perished,   130
And have vanished from the people,
And have perished in the battle?"

Then his mother gave him answer,
And she spoke the words which follow:
"Not thou knowest a mother's feelings,
Nor a mother's heart esteemest.
I shall weep for thy destruction,
If I hear that thou hast perished,
And from out the people vanished,
And have perished in a battle: 140
Weep until the house is flooded,
Weep until the floor is swimming,
Weep until the paths are hidden,
And with tears the cowsheds weighted,
Weep until the snows are slippery,
Till the ground is bare and slippery,
Lands unfrozen teem with verdure,
And my tears flow through the greenness.
If I cannot keep on weeping,
And no strength is left for grieving,   150
Weeping in the people's presence,
I will weep in sauna hidden,
Till the seats with tears are flowing,
And the flooring all is flooded."

Kullervo, Kalervo's offspring,
With the very bluest stockings,
Went with music forth to battle,
Joyfully he sought the conflict,
Playing tunes through plains and marshes,
Shouting over all the heathland,   160
Crashing onwards through the meadows,
Trampling down the fields of stubble.
And a messenger o'ertook him,
In his ear these words he whispered:
"At thy home has died thy father,
And thy aged parent perished.
Now return to gaze upon him,
And arrange for his interment!"

Kullervo, Kalervo's offspring,
Made him answer on the instant: 170
"Is he dead, so let him perish.
In the house there is a gelding,
Which unto the grave can drag him,
And can sink him down to Kalma!"

Played he, as he passed the marshes,
And he shouted in the clearings,
And a messenger o'ertook him,
In his ear these words he whispered:
"At thy home has died thy brother,
And thy parent's child has perished.   180
Now return to gaze upon him,
And arrange for his interment!"

Kullervo, Kalervo's offspring,
Made him answer on the instant:
"Is he dead, so let him perish.
In the house there is a stallion,
Which unto the grave can drag him,
And can sink him down to Kalma!"

Through the marshes passed he, playing,
Blew his horn amidst the fir-woods,   190
And a messenger o'ertook him,
In his ear these words he whispered:
"At thy home has died thy sister,
And thy parent's child has perished.
Now return to gaze upon her,
And arrange for her interment!"

Kullervo, Kalervo's offspring,
Made him answer on the instant:
"Is she dead, so let her perish.
In the house a mare is waiting,   200
Which unto the grave can drag her,
And can sink her down to Kalma!"

Through the meadows pranced he shouting,
In the grassfields he was shouting,
And a messenger o'ertook him,

In his ear these words he whispered:
"Now has died thy tender mother,
And thy darling mother perished.
Now return to gaze upon her,
And arrange for her interment!"   210

Kullervo, Kalervo's offspring,
Answered in the words which follow:
"Woe to me, a youth unhappy,
For my mother now has perished,
Wearied she who wove the curtains,
And the counterpane embroidered.
With her long thread she was working,
As she turned around her spindle.
I was not at her departure,
Near her when her soul was parting.   220
Perhaps the cold was great and killed her,
Or perchance was bread too scanty!
In the house with care, O wash her,
With the Saxon soap, the finest,
Wind her then in silken wrappings,
Wrap her in the finest linen,
Thus unto the grave convey her,
Sink her gently down to Kalma,
Then upraise the songs of mourning,
Let resound the songs of mourning,   230
For not yet can I turn homeward:
Untamo is still unfallen,
Yet unfelled the man of evil,
Undestroyed is yet the villain."

Forth he went to battle, playing,
Went to Untola rejoicing,
And he said the words which follow:
"Ukko, thou, of Gods the highest!
Give me now a sword befitting,
Give me now a sword most splendid,   240
Which were worth an army to me,
Though a hundred came against me!"

Then the sword he asked was granted,
And a sword of all most splendid,

And he slaughtered all the people,
Untamo's whole tribe he slaughtered,
Burned the houses all to ashes,
And with flame completely burned them,
Leaving nothing but the hearthstones,
Nought but in each yard the rowan.   250

Kullervo, Kalervo's offspring,
Then to his own home retired,
To his father's former dwelling,
To the home-fields of his parents.
Empty did he find the homestead,
Desolate the open places;
No one forward came to greet him,
No one came his hand to offer.

To the hearth he stretched his hand out,
On the hearth the coals were frozen,   260
And he knew on his arrival,
That his mother was not living.

To the stove he stretched his hand out,
At the stove the stones were frozen,
And he knew on his arrival,
That his father was not living.

On the floor his eyes then casting,
All he noticed in confusion,
And he knew on his arrival,
That his sister was not living.   270

To the mooring-place he hastened,
But no boats were at their moorings,
And he knew on his arrival,
That his brother was not living.

Thereupon he broke out weeping,
And he wept one day, a second,
And he spoke the words which follow:
"O my mother, O my dearest,
Hast thou left me nought behind thee,
When thou livedst in this country?   280

But thou hearest not, O mother,
Even though my eyes are sobbing,
And my temples are lamenting,
And my head is all complaining!"

In the grave his mother wakened,
And beneath the mould made answer:
"Still there lives the black dog, Musti,
Go with him into the forest,
At thy side let him attend thee,
Take him to the wooded country,   290
Where the forest rises thickest,
Where reside the forest-maidens,
Where the Blue Maids have their dwelling,
And the birds frequent the pine-trees,
There to seek for their assistance,
And to seek to win their favour!"

Kullervo, Kalervo's offspring,
At his side the black dog taking,
Tracked his path through trees of forest,
Where the forest rose the thickest.   300
But a short way had he wandered,
But a little way walked onward,
When he reached the stretch of forest,
Recognized the spot before him,
Where he had seduced the maiden,
And his mother's child dishonoured.

There the tender grass was weeping,
And the lovely spot lamenting,
And the young grass was deploring,
And the flowers of heath were grieving,   310
For the ruin of the maiden,
For the mother's child's destruction.
Neither was the young grass sprouting,
Nor the flowers of heath expanding,
Nor the spot had covered over,
Where the evil thing had happened,
Where he had seduced the maiden,
And his mother's child dishonoured.

Kullervo, Kalervo's offspring,
Grasped the sharpened sword he carried,   320
Looked upon the sword and turned it,
And he questioned it and asked it,
And he asked the sword's opinion,
If it was disposed to slay him,
To devour his guilty body,
And his evil blood to swallow.

Understood the sword his meaning,
Understood the hero's question,
And it answered him as follows:
"Wherefore at thy heart's desire   330
Should I not thy flesh devour,
And drink up thy blood so evil?
I who guiltless flesh have eaten,
Drunk the blood of those who sinned not?"

Kullervo, Kalervo's offspring,
With the very bluest stockings,
On the ground the haft set firmly,
On the heath the hilt pressed tightly,
Turned the point against his bosom,
And upon the point he threw him,   340
Thus he found the death he sought for,
Cast himself into destruction.

Even so the young man perished,
Thus died Kullervo the hero,
Thus the hero's life was ended,
Perished thus the hapless hero.

Then the aged Väinämöinen,
When he heard that he had perished,
And that Kullervo had fallen,
Spoke his mind in words that follow: 350
"Never, people, in the future,
Rear a child in crooked fashion,
Rocking them in stupid fashion,
Soothing them to sleep like strangers!
Children reared in crooked fashion,

Boys thus rocked in stupid fashion,
Grow not up with understanding,
Nor attain to man's discretion,
Though they live till they are aged,
And in body well-developed."   360

XXXVII   The gold and silver bride

Ilmarinen weeps long for his dead wife and then forges himself a wife
of gold and silver with great labour and trouble (1–162). At night he
rests by the golden bride, but finds in the morning that the side which
he has turned towards her is quite cold (163–96). He offers his golden
bride to Väinämöinen, who declines to receive her, and advises him to
forge more useful things, or to send her to other countries where
people wish for gold (197–250).

Afterwards smith Ilmarinen
Mourned his wife throughout the evenings,
And through sleepless nights was weeping,
All the days bewailed her fasting,
And he mourned her all the mornings,
In the morning hours lamented,
Since the time his young wife perished,
Death the fair one had o'ertaken.
In his hand he swung no longer,
Copper handle of his hammer,   10
Nor his hammer's clang resounded,
While a month its course was running.

Said the smith, said Ilmarinen,
"Hapless youth, I know no longer,
How to pass my sad existence,
For at night I sit and sleep not,
Always in the night comes sorrow,
And my strength grows weak from trouble.

All my evenings now are weary,
Sorrowful are all my mornings,
And the nights indeed are dismal,   20
Worst of all when I am waking.
Grieve I not because 'tis evening,
Sorrow not because 'tis morning,
Trouble not for other seasons;

But I sorrow for my fair one,
And I sorrow for my dear one,
Grieve for her, my dark-browed beauty.
Sometimes in these times so dismal,
Often in my time of trouble,
Often in my dreams at midnight,   30
Has my hand felt out at nothing,
And my hand seized only trouble,
As it strayed about in strangeness."

Thus the smith awhile lived wifeless,
And without his wife grew older,
Wept for two months and for three months,
But upon the fourth month after,
Gold from out the lake he gathered,
Gathered silver from the billows,   40
And a pile of wood collected,
Nothing short of thirty sledgeloads,
Then he burned the wood to charcoal,
Took the charcoal to the smithy.

Of the gold he took a portion,
And he chose him out some silver,
Even like a ewe of autumn,
Even like a hare of winter,
And the gold to redness heated,
Cast the silver in the furnace,   50
Set his slaves to work the bellows,
And his workers pressed the bellows.

Toiled the slaves, and worked the bellows,
And the workers pressed the bellows,
With their ungloved hands they pressed them,
Worked them with their naked shoulders,
While himself, smith Ilmarinen,
Carefully the fire was tending,
As he strove a bride to fashion
Out of gold and out of silver.   60

Badly worked the slaves the bellows,
And the workers did not press them,
And on this smith Ilmarinen

Went himself to work the bellows;
Once and twice he worked the bellows,
For a third time worked the bellows,
Then looked down into the furnace,
Looking closely to the bellows,
What rose up from out the furnace,
What from out the flames ascended.   70

Then a ewe rose from the furnace,
And it rose from out the fire.
One hair gold, another copper,
And the third was all of silver;
Others might therein feel pleasure,
Ilmarinen felt no pleasure.

Said the smith, said Ilmarinen,
"Such as you a wolf may wish for!
But I want a golden consort,
One of silver half constructed."   80

Thereupon smith Ilmarinen
Thrust the ewe into the furnace,
Gold unto the mass he added,
And he added silver to it,
Set his slaves to work the bellows,
And his workers pressed the bellows.

Toiled the slaves and worked the bellows,
And the workers pressed the bellows,
With their ungloved hands they pressed them,
Worked them with their naked shoulders,   90
While himself, smith Ilmarinen,
Carefully the fire was tending,
As he strove a bride to fashion
Out of gold and out of silver.

Badly worked the slaves the bellows,
And the workers did not press them,
And on this smith Ilmarinen
Went himself to work the bellows;
Once and twice he worked the bellows,
For the third time worked the fire,   100

Then looked down into the furnace,
Looking closely to the fire,
What rose up from out the furnace,
What from out the flames ascended.

Then a foal rose from the furnace,
And it rose from out the bellows,
Mane of gold, and head of silver,
And his hoofs were all of copper;
But though others it delighted,
Ilmarinen felt no pleasure.   110

Said the smith, said Ilmarinen,
"Such as you a wolf may wish for,
But I want a golden consort,
One of silver half constructed."

Thereupon smith Ilmarinen
Thrust the foal into the furnace,
Gold unto the mass he added,
And he added silver to it,
Set his slaves to work the bellows,
And his workers pressed the bellows.   120

Toiled the slaves and worked the bellows,
And the workers pressed the bellows,
With their ungloved hands they pressed them,
Worked them with their naked shoulders,
While himself, smith Ilmarinen,
Carefully the fire was tending,
As he strove a bride to fashion,
Out of gold and out of silver.

Badly worked the slaves the bellows,
And the workers did not press them,   130
And on this, smith Ilmarinen
Went himself to work the bellows;
Once and twice he worked the bellows,
For a third time worked the bellows,
Then looked down into the furnace,
Looking closely to the fire,

What rose up from out the furnace,
What from out the flames ascended.

Then a maid rose from the furnace,
Golden-locked, from out the fire,   140
Head of silver, hair all golden,
And her figure all was lovely.
Others greatly shuddered at her,
Ilmarinen was not frightened.

Thereupon smith Ilmarinen
Set to work to shape the image,
Worked at night without cessation,
And by day he worked unresting.
Feet he fashioned for the maiden,
Fashioned feet; and hands he made her.   150
But the feet would not support her,
Neither would the arms embrace him.

Ears he fashioned for the maiden,
But the ears served not for hearing;
And a dainty mouth he made her,
Tender mouth and shining eyeballs,
But the mouth served not for speaking,
And the eyes served not for smiling.

Said the smith, said Ilmarinen,
"She would be a pretty maiden,   160
If she had the art of speaking,
And had sense, and spoke discreetly."

After this he laid the maiden
On the softest of the blankets,
Smoothed for her the softest pillows,
On the silken bed he laid her.

After this smith Ilmarinen,
Quickly warmed the steaming sauna,
Took the soap into the bath-house,
And provided twigs for bath-whisks,   170
And of water took three tubs full,

That the little finch should wash her,
And the little goldfinch cleanse her,
Cleanse her beauty from the ashes.

When the smith had also bathed him,
Washed him to his satisfaction,
At the maiden's side he stretched him,
On the softest of the blankets,
'Neath the steel-supported hangings,
'Neath the over-arching iron.   180

After this smith Ilmarinen,
Even on the very first night,
Asked for coverlets in plenty,
And for blankets to protect him,
Also two and three of bearskins,
Five or six of woollen mantles,
All upon one side to lay him,
That towards the golden image.

And one side had warmth sufficient
Which was covered by the bedclothes;   190
That beside the youthful damsel,
Turned towards the golden image,
All that side was fully frozen,
And with frost was quite contracted,
Like the ice on lake when frozen,
Frozen into stony hardness.

Said the smith, said Ilmarinen,
"This is not so pleasant for me;
I might take the maid to Väinö,
Pass her on to Väinämöinen,   200
On his knee as wife to seat her,
Dovelike in his arms to nestle."

So to Väinölä he took her,
And he said upon his coming,
In the very words which follow:
"O thou aged Väinämöinen,
Here I bring a damsel for you,
And a damsel fair to gaze on,

And her mouth gapes not too widely,
And her chin is not too broadened." 210

Väinämöinen, old and steadfast,
Looked upon the golden image,
Looked upon her head all golden,
And he spoke the words which follow:
"Wherefore have you brought her to me,
Brought to me this golden spectre?"

Said the smith, said Ilmarinen,
"With the best intent I brought her,
On your knee as wife to rest her,
Dovelike in your arms to nestle." 220

Said the aged Väinämöinen,
"O thou smith, my dearest brother!
Thrust the damsel in the furnace,
Forge all sorts of objects from her,
Or convey her hence to Russia,
Take your image to the Saxons,
Since they wed the spoils of battle,
And they woo in fiercest combat;
But it suits not my position,
Nor to me myself is suited, 230
Thus to woo a bride all golden,
Or distress myself for silver."

Then dissuaded Väinämöinen,
And forbade the wave-sprung hero,
All the rising generation,
Likewise those upgrown already,
For the sake of gold to bow them,
Or debase themselves for silver,
And he spoke the words which follow,
And in words like these expressed him: 240
"Never, youths, however wretched,
Nor in future, upgrown heroes,
Whether you have large possessions,
Or are poor in your possessions,
In the course of all your lifetime,
Ever while the moon is shining,

May you woo a golden woman,
Or distress yourselves for silver,
For the gleam of gold is freezing,
Only frost is breathed by silver!"   250

XXXVIII   Ilmarinen's new bride from Pohjola

Ilmarinen goes to Pohjola to woo the younger sister of his first wife, but as he receives only insulting words in reply, he becomes angry, seizes the maiden, and starts on his homeward journey (1–124). On the way the maiden treats Ilmarinen with contempt, and provokes him till he changes her into a seagull (125–286). When Illmarinen comes home, he relates to Väinämöinen how the inhabitants of Pohjola live free from care since they possessed the *Sampo*; and also tells him how badly his wooing has prospered (287–328).

> Thereupon smith Ilmarinen,
> He the great primeval craftsman,
> Cast away the golden image,
> Cast away the silver damsel;
> Afterwards his horse he harnessed,
> Yoked before the sledge the chestnut,
> On the sledge himself he mounted,
> And within the sledge he sat him,
> And departed on his journey,
> And proposed, as he was driving,   10
> He to Pohjola would travel,
> There to ask another daughter.

> So he drove for one day onward,
> Journeyed also on the second,
> And at length upon the third day,
> Came to Pohjola's broad courtyard.

> Louhi, Pohjola's old Mistress
> Came into the yard to meet him,
> And began the conversation,
> And she turned to him and asked him   20

How her child's health was at present,
If her daughter was contented,
As the daughter-in-law of master,
And the daughter-in-law of mistress.

Thereupon smith Ilmarinen,
Head bowed down, and deeply grieving,
And his cap so sad askew,
Answered in the words which follow:
"Do thou not, O mother, ask me,
Do not question me in thiswise   30
How your daughter may be living,
How your dear one now is dwelling!
Death has borne her off already,
Grisly death has seized upon her.
In the ground is now my berry,
On the heath is now my fair one,
And her dark locks 'neath the stubble,
'Neath the grass my silver-fair one.
Give me now your second daughter,
Give me now that youthful maiden,   40
Give her to me, dearest mother,
Give me now your second daughter,
Thus to occupy the dwelling,
And the station of her sister!"

Louhi, Pohjola's old Mistress,
Answered in the words which follow:
"Ill have I, unhappy, acted,
And it was a sad misfortune
When to thee my child I promised,
And I gave to thee the other,   50
In her early youth to slumber,
For the rosy-cheeked one perished.
To the mouth of wolf I gave her,
To the jaws of bear when growling.

No more daughters will I give you,
Nor my daughter will I give you,
Soot to wash from off your wallspace,
Scratch the crust from off your ceilings,
Sooner would I give my daughter,

And would give my tender daughter,　　　60
To the fiercely-foaming cataract,
To the ever-seething whirlpool,
As a prey to worms of Mana,
To the teeth of pike of Tuoni."

Thereupon smith Ilmarinen,
Altogether sad and gloomy,
With his black hair in disorder,
As his head he shook in anger,
Pushed his way into the chamber,
And beneath the roof he entered,　　　70
And he spoke the words which follow:
"Come thou now with me, O maiden,
In the station of thy sister,
And to occupy her dwelling,
Cakes of honey there to bake me,
And the best of ale to brew me!"

From the floor there sang a baby,
Thus he sang, and thus made answer:
"Quit our castle, guest unwelcome,
From our doors, O stranger, hasten!　　　80
Thou before hast harmed our castle,
Evil much hast wrought our castle,
When the first time here thou camest,
And within our doors hast entered.

Maiden, O my dearest sister,
O rejoice not in this lover,
Neither in his mouth so subtle,
Neither in his feet well-shapen!
For his gums are like a wolf's gums,
Curved his claws like those of foxes,　　　90
And the claws of bears conceals he,
And his belt-knife blood is drinking,
'Tis with this that heads he severs,
And with this the backs lays open."

Then the maiden's self made answer,
Thus she spoke to Ilmarinen:
"I myself will not go with you,

Trouble not for such a scoundrel;
For your first wife you have murdered,
And my sister you have slaughtered.   100
You perchance would also slay me,
Murder me, as her you murdered.
Such a maiden is deserving
Of a man of greater standing,
And whose form is far more handsome,
In a finer sledge to take me,
To a larger, finer dwelling,
To a better home than thou hast,
Not unto a smith's black coalhouse
To a stupid husband's homestead."   110

Thereupon smith Ilmarinen,
He the great primeval craftsman,
Altogether sad and gloomy,
And his black hair in disorder,
Seized without ado the maiden,
In his grasp he seized the maiden,
From the room he rushed like snowstorm,
Dragged her where his sledge was standing,
In the sledge he pushed the maiden,
And within the sledge he cast her,   120
Started quickly on his journey,
And prepared him for his journey,
With one hand the horse he guided,
On the girl's breast laid the other.

Wept the maiden and lamented,
And she spoke the words which follow:
"Now I come where grow the cranberries,
To the swamps where grow the arums,
Now the dove approaches ruin,
And the bird is near destruction.   130

Hear me now, smith Ilmarinen!
If you will not now release me,
I will smash your sledge to pieces,
And will break it into fragments,

Break it with my knees asunder,
Break it with my legs to fragments."

Thereupon smith Ilmarinen
Answered in the words that follow:
"Know, the sledge by smith was fashioned,
And the boards are bound with iron,   140
And it can withstand the pushing,
And the noble maiden's struggles."

Then the hapless girl lamented,
And bewailed the copper-belted,
Struggled till she broke her fingers,
Struggled till her hands were twisted,
And she spoke the words which follow:
"If you will not now release me,
To a lake-fish I'll transform me,
In the deepest waves a powan."   150

Thereupon smith Ilmarinen
Answered in the words which follow:
"Even so you will not 'scape me,
I myself as pike will follow."

Then the hapless girl lamented,
And bewailed the copper-belted,
Struggled till she broke her fingers,
Struggled till her hands were twisted,
And she spoke the words which follow:
"If you will not now release me,   160
To the wood will I betake me,
Hiding in the rocks like ermine."

Thereupon smith Ilmarinen
Answered in the words which follow:
"Even thus you will not 'scape me,
For as otter I'll pursue you."

Then the hapless girl lamented,
And bewailed the copper-belted,

Struggled till she broke her fingers,
Struggled till her hands were twisted,   170
And she spoke the words which follow:
"If you will not now release me,
As a lark I'll soar above you,
And behind the clouds will hide me."

Thereupon smith Ilmarinen,
Answered in the words which follow:
"Even thus you will not 'scape me,
For as eagle I'll pursue you."

But a little way they journeyed,
Short the distance they had traversed,   180
When the horse pricked ears to listen,
And the long-eared steed was shying.

Then her head the maiden lifted,
In the snow she saw fresh footprints,
And she thereupon inquired:
"What has passed across our pathway?"
Said the smith, said Ilmarinen,
"'Twas a hare that ran across it."

Then the hapless girl was sighing,
Much she sobbed, and much was sighing,   190
And she spoke the words which follow:
"Woe to me, unhappy creature!
Better surely had I found it,
And my lot were surely better
If the hare's track I could follow,
In the traces of the Crook-leg,
Than in sledge of such a suitor,
'Neath the rug of one so wrinkled,
For the hairs of hare are finer,
And his mouth-cleft is more handsome."   200

Thereupon smith Ilmarinen,
Bit his lips, his head turned sideways,
And the sledge drove rattling onward,
And a little way they journeyed,

When the horse pricked ears to listen,
And the long-eared steed was shying.

Then her head the maiden lifted,
In the snow she saw fresh footprints,
And she thereupon inquired:
"What has passed across our pathway?"   210
Said the smith, said Ilmarinen,
"'Twas a fox that ran across it."

Then the hapless girl was sighing,
Much she sobbed, and much was sighing,
And she spoke the words which follow:
"Woe to me, unhappy creature,
Better surely had I found it,
And my lot were surely better,
Were I riding in a fox-sledge,
And in Lapland sledge were fleeing,   220
Than in sledge of such a suitor,
'Neath the rug of one so wrinkled,
For the hairs of fox are finer,
And his mouth-cleft is more handsome."

Thereupon smith Ilmarinen
Bit his lips, his head turned sideways,
And the sledge drove rattling onward,
And a little way they journeyed,
When the horse pricked ears to listen,
And the long-eared steed was shying.   230

Then her head the maiden lifted,
In the snow she saw fresh footprints,
And she thereupon inquired:
"What has passed across our pathway?"
Said the smith, said Ilmarinen,
"'Twas a wolf that ran across it."

Then the hapless girl was sighing,
Much she sobbed, and much was sighing,
And she spoke the words which follow:
"Woe to me, unhappy creature!   240

Better surely had I found it,
And my lot were surely better
If a growling wolf I followed,
Tracked the pathway of the Snouted,
Than in sledge of such a suitor,
'Neath the rug of one so wrinkled,
For the hair of wolf is finer,
And his mouth-cleft is more handsome."

Thereupon smith Ilmarinen
Bit his lips, his head turned sideways,   250
And the sledge drove rattling onwards,
And at night they reached a village.

With the journey overwearied,
Slept the smith, and slept profoundly,
And another than her husband
Made the girl laugh as he slept there.

Thereupon smith Ilmarinen
In the morning when he wakened,
Altogether sad and gloomy,
Tossed his black hair in disorder.   260

After this, smith Ilmarinen
Pondered till he spoke as follows:
"Shall I now commence my singing,
Shall I sing a bride like this one,
To a creature of the forest,
Or a creature of the water?

Not to forest beast I'll sing her,
All the forest would be troubled;
Neither to a water-creature,
Lest the fishes all should shun her;   270
Better slay her with my hanger,
With my sword will I dispatch her."

But the sword perceived his object,
Understood the hero's language,
And it spoke the words which follow:
"Not for this was I constructed,

That I should dispatch the women,
And the weak I thus should slaughter."

Thereupon smith Ilmarinen
Presently commenced his singing,   280
And began to speak in anger,
Sung his wife into a seamew,
Thenceforth round the cliffs to clamour,
Scream upon the rocks in water,
Moan around the jutting headlands,
Struggle with the winds against her.

After this smith Ilmarinen
In his sledge again dashed forward,
And the sledge drove rattling onward,
Head bowed down in great depression,   290
Back he journeyed to his country,
Till he reached the well-known regions.

Väinämöinen, old and steadfast,
Came upon the road to meet him,
And began to speak as follows:
"Ilmarinen, smith and brother,
Wherefore is your mood so gloomy,
Wherefore is your cap so sad askew,
As from Pohjola thou comest?
How at Pohjola exist they?"   300

Said the smith, said Ilmarinen,
"How at Pohjola exist they?
There the Sampo grinds for ever,
And revolves the pictured cover;
On one day it grinds provisions,
Grinds for sale upon the second,
On the third what needs the household.
Thus I speak, and tell you truly,
And again repeat it to you,
How at Pohjola exist they,   310
When at Pohjola's the Sampo!
There is ploughing, there is sowing,
There is every kind of increase,
And their welfare is eternal."

Said the aged Väinämöinen,
"Ilmarinen, smith and brother,
Where hast thou thy wife abandoned,
Where thy youthful bride so famous,
That you here return without her,
Ever driving homeward wifeless?"   320

Thereupon smith Ilmarinen,
Answered in the words which follow:
"Such a wife she was, I sang her
To the sea-cliffs as a seamew;
Now she screams aloud as seagull,
Shrieks aloud without cessation,
Moans about the rocks in water,
And around the cliffs she clamours."

XXXIX   The expedition against Pohjola

Väinämöinen persuades Ilmarinen to go with him to Pohjola to bring
away the *Sampo*. Ilmarinen consents, and the heroes start off on their
journey in a boat (1–330). Lemminkäinen hails them from the shore,
and on hearing where they are going, proposes to join them, and is
accepted as a third comrade (331–426).

Väinämöinen, old and steadfast,
Uttered then the words which follow:
"O thou smith, O Ilmarinen,
Unto Pohjola we'll travel,
And will seize this splendid Sampo,
And behold its pictured cover!"

Thereupon smith Ilmarinen
Answered in the words which follow:
"No, we cannot seize the Sampo,
Cannot bring the pictured cover,   10
From the gloomy land of Pohja,
Sariola for ever misty.
There the Sampo has been carried,
And removed the pictured cover
Unto Pohjola's stone mountain,
And within the hill of copper.
There by nine locks is it fastened;
And three roots have sprouted from it,
Firmly fixed, nine fathoms deeply.
In the earth the first is rooted,   20
By the water's edge the second,
And the third within the home-hill."

Said the aged Väinämöinen,
"O thou smith, my dearest brother,
Unto Pohjola we'll travel,
And will carry off the Sampo.

Let us build a ship enormous,
Fit to carry off the Sampo,
And convey the pictured cover,
Forth from Pohjola's stone mountain,   30
From within the hill of copper,
And the ninefold locks that hold it!"

Said the smith, said Ilmarinen,
"Safest is by land the journey.
Lempo on the sea is brooding,
Death upon its mighty surface!
And the wind might drive us onward,
And the tempest might o'erturn us;
We might have to row with fingers,
And to use our hands for steering."   40

Said the aged Väinämöinen,
"Safest is by land the journey,
Safest, but the most fatiguing,
And moreover, full of windings.
Pleasant 'tis in boat on water,
Swaying as the boat glides onward,
Gliding o'er the sparkling water,
Driving o'er its shining surface,
While the wind the boat is rocking,
And the waves drive on the vessel,   50
While the west-wind rocks it gently,
And the south-wind drives it onward;
But let this be as it may be,
If you do not like the sea-voyage,
We by land can journey thither,
And along the shore can journey!

First a new sword do you forge me,
Make me now a keen-edged weapon,
So that I with beasts can struggle,
Chase away the folks of Pohja.   60
Forth I go to seize the Sampo,
From the cold and dismal village,
From the gloomy land of Pohja,
Sariola for ever misty!"

Thereupon smith Ilmarinen,
He the great primeval craftsman,
Cast some iron in the fire,
Steel upon the glowing charcoal,
And of gold he took a handful,
And of silver took a handful,   70
Set the slaves to work the bellows,
And he made the workers press them.

Worked the slaves the bellows strongly,
Well the workers pressed the bellows,
Till like soup spread out the iron,
And like dough the steel was yielding,
And the silver shone like water,
And the gold swelled up like billows.

Thereupon smith Ilmarinen,
He the great primeval craftsman,   80
Stooped to look into the furnace,
At the edges of the bellows:
And he saw a sword was forming,
With a hilt of gold constructed.

From the fire he took the weapon,
Took the work so finely fashioned
From the furnace to the anvil,
To the hammer and the mallet,
Forged the sword as he would wish it,
And a blade the best of any,   90
And with finest gold inlaid it,
And with silver he adorned it.

Väinämöinen, old and steadfast,
Entered then to view the weapon,
And he took the keen-edged sword-blade.
Straightway in his hand he raised it,
And he turned it and surveyed it,
And he spoke the words which follow:
"Does this sword befit a hero,
Is the sword to bearer suited?"
And the sword the hero suited,   100

Well did it befit the bearer.
On its point the moon was shining,
On its side the sun was shining,
On the haft the stars were gleaming,
On the tip a horse was neighing,
On the knob a cat was mewing,
On the sheath a dog was barking.

After this the sword he brandished,
And he cleft an iron mountain,   110
And he spoke the words which follow:
"Thus, with such a blade as this is,
Can I cleave the mountains open,
Cleave the rocky hills asunder!"

After this did Ilmarinen
Speak aloud the words which follow:
"How shall I myself, unhappy,
How shall I, the weak, defend me,
And shall armour me, and belt me,
'Gainst the risks of land and water?   120
Shall I clothe myself in armour,
In a coat of mail the strongest,
Gird a belt of steel around me?
Stronger is a man in armour,
In a coat of mail is better,
With a belt of steel more mighty."

Then arrived the time for starting,
And preparing for departure;
First the aged Väinämöinen,
Secondly smith Ilmarinen,
And they went to seek the courser,   130
And to find the yellow-maned one,
And the one-year old to bridle,
And to see the foal was rough-shod.
Then they went to seek the courser,
Went to seek him in the forest,
And they gazed around them keenly,
And they sought around the blue wood,
Found the horse among the bushes,
Found the yellow-maned in firwood.   140

Väinämöinen, old and steadfast,
Secondly smith Ilmarinen,
On his head the bit adjusted,
And the one-year old they bridled,
And they drove upon their journey.
On the shore drove both the heroes;
On the shore they heard lamenting,
From the haven heard complaining.

Then the aged Väinämöinen
Spoke aloud the words which follow: 150
"Perhaps it is a girl complaining,
Or perchance a dove lamenting.
Shall we go to look about us?
Shall we nearer go to listen?"

Therefore to the spot they sauntered,
Nearer went to gaze around them,
But no maiden there was weeping,
And no dove was there lamenting;
But they found a vessel weeping,
And a boat was there lamenting;   160

Said the aged Väinämöinen
As he went towards the vessel,
"Wherefore weep, O wooden vessel:
Boat with rowlocks, why lamentest?
Dost thou weep that thou art clumsy,
And art dreaming at thy moorings?"

Then the wooden boat made answer,
Thus replied the boat with rowlocks:
"Know, a vessel longs for water,
And its tarry sides desire it,   170
As a maiden may be longing
For the fine home of a husband.
Therefore weeps the boat unhappy,
And the hapless boat lamenteth,
And I weep to speed through water,
And to float upon the billows.

It was said when I was fashioned,
When my boards were sung together,
That I should become a warship,
And should be employed for warboat,   180
And should bear the plunder homeward,
In my hold should carry treasure;
But I have not been in battle,
Neither have been stored with plunder!
Other boats, and even bad ones,
Always wander forth to battle,
And are led to battle-struggle
Three times in the course of summer,
And return with money loaded,
In their hold they carry treasure;   190
But for me, though well constructed,
Of a hundred boards constructed,
Here upon my rests I'm rotting,
Lying idly at my moorings;
And the worst worms of the country
Underneath my ribs are lurking,
While the birds, of all most horrid,
In my masts their nests are building,
All the toads from out the forest
Over all my deck are leaping.   200
Twice it had been better for me,
Two or three times were it better
Had I been a mountain pine-tree,
Or upon the heath a fir-tree,
With a squirrel in my branches,
Underneath my boughs a puppy."

Väinämöinen, old and steadfast,
Answered in the words which follow:
"Do not weep, O wooden vessel,
Fret thyself, O boat with rowlocks!   210
Soon shalt thou go forth to battle,
There to mix in furious conflict!
Boat, who wast by builder fashioned,
'Twas this gift the builder gave thee,
That thy prow should reach the water,
And thy sides the billows traverse,

Even though no hand should touch thee,
Neither arm be thrust against thee,
Though no shoulder should direct thee,
And although no arm should guide thee!"   220

Then replied the wooden vessel,
Answered thus the boat with rowlocks:
"None of all my race so mighty,
Neither will the boats, my brothers,
Move unpushed into the water,
Nor unrowed upon the billows,
If no hand is laid upon us,
And no arm should urge us forward."

Said the aged Väinämöinen,
"If I push you in the water,   230
Will you make, unrowed, your journey,
Unassisted by the oars,
By the rudder undirected,
When the sails no breeze is filling?"

Answer made the wooden vessel,
Thus replied the boat with rowlocks:
"None of all my race so noble,
Nor the host of other vessels,
Speed along unrowed by fingers,   240
Unassisted by the oars,
By the rudder undirected,
When the sails no breeze is filling."

Väinämöinen, old and steadfast,
Answered in the words which follow:
"Can you speed if some one rows you,
If assisted by the oars,
By the rudder if directed,
When the sails the breeze is filling?"

Answered then the wooden vessel,
Thus replied the boat with rowlocks: 250
"Yes, my race would hasten onward,
All the other boats my brothers,

Speed along if rowed by fingers,
If assisted by the oars,
By the rudder if directed,
When the sails the breeze is filling."

Then the aged Väinämöinen
Left his horse upon the sandhills,
On a tree he fixed the halter,
Tied the reins upon the branches,   260
Pushed the boat into the water,
Sang the vessel in the billows;
And he asked the wooden vessel,
And he spoke the words which follow:
"O thou boat, of shape so curving,
O thou wooden boat with rowlocks!
Art thou just as fit to bear us,
As thyself art fair to gaze on?"

Answered thus the wooden vessel,
Thus replied the boat with rowlocks: 270
"I am fitted well to bear you,
And my floor is very spacious,
And a hundred men might row me,
And a thousand others stand there."

So the aged Väinämöinen
Softly then began to carol,
Sang on one side of the vessel
Handsome youths, with hair all tufted,
Bristlehaired and fists of iron,
Noble ones all finely booted;   280
Sang on other side of vessel
Girls with tin upon their head-dress,
Head-dress tin, and belts of copper,
Golden rings upon their fingers.

And again sang Väinämöinen,
Till the seats were full of people,
Some were very aged people,
Men whose lives were nearly over,
But for these the space was scanty,
For the young men came before them.   290

In the stern himself he seated,
Sat behind the birchwood vessel,
And he steered the vessel onward,
And he spoke the words which follow:
"Speed thou on through treeless regions,
O'er the wide expanse of water,
O'er the sea do thou float lightly,
As on waves a water-lily!"

Then he set the youths to rowing,
But he left the maidens resting;   300
Rowed the youths, and bent the oars,
Yet the vessel moved not onward.

Then he set the girls to rowing,
But he left the youths reposing;
Rowed the girls, and bent their fingers,
Yet the vessel moved not onward.

Then the old folks set to rowing,
While the young folks gazed upon them;
Rowed they till their heads were shaking,
Still the vessel moved not onward.   310

Thereupon smith Ilmarinen
Sat him down, and set to rowing;
Now moved on the wooden vessel,
Sped the boat and made good progress,
Far was heard the splash of oars,
Far the splashing of the rudder.

On he rowed, while splashed the water,
Cracked the seats, and shook the planking,
Clashed the mountain-ashwood oars,
Creaked like hazel-grouse the rudders,   320
And their tips like cry of blackcock.
Like a swan the prow clove onward,
Croaked the stern as croaks a raven,
Hissed the rowlocks just as geese hiss.

And the aged Väinämöinen
Steered the vessel quickly onward,

From the stern of the red vessel,
With the aid of the strong rudder,
Till they saw a cliff before them,
And perceived a wretched village.   330

On the cape was Ahti dwelling,
In its bend was Kauko living,
Weeping that the fish had failed him,
Weeping that the bread had failed him;
For the smallness of his storehouse,
Wept the scamp his wretched fortune.
At a boat's planks he was working,
At a new boat's keel was working,
On this hungry promontory,
And beside the wretched village.   340

Very keen was Ahti's hearing,
But his sight was even keener;
As he gazed afar to north-west,
And to south his head was turning;
Suddenly he saw a rainbow,
And a single cloud beyond it.
What he saw was not a rainbow,
Nor a little cloud beyond it;
But a boat that speeded swiftly,
And a vessel rushing onward   350
O'er the broad sea's shining surface,
Out upon the open water,
In the stern a noble hero,
And a handsome man was rowing.

Said the lively Lemminkäinen,
"What this boat may be I know not,
Whose may be this handsome vessel,
Which is hither rowed from Suomi,
From the east, with strokes of oars,
And its rudder to the north-west."   360

Then with all his might he shouted,
Shouted, and continued shouting,
From the cape the hero called out,

Called out loudly o'er the water,
"Whose the boat that cleaves the water,
Whose the vessel on the billows?"

From the boat the men made answer,
And the women answered likewise:
"Who art thou, O forest-dweller,
Hero, breaking through the thicket,   370
That thou dost not know this vessel,
Whose from Väinölä this vessel,
Dost not even know the steersman,
Nor the hero at the oars?"

Said the lively Lemminkäinen,
"Now do I perceive the steersman,
And I recognize the oarsman:
Väinämöinen, old and steadfast,
In the vessel's stern is sitting,
Ilmarinen at the oars.   380
Whither then away, O heroes,
Whither do you journey, heroes?"

Said the aged Väinämöinen,
"To the northward do we journey,
Journey through the foaming billows,
And above the foam-flecked billows.
Forth we go to seize the Sampo,
Gaze upon its pictured cover,
There in Pohjola's stone mountain,
And within the hill of copper."   390

Said the lively Lemminkäinen,
"O thou aged Väinämöinen!
Take me with you as your comrade,
As the third among the heroes,
When you go to seize the Sampo,
Bear away the pictured cover.
Perhaps my manly sword may aid you,
In the combat may be useful,
As my hands may bear you witness,
And my shoulders witness to you."   400

Väinämöinen, old and steadfast,
Took the man upon his journey,
In the boat he took the rascal;
And the lively Lemminkäinen
Hurried on to climb upon it,
And he hastened quick to board it,
And his planks he carried with him
To the boat of Väinämöinen.

Said the aged Väinämöinen,
"In my boat is wood in plenty,   410
Planks sufficient for the vessel,
And besides 'tis heavy laden.
Wherefore do you bring more planking,
Bringing timber to the vessel?"

Said the lively Lemminkäinen,
"Foresight will not sink the vessel,
Nor o'erturns a prop the haystack;
Often on the sea of Pohja,
Does the wind demand strong planking,
And the head wind tests your boatsides."   420

Said the aged Väinämöinen,
"Therefore in a ship for battle,
Are the sides composed of iron,
And the prow of steel constructed,
Lest the wind aside should turn it,
Storms should shatter it to pieces."

XL The pike and the *kantele*

The *Sampo*-raiders come to a waterfall, beneath which the boat is caught fast on the back of a great pike (1–94). The pike is killed, and the front part is taken into the boat, cooked, and eaten (94–204). Väinämöinen makes the jaws of the pike into a *kantele*, on which several of the party attempt to play, but without success (205–342).

Väinämöinen, old and steadfast,
Steered the vessel swiftly forward,
On beyond the jutting headland,
On beyond the wretched village,
Singing songs upon the water,
Joyous songs upon the billows.

On the cape were maidens standing,
And they looked around and listened:
"From the sea there comes rejoicing,
And what song from sea re-echoes,   10
Far more joyous than aforetime,
And a finer song than any?"

Onward steered old Väinämöinen,
For a day o'er lake was steering,
For the next through marshy waters,
For the third day past a cataract.

Then the lively Lemminkäinen
Thought of spells he heard aforetime,
Once nearby a roaring cataract,
And the sacred river's whirlpool.   20
And he spoke the words which follow,
And expressed himself in singing:

"Cease, O Cataract, thy foaming,
Mighty water, cease thy rushing,
Thou, foam-maiden, Rapids's daughter,
On the foam-flecked stones, O seat thee,
On the wet stones do thou seat thee,
In thy lap the waters gather,
And in both thy hands collect them,
With thy hands repress their fury,   30
That upon our breasts they splash not,
Nor upon our heads are falling!

Thou, old dame, beneath the billows,
Lady, pillowed on the waters!
Raise thy head above the waters,
Rise from bosom of the waters,
That the foam be heaped together,
And that thou mayst watch the foam-wreaths,
Lest they should o'erwhelm the guiltless,
And should overthrow the faultless!   40

Stones that stand amid the river,
Slabs of stone with foam o'ercovered,
Be ye sunk into the water,
And your heads be pressed beneath it,
From the red boat's pathway banished,
From the course the tarred boat follows!

If this is not yet sufficient,
Stony Kimmo, son of Kammo,
Make an opening with thy auger,   50
With thy wimble pierce a deep hole,
Through the stones in river standing,
And the dangerous slabs that border,
That the boat may pass uninjured,
And the vessel pass undamaged!

If this is not yet sufficient,
Water-Father, 'neath the river,
Into moss the rocks transform thee,
Make the boat like pike's light bladder,
As amid the foam it rushes,
As beneath the banks it passes!   60

"Maiden in the rapids dwelling,
Girl who dwell'st beside the river,
Do thou spin a thread of softness,
In a soft ball do thou wind it,
Drop thy thread into the water,
Through the blue waves do thou guide it,
That the boat its track may follow,
While its tarry prow speeds onward,
So that men the least instructed,
E'en the inexperienced find it!   70

Melatar, thou gracious matron!
Of thy favour, take the rudder,
That with which thou guid'st the vessel,
Safely through the streams enchanted,
Pass the house that jaundiced eyes has,
Underneath the sorcerer's windows!

If this is not yet sufficient,
Ukko, Jumala in heaven,
With thy sword direct the vessel!
With thy naked sword direct it,   80
That the wooden boat speed onward,
Journey on, the pinewood vessel."

Then the aged Väinämöinen,
Steered the vessel swiftly forward,
Through the river-rocks he steered it,
Steered it through the foaming waters,
And the wooden vessel wedged not,
Nor the wise man's boat was grounded.

But as they their voyage continued
Once again in open water,   90
Suddenly the vessel halted,
Stopped the boat upon its journey;
In its place remained it fastened,
And the vessel rocked no longer.

Thereupon smith Ilmarinen,
With the lively Lemminkäinen,
Pushed into the sea the rudder,

In the waves the spar of pinewood,
And they tried to loose the vessel,
And to free the wooden vessel;   100
But they could not move the vessel,
Nor release the wooden vessel.

Väinämöinen, old and steadfast,
Uttered then the words which follow:
"O thou lively son of Lempi,
Stoop thou down, and look around thee.
Look what stops the boat from moving,
Look what keeps the the boat in standstill.
Here amid the open water;
What the force beneath that holds it,   110
Whether stopped by rocks or branches,
Or by any other hindrance!"

Then the lively Lemminkäinen
Stooped him down to look about him,
And he looked beneath the vessel,
And he spoke the words which follow:
"Not on rock the boat is resting,
Not on boat, and not on branches,
But upon a pike's broad shoulders,
And on water-dog's great backbone."   120

Väinämöinen, old and steadfast,
Answered in the words which follow:
"All things may be found in rivers,
Whether they are pikes or branches;
If we rest on pike's broad shoulders,
And on water-dog's great backbone,
Plunge your sword into the water,
Thus in twain the fish to sever!"

Then the lively Lemminkäinen
Ruddy youth, accomplished rascal,   130
Drew his sword from out his sword-belt,
From his side the bone-destroyer;
In the lake his sword plunged deeply,
Thrust it underneath the vessel,

But he splashed into the water,
Plunged himself into the billows.

Thereupon smith Ilmarinen
By the hair seized fast the hero,
Dragged from out the sea the hero,
And he spoke the words which follow: 140
"All pretend to grow to manhood,
And are ready to be bearded,
Such as these we count by hundreds,
And their number mounts to thousands!"

From his belt he drew his sword-blade,
From the sheath the keen-edged weapon,
And he struck the fish with fury,
Striking down beneath the vessel;
But the sword in pieces shivered,
And the pike was injured nothing.   150

Väinämöinen, old and steadfast,
Uttered then the words which follow:
"Not the half of manhood have you,
Not the third part of a hero!
But a man is now required,
And a man's sense now is needed,
All the sense of the unskilful,
All the efforts of the others."

Then himself he drew his sword-blade,
Firmly grasped the keen-edged weapon,   160
In the sea his sword then thrust he,
Underneath the boat he struck it,
At the pike's great shoulders striking
At the water-dog's great backbone.

But the sword was fixed securely,
In the fish's jaws fixed firmly;
Then the aged Väinämöinen
Presently the fish uplifted,
Dragged it up from out the water;
And the pike in twain he severed.   170

To the bottom sank the fish-tail,
In the boat the head he hoisted.

Now again moved on the vessel,
And the boat-prow now was loosened.
Väinämöinen, old and steadfast
To the shoals steered on the vessel,
To the shore the boat he guided,
And he turned and looked about him,
And the pike's great head examined,
And he spoke the words which follow: 180
"Let the eldest of the yeomen,
Come and cleave the pike to pieces,
Let him carve it into slices,
Let him hew the head to pieces!"

From the boat the men made answer,
From the boat replied the women:
"But the captor's hands are finer,
And the speaker's fingers better."

Väinämöinen, old and steadfast,
Drew from out the sheath his knife-blade,   190
From his side the cold sharp iron,
That the pike might be divided,
And he cut the fish to pieces,
And he spoke the words which follow:
"Let the youngest of the maidens,
Cook the pike that we have captured,
Let her mince it for our breakfast,
That on fish we make our repast."

Then the maidens set to cooking,
Ten there were who made the effort,   200
And they cooked the pike for eating,
And they minced it for their breakfast;
On the reefs the bones they scattered,
On the rocks they left the fishbones.

Väinämöinen, old and steadfast,
Saw the bones where they were lying,
And he turned to look upon them,

And he spoke the words which follow:
"What might well be fashioned from them,
From the pike's teeth be constructed,   210
From the fragments of the jawbones,
Were they to the smithy taken,
To the skilful smith entrusted,
To the hands of one most skilful?"

Said the smith, said Ilmarinen,
"Nothing comes from what is useless,
Nothing can be made of fishbones,
By a smith in smithy working,
Though to skilful smith entrusted,
To the hands of one most skilful."   220

Väinämöinen, old and steadfast,
Answered in the words which follow:
"Yet a harp might be constructed
Even of the bones of fishes,
If there were a skilful workman,
Who could from the bones construct it."

As no craftsman there was present,
And there was no skilful workman
Who could make a sound from fishbones,
Väinämöinen, old and steadfast,   230
Then began the harp to fashion,
And himself the work accomplished,
Of the pike bones he made music,
Fit to give unending pleasure.

Out of what did he construct it?
Chiefly from the great pike's jawbones,
Whence obtained he pegs to suit it?
Of the teeth of pike he made them;
Out of what were harpstrings fashioned?
From the hairs of Hiisi's gelding.   240

Now the instrument was ready,
And the kantele completed,
Fashioned from the pike's great jawbones,
And from fins of fish constructed.

Thereupon the youths came forward,
Forward came the married heroes,
And the half-grown boys came forward,
And the little girls came likewise,
Maidens young, and aged women,
And the women middle-agèd,   250
All advanced the harp to gaze on,
And the instrument examine.

Väinämöinen, old and steadfast,
Bade the young folks and the old ones,
And the people middle-agèd,
With their fingers play upon it,
On the instrument of fishbone,
On the kantele of fishbone.

Played the young and played the aged,
Likewise played the middle-agèd,   260
Played the young, and moved their fingers,
Tried the old, whose heads were shaking,
But they drew no music from it,
Nor composed a tune when playing.

Said the lively Lemminkäinen,
"O ye boys half-witted only,
And ye maidens, all so stupid,
And you other wretched people!
'Tis not thus you play upon it,
Neither are you skilled musicians.   270
Give me now the harp of fishbone,
Let me try to play upon it,
On my knees now place it for me,
At the tips of my ten fingers!"

Then the lively Lemminkäinen
In his hands the harp uplifted
And he drew it nearer to him,
Held it underneath his fingers;
And he tried to play upon it,
And the kantele he twisted;   280
But could play no tune upon it,
Draw no cheerful music from it.

Said the aged Väinämöinen,
"There are none among the youthful,
Nor among the growing people,
Nor among the aged people,
Who can play upon these harpstrings,
Drawing cheerful music from them.
Perhaps in Pohjola 'twere better,
Tunes perhaps might be played on it,   290
Cheerful music played upon it,
If to Pohjola I took it."

So to Pohjola he took it,
And to Sariola he brought it,
And the boys they played upon it,
Boys and girls both played upon it,
And the married men played on it,
Likewise all the married women,
And the Mistress played upon it,
And they turned the harp and twisted,   300
Held it firmly in their fingers,
At the tips of their ten fingers.
Thus played all the youths of Pohja,
People played of every station,
But no cheerful notes came from it,
And they played no music on it;
For the strings were all entangled,
And the horsehair whined most sadly,
And the notes were all discordant,
And the music all was jarring.   310

In the corner slept a blind man,
By the stove there lay an old man,
And beside the stove he wakened,
From the stove he raised an outcry,
From his couch he grumbled loudly,
And he grumbled, and he mumbled:
"Leave it off, and stop your playing,
Cut it short and finish quickly!
For the noise my ears is bursting,
Through my head the noise is echoing,   320
And through all my hair I feel it,
For a week you've made me sleepless.

"If the harp of Suomi's people
Cannot really give us pleasure,
Lulls us not to sleep when weary,
Nor to rest does it incline us,
Cast it forth upon the waters,
Sink it down beneath the billows,
Send it back to where it came from,
And the instrument deliver   330
To the hands of those who made it,
To the fingers which have shaped it."

With its tongue the harp made answer,
As the kantele resounded:
"No, I will not sink in water,
Nor will rest beneath the billows,
But will play for a musician,
Play for him who toiled to make me."

Carefully the harp they carried,
And with greatest care conveyed it   340
Back to him whose hands had made it,
To the knees of its constructor.

XLI   Väinämöinen's music

Väinämöinen plays on the *kantele*, and all living things, whether belonging to the air, earth, or water, hasten to the spot to listen (1–168). The hearts of all listeners are so affected by the music that tears fall from their eyes, and Väinämöinen's own eyes shed large drops which fall to the ground and trickle into the water, where they are changed into beautiful blue pearls (169–266).

Väinämöinen, old and steadfast,
He the great primeval minstrel,
Presently stretched out his fingers,
Washed his thumbs, the harp for playing,
On the stone of joy he sat him,
On the singer's stone he sat him,
On a hill all silver-shining,
From a golden heath arising.

Then the harp he grasped with fingers,
And upon his knee he propped it,   10
And his hands he placed beneath it,
Then he spoke the words which follow:
"Come ye now to listen to me,
Ye before who never heard me,
Hear with joy my songs primeval,
While the kantele is sounding!"

Then the aged Väinämöinen,
Quick commenced his skilful playing
On the instrument of pikebone,
On the kantele of fishbone,   20
And he raised his fingers nimbly,
And his thumb he lifted lightly.

Now came pleasure after pleasure,
As the sweet notes followed others,
As he sat and played the music,
As he sang his songs melodious,
As he played upon the pike-teeth,
And he lifted up the fish-tail,
And the horsehair sounded sweetly,   30
Clearly sang the strings of horsehair.

Played the aged Väinämöinen.
Nothing was there in the forest,
Which upon four feet was running,
Or upon their legs were hopping,
And which came not near to listen,
Came not to rejoice and wonder.

Gathered round him all the squirrels,
As from branch to branch they clambered,
And the ermines flocked around him,
Laid them down upon the fences,   40
On the plains the deer were springing,
And the lynxes shared the pleasure.

In the swamp each wolf awakened,
From the heath the bear aroused him,
From his lair among the pine-trees,
And the thickly growing fir-trees,
And the wolves ran lengthy journeys,
And the bears came through the heather,
Till they sat upon the fences,
Side by side against the gateway.   50
On the rocks the fence fell over,
On the field the gate fell over,
Then they climbed upon the fir-trees,
And they ran around the pine-trees,
Just to listen to the music,
All rejoicing, and in wonder.

Sage of Tapiola illustrious,
He of Metsola the Master,
And the whole of Tapio's people,
All the boys and all the maidens,   60

Climbed upon a mountain summit,
That they might enjoy the music,
While the Mistress of the Forest,
Keen-eyed matron of Tapiola,
Fine her stockings, blue in colour,
Firmly tied with crimson ribands,
Climbed into a crooked birch-tree,
Rested in a curving alder,
To the kantele to listen,
That she might enjoy the music.   70

And the birds of air assembled,
Those upon two wings that raise them,
Backwards sailing, forwards sailing,
And with all their speed came flying,
Swift to listen to the music,
All in wonder and rejoicing.

When the eagle in his aerie,
Heard the sweet tones sound from Suomi,
In the nest she left her fledgelings,
And she hovered round to listen   80
To the gallant hero's playing,
And to Väinämöinen's singing.

High in air there soared the eagle,
Through the clouds the hawk was sailing,
Came the ducks from deepest waters,
Came the swans from snow-wreathed marshes,
And the smallest of the finches,
All the twittering birds assembled,
Singing-birds flocked round by hundreds,
And in thousands they assembled   90
In the air, and heard delighted,
And alighted on his shoulders,
All rejoicing in the patriarch,
And in Väinämöinen's playing.

E'en the Daughters of Creation,
Of the air the charming maidens,
Gathered to rejoice and wonder,
To the kantele to listen.

Some on arch of air were seated,
Seated on the dazzling rainbow,   100
Some on little clouds were seated,
Resting on their crimson borders.

There were Kuutar, slender damsel;
Päivätär, the maid accomplished;
Casting with their hands the shuttle,
Drawing threads that they were weaving,
As they wove a golden fabric,
And they wove the threads of silver,
High upon the red cloud-borders,
On the borders of the rainbow.   110

But when they began to listen
To the notes of charming music,
From their hands they let the comb fall,
Cast from out their hands the shuttle,
And the golden bands were broken,
And the silver shaft was broken.

There remained no living creature,
None of those who dwell in water,
None who with six fins are moving,
Nor the largest shoals of fishes,   120
Which assembled not to listen,
Came not to rejoice and wonder.

Thither came the pikes all swimming,
And the water-dogs swam forward,
From the rocks swam swift the salmon,
From the deeps there came the powans,
Perch and little roach came also,
Powans white, and other fishes;
Through the reeds they pushed their bodies,
Straightway to the shore they hastened,   130
There to hear the songs of Väinö,
And to listen to his playing.

Ahto, king of all the billows,
Grass-beard ancient of the waters,
Mounted to the water's surface,

Climbed upon a water-lily,
To the notes with joy he listened,
And he spoke the words which follow:
"Never have I heard such music,
In the course of all my lifetime,   140
As is played by Väinämöinen,
Joyous and primeval minstrel."

And the sisters, Sotko's daughters,
Cousins of the reeds on lakeshore,
At the time their hair were brushing,
And their locks were deftly combing,
With a comb composed of silver,
And with golden brush they stroked it;
When they heard the strains unwonted,
And they heard the skilful playing;   150
In the waves they dropped the brushes,
Dropped the comb among the lake-waves,
And their hair unsmoothed was hanging,
Nor they smoothed it in the middle.

E'en the Mistress of the Waters,
Water-Mother, towards the rushes,
From the lake herself ascended,
Raised herself from out the billows,
Quickly moved her to the rushes,
Climbed a rock in water standing,   160
And she listened to the music,
And to Väinämöinen playing,
Listened to the wondrous music,
And to the delightful playing,
And she fell in deepest slumber,
Sank upon the ground in slumber,
On the mottled rocky surface,
Underneath a great rock's shelter.

Then the aged Väinämöinen,
Played one day, and played a second.   170
There was none among the heroes,
None among the men so mighty,
None among the men or women,
None of those whose hair is plaited,

Whom he did not move to weeping,
And whose hearts remained unmelted;
Wept the young and wept the aged,
All the married men were weeping,
Likewise all the married women,
And the half-grown boys were weeping,   180
All the boys, and all the maidens,
Likewise all the little children,
When they heard the tones so wondrous,
And the noble sage's music.

He himself, old Väinämöinen,
Felt his own tears rolling downward,
From his eyes the tears dropped downward,
And the water-drops fell downward;
They were tears than cranberries larger,
They were tears than peas much larger,   190
Than the eggs of grouse still rounder,
Larger than the heads of swallows.

From his eyes there fell the tear-drops,
Others followed after others,
Tears upon his cheeks were falling,
Down upon his cheeks so handsome,
Rolling from his cheeks so handsome,
Down upon his chin's expansion,
Rolling from his chin's expansion,
Down upon his panting bosom,   200
Rolling from his panting bosom,
Down upon his strong knee's surface,
Rolling from his strong knee's surface,
Down upon his feet so handsome,
Rolling from his feet so handsome,
Down upon the ground beneath them;
And five woollen cloaks were soaking,
Likewise six of gilded girdles,
Seven blue dresses too were soaking,
And ten overcoats were soaking.   210

And the tear-drops still were falling,
From the eyes of Väinämöinen,
Till they reached the blue sea's margin,

Overflowed the blue sea's margin,
Down below the sparkling water,
To the black ooze at the bottom.

Then the aged Väinämöinen
Spoke aloud the words which follow:
"Is there in this youthful party,
'Mid the young and fair here gathered,   220
'Mid these high-descended people,
Any darling child of father,
Who the tears I shed can gather,
From beneath the sparkling water?"

And the young folks gave him answer,
And the old folks likewise answered:
"There are none among the youthful,
In this young and fair assemblage,
'Mid these high-descended people,
Not a darling child of father,   230
Who the tears you shed can gather,
From beneath the sparkling water."

Then the aged Väinämöinen,
Spoke again in words that follow:
"He who brings my tears unto me,
And the tears again can gather,
From beneath the sparkling waters,
Shall receive a dress of feathers!"

Forth there came a raven passing;
Said the aged Väinämöinen: 240
"Bring me now my tears, O raven,
From beneath the sparkling water,
And receive the dress of feathers."
But the raven could not do it.

And the blue duck heard him likewise,
And the blue duck next came forward.
Said the aged Väinämöinen:
"Often, blue duck, does it happen
That thy beak thou plungest downward,
As thou speedest through the water.   250

Go thou forth my tears to gather,
From beneath the sparkling water,
Bounteous guerdon will I give thee,
And will give a dress of feathers."

Then the duck went forth to seek them,
Seek the tears of Väinämöinen,
Underneath the sparkling water,
On the black ooze of the bottom.
In the sea she found the tear-drops,
And to Väinö's hands she brought them,   260
But they were transformed already,
Suffered beauteous transformation.
Into pearls were they developed,
Like the blue pearls of the mussel,
Fit for every king's adornment,
To the great a lifelong pleasure.

XLII   The capture of the *Sampo*

The heroes arrive at Pohjola, and Väinämöinen announces that he has come to take possession of the *Sampo*, either with good-will, or by force (1–58). The Mistress of Pohjola refuses to yield it either by consent or by compulsion, and calls together her people to oppose him (59–64). Väinämöinen takes the *kantele*, begins to play, and lulls to sleep all the people of Pohjola, and goes with his companions to search for the *Sampo*; they take it from the stone mountain and convey it to the boat (65–164). They sail homewards well satisfied, carrying the *Sampo* with them (165–308). On the third day the Mistress of Pohjola wakes from her sleep, and when she finds that the *Sampo* has been carried off, she prepares a thick fog, a strong wind, and other impediments, to oppose the robbers of the *Sampo*, which reach the vessel, and during the tempest Väinämöinen's *kantele* falls into the water (309–562).

Väinämöinen, old and steadfast,
Secondly, smith Ilmarinen,
Third, the lively son of Lempi,
He the handsome Kaukomieli,
Sailed upon the sea's broad surface,
O'er the far-extending billows,
To the cold and dreary village,
To the misty land of Pohja,
To the land where men are devoured,
Where the heroes will be drowned.   10

Who should row the vessel onward?
First, the smith named Ilmarinen.
He it was who rowed the vessel,
He was first among the rowers,
And the lively Lemminkäinen
Was the last among the rowers.

Väinämöinen, old and steadfast,
In the stern himself was seated,
And he steered the vessel onward,
Through the waves he steered it onward,   20
Through the foaming waves he steered it,
Steered it o'er the foam-capped billows,
Unto Pohja's distant havens,
To his well-known destination.

When they reached the goal they sought for,
And the voyage at length was ended,
To the land they drew the vessel,
Up they drew the tarry vessel,
Laid it on the steely rollers,
At the quay with copper edging.   30

After this the house they entered,
Crowding hastily within it;
Then did Pohjola's old Mistress,
Ask the purport of their coming:
"Men, what tidings do you bring us,
What fresh news, O heroes, bring you?"

Väinämöinen, old and steadfast,
Answered in the words which follow:
"Men are speaking of the Sampo,
Heroes, of its pictured cover.   40
We have come to share the Sampo,
And behold its brilliant cover."

Then did Pohjola's old Mistress
Answer in the words which follow:
"Two men cannot share a grouseling,
Nor can three divide a squirrel,
And the Sampo loud is whirring,
And the pictured cover grinding,
Here in Pohjola's stone mountain,
And within the hill of copper.   50
I myself rejoice in welfare,
Mistress of the mighty Sampo."

Väinämöinen, old and steadfast,
Answered in the words which follow:
"If you will not share the Sampo,
Give us half to carry with us,
Then the Sampo, all entire,
To our vessel will we carry."

Louhi, Pohjola's old Mistress,
Heard him with the greatest anger,   60
Called together all her people,
Summoned all her youthful swordsmen,
Bade them all to aim their weapons
At the head of Väinämöinen.

Väinämöinen, old and steadfast,
Took the kantele and played it,
Down he sat and played upon it,
And began a tune delightful;
All who listened to his playing
Heard it with delight and wonder,   70
And the men were all delighted,
And the women's mouths were laughing,
Tears from heroes' eyes were falling,
Boys upon the ground were kneeling.
At the last their strength forsook them,
And the people all were wearied;
All the listeners sank in slumber,
On the ground sank all beholders,
Slept the old and slept the youthful,
All at Väinämöinen's playing.   80

Then the crafty Väinämöinen,
He the great primeval minstrel,
Put his hand into his pocket,
And he drew his purse from out it,
And sleep-needles took he from it,
And their eyes he plunged in slumber,
And their eyelashes crossed tightly,
Locked their eyelids close together,
Sank the people all in slumber.

Into sleep he plunged the heroes,   90
And they sank in lasting slumber,
And he plunged in languid slumber
All the host of Pohja's people,
All the people of the village.

Then he went to fetch the Sampo,
And behold its pictured cover,
There in Pohjola's stone mountain,
And within the hill of copper.
Nine the locks that there secured it,
Bars secured it, ten in number.   100

Then the aged Väinämöinen
Gently set himself to singing
At the copper mountain's entrance,
There beside the stony fortress;
And the castle doors were shaken,
And the iron hinges trembled.

Thereupon smith Ilmarinen,
Aided by the other heroes,
Overspread the locks with butter,
And with lard he rubbed the hinges,   110
That the doors should make no jarring,
And the hinges make no creaking.
Then the locks he turned with fingers,
And the bars and bolts he lifted,
And he broke the locks to pieces,
And the mighty doors were opened.

Then the aged Väinämöinen
Spoke aloud the words which follow:
"O thou lively son of Lempi,
Of my friends the most illustrious,   120
Come thou here to take the Sampo,
And to seize its brilliant cover!"

Then the lively Lemminkäinen,
He the handsome Kaukomieli,
Always eager, though unbidden,
Ready, though men did not praise him,

Came to carry off the Sampo,
And to seize its pictured cover,
And he said as he was coming,
Boasted as he hastened forward: 130
"O, I am a man of mettle,
And a hero-son of Ukko!
I can surely move the Sampo,
And can seize its brilliant cover,
Standing on my right foot only,
If I touch it with my shoe-heel!"

Lemminkäinen pushed against it,
Turned himself, and pushed against it,
Pushed his arms and breast against it,
On the ground his knees down-pressing;   140
But he could not move the Sampo,
Could not stir its pictured cover,
For the roots were sunken firmly
In the depths nine fathoms under.

There was then a bull in Pohja,
Which had grown to size enormous,
And his sides were sleek and fattened,
And his sinews of the strongest;
Horns he had in length a fathom,
One-half more his muzzle's thickness.   150

So they led him from the meadow,
On the borders of the ploughed field,
Up they ploughed the roots of Sampo,
Those which fixed the brilliant cover!
Then began to move the Sampo,
And to sway the pictured cover.

Then the aged Väinämöinen,
Secondly, smith Ilmarinen,
Third, the lively Lemminkäinen
Carried forth the mighty Sampo,   160
Forth from Pohjola's stone mountain,
From within the hill of copper;
To the boat away they bore it,
And within the ship they stowed it.

In the boat they stowed the Sampo,
In the hold the pictured cover,
Pushed the boat into the water,
In the waves the hundred-boarded;
Splashed the boat into the water,
In the waves its sides descended.   170

Asked the smith, said Ilmarinen,
And he spoke the words which follow:
"'Whither shall we bear the Sampo,
Whither shall we now convey it,
Take it from this evil country,
From the wretched land of Pohja?"

Väinämöinen, old and steadfast,
Answered in the words which follow:
"Thither shall we bear the Sampo,
And will take the pictured cover,   180
To the misty island's headland,
At the end of shady island,
There in safety can we keep it,
There it can remain for ever.
There's a little spot remaining,
Yet a little plot left over,
Where they eat not and they fight not,
Whither swordsmen never wander."

Then the aged Väinämöinen
Steered away from Pohja's borders,   190
Sailed away in great contentment,
Joyous to his native country;
And he spoke the words which follow:
"Speed from Pohjola, O vessel,
Make thy way directly homeward,
Leave behind the foreign country!

Blow, thou wind, and sway the vessel,
Urge the boat upon the water,
Lend assistance to the rowers,
To the rudder give thou lightness,   200

On the wide expanse of water,
Out upon the open water!

If the oars should be too little,
And too weak should be the oarsmen,
In the stern too small the steerer,
And the vessel's masters children,
Ahto, give thyself thy oars
To the boat, O Water-Master,
Give the best and newest oars,
Give us, too, a stronger rudder!   210
Do thou seat thee at the oars,
Do thou undertake the rowing,
Speed thou on this wooden vessel,
Urge the iron-rowlocked forward,
Drive it through the foaming billows,
Through the foam-capped billows drive it!"

Then the aged Väinämöinen
Steered the vessel swiftly forward,
While the smith named Ilmarinen,
And the lively Lemminkäinen,   220
Set themselves to work the oars,
And they rowed, and speeded onward
O'er the sparkling water's surface,
O'er the surface of the billows.

Said the lively Lemminkäinen,
"Formerly when I was rowing,
There was water for the rowers,
There was singing for the minstrels,
But at present time, when rowing,
Nothing do we hear of singing,   230
In the boat we hear no singing,
On the waves we hear no chanting."

Väinämöinen, old and steadfast,
Answered in the words which follow:
"Do not sing upon the waters,
Do not chant upon the billows:

Singing brings the boat to halting,
Songs would but impede the rowing,
Then would wane the golden daylight,
And the night descend upon us,   240
On the wide expanse of water,
On the surface of the billows."

Then the lively Lemminkäinen
Answered in the words which follow:
"Anyway, the time is passing,
Fades away the lovely daylight,
And the night is swift approaching,
And the twilight comes upon us,
Though no song our life enlivens,
Nor the time is given to chanting."   250

Steered the aged Väinämöinen
O'er the blue sea's shining water,
And he steered one day, a second.
And at length upon the third day
Then the lively Lemminkäinen
For a second time inquired:
"Wherefore sing not, Väinämöinen?
O thou great one, sing unto us!
We have won the splendid Sampo;
Straight the course that now we follow."   260

Väinämöinen, old and steadfast,
Gave him a decided answer:
"'Tis too early yet for singing,
'Tis too early for rejoicing.
Soon a time will come for singing,
Fitting time for our rejoicing,
When we see our doors before us,
And we hear our own doors creaking."

Said the lively Lemminkäinen,
"In the stern I'll take position,   270
And with all my might will sing there,
And with all my force will bellow.
Perhaps indeed I cannot do so,
Loud enough I cannot bellow:

If you will not sing unto us,
Then will I commence the singing."

Then the lively Lemminkäinen,
He the handsome Kaukomieli,
Quickly pursed his mouth for singing,   280
And prepared himself to carol,
And began to sing his carols,
But his songs were most discordant,
And his voice it sounded hoarsely,
And his tones were sharp and tuneless.

Sang the lively Lemminkäinen,
Shouted loudly Kaukomieli,
Moved his mouth, his beard was wagging,
And his chin was likewise shaking.
Far away was heard his singing;
Far away across the water,   290
In six villages they heard it,
Over seven the song resounded.

On a stump a crane was sitting,
On a mound from swamp arising,
And his toe-bones he was counting,
And his feet he was uplifting,
And was terrified extremely
At the song of Lemminkäinen.

Left the crane his strange employment,
With his harsh voice screamed in terror,   300
From the marsh he flew in terror,
Over Pohjola in terror,
And upon his coming thither,
When he reached the swamp of Pohja,
Screamed again, and screamed harshly,
Screamed out at his very loudest:
Waked in Pohjola the people,
And aroused that evil nation.

Up rose Pohjola's old Mistress
From her long and heavy slumber,   310
And she hastened to the farmyard,

Ran to where the corn was drying,
And she looked upon the cattle,
And the corn in haste examined.
Nought was missing from the cattle,
And the corn had not been plundered.

To the hill of stone she wandered,
And the copper mountain's entrance,
And she said as she was coming:
"Woe to me, this day unhappy!   320
For a stranger here has entered,
And the locks have all been opened,
And the castle's doors been opened,
And the iron hinges broken.
Has the Sampo then been stolen,
And the whole been taken from us?"

Yes, the Sampo had been taken,
Carried off the pictured cover,
Forth from Pohjola's stone mountain,
From within the hill of copper,   330
Though by ninefold locks protected,
Though ten bars protected likewise.

Louhi, Pohjola's old Mistress,
Fell into the greatest fury,
But she felt her strength was failing,
And her power had all departed,
So she prayed to the Cloud-Maiden:
"Maiden of the Clouds, Mist-Maiden,
Scatter from thy sieve the cloudlets,
And the mists around thee scatter,   340
Send the thick clouds down from heaven,
Sink thou from the air of vapour,
O'er the broad sea's shining surface,
Out upon the open water,
On the head of Väinämöinen,
Falling on Uvantolainen!

But if this is not sufficient,
Iku-Turso, son of Äijö,
Lift thy head from out the water,

Raise thy head above the billows, 350
Crush thou Kaleva's vile children,
Sink thou down Uvantolainen,
Sink thou down the wicked heroes
In the depths beneath the billows,
Bring to Pohjola the Sampo,
Let it fall not from the vessel!
But if this is not sufficient,
Ukko, thou, of Gods the highest,
Golden king in airy regions,
Mighty one, adorned with silver! 360
Let the air be filled with tempest,
Raise a mighty wind against them,
Raise thou winds and waves against them,
With their boat contending ever,
Falling on the head of Väinö,
Rushing on Uvantolainen!"

Then the Maid of Clouds, Mist-Maiden,
From the sea a cloud breathed upward,
Through the air the cloud she scattered,
And detained old Väinämöinen, 370
And for three whole nights she kept him
Out upon the sea's blue surface,
And he could not move beyond it,
Nor could he escape beyond it.

When for three nights he had rested
Out upon the sea's blue surface,
Spoke the aged Väinämöinen,
And expressed himself in thiswise:
"There's no man, how weak soever,
Not among the laziest heroes, 380
Who by clouds would thus be hindered,
And by mists would thus be worsted."

With his sword he clove the water,
In the sea his sword plunged deeply,
Mead along his blade was flowing,
Honey from his sword was dropping.
Then the fog to heaven ascended,
And the cloud in air rose upward,

From the sea the mist ascended,
And the vapour from the sea-waves,   390
And the sea extended widely,
Wider spread the whole horizon.

But a little time passed over,
Short the time that then passed over,
When they heard a mighty roaring,
At the red boat's side they heard it,
And the foam flew wildly upwards,
'Gainst the boat of Väinämöinen.

Thereupon smith Ilmarinen,
Felt the very greatest terror.   400
From his cheeks the blood departed,
From his cheeks the ruddy colour;
O'er his head he drew his felt-cap,
And above his ears he drew it,
And his cheeks with care he covered,
And his eyes he covered better.

Then the aged Väinämöinen
Looked into the water round him,
Cast his gaze beside the vessel,
And he saw a mighty wonder: 410
Iku-Turso, son of Äijö,
By the red boat's side was lifting
High his head from out the water,
Raising it from out the billows!

Väinämöinen, old and steadfast,
Grasped his ears upon the instant,
By the ears he dragged him upward,
And he sang aloud, and questioned,
And he said the words which follow:
"Iku-Turso, son of Äijö,   420
Wherefore from the sea uplift thee,
Wherefore rise above the billows,
Thus thyself to men revealing,
Even Kaleva's own children?"

Iku-Turso, son of Äijö,
Was not pleased with this reception,
But he was not very frightened,
And no answer he returned him.

Väinämöinen, old and steadfast,
Asked again an explanation,   430
And a third time asked him loudly:
"Iku-Turso, son of Äijö!
Wherefore from the sea uplift thee,
Wherefore rise above the billows?"

Iku-Turso, son of Äijö,
When he asked him for the third time,
Answered in the words which follow:
"Therefore from the sea I raise me,
Therefore rise above the billows:
For that in my mind I purpose   440
Kaleva's great race to ruin,
To bear to Pohjola the Sampo.
In the waves if you will send me,
And my wretched life concede me,
Not another time ascending,
In the sight of men I'll venture."

Then the aged Väinämöinen
Cast the wretch into the billows,
And he said the words which follow:
"Iku-Turso, son of Äijö!   450
Nevermore from sea arising,
Or ascending from the billows,
Venture forth where men can see thee,
From this very day henceforward."

Therefore from that day thenceforward,
Never from the sea rose Turso,
In the sight of men to venture,
Long as sun and moon are shining,
Or the pleasant day is dawning,
And the air is most delightful.   460

Then the aged Väinämöinen
Once again steered on the vessel;
But a little time passed over,
Short the time that then passed over,
When did Ukko, God the Highest,
Of the air the mighty ruler,
Winds arouse in magic fury,
Made the tempests rage around them.

Then the winds arose in fury,
And the tempests raged around them,   470
And the west wind blew most fiercely,
From the south-west just as fiercely,
And the south wind still more fiercely,
And the east wind whistled loudly,
Roared the south-east wind tremendous,
And the north wind howled in fury.

From the trees the leaves were scattered,
And the fir-trees lost their needles,
And the heather lost its flowerets,
And the grasses lost their tassels,   480
And the black ooze was uplifted
To the sparkling water's surface.

Still the winds were wildly blowing,
And the waves assailed the vessel,
Swept away the harp of pikebone,
And the kantele of fish-fins,
Joy for Vellamo's attendants,
And to Ahtola a pleasure.
Ahto on the waves perceived it,
On the waves his children saw it,   490
And they grasped the harp so charming,
And unto their home conveyed it.

Then the aged Väinämöinen
From his eyes wept tears of sadness,
And he spoke the words which follow:
"Thus has gone what I constructed,
And my cherished harp has vanished,
And is lost my life-long pleasure.

Never will it happen to me,
In the course of all my lifetime   500
To rejoice again in pike-teeth,
Or to play on bones of fishes."

Thereupon smith Ilmarinen
Felt the very greatest sadness,
And he spoke the words which follow:
"Woe to me, this day unhappy,
That upon the sea I travel,
On this wide expanse of water,
That I tread on wood that's rolling,
And on planks that shake beneath me!   510
Now my hair has seen the tempest,
And my hair begins to shudder,
And my beard ill days has witnessed,
Which it saw upon the water,
Yet have we but seldom witnessed,
Such a storm as rages round us,
Witnessed such tremendous breakers,
Or have seen such foam-capped billows.
Let the wind be now my refuge,
And the waves have mercy on me."   520

Väinämöinen, old and steadfast,
Heard his words, and thus responded:
"In the boat's no place for weeping,
Room is none for lamentation;
Weeping helps not in misfortune,
Howling, not when days are evil!"
Then he spoke the words which follow,
And he sang and thus expressed him:
"Water, now restrain thy children,
And, O wave, do thou restrain them!   530
Ahto, do thou calm the billows,
Vellamo, o'ercome the waters,
That they splash not on our timbers,
Nor may overwhelm my boat-ribs!

Rise, O wind, aloft to heaven,
And among the clouds disport thee,
To thy race, where thou wast nurtured,

To thy family and kindred!
Do not harm this wooden vessel,
Sink thou not this boat of pinewood.   540
Rather fell burnt trees in clearings,
On the slopes o'erthrow the fir-trees!"

Then the lively Lemminkäinen,
He the handsome Kaukomieli,
Spoke aloud the words which follow:
"Come, O eagle, thou from Turja,
Do thou bring three feathers with thee,
Three, O eagle, two, O raven,
To protect this little vessel,
To protect this poor boat's timbers!"   550

He himself enlarged the bulwarks,
Fixed the timbers in their places,
And to these fresh boards he added,
And to fathom-height he raised them,
Higher than the waves were leaping,
Nor upon his beard they splashed him.

All his work was now completed,
And the bulwarks raised protecting,
Though the winds might blow most fiercely,
And the waves might beat in fury,   560
And the foam be wildly seething,
And like hillocks be uprising.

XLIII   The fight for the *Sampo*

The Mistress of Pohjola equips a war-vessel and goes in pursuit of the robbers of the *Sampo* (1–22). When she overtakes them a fight ensues between the forces of Pohjola and Kalevala in which the latter conquer (23–258). Nevertheless the Mistress of Pohjola succeeds in dragging the *Sampo* from the boat into the sea, where it breaks to pieces (259–66). The larger portions sink in the sea, and form its riches, while the smaller pieces are thrown on shore by the waves, at which Väinämöinen is much pleased (267–304). The Mistress of Pohjola threatens to send all evil upon Kalevala, to which Väinämöinen pays no attention (305–68). The Mistress of Pohjola returns home in great distress, taking with her only a small fragment of the cover of the *Sampo* (369–84). Väinämöinen carefully collects the fragments of the *Sampo* on the shore, and plants them, hoping for continuous good fortune (385–434).

Louhi, Pohjola's old Mistress,
Called together all her forces,
Bows delivered to her army,
And the men with swords provided,
Fitted out a ship of Pohja,
As a war-ship she prepared it.

In the ship the men she stationed,
And equipped for war the heroes,
As the duck her ducklings musters,
Or the teal her children marshals;   10
There she ranged a hundred swordsmen,
And a thousand men with crossbows.

In the boat the mast she lifted,
Put the yards and spars in order,
On the mast the sails adjusted,
Spread the canvas o'er the sailyards;

Like a hanging cloud it waved there,
Like a cloud in heaven suspended;
Then upon her voyage she started,
Sailed away and speeded onward,   20
Soon to struggle for the Sampo,
With the boat of Väinämöinen.

Väinämöinen, old and steadfast,
O'er the blue sea steered his vessel,
And he spoke the words which follow,
From the stern where he was seated:
"O thou lively son of Lempi,
Of my friends the dearest to me,
Climb thou quickly to the masthead,
And among the canvas hasten.   30
Look thou to the air before thee,
Look thou to the sky behind thee,
Whether clear is the horizon,
If the skies are clear or cloudy!"

Then the lively Lemminkäinen,
Ruddy youth, accomplished scoundrel,
Very active, though unbidden,
Very quick, though never boastful,
To the masthead then ascended,
Up aloft among the canvas.   40

East he looked, and looked to westward,
Looked to north-west and to southward,
Looked across to Pohja's coast-line,
And he spoke the words which follow:
"Clear in front is the horizon,
Dark behind is the horizon:
Rises north a cloud, a small one,
Hangs a single cloud to north-west."

Said the aged Väinämöinen,
"What you say is surely nonsense,   50
For no cloud is there ascending,
Nor a single cloud arising,
But perchance a sailing vessel;
Look again, and look more sharply!"

Then he looked again more sharply,
And he spoke the words which follow:
"Far away I see an island,
Dimly looming in the distance,
Aspens covered o'er with falcons,
Speckled grouse upon the birchtrees."   60

Said the aged Väinämöinen,
"What you say is surely nonsense,
For no falcons do you see there,
And no speckled grouse you see there,
But perchance the sons of Pohja;
Look more sharply for the third time!"

Then the lively Lemminkäinen
For the third time looked around him,
And he spoke the words which follow,
And in words like these expressed him: 70
"'Tis a ship from Pohja sailing,
With a hundred rowlocks fitted,
And I see a hundred oarsmen,
And a thousand men beside them!"

Then the aged Väinämöinen,
All the truth at once perceiving,
Spoke aloud the words which follow:
"Row, thou smith, row, Ilmarinen!
Row, O lively Lemminkäinen!
Row ye also, all ye people,   80
That the boat be hurried forward,
And the vessel onward driven!"

Rowed the smith, rowed Ilmarinen,
Rowed the lively Lemminkäinen;
All the people joined in rowing.
Swayed about the pinewood oars,
Loudly rang the rowan rowlocks,
And the pinewood boat was swaying.
Like a seal the prow dashed onward,
Boiled the waves behind like rapids,   90
Like a bell uprose the water,
And the foam flew up in masses.

As for wager rowed the heroes,
As in race the heroes struggled,
But they rowed, and made no progress,
Nor could urge the wooden vessel
Further from the sailing vessel,
And the ship that came from Pohja.

Then the aged Väinämöinen
Saw misfortune fast approaching.   100
On his head was doomsday falling,
And he pondered and reflected,
How to act and how to save him,
And he spoke the words which follow:
"Still I know a plan of safety,
Still I see a little marvel."

Then he took a piece of tinder,
In his tinder-box he found it,
And of pitch he took a little,
And a little piece of tinder,   110
And into the sea he threw it,
O'er his shoulder left he threw it,
And he spoke the words which follow,
And in words like these expressed him:
"Let a reef of this be fashioned,
And a cliff be fashioned from it,
Where may run the ship of Pohja,
Fitted with a hundred rowlocks,
And may strike in sea tempestuous,
And amid the waves be shattered!"   120

Thereupon a reef grew upward,
In the sea a cliff was fashioned,
Half its length to east directed,
And its breadth to north directed.

Onward sped the ship of Pohja,
Gliding swiftly through the sea-waves,
And upon the reef came rushing,
And upon the rocks wedged firmly.
Broke across the wooden vessel,
And to splinters it was broken;   130

In the sea the masts fell crashing,
And the sails fell drooping downward,
By the wind away were carried,
And the spring wind all dispersed them.

Louhi, Pohjola's old Mistress,
Plunged her feet into the water,
And she tried to push the vessel,
And she tried to raise the vessel;
But no spear could lift the vessel,
And she could not even move it,   140
For the ribs had all been shattered,
All the rowlocks had been broken.
And she pondered and reflected,
And she spoke the words which follow:
"Who can aid me now with counsel?
Who can help me in this trouble?"

Then her form she quickly altered,
To another shape transformed her,
And she took five scythes the sharpest,
And six hoes, worn out completely;   150
These she fashioned into talons,
Into claws did she convert them;
Half the broken vessel's fragments
Did she then arrange beneath her,
And the sides to wings she fashioned,
And to tail she turned the rudder,
'Neath her wings took men a hundred,
On her tail she took a thousand,
And the hundred men were swordsmen,
And the thousand men were archers.   160

Then she flew, her wings extending,
And she soared aloft as eagle,
And she poised herself and hovered,
To attack old Väinämöinen;
In the clouds one wing was flapping,
In the water splashed the other.

Then the fairest Water-Mother
Spoke aloud the words which follow:

"O thou aged Väinämöinen!
Turn thy head beneath the sunrise,   170
Do thou turn thine eyes to north-west,
Look a little now behind thee!"

Väinämöinen, old and steadfast,
Turned his head beneath the sunrise,
And he turned his eyes to north-west,
Looked a little just behind him:
Onward came the crone of Pohja,
And the wondrous bird was hovering
Like a hawk about his shoulders,
With the body of an eagle.   180

Soon she came near Väinämöinen,
And she flew upon the masthead,
Clambered out upon the sailyard,
And upon the pole she sat her,
And the boat was nearly sinking,
And the vessel's side lurched downward.

Thereupon smith Ilmarinen
Sought from Jumala assistance,
And invoking the Creator,
Then he spoke the words which follow: 190
"Save us, O thou good Creator,
Gracious Jumala, protect us,
That thy son may not be buried,
Nor the mother's child hurled downward,
From among the living creatures,
From the creatures whom thou rulest!

Ukko, Jumala the Highest,
Thou our Father in the heavens!
Cast a fiery robe around me,
Over me a shift of fire,   200
That I thus may fight protected,
And may thus contend protected,
That my head may fear no evil,
Nor my hair may be disordered,
When the shining swords are clashing,
And the steely points are meeting!"

Said the aged Väinämöinen,
And he spoke the words which follow:
"Hail, O Pohjola's great Mistress!
Wilt thou now divide the Sampo,   210
Out upon the jutting headland,
On the hazy island's summit?"

Then said Pohjola's old Mistress,
"No, I'll not divide the Sampo,
Not with thee, thou wretched creature,
Not with thee, O Väinämöinen!"
And she swooped to snatch the Sampo
From the boat of Väinämöinen.

Then the lively Lemminkäinen
Drew his sword from out his swordbelt,   220
Firm he grasped the sharpened iron,
And from his left side he drew it,
Striking at the eagle's talons,
At the claws of eagle striking.

Struck the lively Lemminkäinen,
As he struck, these words he uttered:
"Down ye men, and down ye swordsmen,
Down with all the sleepy heroes!
From her wings, ye men a hundred,
Ten from ends of every feather!"   230

Answered then the crone of Pohja,
And she answered from the masthead:
"O thou lively son of Lempi,
Wretched Kauko, worthless fellow,
For thou hast deceived thy mother,
Lied unto thy aged mother!
Thou wast pledged to seek no battle
In the space of six, ten summers,
Whether need of gold should tempt thee,
Or the love of silver urge thee!"   240

Väinämöinen, old and steadfast,
He the great primeval minstrel,
Thought his doom had come upon him,

And he felt his bane approaching;
From the sea he drew the rudder,
Took the oak-spar from the billows,
And with this he struck the monster,
On the claws he struck the eagle,
All the other claws he shattered,
There remained the smallest only.   250

From her wings the youths dropped downward,
In the sea the men splashed downward,
From beneath her wings a hundred,
From her tail a thousand heroes;
Down there dropped the eagle likewise,
Crashing down upon the boat-ribs,
As from tree the capercailzie,
Or from fir-branch drops the squirrel.

Then she tried to seize the Sampo,
Seized it with her nameless finger,   260
From the boat she dragged the Sampo,
Down she pulled the pictured cover,
From the red boat's hold she pulled it,
'Mid the blue sea's waters cast it,
And the Sampo broke to pieces,
And was smashed its pictured cover.

Then the fragments all were scattered,
And the Sampo's larger pieces
Sank beneath the peaceful waters
To the black ooze at the bottom;   270
Thence there springs the water's riches,
And the wealth of Ahto's people.
Nevermore in all his lifetime,
While the golden moon is shining,
Shall the wealth of Ahto fail him,
Neither shall his watery honours.

Other pieces were remaining,
Rather small those other fragments,
On the blue sea's surface floating,
Tossing on the broad sea's billows,   280

And the wind for ever rocked them,
And the billows drove them onward.

And the wind still rocked the fragments,
And the sea-waves ever tossed them,
On the blue sea's surface floating,
Tossing on the broad sea's billows;
To the land the wind impelled them,
To the shore the billows drove them.

Väinämöinen, old and steadfast,
In the surf beheld them floating,   290
Through the breakers shoreward driving,
Then on shore upcast by billows,
Saw the fragments of the Sampo,
Splinters of its brilliant cover.

Very greatly did it please him,
And he spoke the words which follow:
"From these seeds the plant is sprouting,
Lasting welfare is commencing,
Here is ploughing, here is sowing,
Here is every kind of increase,   300
Thence there comes the shining moonlight,
Thence there comes the lovely sunlight,
O'er the mighty plains of Suomi,
And the lovely land of Suomi."

Then did Pohjola's old Mistress
Speak aloud the words which follow:
"Still can I devise a method,
Find a method and contrivance,
'Gainst thy ploughing and thy sowing,
'Gainst thy cattle and thine increase,   310
That thy moon shall cease its shining,
And thy sun shall cease its shining.
In the rocks the moon I'll carry,
Hide the sun in rocky mountains,
And will send the Frost to freeze you,
That the frozen air destroyeth
What thou ploughest and thou sowest,

Thy provisions and thy harvests.
I will send a hail of iron,
And a hail of steel o'erwhelming,   320
Over all thy finest clearings,
And the best among the cornfields.
On the heath the bear I'll waken,
From the pines the wide-toothed monster,
That he may destroy thy geldings,
And that he thy mares may slaughter,
And that he may kill thy cattle,
And that he thy cows may scatter.
I'll with sickness slay thy people,
And thy race will wholly slaughter,   330
That so long as shines the moonlight,
In the world no more 'tis mentioned."

Then the aged Väinämöinen
Answered in the words that follow:
"Never Lapland spell affects me,
Neither threats from Turjalainen.
Jumala is lord of weather
Keys of fate are the Creator's,
Not to wicked men entrusted,
Neither to malicious fingers.   340

If I turn to my Creator,
To my Jumala upreaching,
From my corn he'll banish maggots,
That they do not spoil my harvests,
That they may not harm my seed-corn,
Nor destroy my corn when growing,
Nor may take my seed-corn from me,
Nor my splendid corn when growing.

Go thou, Pohjola's great Mistress,
Drag unto the stones the lost ones,   350
Crush thou in the rocks the wicked,
Evils in thy chosen mountain,
Not the shining of the moonlight,
Nor the shining of the sunlight!

Send the Frost to freeze the country,
Send the frozen air destroying,
Send it only on thy seed-corn,
That thy corn when sown be injured.
Send thou forth a hail of iron,
And a hail of steel o'erwhelming,   360
Let it fall on thine own ploughing,
Only on the fields of Pohja!

On the heath the bear awaken,
And the fierce cat in the bushes,
From the wood the curving-clawed one,
'Neath the pines the wide-toothed monster,
But to range the paths of Pohja,
And to prey on Pohja's cattle!"

Then did Pohjola's old Mistress
Answer in the words which follow: 370
"Now my might has all departed,
And my strength has greatly weakened.
By the sea my wealth was taken,
By the waves was crushed the Sampo!"

Then she hastened homeward weeping,
Back to Pohjola lamenting.
Nothing worthy to be mentioned
Of the Sampo brought she homeward,
Nothing but a little fragment,
By her nameless finger carried,   380
But a fragment of the cover
Which to Sariola she carried:
Hence the poverty of Pohja,
And the starving life of Lapland.

Väinämöinen, old and steadfast,
Went back likewise to his country,
But he took the Sampo's fragments,
And the fragments of the cover,
From the seashore where he found them,
From the fine sand of the margin.   390

And he sowed the Sampo's fragments,
And the pieces of the cover,
Out upon the jutting headland,
On the hazy island's summit,
That they there might grow and flourish,
Might increase and yield their produce,
As the ale obtained from barley,
As the bread that rye is yielding.

Then the aged Väinämöinen
Spoke aloud the words which follow: 400
"Grant, O Jumala, Creator,
That we now may live in comfort,
And be joyous all our lifetime,
And thereafter die in honour,
In our pleasant land of Suomi,
And in beautiful Carelia!

Keep us, O thou great Creator,
Guard us, Jumala most gracious,
From the men to us unfriendly,
And from that old woman's malice.   410
Guard us from terrestrial evils,
And the spells of water-sorcerers!

O protect thy sons for ever,
May'st thou always aid thy children,
Guard them always in the night-time,
And protect them in the daytime,
Lest the sun should cease from shining,
Lest the moon should cease from beaming,
Lest the winds should cease from blowing,
Lest the rain should cease from falling,   420
Lest the Frost should come and freeze us,
And the evil weather harm us!

Build thou up a fence of iron,
And of stone a castle build us,
Round the spot where I am dwelling,
And round both sides of my people.
Build it up from earth to heaven,
Build it down to earth from heaven,

As my own, my lifelong dwelling,
As my refuge and protection,　　　430
That the proud may not devour us
And they may not spoil our harvests
In the course of all our lifetime
Through the golden years that passeth."

XLIV Väinämöinen's new *Kantele*

Väinämöinen goes to seek for his *kantele* which was lost in the lake, but cannot find it (1–76). He makes himself a new *kantele* of birchwood, on which he plays, and delights every creature in the neighbourhood (77–334).

Väinämöinen, old and steadfast,
In his mind was thus reflecting:
"Now the time has come for music,
Time to give ourselves to pleasure,
In our dwelling newly chosen,
In our homestead now so charming;
But the kantele is sunken,
And my joy has gone for ever
To the dwelling-place of fishes,
To the rock-caves of the salmon,   10
Where it may enchant the sea-pike,
Likewise Vellamo's attendants;
But they never will return it,
Ahto will no more return it.

O thou smith, O Ilmarinen!
Yestreen and before thou workedst,
Work to-day with equal vigour.
Forge me now a rake of iron,
Let the teeth be close together,
Close the teeth, and long the handle   20
That I rake among the billows,
And may rake the waves together,
And may rake among the sea-weeds,
With the rake rake all the margins,
And my instrument recover,
And the kantele recover,
From the devious paths of fishes,
From the rocky caves of salmon!"

Thereupon smith Ilmarinen,
He the great primeval craftsman,   30
Forged for him a rake of iron,
Furnished with a copper handle,
Teeth in length a hundred fathoms,
And the handle full five hundred.

Then the aged Väinämöinen
Took the mighty rake of iron,
And a little way he wandered,
Made a very little journey,
Till he reached the quay, steel-fitted,
And the landing-stage of copper.   40

There he found a boat, found two boats,
Both the boats were waiting ready
On the quay, with steel all fitted,
On the landing-stage of copper,
And the first boat was a new one,
And the second was an old one.

Said the aged Väinämöinen,
To the new boat firstly speaking:
"Go, thou boat, into the water,
To the waves, O vessel, rush thou,   50
Even though no arm should turn thee,
Even though no thumbs should touch thee!"

Sped the boat into the water,
Rushed amid the waves the vessel.
Old and steadfast Väinämöinen,
In the stern made haste to seat him,
And he went to sweep the water,
And to sweep among the billows.
Scattered leaves of water-lilies,
Raked he up among the shore-drift,   60
All the rubbish raked together,
All the rubbish, bits of rushes,
Every scrap he raked together,
All the shoals with care raked over,
But he found not, nor discovered,
Where his pike-bone harp was hidden,

And this joy was gone for ever,
With the kantele was sunken.

Väinämöinen, old and steadfast,
Then returned unto his dwelling,   70
Head bowed down, and sadly grieving,
And his cap askew and drooping,
And he said the words which follow:
"Unto me is lost for ever
Pleasure from the harp of pike-teeth,
From the harp I made of fish-bone!"

As he wandered through the meadows,
On the borders of the woodlands,
Then he heard a birch-tree weeping,
And a speckled tree lamenting,   80
And in that direction hastened,
Walking till he reached the birch-tree.

Thereupon he spoke and asked it:
"Wherefore weep'st thou, beauteous birch-tree,
Shedding tears, O green-leaved birch-tree,
By thy belt of white conspicuous?
To the war thou art not taken,
Longest not for battle-struggle."

Answer made the leaning birch-tree,
And the green-leaved tree responded: 90
"There is much that I could speak of,
Many things I might reflect on,
How I best might live in pleasure,
And I might rejoice for pleasure.
I am wretched in my sorrow,
And can but rejoice in trouble,
Living with my life o'erclouded,
And lamenting in my sorrow.

And I weep my utter weakness,
And my worthlessness lament for,   100
I am poor, and all unaided,
Wholly wretched, void of succour,
Here in such an evil station,
On a plain among the willows.

Perfect happiness and pleasure
Others always are expecting,
When arrives the beauteous summer.
In the warm days of the summer.
But my fate is different, wretched,
Nought but wretchedness awaits me;   110
And my bark is peeling from me,
Down are hewed my leafy branches.

Often unto me defenceless
Oft to me, unhappy creature,
In the short spring come the children,
Quickly to the spot they hurry,
And with sharpened knives they score me,
Draw my sap from out my body,
And in summer wicked herdsmen,
Strip from me my white bark-girdle,   120
Cups and sheaths therefrom constructing,
Baskets too, for holding berries.

Often unto me defenceless,
Oft to me, unhappy creature,
Come the girls beneath my branches,
Come beneath, and dance around me.
From my crown they cut the branches,
And they bind them into bath-whisks.

Often too, am I, defenceless,
Oft am I, unhappy creature,   130
Hewed away to make a clearing,
Cut to pieces, into faggots.
Thrice already in this summer,
In the warm days of the summer,
Unto me have come the woodmen,
And have hewed me with their axes,
Hewed the crown from me unhappy,
And my weak life has departed.

This has been my joy in summer,
In the warm days of the summer,   140
But no better was the winter,
Nor the time of snow more pleasant.

And in former times already,
Has my face been changed by trouble,
And my head has drooped with sadness,
And my cheeks have paled with sorrow,
Thinking o'er the days of evil,
Pondering o'er the times of evil.

And the wind brought ills upon me,
And the frost brought bitter sorrows;   150
Tore the wind my green cloak from me,
Frost my pretty dress from off me.
Thus am I of all the poorest,
And a most unhappy birch-tree,
Standing stripped of all my clothing,
As a naked trunk I stand here,
And in cold I shake and tremble,
And in frost I stand lamenting."

Said the aged Väinämöinen:
"Weep no more, O verdant birch-tree!   160
Leafy sapling, weep no longer,
Thou, equipped with whitest girdle!
For a pleasant future waits thee,
New and charming joys await thee.
Soon shalt thou with joy be weeping,
Shortly shalt thou sing for pleasure!"

Then the aged Väinämöinen
Carved into a harp the birch-tree,
On a summer day he carved it,
To a kantele he shaped it,   170
At the end of cloudy headland,
And upon the hazy island,
And the harp-frame he constructed,
From the trunk he formed new pleasure,
And the frame of toughest birchwood;
From the mottled trunk he formed it.

Said the aged Väinämöinen
In the very words which follow:
"Now the frame I have constructed,
From the trunk for lasting pleasure.   180

Whence shall now the screws be fashioned,
Whence shall come the pegs to suit me?"

In the yard there grew an oak-tree,
By the farmyard it was standing,
'Twas an oak with equal branches,
And on every branch an acorn,
In the acorns golden kernels,
On each kernel sat a cuckoo.

When the cuckoos all were calling,
In the call five tones were sounding,   190
Gold from out their mouths was flowing,
Silver too they scattered round them,
On a hill the gold was flowing,
On the ground there flowed the silver,
And from this he made the harp-screws,
And the pegs from that provided!

Said the aged Väinämöinen
In the very words which follow:
"Now the harp-screws are constructed,
And the harp-pegs are provided.   200
Something even now is wanting,
And five strings as yet are needed.
How shall I provide the harp-strings,
Which shall yield the notes in playing?"

Then he went to seek for harp-strings,
And along the heath he wandered.
On the heath there sat a maiden,
Sat a damsel in the valley,
And the maiden was not weeping,
Neither was she really joyful.   210
To herself she sang full softly,
Sang, that soon might come the evening,
Hoping for her lover's coming,
For the dear one she had chosen.

Väinämöinen, old and steadfast,
Crept without his shoes towards her,
Sprang to her without his stockings,

And as soon as he approached her,
He besought her hair to give him,
And he spoke the words which follow: 220
"Give thy hair to me, O maiden,
Give me of thy hair, O fair one,
Give me hair to form my harp-strings,
For the tones of lasting pleasure!."

Then her hair the maiden gave him,
From her soft locks hair she gave him,
And she gave him five and six hairs,
Seven the hairs she gave unto him,
That he thus might form his harp-strings,
For the tones of lasting pleasure.   230

Now the harp at last was finished,
And the aged Väinämöinen
On a rock his seat selected,
Near the steps, upon a stone bench.

In his hands the harp then taking,
Very near he felt his pleasure,
And the frame he turned to heaven,
On his knees the knob then propping,
All the strings he put in order,
Fit to make melodious music.   240

When he had the strings adjusted,
Then the instrument was ready;
Underneath his hands he placed it,
And across his knees he laid it,
With his ten nails did he play it,
And he let five active fingers
Draw the tunes from out the harp-strings,
Making most delightful music.

When the aged Väinämöinen
Thus upon his harp was playing,   250
Fine his hands, his fingers tender,
And his thumbs were gently curving.
Soon rang out the wood so speckled,
Sang the sapling green full loudly,

Loudly called the golden cuckoo,
And rejoiced the hair of maiden.

Thus played Väinämöinen's fingers,
And the harp-strings loud resounded,
Mountains shook and plains resounded,
All the rocky hills resounded,   260
In the waves the stones were rocking,
In the water moved the gravel,
And the pine-trees were rejoicing,
On the heath the stumps were skipping.

All of Kaleva's fair women,
All the fair ones flocked together,
And in streams they rushed together,
Like a river in its flowing.
Merry laughed the younger women,
And the mistresses were joyful,   270
As they heard the music playing,
And they wondered at their pleasure.

Likewise many men were present,
In their hands their caps all holding,
All the old dames in the party
To their cheeks their hands were holding,
And the maidens' eyes shed tear-drops,
On the ground the boys were kneeling,
To the kantele all listening,
And they wondered at their pleasure.   280
With one voice they all were singing,
With one tongue they all repeated:
"Never have we heard aforetime,
Heard before such charming music,
In the course of all our lifetime,
Through the golden years that have passed."

Far was heard the charming music,
In six villages they heard it,
There was not a single creature
But it hurried forth to listen,   290
And to hear the charming music
From the kantele resounding.

All the wild beasts of the forest,
Upright on their claws were resting
To the kantele to listen,
And they wondered at their pleasure.
All the birds in air then flying,
Perched upon the nearest branches,
All the fish that swam the waters,
To the margin hastened quickly,   300
And the worms in earth then creeping,
Up above the ground then hastened,
And they turned themselves and listened,
Listened to the charming music,
In the kantele rejoicing,
And in Väinämöinen's singing.

Then the aged Väinämöinen
Played in his most charming manner,
Most melodiously resounding;
And he played one day, a second,   310
Playing on, without cessation,
Every morning all through breakfast,
Girded with the selfsame girdle,
And the same shirt always wearing.

When he in his house was playing,
In his house of fir constructed,
All the roofs resounded loudly,
And the boards resounded likewise,
Ceilings sang, the doors were creaking,
All the windows were rejoicing,   320
And the hearthstones all were moving,
Birchwood columns sang in answer.

When he walked among the firwoods,
And he wandered through the pinewoods,
All the firs bowed down before him,
To the very ground the pine-trees;
On the grass the cones rolled round him,
On the roots the needles scattered.

When he hurried through the greenwood,
Or across the heath was hastening,   330

All the leaves called gaily to him,
And the heath was all rejoicing,
And the flowers breathed fragrance round him,
And the young shoots bowed before him.

XLV   The pestilence in Kalevala

The Mistress of Pohjola sends terrible diseases to Kalevala (1–190).
Väinämöinen heals the people by powerful incantations and un-
guents (191–362).

Louhi, Pohjola's old Mistress,
In her ears received the tidings
That in Väinölä it prospered,
And that Kalevala had flourished,
Through the fragments of the Sampo,
Pieces of the pictured cover.

Thereupon she grew most envious,
And for evermore reflected
On the death that she might fashion,
How she best might bring destruction   10
On the people in Väinölä,
And on Kalevala's whole people.

Then she prayed aloud to Ukko,
And she thus implored the Thunderer:
"Ukko, thou of Gods the highest!
Slay thou Kaleva's whole people,
Slay them with thy hail of iron,
With thy steely needles slay them,
Or by sickness let them perish,
Let the evil nation perish,   20
Let the men die in the farmyard,
On the cowshed floor the women!"

Lived in Tuonela a blind maid,
Loviatar, an aged woman,
She the worst of Tuoni's daughters,
And of Mana's maids most hideous,

She, the source of every evil,
Origin of woes a thousand,
With a face of swarthy colour,
And a skin of hue most hideous.   30

Then this daughter black of Tuoni,
Ulappala's blind-eyed damsel,
Made her bed upon the pathway,
On the straw in evil country;
And her back she turned to windward,
Sideways to the bitter weather,
Backwards to the blast so freezing,
And the chilling winds of morning.

Then a great wind rose in fury,
From the east a mighty tempest,   40
Blew this wretched creature pregnant,
And she quickened from the tempest,
On a barren waste all treeless,
On the bare and grassless meadows.

And she bore a heavy burden,
Bore a heavy painful burden,
Bore it two months, bore it three months,
And for four and five months bore it,
Bore it seven, bore it eight months,
For the ninth month also bore it,   50
As old wives are wont to reckon,
And for half the tenth month likewise.

When the ninth month had passed over,
And the tenth month was beginning,
Then she writhed about in anguish,
And the greatest pain oppressed her,
But as yet she brought forth nothing,
And no brood as yet resulted.

From her lair at length she moved her,
In another place she laid her,   60
And the wench in childbed laid her,
Sport of winds, to bear her children.
There betwixt two rocks she laid her,

In the clefts among five mountains,
But as yet she brought forth nothing,
And no brood as yet resulted.

And she sought a place for breeding,
Sought a place for bearing suited:
In the quaking swamps she sought it,
And among the waves she sought it;   70
But she found no place to suit her,
Where she could relieve her burden.

Then she fain would bring forth children,
And relieve her body's burden
In the foam of furious cataract,
'Neath the whirl of roaring waters,
Where three waterfalls are falling,
Under nine of precipices,
But as yet she brought forth nothing,
Nor the foul one eased her burden.   80

Then began to weep the foul one,
And to howl the wicked monster.
Whither now to go she knew not,
And in what direction wander,
Where she might relieve her burden,
Where to go to cast her offspring.

From the clouds then bespoke her Jumala,
The Creator spoke from heaven:
"Stands in swamp a hut three-cornered,
Just upon a lakelet's margin,   90
In the gloomy land of Pohja,
Near where Sariola's bay stretches.
There thou may'st bring forth thy offspring,
There lay down thy heavy burden,
There it is that people need thee,
There do they expect thy offspring!"

Therefore Tuoni's blackest daughter,
Manala's most hideous damsel,
Came unto the house of Pohja,
Came to Sariola's great sauna,   100

That she there might bear her children,
And she might bring forth her offspring.

Louhi, Pohjola's old Mistress,
Old and gap-toothed dame of Pohja,
Secret led her to the sauna,
Secretly into the bath-house,
And the village did not know it,
Nought was spoken in the village.

Secretly she warmed the sauna,
Hastily she made it ready,   110
And with ale the doors smeared over,
And with beer the hinges wetted,
That the doors should make no jarring,
And the hinges make no creaking.

Then she spoke the words which follow,
And expressed herself in thiswise:
"Noble dame, Creation's daughter,
Noble one, as gold all lustrous,
Thou the oldest of all women,
Thou the first of all the mothers!   120
Knee-deep in the sea descend thou,
To thy waist among the billows,
From the perch the slime obtain thou,
And the slime from swimming burbot,
Do thou smear with this the gateway,
And upon the sides anoint it,
Free the damsel from her burden,
And the woman from her sufferings,
Free her from this grievous torment,
And release her from her sufferings!   130

But if this is not sufficient,
Ukko, thou of Gods the highest,
Hither come where thou art needed,
Come thou at our supplication!
Here there is a dame in childbed,
And a woman suffering greatly,
Here amid the sauna's vapour,
Brought into the village bathhouse.

Do thou take thy club all golden
In thy right hand do thou take it,   140
Each impediment remove thou,
And the door-posts move asunder,
Bend thou the Creator's castles,
Break thou all the bars asunder,
Push the large ones and the small ones,
Even push the very smallest!"

Then this foul and wicked creature,
She, the daughter blind of Tuoni,
Presently relieved her burden,
And she brought forth evil children,   150
'Neath a rug adorned with copper,
Underneath the softest blankets.

Thus became she nine sons' mother,
In a single night of summer,
With the bath prepared once only,
With the bath but once made ready,
With a single effort only,
From the fulness of her body.

To the boys their names assigned she,
And she nurtured well the children,   160
Just as each one names the children
Whom themselves have brought to being:
One as Pleurisy she destined,
One did she send forth as Colic,
And as Gout she reared another,
One as Scrofula she fashioned,
Boil, another designated,
And as Itch proclaimed another,
Thrust another forth as Cancer,
And as Plague she formed another.   170

One remained, and he was nameless,
In the straw the lowest lying,
Therefore did she send him onward,
As a sorcerer on the waters,
Also to bewitch the lowlands,
Everywhere to practise malice.

Louhi, Pohjola's old Mistress,
Sent the others forth to journey
To the cloud-encompassed headland,
And the hazy island's summit,   180
Sent in rage these evil monsters,
These diseases all unheard of,
Forth to Väinölä she sent them,
Kaleva's great race to slaughter.

Sickened Väinölä's own people,
Kaleva's descendants sickened,
With diseases all unheard of,
And whose names were known to no one,
And the floors beneath them rotted,
And the sheet above corrupted.   190

Then the aged Väinämöinen,
He the great primeval sorcerer,
Went to drive away the evil,
And his people's lives to succour;
Forth he went to war with Tuoni,
And against disease to struggle.

Thereupon he warmed the sauna,
And the stones prepared to heat it,
And the finest wood provided,
Faggots, too, picked up from sea shore,   200
Water brought in covered vessels,
Bath-whisks also, fresh and leafy,
Warmed the bath-whisks to perfection,
And the hundred twigs he softened.

Then he raised a warmth like honey,
Raised a heat as sweet as honey,
From the heated stones he raised it,
From the glowing stones he raised it,
And he spoke the words which follow,
And in words like these expressed him: 210
"Now the bath approach, O Jumala,
To the warmth, O heavenly Father,
Healthfulness again to grant us,
And our peace again secure us!
Drive away these foul diseases,
From these dread diseases save us,

Calm thou down the heat excessive
Drive away the heat that's evil,
That it may not burn thy children,
Neither may destroy thy offspring!					220

Therefore will I sprinkle water,
On the glowing stones I cast it,
Let it now be changed to honey,
May it trickle down like honey,
Let it flow a stream like honey,
Flowing to a lake of honey,
As it flows along the hearthstones,
Flowing through the mossy sauna!

Do not let us guiltless perish,
Nor be overcome by sickness,					230
'Gainst the great Creator's mandate,
When sends Jumala our death not.
He who slaughters us, the sinless,
Let his mouth his own words swallow,
On his head cast back the evils,
Evil thoughts recoil upon him!

If myself I am not manly,
Nor is Ukko's son a hero,
Nor can drive away these evils,
Nor from off my head can lift them,					240
Ukko is a man and hero,
He it is the clouds who marshals,
And the rainless clouds he governs,
Ruling o'er the scattered cloudlets.

Ukko, thou of Gods the highest,
Thou above the clouds who dwellest!
Come thou here where thou art needed,
Listen to our supplications:
Do thou look upon our sufferings,
Do thou end our days of anguish,					250
Free us from this evil magic,
Free us now from every evil!

Bring me now a sword of fire,
Bring me now a flashing sword-blade,
That I may oppose these evils
Quite subdue these frightful evils,
On the wind's path drive our sufferings,
Drive them far amid the deserts!

Thence I'll drive these sorcerers' torments,
Thence these sufferings will I banish, 260
Far away to rocky caverns,
Rocky caves as hard as iron,
Torments to the stones to carry,
And upon the rocks heap suffering.
Never weeps the stone for anguish,
Nor the rock complains of suffering,
Though it should be greatly beaten,
And though blows be heaped upon it.

Kiputyttö, Tuoni's maiden,
Sitting on the Stone of Sickness, 270
In the rush of three great rivers,
Where three waters are divided,
Turning round the torture-millstone.
And the Mount of Sickness turning!
Go and turn away these sufferings,
To the blue stone gorge direct them,
Or amid the waters send them,
To the deep sea, O condemn them,
Which by wind is never troubled,
Where the sun is never shining. 280

If this be not yet sufficient,
Kivutar, O noble Mistress,
Vammatar, O noble matron,
Come ye all, and come together,
Once again to work us healing,
And restore our peace unto us!
Take the sufferings from the suffering,
And the ulcers from the ulcered,
That the sick may fall in slumber,

And the weak may rise from weakness,   290
And the sufferer hope recover,
And our mourning have an ending!

Put the sufferings in a bucket,
All the pains in copper caskets,
Carry thou away the sufferings,
And do thou cast down the tortures,
In the midst of Torture-Mountain;
On the peak of Mount of Suffering,
Do thou there boil up the tortures
In the very smallest kettle,   300
Larger not than round a finger,
And no wider than a thumb-breadth!

There's a stone in midmost mountain,
'Mid the stone there is an opening,
Which has there been bored by auger,
Where the auger has transpierced it:
Do thou thrust therein the sufferings,
Overcome these painful ulcers,
Crush thou in these raging tortures,
Do thou end our days of suffering,   310
That by night they may be harmless,
And be harmless in the daytime."

Then the aged Väinämöinen,
He the great primeval sorcerer,
Salved o'er all the ulcered places,
And the open wounds anointed,
With nine various salves anointed,
With eight magic drugs he rubbed them,
And he spoke the words which follow,
And in words like these expressed him: 320
"Ukko, thou of Gods the highest,
O thou aged man in heaven!
Let a cloud appear to eastward,
Let another rise from north-west,
Send thou from the west another;
Grant us honey, grant us water,
That our sores may be anointed,
And our wounds be all salved over!

Yet to me no power is given,
Save by my Creator granted.   330
Grant us now thy grace, Creator,
Grant us, Jumala, thy mercy.
With my eyes have I been seeing,
And my hands have been uplifting,
With my mouth have I been speaking,
With my breath have I been sighing!

Where my hands avail to reach not,
Let the hands of God be resting;
Where I cannot reach my fingers,
There let God extend his fingers;   340
Far more skilful are his fingers,
The Creator's hands more active!

O Creator, work thy magic,
Speak, O Jumala, unto us,
Deign to gaze on us, Almighty!
Let those who at night are healthy,
Likewise in the day be healthy,
Let no suffering fall upon them,
And no sickness come among them,
Nor their hearts be filled with anguish,   350
That they feel no slightest evil,
Feel no more the slightest suffering,
In the course of all their lifetime,
In the course of years that passeth!"

Väinämöinen, old and steadfast,
He the great primeval sorcerer,
Thus at length dispelled the evils,
Raised their burdens from his people,
Drove away the plagues of magic,
Healed the magical diseases,   360
And from death he saved his people,
Thus saved Kaleva's descendants.

XLVI Väinämöinen and the bear

The Mistress of Pohjola sends a bear to destroy the herds of Kalevala (1–20). Väinämöinen kills the bear, and a great feast is held in Kalevala in honour of the occasion (21–606). Väinämöinen sings, plays on the *kantele*, and hopes that a time of great happiness and prosperity is coming to Kalevala (607–44).

Unto Pohjola came tidings,
To the village cold the tidings
That in Väinölä 'twas healthy;
Freed was Kalevala completely
From the evil plagues of magic,
And the scourge of nameless sickness.

Louhi, Pohjola's old Mistress,
Old and gap-toothed dame of Pohja,
Thereupon again grew furious,
And she spoke the words which follow: 10
"Still I know another method,
And a cunning scheme have thought on:
On the heath the Bear I'll waken,
On the waste the curving-clawed one,
Väinölä's fine flocks to ravage,
Kalevala's herds to slaughter."

On the heath the bear she wakened,
From his native land she drove him
To the heathlands of Väinölä,
And to Kalevala's green pastures.   20

Väinämöinen, old and steadfast,
Uttered then the words which follow:
"Ilmarinen, smith and brother,
Make a new spear quickly for me,

Make it with three cutting edges,
With a copper shaft construct it!
With the bear I now must struggle,
Overthrow the shaggy monster,
That he slay no more my geldings,
Nor shall fall upon my brood-mares,   30
Neither shall destroy my cattle,
Or attempt my cows to injure."

Then the smith a spear constructed,
Not a long one, not a short one,
But of middle length he forged it;
On the blade a wolf was sitting,
On the edge a bear was standing,
At the joint an elk was trotting,
On the shaft a colt was running,
At the end a reindeer leaping.   40
Then fresh snow was gently falling,
And a little snow had drifted
As it drifts in early autumn,
White as is the hare in winter.

Said the aged Väinämöinen,
And he spoke the words which follow:
"Now my inclination leads me
Unto Metsola to travel;
To the forest's daughter's dwelling,
And to the Blue Maiden's homestead.   50

Leaving men, I seek the forest,
Heroes leave, for distant regions;
Take me as thy man, O forest,
Take me, Tapio, for thy hero.
May good fortune now be granted,
And to fell the forest-beauty!

Mielikki, the forest's Mistress,
Tellervo, the wife of Tapio!
Do thou bind thy dogs securely,
Do thou keep thy whelps in order,   60
In the paths, 'mid honeysuckle,
And beneath the roof of oakwood!

Otso, apple of the forest,
O thou lazy honey-pawed one!
If thou hearest me approaching,
Hearest me, the hero, coming,
In thy hair thy claws conceal thou,
In thy gums thy teeth conceal thou,
That thou never more may'st move them,
That they motionless remain there!   70

O my Otso, O my darling,
Fair one with the paws of honey!
Do thou rest in hilly country,
And among the rocks so lovely,
Where the pines above are waving,
And the firs below are rustling.
Turn thyself around, O Otso,
Turn thee round, O honey-pawed one,
As upon her nest the woodgrouse,
Or as turns the goose when brooding!"   80

Then the aged Väinämöinen
Heard his dog was barking loudly,
And the hound was fiercely baying
Just beside the Small-eye's dwelling,
In the pathway of the Broad-nose;
And he spoke the words which follow:
"First I thought it was a cuckoo,
Thought I heard a love-bird singing;
But no cuckoo there is calling,
And no love-bird there is singing,   90
But it is my dog that's baying,
Here my faithful hound awaits me,
At the door of Otso's dwelling,
At the handsome hero's homestead!"

Then the aged Väinämöinen
Struck the bear where he was lying,
Overturned his bed of satin,
Overthrew his lair so golden,
And he spoke the words which follow,
And in words like these expressed him: 100

"Praise, O Jumala, unto thee,
Praise to thee alone, Creator,
Unto me the bear who gavest,
And the forest gold hast granted!"

Gazed he on the golden booty,
And he spoke the words which follow:
"O my Otso, O my darling,
Fair one with the paws of honey!
Be not filled with causeless anger,
I myself have not o'erthrown thee,   110
Thou thyself hast left the forest,
Wandered from thy pine-tree covert,
Thou hast torn away thy clothing,
Ripped thy grey cloak in the thicket.
Slippery is this autumn weather,
Cloudy are the days and misty.

Golden cuckoo of the forest,
Shaggy-haired and lovely creature!
Do thou quit thy chilly dwelling,
Do thou quit thy native desert,   120
And thy home of birchen branches,
Wattled wigwam where thou dwellest.
Go to wander in the open,
O thou beauty of the forest,
On thy light shoes wandering onward,
Marching in thy blue-hued stockings,
Leaving now this little dwelling.
Do thou leave this narrow dwelling,
Leave it for the mighty heroes,
To the race of men resign it!   130
There are none will treat thee badly,
And no wretched life awaits thee.
For thy food they'll give thee honey,
And for drink, of mead the freshest,
When thou goest to a distance,
Whither with the staff they guide thee.

From this place depart thou quickly,
From thy little nest depart thou,

Till you reach the famous rafters,
And you rest beneath the shelter,   140
Glide along upon thy snowpaws,
As on pond a water-lily,
Patter on among the fir-trees,
Like a squirrel in the branches!"

Then the aged Väinämöinen,
He the great primeval minstrel,
Walked across the plains, loud-playing,
O'er the heath he wandered singing,
And he brought the noble stranger.
With his shaggy friend he wandered;   150
In the house was heard his playing,
'Neath the roofs they heard his singing.

In the house there cried the people,
And exclaimed the handsome people:
"Listen to the noise resounding,
To the music from the forest,
Like the singing of the crossbill,
Or a maiden's flute in forest!"

Väinämöinen, old and steadfast,
Then the house was fast approaching.   160
From the house there called the people,
And the handsome people asked him:
"Have you brought the bright gold with you,
Have you brought the silver hither,
Brought the precious treasure with you,
Gathered money on your journey?
Gave the wood the honey-eater,
Or a lynx, the lord of forest,
That you come among us singing,
On your skis you come rejoicing?"   170

Väinämöinen, old and steadfast,
Answered in the words which follow:
"Singing would I bring the otter,
Give to Jumala my praises,

So I sing as I am coming,
On my skis I come rejoicing.

What I bring is not an otter,
Not a lynx, and not an otter:
One more famous is approaching,
Comes the pride of all the forest.   180
Comes an old man wandering hither,
With his overcoat he cometh.
If it be a pleasure to you,
Let the doors be widely opened;
But if you dislike the stranger,
Close the doors against him firmly!"
And the people gave him answer,
Shouted all the handsome people:
"Welcome, Otso, be thy coming,
Honey-pawed, who now approachest   190
To our dwelling, freshly scoured,
To our household, now so charming!

This I wished for all my lifetime,
All my youth I waited for it,
Tapio's horn to hear resounding,
And to hear the wood-pipe whistling,
Darling wandering through the forest,
Coming through the silver woodland,
Our little house approaching,
On along the narrow pathways.   200

I had hoped a year of fortune,
Waiting for the coming summer,
As a ski for crusty snow drifts,
Or a trail for gliding suited,
As a maiden for her lover,
Or a consort for a red-cheek.

In the eve I sat at window,
Morning, at the door of storehouse,
At the gate a week I waited,
And a month at pathway's opening.   210

In the lane I stayed a winter;
Stood in snow while ground was hardened,
Till the hardened land grew softer,
And the soft ground turned to gravel,
And to sand was changed the gravel,
And the sand at length grew verdant,
And I pondered every morning,
In my head reflected daily:
'Wherefore is the Bear delaying?
Why delays the forest's darling?   220
Has he travelled to Esthonia,
Wandered from the land of Suomi?' "

Then the aged Väinämöinen
Answered in the words that follow:
"Where's my guest to be conducted,
Whither shall I lead my gold one?
To the barn shall I conduct him
On a bed of straw to lay him?"

And the people gave him answer,
Shouted all the handsome people: 230
"Better lead our guest illustrious,
And conduct our golden beauty
Underneath these famous rafters,
Underneath this roof so handsome.
There is food arranged for eating,
There is drink poured out for drinking,
All the floors have there been dusted,
And the floors been swept most cleanly,
All the women finely dressed them,
In their very finest garments,   240
Donned their head-dresses the finest,
In their brightest robes arrayed them."

Then the aged Väinämöinen
Spoke aloud the words which follow:
"O my Otso, O my birdling,
O my charge, with paws of honey!
Still there's ground for thee to walk on,
And upon the heath to wander.

Golden one, go forth to wander,
Dear one, range about the country,   250
Forth to march with sable stockings,
Wander in thy cloth-made trousers,
On the pathway of the titmouse,
And the path where sparrows wander,
Underneath five rafters straying,
Underneath six roof-trees walking!

Now be careful, luckless woman,
That the herd may not be frightened,
Terrified the little cattle,
Nor the mistress' calves be frightened,   260
If the bear approach the homestead,
And his shaggy jaws should seize them!

Now, ye boys, the porch abandon,
Girls, depart ye from the door-posts,
To the house there comes the hero,
And the pride of men approaches!

Otso, apple of the forest,
Fair and bulky forest dweller,
Be not frightened at the maidens,   270
Fear not the unbraided maidens,
Be not fearful of the women,
They the wearers of the stockings.
All the women of the household
Quickly round the stove will gather,
When they see the hero enter,
And behold the youth advancing!"

Said the aged Väinämöinen,
"Jumala be gracious to us,
Underneath these famous rafters,
Underneath this roof so handsome!   280
Whither shall I take my darling,
And shall bring the shaggy creature?"

And the people spoke in answer:
"Hail, all hail to thee who comest!

Thither shalt thou bring thy birdling,
Thither take thy golden beauty
To the end of pole of pinewood,
To the end of bench of iron,
That his shaggy coat we gaze on,
And his hair may well examine!   290
Be not grieved for this, O Otso,
Neither let it make thee angry,
That we take thy hide an hour,
And thy hair to gaze on always!
For thy hide will not be injured,
And thy hair will not be draggled,
Like the rags of evil people,
Or the clothing of the beggars."

Then the aged Väinämöinen
From the bear stripped off the bearskin,   300
In the storehouse loft he hung it,
Put the flesh into the kettles,
Put it in the gilded kettles,
In the copper caldrons placed it.

On the fire the pots arranged he,
In the blaze their sides of copper,
Filled them up, and overfilled them,
With the meat he overfilled them.
Salt unto the stew he added,
Brought from very distant regions,
From the Saxon land they brought it,   310
And from distant waters brought it,
Through the Sound of Salt they rowed it,
And they from the ships conveyed it.

When the meat enough was sodden,
From the fire they took the kettles,
And the booty then was carried,
And the crossbill then they carried
Quickly to the long deal table,
In the golden dishes laid it,   320
Where they sat the mead enjoying,
And the beer they were imbibing.
And of firwood was the table,

And the dishes were of copper,
And the spoons were all of silver,
And the knives of gold constructed.
All the plates were overloaded,
Brimming o'er were all the dishes,
With the darling of the forest,
Booty of the golden woodland.   330

Then the aged Väinämöinen
Spoke aloud the words that follow:
"Comrade old, with golden bosom,
Master thou of Tapio's household;
Thou of Metsola, sweet matron,
Gracious Mistress of the Forest;
Handsome man, the son of Tapio,
Handsome red-capped son of Tapio;
Tellervo, the maid of Tapio;
All the rest of Tapio's people,   340
Come ye to the feast of cattle,
Where the shaggy beast is eaten!
Here is plenty to be eaten,
Here is food and drink abundant,
Here there is enough for storage,
Plenty too, to give the village."

And the people then responded,
Answered thus the handsome people:
"Where was Otso born and nurtured,
Whence was formed his hide so shaggy;   350
Was he born perchance in straw-bed,
Was he born near stove in sauna?"

Then the aged Väinämöinen
Answered in the words which follow:
"Otso was not born in straw-bed.
Nor was born on chaff in malt-house;
There was Otso brought to being,
There was born the honey-pawed one,
Near the morn, in gleams of sunshine,
And upon the Great Bear's shoulders,   360
There beside the Air's fair maiden,
Near the daughter of Creation.

On Air's borders walked a maiden,
Through mid-heaven there walked a damsel,
Through the rifted clouds she wandered,
On the borders of the heavens,
Clad in stockings, blue in colour,
And with shoes most gaily coloured,
In her hand a wool-filled satchel,
'Neath her arm a hair-filled basket;   370
Wool she cast upon the waters,
Hair she threw among the billows,
And the wind arose and tossed it,
And the air unceasing rocked it,
And the breeze on water rocked it,
To the shore the waves impelled it,
To the edge of honeyed forest,
To the end of honeyed headland.

Mielikki, the forest's Mistress,
Tapiola's accomplished matron,   380
Took the wool from out the water,
Took the soft wool from the billows.

Then she wrapped it all together,
With a handsome band she wrapped it,
Put it in her maple basket,
In a beauteous cradle laid it,
Then she lifted up the bundle,
And the golden chains she carried
Where the branches were the thickest
And the leaves were most abundant.   390

Then she rocked the charming object,
And she rocked the lovely creature
Underneath a spreading fir-tree,
Underneath a blooming pine-tree;
Thus it was the bear was nurtured,
And the furry beast was fostered,
There beside a bush of honey,
In a forest dripping honey.

Now the bear grew up most handsome,
And attained his perfect stature: 400

Short his legs, his knees were crooked,
Broad his nose, both thick and stumpy,
Broad his head and short his muzzle,
And his handsome hair was shaggy,
But as yet the bear was toothless,
And with claws was unprovided.

Mielikki, the forest's Mistress,
Uttered then the words which follow:
'Now let claws be granted to him,
And let teeth be also sought for,   410
If he does no mischief with them,
Nor to evil purpose turns them.'

Then the bear by oath engaged him,
Kneeling by the forest's Mistress,
And in Jumala's high presence,
'Fore the face of Him Almighty,
Never would he work a mischief,
And would work no evil with them.

Mielikki, the forest's Mistress,
Tapiola's accomplished matron,   420
Went to seek the teeth he needed,
And to seek the claws he wanted,
From the wood of mountain ash-tree,
And from juniper the hardest,
From the hardest roots of any,
From the hardest resinous tree-stumps,
But she found no claws among them,
Neither found she teeth among them.

On the heath there grew a pine-tree,
On the hill there rose a fir-tree,   430
And the pine had silver branches,
And the fir-tree golden branches;
With her hands she plucked the branches,
And from these the claws constructed,
Others fixed in Otso's jawbones,
In his gums securely fixed them.

Forth she sent the shaggy creature,
Sent her darling forth to wander,

Let him wander through the marshes,
Let him wander through the forest,   440
Walk along the woodland's borders,
Step along across the heathland;
And she bade him walk discreetly,
And to march along demurely,
And to live a life of pleasure,
And upon fine days to wander,
Through the plains and o'er the marshes,
Past the heaths where men are dancing,
Wandering shoeless in the summer,
Wandering sockless in the autumn,   450
Resting in the worst of weather,
Idling in the cold of winter,
In a hollow stump of cherry,
In the castle of the pine-trees,
At the foot of beauteous fir-trees,
'Mid the junipers close-growing,
Underneath five woollen mantles,
'Neath eight mantles was he hidden,
And from thence I fetched my booty,
There I found it on my journey."   460

Then the younger people asked him,
And the old folks asked him likewise:
"Wherefore was the wood so gracious,
Gracious wood, and forest lavish,
And the greenwood's lord so joyous,
So propitious friendly Tapio,
That he thus his pet has given,
And resigned the honey-eater?
Did you with the spear attack him,
Was he overcome with arrows?"   470

Väinämöinen, old and steadfast,
Answered in the words which follow:
"Very gracious was the forest,
Gracious wood, and forest lavish,
And the greenwood's lord was joyous,
And propitious, friendly Tapio.
Mielikki, the forest's Mistress,
Tellervo, the maid of Tapio,

Fair-haired damsel of the forest,
Little damsel of the forest, 480
Went along the path to guide me,
And to raise the landmarks for me:
By the roadside posts erected,
And directed all my journey,
And the trees she blazed before me,
Marks she set upon the mountains,
To the door of noble Otso,
To the borders of his dwelling.

When I reached the place I sought for,
And arrived upon its borders; 490
With the spear I smote not Otso,
And I shot no arrows at him.
He himself lurched from the archway,
Tumbled from the pine-tree's summit,
And the branches broke his breastbone,
Others ripped his belly open."

Then he spoke the words which follow,
And in words like these expressed him:
"O my Otso, O my dearest,
O my birdling, O my darling! 500
Now resign to us thy headland,
Lay aside thine eye-teeth likewise,
Cast away the few teeth left thee,
And thy wide jaws give us also,
Yet thou needest not be angry,
That I come to thee in thiswise,
And thy bones and skull have broken,
And have dashed thy teeth together.

Now I take the nose from Otso,
That my own nose may be lengthened, 510
But I take it not completely,
And I do not take it only.

Now I take the ears of Otso,
That my own ears I may lengthen,
But I take them not completely,
And I do not take them only.

Now I take the eyes of Otso,
That my own eyes I may better,
But I take them not completely,
And I do not take them only.   520

Now will I take Otso's forehead,
That my forehead I may broaden,
But I take it not completely,
And I do not take it only.

Now I take the mouth of Otso,
That my own mouth may be widened,
But I take it not completely,
And I do not take it only.

Now I take the tongue of Otso,
That my own tongue may be lengthened,   530
But I take it not completely,
And I do not take it only.

He shall be a man respected,
And as hero shall be reckoned,
Who the bear's teeth now can number,
And the rows of teeth can loosen
From the jaws of steely hardness,
With his grasp as strong as iron."

As no other man came forward,
And no hero would attempt it,   540
He himself the bear's teeth numbered,
And the rows of teeth he reckoned,
Kneeling down beneath the jawbones,
With his grasp as strong as iron.

From the bear the teeth then taking,
Uttered he the words which follow:
"Otso, apple of the forest,
Fair and bulky forest-dweller
Thou must go upon thy journey,
Leap along upon the journey,   550
Forth from out this narrow dwelling,
From this low and narrow cottage,

To a lofty house that, 'waits thee,
To a wide and pleasant dwelling.

Golden one, go forth to wander,
Dearest treasure, march thou onward,
On the swine's path march thou onward,
Traversing the road of piglets,
To the firwood so luxuriant,
To the needle-covered pine-trees,   560
To the hills all clothed with forest,
To the lofty-rising mountains!
Here for thee to dwell is pleasant,
Charming is it to abide there,
Where the cattle-bells are ringing,
And the little bells are tinkling."

Väinämöinen, old and steadfast,
After this his dwelling entered,
And the younger people asked him,
All the handsome people asked him: 570
"Where have you bestowed your booty,
Whither did you make your journey?
Have you left him in the icefield,
In the snow-slush have you sunk him,
Pushed him down in the morasses,
Buried him upon the heathland?"

Väinämöinen, old and steadfast,
Answered in the words which follow:
"In the ice I did not leave him,
Sunk him not among the snow-slush;   580
For the dogs from thence would drag him,
Likewise would the birds befoul him.
In the swamp I have not sunk him,
Nor upon the heath have buried,
For the worms would there destroy him
And the black ants would devour him.

Thither have I brought my booty,
There bestowed my little captive,
On a golden mountain's summit,
On a copper mountain's summit.   590
In a splendid tree I laid him,
Pine-tree with a hundred needles,

In the very largest branches,
In the broad and leafy summit,
As a joy to men for ever,
And a pleasure to the travellers.

Then I turned his gums to eastward,
And his eyes I turned to north-west,
Not too high upon the summit,
Lest if they were in the summit,   600
Then the wind might perhaps destroy them,
And the spring wind treat them badly.
Nor too near the ground I placed them,
Lest if I too low had laid them,
Then the pigs might perhaps disturb them,
And the snouted ones o'erturn them."

Then the aged Väinämöinen
Once again prepared for singing,
For a splendid evening's pleasure,
And a charm to day departing.   610

Said the aged Väinämöinen,
And in words like these expressed him:
"Keep thy light, O holder, shining,
So that I can see while singing,
For the time has come for singing,
And my mouth to sing is longing."

Played and sang old Väinämöinen,
Charming all throughout the evening,
And when he had ceased his singing,
Then a speech he made concluding: 620
"Grant, O Jumala, in future,
Once again, O good Creator,
That once more we meet rejoicing,
And may once again assemble
Here to feast on bear so fattened,
Feasting on the shaggy creature!

Grant, O Jumala, for ever,
Grant again, O good Creator,
That the posts be raised to guide us,

And the trees be blazed before us,   630
For the most heroic people,
For the manly race of heroes!

Grant, O Jumala, for ever,
Grant again, O good Creator,
That may sound the horn of Tapio,
And the forest-pipe may whistle
Even in these little courtyards,
Even in these narrow homesteads!

In the day may we be playing,
And at eventide rejoicing,   640
In this firm and solid country,
In the wild expanse of Suomi,
With the young who now are growing,
With the rising generation."

XLVII   The robbery of the sun and moon

The sun and moon descend to listen to Väinämöinen's playing. The Mistress of Pohjola succeeds in capturing them, hides them away in a mountain, and steals the fire from the homes of Kalevala (1–40). Ukko, the Supreme God, is surprised at the darkness in the sky, and kindles fire for a new moon and a new sun (41–82). The fire falls to the ground, and Väinämöinen and Ilmarinen go to search for it (83–126). The Virgin of the Air informs them that the fire has fallen into Lake Alue, and has been swallowed by a fish (127–312). Väinämöinen and Ilmarinen try to catch the fish with a net of bast, but without success (313–64).

Väinämöinen, old and steadfast,
On his kantele was playing,
Long he played, and long was singing,
And was ever full of gladness.

In the moon's house heard they playing,
Came delight to the sun's window,
And the moon came from his dwelling,
Standing on a crooked birch-tree,
And the sun came from his castle,
Sitting on a fir-tree's summit,   10
To the kantele to listen,
Filled with wonder and rejoicing.

Louhi, Pohjola's old Mistress,
Old and gap-toothed dame of Pohja,
Set to work the sun to capture,
In her hands the moon seized likewise.
From the birch the moon she captured,
And the sun from fir-tree's summit;
Straightway to her home she brought them,
To the gloomy land of Pohja.   20

Then she hid the moon from shining,
In the mottled rocks she hid him,
Sang the sun to shine no longer,
Hidden in a steel-hard mountain;
And she spoke the words which follow:
"Never more again in freedom
Shall the moon arise for shining,
Nor the sun be free for shining,
If I come not to release them,
If I do not go to fetch them,   30
When I bring nine stallions with me,
Which a single mare has littered!"

When the moon away was carried,
And the sun had been imprisoned
Deep in Pohjola's stone mountain,
In the rocks as hard as iron,
Then she stole away the brightness,
And from Väinölä the fires,
And she left the houses fireless,
And the rooms no flame illumined.   40

Therefore was the night unending,
And for long was utter darkness,
Night in Kalevala for ever,
And in Väinölä's fair dwellings,
Likewise in the heavens was darkness,
Darkness round the seat of Ukko.

Life without the fire was weary,
And without the light a burden,
Unto all mankind 'twas dismal,
And to Ukko's self 'twas dismal.   50

Ukko, then, of Gods the highest,
In the air the great Creator,
Now began to feel most strangely,
And he pondered and reflected,
What strange thing the moon had darkened,
How the sun had been obstructed,
That the moon would shine no longer,
And the sun had ceased his shining.

Then he stepped to cloudland's borders,
On the borders of the heavens,   60
Wearing now his skyblue stockings,
With the shoes of varied colour;
And he went the moon to seek for,
And he went to find the sunlight,
Yet he could not find the moonlight,
Nor the sun could he discover.

In the air a light struck Ukko,
And a flame did Ukko kindle,
From his flaming sword he struck it,
Sparks he struck from off the sword-blade: 70
From his nails he struck the fire,
From his limbs he made it crackle,
High above aloft in heaven,
On the starry plains of heaven.
When the fire had been kindled,
Then he took the spark of fire,
In his golden purse he thrust it,
Placed it in his silver casket,
And he bade the maiden rock it,
Told the maid of air to rock it,   80
That a new moon might be fashioned,
And a new sun be constructed.

On the long cloud's edge she sat her,
On the verge of air she sat her,
There it was she rocked the fire,
There she rocked the glowing brightness,
In a golden cradle rocked it,
With a silver cord she rocked it.

Then the silver props were shaken,
Rocked about the golden cradle,   90
Moved the clouds and creaked the heavens,
And the props of heaven were swaying,
With the rocking of the fire,
And the rocking of the brightness.

Thus the maid the fire was rocking,
And she rocked the fire to brightness,

With her fingers moved the fire,
With her hands the fire she tended,
And the stupid maiden dropped it,
Dropped the flame the careless maiden,   100
From her hands she dropped it downward
From the fingers of its guardian.

Then the sky was cleft asunder,
All the air was filled with windows,
Burst asunder by the fire-sparks,
As the red drop quick descended,
And a gap gleamed forth in heaven,
As it through the clouds dropped downward.
Through nine heavens the drop descended,
Through six spangled vaults of heaven.   110

Said the aged Väinämöinen,
"Smith and brother, Ilmarinen!
Let us go and gaze around us,
And the cause perchance discover,
What the fire that just descended,
What the strange flame that has fallen
From the lofty height of heaven,
And to earth beneath descended.
Of the moon 'tis perhaps a fragment,
Of the sun perchance a segment!"   120

Thereupon set forth the heroes,
And they wandered on, reflecting
How they might perchance discover,
How they might succeed in finding,
Where the fire had just descended,
Where the brightness had dropped downward.

And a river flowed before them,
And became a lake extensive,
And the aged Väinämöinen
Straight began a boat to fashion,   130
In the wood he worked upon it,
And beside him Ilmarinen
Made a rudder out of firwood,
Made it from a log of pinewood.

Thus the boat at length was ready,
Rowlocks, rudder all completed;
And they pushed it in the water,
And they rowed and steered it onward,
All along the river Neva,
Steering round the Cape of Neva.   140

Ilmatar, the lovely damsel,
Eldest Daughter of Creation,
Then advanced to meet the heroes,
And in words like these addressed them:
"Who among mankind may ye be?
By what names do people call you?"

Said the aged Väinämöinen,
"You may look on us as sailors.
I am aged Väinämöinen,
Ilmarinen, smith, is with me,   150
But inform us of your kindred;
By what name do people call you?"

Then the matron gave them answer:
"I am oldest of all women,
Of the air the oldest damsel,
And the first of all the mothers.
Five times now have I been married,
Six times as a bride attired.
Whither do you take your journey,
Whither, heroes, are you going?"   160

Said the aged Väinämöinen,
And he spoke the words which follow:
"All our fires have been extinguished,
And the flames died down in darkness,
Long already were we fireless,
And in darkness were we hidden,
But at length have we determined
That the fire we ought to seek for,
Which has just dropped down from heaven,
From above the clouds has fallen."   170

Then the woman gave them answer,
And she spoke the words which follow:
"Hard it is to track the fire,
And the bright flame to discover.
It has evil wrought already,
And the flame has crime committed,
For the red spark has shot downward,
And the red ball has descended
From the realms of the Creator,
Where it was by Ukko kindled,   180
Through the level plains of heaven,
Through the void aërial spaces,
Downwards through the sooty smoke-hole,
Downward through the dried-up roof-tree
Of the new-built house of Tuuri,
Of a wretched roofless dwelling.

When the fire at length came thither,
In the new-built house of Tuuri,
Evil deeds he then accomplished,
Shocking deeds he then accomplished: 190
Burning up the maidens' bosoms,
Tearing at the breasts of maidens,
And the knees of boys destroying,
And the master's beard consuming.
And her child the mother suckled,
In a cradle of misfortune.
Thither, too, the fire rushed onward,
And its evil work accomplished:
In the cradle burned the baby,
Burning, too, the mother's bosom,   200
And the child went off to Mana,
And the boy went straight to Tuoni.
Thus it was the infant perished,
And was cast into destruction,
In the red flame's fiery torture,
In the anguish of its glowing.

Great the knowledge of the mother,
And to Manala she went not.

Means she knew to ban the fire,
And to drive away its glowing,   210
Through the little eye of needle,
And across the back of axe-blade,
Through the sheath of glowing sword-blade,
Past the ploughed land did she drive it."

Väinämöinen, old and steadfast,
Heard her words, and then made answer:
"Whither has the fire retreated,
Whither did the pest take refuge,
Was it in the field of Tuuri,
In a lake, or in a forest?"   220

Then the matron made him answer,
And she spoke the words which follow:
"When from thence the fire departed,
And the flame, went wandering onward,
First it burned o'er many districts,
Many districts, many marshes,
Rushed at last into the water,
In the billows of Lake Alue,
And the fire rose up all flaming,
And the sparks arose all crackling.   230

Three times in the nights of summer,
Nine times in the nights of autumn,
Rose the lake the height of fir-trees,
Roaring rose above the lake-banks,
With the strength of furious fire,
With the strength of heat all flaming.

On the banks were thrown the fishes,
On the rocks the perch were stranded,
And the fishes looked around them,
And the perch were all reflecting   240
How they could continue living.
Perch were weeping for their dwellings,
Fish were weeping for their homesteads,
Ruffes for their rocky castles.

And the perch with back all crooked,
Tried to seize the streak of fire,
But the perch was not successful;
Seized upon it the blue powan:
Down he gulped the streak of fire,
And extinguished thus its brightness.   250

Thus retired the Lake of Alue,
And fell back from all its margins,
Sinking to its former level
In a single night of summer.

When a little time passed over,
Fire-pain seized on the devourer,
Anguish came upon the swallower,
Grievous suffering on the eater.

Up and down the fish swam turning,
Swam for one day and a second,   260
All along the powan's island,
Clefts in rocks where flock the salmon,
To the points of capes a thousand,
Bays among a hundred islands.
Every cape made declaration,
Every island spoke in thiswise:
'Nowhere in these sluggish waters,
In the narrow Lake of Alue,
Can the wretched fish be swallowed,
Or the hapless one may perish   270
In the torture of the fire,
In the anguish of its glowing.'

But a salmon-trout o'erheard it,
And the powan blue he swallowed.
When a little time passed over,
Fire-pain seized on the devourer,
Anguish came upon the swallower,
Grievous suffering on the eater.
Up and down the fish swam turning,
Swam for one day and a second,   280

Through the clefts where flock the salmon,
And the depths where sport the fishes,
To the points of capes a thousand,
Bays among a hundred islands.
Every cape made declaration,
Every island spoke in thiswise:
'Nowhere in these sluggish waters,
In the narrow Lake of Alue,
Can the wretched fish be swallowed,
Or the hapless one may perish   290
In the pain of burning fire,
In the anguish of its glowing.'

But a grey pike hurried forward,
And the salmon-trout he swallowed.
When a little time passed over,
Fire-pain seized on the devourer,
Anguish came upon the swallower,
Grievous suffering on the eater.

Up and down the fish swam turning,
Swam for one day and a second,   300
Past the cliffs where flock the seagulls,
And the rocks where sport the seamews,
To the points of capes a thousand,
Bays among a hundred islands.
Every cape made declaration,
Every island spoke in thiswise:
'Nowhere in these sluggish waters,
In the narrow Lake of Alue,
Can the wretched fish be swallowed,
Or the hapless one may perish   310
In the pain of burning fire,
In the anguish of its glowing.' "

Then the aged Väinämöinen,
Secondly, smith Ilmarinen,
Wove a net of bast constructed,
Which from juniper they gathered,
Steeped it in the juice of willow,
And of sallow-bark they made it.

Väinämöinen, old and steadfast,
Sent the women to the drag-net;   320
To the net there went the women,
Sisters came to draw the drag-net;
And they steered, and glided onward
Past the capes and round the islands,
To the clefts where flock the salmon,
And along the powan's island,
Where the red-brown reeds are waving.
And among the beauteous rushes.

Eager now to make a capture,
Then they cast the net and sunk it,   330
But they cast the net out twisted,
And in wrong direction drew it,
And the fish they could not capture,
Though with eagerness they laboured.

In the water went the brethren,
To the net the men proceeded,
And they swung it and they pushed it,
And they pulled it and they dragged it,
Through the deeps, and rocky places,
Drew it o'er Kalevala's shingle;   340
But the fish they could not capture,
Not the fish so greatly needed.
Came the grey pike never near them,
Neither on the placid water,
Nor upon its ample surface;
Fish are small, the meshes larger.

Now the fish were all complaining;
Said one pike unto another,
And the powan asked the ide-fish,
And one salmon asked another: 350
"Can the famous men have perished,
Perished Kaleva's great children,
They who drag the net of linen,
And of yarn have made the fish-net,
With long poles who beat the water,
With long sticks who move the waters?"

Old and famous Väinämöinen
Answered in the words which follow:
"No, the heroes have not perished,
Kaleva's great race has died not;
When one dies, is born another,
And the best of staves they carry,
Longer sticks to sound the water,
And their nets are twice as fearful."

360

XLVIII   The capture of the fire

The heroes prepare a linen net, and at length capture the fish which
has swallowed the fire (1–192). The fire is found in the fish's belly,
but flashes up suddenly, and burns Ilmarinen's cheeks and hands
severely (193–248). The fire rushes into the forest, burns over many
countries, and spreads further and further, till at length it is captured
and carried to the dark dwellings of Kalevala (249–90). Ilmarinen
recovers from his burns (291–372).

Väinämöinen, old and steadfast,
He the great primeval minstrel,
Thereupon began to ponder,
And reflected on the method
How to make a net of linen,
How to make the hundred meshes.

Then he spoke the words which follow,
And expressed himself in thiswise:
"Is there one who flax can sow me,
Who can sow the flax and card it,   10
And of this a net can make me,
Weave for me its hundred meshes,
Thus this wretched fish to slaughter,
And destroy the fish unhappy?"

So a little spot they found him,
Found a place not yet burned over,
In the wide extent of marshes,
There between two stumps they found it.

Thereupon they dug the roots out,
And 'twas there they found the flaxseed,   20
Guarded by the worm of Tuoni,
There protected by the earthworm.

There they found a heap of ashes;
Dry the ashes that they found there,
Of a wooden burned-up vessel,
Of a boat that once had burned there.
There it was they sowed the flaxseed,
In the loose ash did they sow it,
On the shore of Lake of Alue,
There they sowed it in the clayfield.   30

Presently the shoot rose upward,
And the flax grew thick and strongly,
Grew beyond their expectations,
In a single night of summer.

In the night they sowed the flax-seed,
And they plowed the field by moonlight,
And they cleansed the flax and stripped it,
And they beat it and they rubbed it,
With their tools of steel they scraped it,
And with all their strength they stripped it.   40

Then they took the flax to steeping,
And it soon began to soften,
And they hastened then to pound it,
Afterwards in haste they dried it.

Then into the house they brought it,
And they hastened then to strip it,
And they hastened next to beat it,
And they hastened then to clean it.

Then with diligence they brushed it,
In the twilight did they comb it,   50
On the spinning-wheel they bunched it,
Quicker brought it to the spindle,
In a single night of summer;
Thus between two days they worked it.

After this the sisters spun it,
And their brothers' wives were netting,
And the brothers worked the meshes,
And the fathers also aided.

Quickly did they turn the netter,
And the mesh with speed they twisted,   60
Till the net was quite completed,
And the cords were fixed upon it,
In a single night of summer,
Even that one only half ways.
Thus the net was quite completed,
And the cords were fixed upon it.
And its length was hundred fathoms,
And its breadth was hundreds seven;
Stones for weights were fastened to it,
Likewise proper floats provided.   70

With the net the youths were walking,
And at home the old men pondered,
Whether they would make a capture,
And secure the fish they wished for.

Then they drew the net and dragged it,
Much they toiled, and threshed the water,
Drew it lengthwise through the water,
Dragged it crosswise through the water,
Captured many little fishes:
Many luckless ruffes they captured,   80
Many bony perch they captured,
And a large-galled Redeye likewise,
But the fish they could not capture
That for which the net was fashioned.

Said the aged Väinämöinen:
"O thou smith, O Ilmarinen,
Let us now go forth together
Where the net is in the water!"

Thereupon went both the heroes,
And they drew it through the water,   90
And upon one side they spread it
Round the islands in the water,
And the other side directed,
Round about the promontories,
And the pulling-ropes were guided
To the haven of Väinämöinen.

Thus they cast the net and pushed it,
And they drew the net and dragged it,
Captured fishes in abundance,
And they captured perch in plenty,   100
Salmon-trout in great abundance,
Bream and salmon too they captured,
All the fishes of the water;
Only not the fish they sought for,
That for which the net was woven,
And the ropes were fastened to it.

Then the aged Väinämöinen
Worked to make the net yet longer,
Wider yet the sides expanded,
Perhaps five hundred fathoms broader,   110
Netted full seven hundred fathoms,
And he spoke the words which follow:
"To the depths the nets we'll carry,
And will now extend them further,
Once again will drag the water,
Thus another cast attempting."

To the depths the nets they carried,
Further did they then convey them,
And again they dragged the water,
Thus another cast attempting!   120

Then the aged Väinämöinen
Spoke aloud the words which follow:
"Vellamo, O Water-Mother,
Old one with the lavish bosom!
Do thou change the shift upon thee,
Do thou change thy dress completely,
For thou hast a shift of rushes,
On thy head a cap of lake-foam,
Fashioned by the Wind's fair daughter,
Which the billows' daughter gave thee.   130
I'll give you a shift of linen,
Of the finest flax that's woven,
Which by Kuutar has been woven,
Päivätär has wrought when spinning.

Ahto, master of the billows,
Ruler thou of caves a hundred!
Take thy pole in length five fathoms,
Take thy stake, in length full seven,
Thresh with this the open water,
And do thou stir up the lake-bed, 140
Stir thou all the heaps of refuse,
Drive thou on the shoals of fishes,
Where the net is spread to catch them,
And its hundred floats are swimming,
From the bays by fish frequented,
From the caves where hide the salmon,
From the wide lake's seething whirlpool,
And from the profound abysses,
Where the sun was never shining,
Undisturbed the sand for ever!" 150

From the lake a dwarf ascended,
From the waves arose a hero,
Stood upon the lake's broad surface,
And he spoke the words which follow:
"Is there need to thresh the water,
With a long pole to disturb it?"

Väinämöinen, old and steadfast,
Answered in the words that follow:
"There is need to thresh the water,
With a long pole to disturb it." 160
Then the dwarf, the little hero,
Lifted from the bank a pine-tree,
Took a tall tree from the pinewood,
And prepared to thresh the water,
And he asked, and spoke as follows:
"Shall I thresh with strength sufficient,
Putting forth my utmost efforts,
Or as hard as may be needful?"

Old and prudent Väinämöinen
Answered in the words which follow: 170
"If you thresh as hard as needful,
You will have to do much threshing."

Then the man, the little hero,
Set to work to thresh the water,
And he threshed as much as needful,
And he drove the shoals of fishes,
And into the net he drove them,
In the net with floats a hundred.
Rested now the smith his oars;
Väinämöinen, old and steadfast,   180
Now the net himself drew upward,
At the rope as he was pulling.
Said the aged Väinämöinen,
"We have caught a shoal of fishes,
In the net that I am lifting,
With a hundred floats provided."

Then the net was soon drawn upward,
And they drew it up and shook it,
In the boat of Väinämöinen,
Finding mid the shoal of fishes,   190
That for which the net was fashioned,
And the hundred floats provided.

Väinämöinen, old and steadfast,
To the land then urged the vessel,
To the blue bridge-side he brought it,
To the red bridge-end he brought it,
There the shoal of fishes sorted,
Turned the heap of bony fishes,
And the grey pike found among them,
Which he long had sought to capture.   200

Then the aged Väinämöinen
Thus unto himself reflected:
"Is it wise with hands to seize it,
Save with gauntlets made of iron,
Save with gloves of stone constructed,
Save with mittens made of copper?"

And the Sun's son heard him speaking,
And replied in words that follow:
"I myself would rip the pike up,
Venture in my hand to take him,   210

If I had my large knife only,
Which my noble father gave me."

Then from heaven the knife descended,
From the clouds the knife fell downward,
Golden-hafted, silver-bladed,
To the Sun's son's belt dropped downward.
Thereupon the Sun's son seized it,
Firmly in his hand he grasped it,
And with this the pike ripped open,
Cleft the body of the Broad-snout;   220
And within the sleek pike's belly
There the grey trout he discovered,
And within the grey trout's belly
There he found the smooth-skinned powan.

Then he split the smooth-skinned powan,
And a blue clew he discovered,
In the powan's entrails hidden,
In the third fold of the entrails.

Then the blue clew he unwinded;
From the inside of the blue clew   230
Fell a red clew from within it,
And when he unwound the red clew:
In the middle of the red clew,
There he found a spark of fire
Which had once from heaven descended,
Through the clouds had fallen downward,
From above eight heavens descending,
From the ninth aërial region.

Väinämöinen then considered
How the spark might best be carried,   240
To the cold and fireless dwellings,
To the rooms so dark and gloomy.
But the fire flashed up most fiercely,
From the Sun's son's hands who held it,
Singed the beard of Väinämöinen,
Burned the smith much more severely,
For upon his cheeks it burned him,
And upon his hands it scorched him.

And it hastened quickly onward
O'er the waves of Lake of Alue,   250
Through the junipers fled onward,
Burnt its way through all the thicket,
Then rushed upward through the fir-trees,
Burning up the stately fir-trees,
Rushing ever further onward,
Burned up half the land of Pohja,
And the furthest bounds of Savo,
Over both halves of Carelia.

Väinämöinen, old and steadfast,
Followed hard upon its traces,   260
And he hastened through the forest,
Close behind the furious fire,
And at length he overtook it,
'Neath the roots of two great tree-stumps,
In the stumps of alders hidden,
In the rotten stumps he found it.

Then the aged Väinämöinen
Spoke aloud the words which follow:
"Fire, whom Jumala created,
Creature of the bright Creator!   270
Idly to the depths thou goest,
Aimlessly to distant regions.
It were better far to hide thee
In the hearth of stone constructed,
There thy sparks to bind together,
And within the coals enclose them,
That by day thou may'st be flickering
In the kitchen birchen faggots,
And at night thou may'st be hidden
Close within the golden fire-box."   280
Then he thrust the spark of fire
In a little piece of tinder,
In the fungus hard of birch-tree,
And among the copper kettles.
Fire he carried to the kettles,

Took it in the bark of birch-tree,
To the end of misty headland,
And the hazy island's summit.
Now was fire within the dwellings,
In the rooms again 'twas shining. 290

But the smith named Ilmarinen
Quickly hastened to the seashore,
Where the rocks the water washes,
And upon the rocks he sat him,
In the pain of burning fire,
In the anguish of its glowing.

There it was he quenched the fire,
There it was he dimmed its lustre,
And he spoke the words which follow,
And in words like these expressed him: 300
"Fire, whom Jumala created,
And O thou, the Sun's son, Panu!
What has made ye thus so angry,
As to scorch my cheeks in thiswise,
And to burn my hips so badly,
And my sides so much to injure?

How shall I the fire extinguish,
How shall I reduce its glowing,
Make the fire for evil powerless,
And its lustre render harmless, 310
That no longer it may pain me,
And may cause me pain no longer?

Come, thou girl, from land of Turja,
Come, thou maiden, forth from Lapland,
Frosty-stockinged, icy-booted,
And thy skirts all frosted over,
In thy hand the icy kettle,
And the ice-spoon in the kettle.
Sprinkle me with freezing water,
Sprinkle me with icy water, 320
On the places scorched so badly,
And the burns the fire caused me!

But if this is not sufficient,
Come, thou youth, come forth from Pohja,
Come, thou child, from midst of Lapland,
From Pimentola, O tall one,
Tall as is a forest fir-tree,
Tall as pine-tree in the marshes,
On thy hands the gloves of hoarfrost,
On thy feet the boots of hoarfrost,   330
On thy head the cap of hoarfrost,
Round thy waist the belt of hoarfrost!
Bring from Pohjola the hoarfrost,
Ice from out the frozen village!
Hoarfrost's plentiful in Pohja,
Ice enough in frozen village:
Lakes of ice, and frozen rivers,
All the air with ice is laden.
O'er the hoarfrost hares are skipping,
On the ice the bears are sporting,   340
In the middle of the snow-heaps,
On the edge of the snow mountains,
On the rims the swans are walking,
On the ice the ducks are waddling,
In the midst of snow-filled rivers,
Cornices of icy cataracts.

On thy sledge bring thou the hoarfrost,
On thy sledge the ice convey thou,
From the slopes of rugged mountains,
From the lofty mountains' borders!   350
Make them hoary with the hoarfrost,
With the ice, O make them icy,
All the hurts by fire occasioned,
All the burns the fire has caused me!

But if this is not sufficient,
Ukko, thou of Gods the highest,
Ukko, thou the clouds who leadest,
Thou the scattered clouds who herdest,
Send a cloud from out the eastward,
And a thick cloud from the westward,   360
Link the edges close together,
Close thou up the gaps between them,

Send thou ice, and send thou hoarfrost,
Send thou, too, the best of ointment,
For the places scorched so badly,
And the hurts by fire occasioned."

Thus it was smith Ilmarinen
Found a means to quench the fire,
And to dim the brilliant fire.
Thus the smith was healed completely,   370
And regained his former vigour,
Healed from wounds the fire occasioned.

XLIX False and true moons and suns

Ilmarinen forges a new moon and sun but cannot make them shine
(1–74). Väinämöinen discovers by divination that the moon and sun
are hidden in the mountain of Pohjola, goes to Pohjola and conquers
the whole nation (75–230). He sees the moon and sun in the mountain, but cannot enter (231–78). He returns home to procure tools
with which to break open the mountain. While Ilmarinen is forging
them, the Mistress of Pohjola, fearing that it may go ill with her,
releases the moon and sun (279–362). When Väinämöinen sees the
moon and sun reappear in the sky, he salutes them, hoping that they
will always go brightly on their course, and bring happiness to the
country (363–422).

Still the sun was never shining,
Neither gleamed the golden moonlight,
Not in Väinölä's dark dwellings,
Not on Kalevala's broad heathlands.
Frost upon the crops descended,
And the cattle suffered greatly,
And the birds of air felt strangely,
All mankind felt ever mournful,
For the sunlight shone no longer,
Neither did there shine the moonlight.   10

Though the pike knew well the pike deeps,
And the bird-paths knew the eagle,
And the wind the vessel's journey,
Yet mankind were all unknowing
If the time was really morning,
Or if perhaps it still was night-time,
Out upon the cloudy headland,
And upon the hazy island.

And the young men then took counsel,
And the older men considered   20
How to live without the moonlight,
And exist without the sunlight,
In that miserable country,
In the wretched land of Pohja.

And the girls took likewise counsel,
And their cousins too considered;
And they hastened to the smithy,
And they spoke the words which follow:
"Smith, from 'neath the wall arise thou,
From the hearthstone rise, O craftsman,   30
That a new moon thou may'st forge us,
And a new sun thou may'st make us!
Ill it is without the moonlight,
Strange it is without the sunlight."

From the hearth arose the craftsman,
From beneath the wall the forger,
That a new moon he might forge them,
And a new sun he might make them,
And a moon of gold constructed,
And a sun he made of silver.   40

Came the aged Väinämöinen,
And beside the door he sat him,
And he spoke the words which follow:
"O thou smith, my dearest brother,
What art thou in smithy forging,
Hammering thus without cessation?"

Thereupon smith Ilmarinen
Answered in the words that follow:
"Out of gold a moon I'm shaping,
And a sun of silver making,   50
In the sky I then will place them,
Over six of starry heavens."

Then the aged Väinämöinen
Answered in the words that follow:

"O thou smith, O Ilmarinen,
What you make is wholly useless!
Gold will never shine like moonlight,
Silver will not shine like sunlight."

Thus the smith a moon constructed,
And a sun completely finished,   60
Eagerly he raised them upward,
Raised them to the best position,
Raised the moon to fir-tree's summit,
Set the sun upon a pine-tree.
From his head the sweat was streaming,
From his forehead sweat was falling,
With the greatness of his efforts,
And the weight that he was lifting.

Thus the moon was now uplifted,
In his place the sun was stationed,   70
Moon amid the crown of fir-tree,
Sun upon a pine-tree's summit;
But the moon shed forth no lustre,
And the sun was likewise rayless.

Then the aged Väinämöinen
Spoke aloud the words which follow:
"Time it is the lots to shuffle,
And the signs with care to question
Where the sun is hidden from us,
And the moon has vanished from us."   80

Then the aged Väinämöinen,
He the great primeval sorcerer,
Hastened alder-sticks to cut him,
And arranged the sticks in order,
And began the lots to shuffle,
With his fingers to arrange them,
And he spoke the words which follow,
And in words like these expressed him:
"Leave I ask of the Creator,
Seek an answer that misleads not: 90

Tell me, signs of the Creator,
Lots of Jumala, instruct me,
Where the sun is hidden from us,
And the moon has vanished from us,
Since no more as time elapses,
In the sky do we behold them?

Speak, O lot, and tell me truly,
With man's reason speak unto me,
Speak thou faithful words unto us,
Make thou faithful compacts with us!   100
If the lot should lie unto me,
Then its worth I hold as nothing,
And upon the fire will cast it,
And will burn the signs upon it."

And the lot spoke words most faithful,
And the signs made answer truly,
For they said the sun was hidden,
And the moon was also sunken,
Deep in Pohjola's stone mountain,
And within the hill of copper.   110

Väinämöinen, old and steadfast,
Uttered then the words which follow:
"If to Pohjola I'll journey,
On the path of Pohja's children,
I will bring the moon to shining,
And the golden sun to shining."

Forth he journeyed, and he hastened
Unto Pohjola's dark regions,
And he walked one day, a second,
And at length upon the third day   120
Came in view the gate of Pohja,
And appeared the rocky mountains.
Then with all his strength he shouted,
As he came to Pohja's river:
"Bring me here a boat directly
Which shall take me o'er the river!"

As his shouting was not heeded,
And no boat for him provided,
Wood into a heap he gathered,
And the dead twigs of a fir-tree,   130
On the shore he made a fire,
And thick clouds of smoke rose upward;
To the sky the flame rose upward,
In the air the smoke ascended.

Louhi, Pohjola's old Mistress
Came herself unto the window,
And, at the sound's opening gazing,
She then spoke the words which follow:
"What's the flame that's burning yonder,
Where the Sound of Saari opens?   140
For a camp too small I think it,
But 'tis larger than a fisher's."

Then the son of Pohja's country
Hurried out into the open,
And he looked about and listened,
Seeking thus for information:
"On the river's other margin,
Is a stately hero marching."

Then the aged Väinämöinen
Once again commenced his shouting: 150
"Bring a boat, O son of Pohja,
Bring a boat for Väinämöinen!"

Answer made the son of Pohja,
And in words like these responded:
"Here the boats are never ready;
You to row must use your fingers,
And must use your hands for rudder,
Crossing Pohjola's deep river!"

Then the aged Väinämöinen
Pondered deeply and reflected: 160
"Not as man should he be reckoned
Who retreats upon his pathway."

Like a pike in lake then plunging,
Powan-like in sluggish river,
Through the sound he swam right quickly,
Speedily the strait he traversed,
And he moved one foot, a second,
And he reached the shore of Pohja!

Then spoke out the sons of Pohja,
And the evil army shouted: 170
"Go into the yard of Pohja!"
And on this the yard he entered.

Then exclaimed the sons of Pohja,
And the evil army shouted:
"Enter now the house of Pohja!"
And on this the house he entered,
On the floor his foot he planted,
Grasped he the door-handle firmly,
Forced his way into the dwelling,
And beneath the roof he entered,   180
There the men the mead were drinking,
And the honey-drink imbibing.
All the men with swords were girded,
And the heroes aimed their weapons
At the head of Väinämöinen,
Thus to slay Suvantolainen.

Then they questioned the intruder
In the very words that follow:
"What's your news, you wretched fellow,
What's your need, O swimming hero?"   190

Väinämöinen, old and steadfast,
Answered in the words which follow:
"Of the moon are curious tidings,
Of the sun are wondrous tidings.
Where is now the sun imprisoned,
Whither has the moon been taken?"

Answered then the sons of Pohja,
And the evil army uttered:

"Thus it is the sun is hidden,
Sun is hidden, moon imprisoned,   200
In the stones of many colours,
In the rocks as hard as iron,
And from there, escape they cannot,
And release shall never reach them."

Then the aged Väinämöinen
Answered in the words that follow:
"If the sun from rock ascends not,
Nor the moon from rocky mountain,
Let us join in closest conflict,
Let us grasp our trusty sword-blades!"   210

Sword they drew, and tried their sword-blades,
Drew from out the sheaths their weapons;
At the point the moon was shining,
On the hilt the sun was shining,
On the back a horse was standing,
At the knob a cat was mewing.

After this the swords they measured,
And they thus compared their weapons:
And the sword of aged Väinö
Was a little trifle longer,   220
Longer, as a grain of barley,
As the width of straw-stalk longer.
Out into the yard they hastened,
On the grass to meet in conflict;
And the aged Väinämöinen
Struck a blow with lightning swiftness,
Struck a blow, and struck a second,
And he sheared, like roots of turnips,
Off he shore, like heads of flax-plant,
Heads of all the sons of Pohja.   230

Then the aged Väinämöinen
Sought for where the moon was hidden,
Likewise would release the sunlight
From the rocks of varied colour,
From the depths of steely mountain,
From the rocks as hard as iron.

Then he walked a little distance,
But a very little distance,
When he saw a copse all verdant;
In the copse a lovely birch-tree,   240
And a large stone block beneath it,
And a rock beneath the stone block,
And there were nine doors before it,
In the doors were bolts a hundred.

In the stone a crack perceiving,
In the rock some lines engraven,
Then he drew his sword from scabbard,
On the coloured stone he scraped it,
With the sharp point of his sword-blade,
With his gleaming blade he scraped it,   250
Till the stone in two divided,
And in three he quickly split it.

Väinämöinen, old and steadfast,
Looked into the stone all pictured;
Many serpents ale were drinking,
In the wort the snakes were writhing,
In the coloured stone were hiding,
In the cracks of liver-colour.
Väinämöinen, old and steadfast,
Uttered then the words that follow: 260
"Thus it is the hapless Matrons,
Have so little ale acquired,
For the snakes the ale are drinking,
In the wort the snakes are writhing."
Off he cut the heads of serpents,
Broke the necks of all the serpents!
And he spoke the words which follow,
And in words like these expressed him:
"Never while the world existeth,
From this very day henceforward,   270
Let our ale by snakes be drunken,
And our malt-drink by the serpents."

Then the aged Väinämöinen,
He the great primeval sorcerer,
Sought with hands the doors to open,

And the bolts by spells to loosen:
But to hands the doors would yield not,
By his spells the bolts were moved not.

Then the aged Väinämöinen
Spoke his thoughts in words that follow: 280
"Man unarmed is weak as woman;
Weak as frog, without a hatchet."
And at once he wended homeward,
Head bowed down, in great vexation,
For the moon was not recovered,
Neither had the sun been captured.

Said the lively Lemminkäinen,
"O thou aged Väinämöinen,
Wherefore didst forget to take me,
As your very trusty comrade?   290
I had brought the locks to creaking,
And the bars asunder broken,
And released the moon for shining,
And had raised the sun for shining."

Väinämöinen, old and steadfast,
Answered in the words that follow:
"Unto spells the bolts will yield not,
And the locks my magic breaks not;
Strength of hands will never move them,
And no strength of arm will force them."   300

To the smith's forge then he wandered,
And he spoke the words which follow:
"O thou smith, O Ilmarinen!
Forge me now a mighty trident,
And a dozen hatchets forge me,
And a bunch of keys enormous,
From the stone the moon to rescue,
From the rock the sun deliver!"

Thereupon smith Ilmarinen,
He the great primeval craftsman,   310
Forged the hero what he needed,
And a dozen hatchets forged him,

Forged a bunch of keys enormous,
And of spears a mighty bundle,
Not too large and not too little,
But of middle size he forged them.

Louhi, Pohjola's old Mistress,
Old and gap-toothed dame of Pohja,
Then with wings herself provided,
And extended them for flying,   320
Near the house at first was flying,
Then her flight extended further,
Straight across the lake of Pohja
Unto Ilmarinen's smithy.

Then the smith his window opened,
Looking if the wind was blowing;
'Twas no wind that there was blowing,
But a hawk, and grey in colour.

Thereupon smith Ilmarinen
Spoke aloud the words that follow: 330
"Bird of prey, what brings thee hither,
Sitting underneath my window?"

Hereupon the bird spoke language,
And the hawk at once made answer:
"O thou smith, O Ilmarinen,
Thou the most industrious craftsman!
Truly art thou very skilful,
And a most accomplished craftsman!"

Thereupon smith Ilmarinen
Answered in the words that follow: 340
"But indeed 'tis not a wonder,
If I am a skilful craftsman,
For 'twas I who forged the heavens,
And the arch of air who welded."

Hereupon the bird spoke language,
And the hawk at once responded:
"What is this, O smith, thou makest,
What, O blacksmith, art thou forging?"

Thereupon smith Ilmarinen
Answered in the words that follow: 350
"'Tis a neck-ring I am forging,
For the aged crone of Pohja,
That she may be firmly fettered
To the side of a great mountain."

Louhi, Pohjola's old Mistress,
Old and gap-toothed dame of Pohja,
Felt on this her doom was coming,
On her head the days of evil,
And at once to flight betook her,
Swift to Pohjola escaping.   360

From the stone the moon released she,
From the rock the sun released she;
Then again her form she altered,
And to dove herself converted,
And her flight again directed
Unto Ilmarinen's smithy,
To the door in bird-form flying,
Lit as dove upon the threshold.

Thereupon smith Ilmarinen
Asked her in the words which follow: 370
"Why, O bird, hast thou flown hither?
Dove, why sit'st thou on the threshold?"

From the door the wild bird answered,
And the dove spoke from the threshold:
"Here I sit upon the threshold,
That the news I now may bring thee:
From the stone the moon has risen,
From the rock the sun is loosened."

Thereupon smith Ilmarinen
Hastened forth to gaze around him,   380
And he stood at door of smithy,
Gazing anxiously to heaven,
And he saw the moon was gleaming,
And he saw the sun was shining.

Then he went to Väinämöinen,
And he spoke the words which follow:
"O thou aged Väinämöinen,
Thou the great primeval minstrel!
Come to gaze upon the moonlight,
Come to gaze upon the sunlight! 390
Now they stand in midst of heaven,
In their old accustomed places."

Väinämöinen, old and steadfast,
Hurried out into the open,
And at once his head uplifted,
And he gazed aloft to heaven:
Moon was risen, sun was loosened,
In the sky the sun was beaming.

Then the aged Väinämöinen
Made a speech without delaying, 400
And he spoke the words which follow,
And in words like these expressed him:
"Hail, O Moon, who beamest yonder,
Thus thy fair cheeks well displaying,
Golden sun, who risest yonder,
Sun, who once again arisest!
Golden Moon, from stone delivered,
Fairest Sun, from rock arisen,
Like the golden cuckoo rise you,
Like the silver dove arise you, 410
Lead the life ye led aforetime,
And resume your former journeys.

Rise for ever in the morning,
From this present day hereafter.
Bring us always happy greetings,
That our wealth increases ever,
Game for ever in our fingers.
Fortune at the points of fish-hooks!
Go ye on your path with blessings,
Go ye on your charming journey, 420
Let your crescent now be beauteous,
Rest ye joyful in the evening!"

L Marjatta

The virgin Marjatta swallows a cranberry and brings forth a boy
(1–346). The child disappears and after a long search is found in a
swamp (347–430). He is taken to an old man to be baptized, but the
latter will not baptize the fatherless child until after due consideration
(431–40). Väinämöinen comes to inquire into the matter, and
advises that the ill-omened boy should be put to death, but the child
reproaches him for his unjust sentence (441–74). The old man bap-
tizes the boy as King of Carelia, at which Väinämöinen is grievously
offended and leaves the country, but first declares that he will again
make a new *Sampo* and *kantele*, and light for the people. He sails away
in a copper boat to a land between earth and heaven, but he leaves
behind his *kantele* and his great songs as a parting gift to his people
(475–512). Concluding verses (513–620).

Marjatta, the graceful damsel,
In her home long time was growing,
In the home of her great father,
In her tender mother's dwelling,
And five chains wore out completely,
And six rings she wore out likewise;
For her father's keys she used them,
Which around her waist were hanging.

And she wore out half the threshold,
With her skirts as she was passing,
And she half frayed off the rafters
Where she hung her silken ribands,
And she half wore out the door-posts
As her fine sleeves rubbed against them,
And the planking of the flooring
Wore away beneath her slippers.

Marjatta, the graceful damsel,
Was a very little damsel,
And was always pure and holy,
And was ever very modest, 20
And she fed on fish the finest,
And the soft bark of the fir-tree,
But the eggs of hens ate never,
Over which the cocks were crowing,
And the flesh of ewe she ate not,
Had the ewe with ram been running.

If her mother sent her milking,
Yet she did not go to milking,
And she spoke the words which follow:
"Never such a maid as I am 30
Udders of the cows should handle,
Which with bulls have been disporting,
If no milk from calf is flowing,
Or from calf it is not running."

If her father sent her sledging,
In a stallion's sledge she went not;
If a mare her brother brought her,
Then these words the maiden uttered:
"Never will I sit in mares' sledge,
Which with stallion has been running, 40
If no foals the sledge are drawing,
Which have numbered six months only."

Marjatta, the graceful damsel,
She who always lived a virgin,
Always greeted as a maiden,
Modest maid with locks unbraided,
Went to lead the herds to pasture,
And beside the sheep was walking.

On the hill the sheep were straying,
To the top the lambs were climbing, 50
On the plain the maiden wandered,
Tripping through the alder bushes,
While there called the golden cuckoo,
And the silvery birds were singing.

Marjatta, the graceful damsel,
Looked around her and she listened,
Sitting on the hill of berries,
Resting on the sloping hillside,
And she spoke the words which follow,
And in words like these expressed her: 60
"Call thou on, O golden cuckoo,
Sing thou still, O bird of silver,
Sing thou from thy breast of silver!
Tell me true, O Saxon strawberry,
Shall I long remain unhooded,
Long among the flocks as herd-girl,
On the wide-extending meadows,
And the far-extending woodlands,
For one summer, for two summers,
Or for five or six of summers,   70
Or perchance for ten long summers,
Or the time fulfilled already?"

Marjatta, the graceful damsel,
For a while lived on as herd-girl.
Evil is the life of shepherd,
Far too heavy for a maiden;
In the grass a snake is creeping,
In the grass the lizards wriggling.

But not there a snake was writhing,
Nor in grass the lizards wriggling.   80
From the hill there cried a berry,
From the heath there cried a cranberry:
"O thou maiden, come and pluck me,
Rosy-cheeked one, come and gather,
Tin bedecked one come and pluck me,
With thy copper belt to choose me,
Ere the slug should come to eat me,
Or the black worm should disturb me!
There are hundreds who have seen me,
Thousands more have sat beside me,   90
Girls by hundreds, wives by thousands,
Children, too, that none can number;
None among them yet has touched me,
None has gathered me, the wretched."

Marjatta, the graceful damsel,
Went a very little distance,
Went to look upon the berry,
And the cranberry to gather,
With her skilful hands to pluck it,
With her beauteous hands to pluck it.   100

On the hill she found the berry,
On the heath she found the cranberry;
'Twas a berry in appearance,
And it seemed to be a cranberry,
But from ground too high for eating,
On a tree too low for climbing!
From the heath a stick she lifted,
That she might pull down the berry;
Then from ground the berry mounted
Upward to her shoes so pretty,   110
From her pretty shoes arose it,
Upward to her knees of whiteness,
Rising from her knees of whiteness
Upward to her skirts that rustled.

To her buckled belt arose it,
To her breast from buckled girdle,
From her breast to chin arose it,
To her lips from chin arose it,
Then into her mouth it glided,
And along her tongue it hastened,   120
From her tongue to throat it glided,
And it dropped into her stomach.

Marjatta, the graceful damsel,
After this had chanced, grew pregnant,
And it soon increased upon her,
And her burden soon grew heavy.
Then she cast aside her girdle,
Loosely dressed, without a girdle,
Secretly she sought the sauna,
And she hid her in the darkness.   130

Always was her mother thinking,
And her mother pondered ever:

"What has chanced to our Marjatta,
What has happened to our house-dove,
That she casts aside her girdle,
Always dresses loosely, beltless,
Goes in secret to the sauna,
And she hides her in the darkness?"

And a baby gave her answer,
And the little child made answer: 140
"This has chanced to our Marjatta,
This befel the wretched creature,
She has been too long a herd-girl,
With the flocks too far has wandered."

And she bore her heavy burden,
And the pain it brought upon her,
Bore it seven months, bore it eight months,
Bore it through the ninth month also,
By the reckoning of old women,
And for half the tenth month also.   150

While the tenth month thus was passing,
Then the girl was filled with anguish,
Pains of labour came upon her,
And the weight oppressed her sorely.

For a bath she asked her mother:
"O my very dearest mother!
Make a warm place ready for me,
And a warm room ready for me,
Where the girl awhile may rest her
In the house of suffering women!"   160

But her mother gave her answer,
Answered thus, the aged woman:
"Woe to thee, O whore of Hiisi!
Tell me now with whom thou restedst,
With a man as yet unmarried,
Or beside a married hero?"

Marjatta, the graceful damsel,
Then replied to her in thiswise:

"Neither with a man unmarried,
Nor with any married hero;   170
But I sought the hill of berries,
And I went to pluck the cranberries,
And I took what seemed a berry,
And upon my tongue I laid it,
Quickly in my throat it glided,
And it dropped into my stomach.
Thus it is that I am pregnant,
That is how I got my burden."

For a bath she asked her father:
"O my very dearest father!   180
Give me now a well-warmed refuge,
Make a warm room ready for me,
Where the wretched one may rest her,
And the girl endure her suffering!"

But her father gave her answer,
Gave her back a shameful answer;
"Go thou forth from here, O strumpet,
Wander forth, O wench for burning,
To the bears' own rocky caverns,
To the caves where bears are lurking,   190
Thither forth to bear, O strumpet,
Bear thy children, wench of fire!"

Marjatta, the graceful damsel,
Then returned submissive answer:
"Not at all am I a strumpet,
Neither am a wench for burning;
I shall bear a mighty hero,
And shall bear a noble offspring,
He shall be a mighty conqueror,
Strong as even Väinämöinen."   200

Then the maid was greatly troubled,
Where to go, and how to journey,
Where a bath she might provide her,
And she spoke the words which follow:
"O my little damsel Piltti,
Thou the best of all my handmaids!

Find me now a bath in village,
Find a bath near reed-fringed brooklet,
Where the wretched one may rest her,
And the girl endure her suffering.   210
Go at once, and hasten quickly,
For my need is of the greatest!"

Then the little damsel Piltti,
Answered in the words that follow:
"Where am I to ask for sauna,
Who will help me to obtain it?"

Thereupon did our Marjatta
Answer in the words which follow:
"Go and ask a bath from Ruotus,
Near where issues forth the Reed-brook!"   220

Then the little maiden Piltti,
Listened to her words obedient,
Always ready, heedless never,
Always quick, avoiding gossip,
Like a mist, away she hurried,
To the yard like smoke she hastened,
With her hands her skirts she lifted,
In her hands her dress she twisted,
And upon her course she hastened
Straight unto the house of Ruotus.   230
Hills re-echoed to her footsteps,
Shook the mountains as she climbed them,
On the heath the cones were dancing,
Gravel scattered o'er the marshes;
Thus she came to Ruotus' dwelling,
And the house she quickly entered.
In his shirt sat wicked Ruotus,
Eating, drinking like the great ones,
In his shirt at end of table,
In a shirt of finest linen,   240

And he asked as he was eating,
Grunted, leaning o'er the table:
"What have you to say, you beggar,
Wretch, why come you running hither?"

Then the little damsel Piltti
Answered in the words that follow:
"Here I seek a village sauna,
Seek a bath near reed-fringed brooklet,
That relief may reach the suffering,
For the need is very pressing."   250

Then the wicked wife of Ruotus
Presently with arms a-kimbo,
Slouched along upon the flooring,
Swept to middle of the flooring,
And she asked upon her coming,
Speaking in the words which follow:
"Who is seeking for a sauna,
Who is seeking for assistance?"
Said the little damsel Piltti:
"Needed 'tis for our Marjatta."   260

Then the wicked wife of Ruotus
Answered in the words that follow:
"Vacant baths are rare in village,
None at mouth of reed-fringed streamlet.
There's a bath upon the clearing,
And a stable in the pinewood,
Where the whore may bear her children,
And the vile one cast her offspring,
While the horses there are breathing,
Let her take a bath and welcome!"   270

Then the little maiden Piltti,
Hurried back with rapid footsteps,
And upon her course she hastened,
And she said on her arrival:
"In the village is no sauna,
None beside the rush-fringed streamlet;
And the wicked wife of Ruotus,
Only spoke the words which follow:
'Vacant baths are none in village,
None at mouth of reed-fringed streamlet.   280
There's a bath upon the clearing,
And a stable in the pinewood,
Where the whore may bear her children,

And the vile one cast her offspring,
While the horses there are breathing,
Let her take a bath and welcome!'
This was all she said unto me,
This is truly what she answered."

Marjatta, the hapless maiden,
When she heard, burst forth in weeping,   290
And she spoke the words that follow:
"Thither must I then betake me,
Even like an outcast labourer,
Even like a hired servant,
I must go upon the clearing,
And must wander to the pinewood."

In her hands her skirt she lifted,
With her hands her skirt she twisted,
And she took the bath-whisks with her,
Of the softest leaves and branches,   300
And with hasty steps went onward,
In the greatest pain of body,
To the stable in the pinewood,
And the stall on hill of Tapio.

And she spoke the words which follow,
And in words like these expressed her:
"Come thou to my aid, Creator,
To my aid, O thou most gracious,
In this anxious time of labour.
In this time of hardest labour!   310
Free the damsel from her burden,
From her pains release the woman,
That she perish not in torment,
May not perish in her anguish!"

When at length her journey ended,
Then she spoke the words which follow:
"O thou good horse, breathe upon me,
O thou draught-foal, snort upon me,
Breathe a vapour-bath around me,
Send thou warmth throughout the sauna,   320

That relief may reach the sufferer,
For the need is very pressing!"

Then the good horse breathed upon her,
And the draught-foal snorted on her,
Over all her suffering body.
When the horse desisted breathing,
Steam was spread throughout the stable,
Like the steam of boiling water.

Marjatta, the hapless maiden,
She, the holy little maiden,   330
Bathed her in a bath sufficient,
Till she had relieved her suffering;
And a little boy was born her,
And a sinless child was given,
On the hay in horses' stable,
On the hay in horses' manger.
Then she washed the little infant,
And in swaddling-clothes she wrapped him,
On her knees she took the infant,
And she wrapped her garments round him.   340
There she reared the little infant,
Thus she reared the beauteous infant,
Reared her little golden apple,
And her little staff of silver,
And upon her lap she nursed it,
With her hands did she caress it.

On her knees she laid the infant,
On her lap she laid her baby,
And began to brush his hair straight,
And began to smooth his hair down,   350
When from off her knees he vanished,
From her lap the infant vanished.

Marjatta, the hapless maiden,
Fell into the greatest trouble,
And she hurried off to seek him,
Seek her little boy, the infant,
And she sought her golden apple,

Sought her little staff of silver,
Sought him underneath the millstones,
Underneath the sledge while running,   360
Underneath the sieve while sifting,
Underneath the lidless basket;
Trees she searched, and grass divided,
Spreading out the tender herbage.

Long the little boy she sought for,
Sought her son, the little infant,
Sought him through the hills and pinewoods,
On the heath among the heather,
Searched through every tuft of heather,
And in every bush she sought him,   370
Roots of juniper updigging,
And of trees the branches straightening.

Then she thought to wander further,
And she went upon her wanderings;
And there came a star to meet her,
And before the star she bowed her:
"Star, whom Jumala created!
Know you nothing of my infant,
Where my little son is hidden,
Where is hid my golden apple?"   380

And the star made answer to her:
"If I knew, I would not tell it.
He it was who me created,
Made me, through these days of evil
In the cold to shine for ever,
And to glimmer through the darkness."

Then she thought to wander further,
And she went upon her wanderings,
And the moon came next to meet her,
And she bowed herself before him: 390
"Moon, whom Jumala created!
Know you nothing of my infant,
Where my little son is hidden,
Where is hid my golden apple?"

And the moon made answer to her:
"If I knew, I would not tell it.
He it was who me created,
Always in these days of evil
Through the night to watch all lonely,
And to sleep throughout the daytime."   400

Then she thought to wander further,
And she went upon her wanderings,
And there came the sun to meet her,
And she bowed herself before him:
"Sun, whom Jumala created!
Know you nothing of my infant,
Where my little son is hidden,
Where is hid my golden apple?"

And the sun made answer wisely:
"Well, indeed I know your infant,   410
He it was who me created,
In those days of finest weather,
Golden rays to shed about me,
Silver rays to scatter round me.

Well indeed I know your infant,
Know your son, unhappy mother!
There thy little son is hidden,
There is hid thy golden apple,
In the swamps to waistband sunken,
To his arm-pits in the marshlands."   420

Marjatta, the hapless maiden,
Sought her infant in the marshes;
In the swamps her son discovered,
And she brought him home in triumph.

Then the son of Marjatta maiden,
Grew into a youth most beauteous,
But they knew not what to call him,
Did not know what name to give him,
But his mother called him Floweret,
And the strangers called him Sluggard.   430

And they sought a man to name him,
And to sprinkle him with water;
And an old man came to name him,
Virokannas to baptize him.

Then these words the old man uttered,
And in words like these expressed him:
"With the cross I will not sign him,
Nor will I baptize the infant,
Not till he has been examined,
And a judgment passed upon him."　　　　　　　440

Who shall dare to come to try him,
Test him, and pass sentence on him?
Väinämöinen, old and steadfast,
He the great primeval sorcerer,
He alone came forth to try him,
And to test him and pass sentence.

Väinämöinen, old and steadfast,
Sentence gave in words that follow:
"As the boy from marsh has risen,
From the ground, and from a berry,　　　　　　　450
On the ground they now shall lay him,
Where the hills are thick with berries,
Or shall to the swamps conduct him,
With a club his head to shatter!"

Then the half-month old spoke loudly,
And the fortnight-old re-echoed:
"O thou old and wretched creature,
Wretched old man, void of insight,
O how stupid is your judgement,
How contemptible thy sentence!　　　　　　　460
Thou hast grievous crimes committed,
Likewise deeds of greatest folly,
Yet to swamps they did not lead thee,
Shattered not thy head with wood clubs,
When thyself, in youthful folly,
Gave the child of thine own mother,
That thou thus mightst 'scape destruction,
And release thyself in thiswise.

And again thou wast not carried,
And abandoned in the marshes,   470
When thyself in youthful folly,
Caused the young maids to be sunken,
In the depths beneath the billows,
To the black ooze at the bottom."

Then the old man quickly named him,
Quick baptized the child with water,
As the king of all Carelia,
And the lord of all the mighty.

Then was Väinämöinen angry,
Greatly shamed and greatly angry,   480
And prepared himself to journey
To the far extending seashore,
And began his songs of magic,
For the last time sang them loudly,
Sang himself a boat of copper,
With a copper deck provided.

In the stern himself he seated,
Sailing o'er the sparkling billows,
Still he sang on his departure,
And he sang as he was sailing: 490
"May the time pass quickly o'er us,
Let one day pass, let come another,
And again shall I be needed.
Men will look for me, and miss me,
To construct another Sampo,
And another harp to make me,
Make another moon for gleaming,
And another sun for shining.
When the sun and moon are absent,
In the air no joy remaineth."   500

Then the aged Väinämöinen
Went upon his journey singing,
Sailing in his boat of copper,
In his vessel made of copper,
Sailed away to loftier regions,
To the sky beneath the heavens.

There he rested with his vessel,
Rested weary, with his vessel,
But his kantele he left us,

Left his charming harp in Suomi,   510
For his people's lasting pleasure,
Mighty songs for Finnish children.

    *   *   *   *   *

Now my mouth must cease from speaking,
And my tongue be bound securely,
Cease the chanting of my verses,
And my lively songs abandon;
Even thus must horses rest them,
When a long course is completed,
Even iron must be wearied
When the grass is mown in summer,   520
And the water-drops be weary,
As they trace the river's windings,
And the fire is extinguished
When throughout the night 'tis burning.
Why should not our songs be wearied,
Those sweet songs that we are singing,
For the lengthy evenings' pleasure,
Singing later than the sunset?

Thus I heard the people talking,
And again it was repeated: 530
"E'en the waterfall when flowing
Yields no endless stream of water,
Nor does an accomplished singer,
Sing till all his knowledge fails him.
Better 'tis to sit in silence
Than to break off in the middle."

Now my song remains completed,
'Tis completed and abandoned.
In a ball I wind my lays up,
As a ball I cast them from me,   540
In the storehouse loft I lay them,
With a lock of bone secure them,
That from thence escape they never,
Nor in time may be untwisted,
Not unless the lock be opened,
And its jaws should be extended,
Not unless the teeth be opened,
And the tongue again is moving,

What would now avail my singing,
If the songs I sang were bad ones,   550
If I sang in every valley,
And I sang in every firwood?
For my mother lives no longer,
Wakes no more my own old mother,
Nor my golden one can hear me,
Nought can learn my dear old mother,
None would hear me but the fir-trees,
Learn, save branches of the pine-trees,
Or the tender leaves of birch-trees,
Or the charming mountain ash-tree.   560

I was small when died my mother,
Weak was I without my mother;
On the stones like lark she left me,
On the rocks like thrush she left me,
Left me like a lark to sing there,
Or to sing as sings the throstle,
In the wardship of a stranger,
At the will of a step-mother;
And she drove me forth, unhappy,
Forth she drove the unloved infant,   570
To a wind-swept home she drove me,
To the north-wind's home she drove me,
That against the wind defenceless,
Winds might sweep away the orphan.

Like a lark away I wandered,
Like a hapless bird I wandered
Shelterless about the country;
Wearily I wandered onward,
Till with every wind acquainted,
I their roaring comprehended;   580
In the frost I learned to shudder,
And I learned to cry with freezing,
Even now do many people,
Many people I encounter,
Speak to me in angry accents,
Rudest speeches hurl against me,
Curses on my tongue they shower,
And about my voice cry loudly,
Likewise they abuse my grumbling,

And they call my songs too lengthy,   590
And they say I sing too badly,
And my song's accented wrongly.

May you not, O friendly people,
As a wondrous thing regard it
That I sang so much in childhood,
And when small, I sang so loudly!
I received no store of learning,
Never travelled to the learned.
Foreign words were never taught me,
Neither songs from distant countries.   600

Others all have had instruction,
From my home I journeyed never,
Always did I help my mother,
And I dwelt for ever near her,
In the house received instruction,
'Neath the rafters of my storehouse,
By the spindle of my mother,
By my brother's heap of shavings,
In my very earliest childhood,
In a shirt that hung in tatters.   610

But let this be as it may be,
I have shown the way to singers,
Showed the way, and left the markers,
Cut the branches, shown the pathways.
This way therefore leads the pathway,
Here the course lies newly opened,
Open for the greater singers,
For the bards and ballad singers,
For the young, who now are growing,
For the rising generation.   620

Notes

These are by the translator, when not otherwise stated. K.K. indicates Professor Kaarle Krohn; A.M., Madame Aino Malmberg; and M.B., Dr M.A. Branch. For proper names, refer to the Glossary.

RUNO I

11 Kulta, 'golden', here rendered 'dearest', is a term constantly applied in the *Kalevala* to anything dear or precious.

20 'Pohja, the North, or Pohjola, the North Land, is chiefly used for the dark North, where the sun is hidden. Poetically used for a homestead in the *Kalevala*. Occasionally it is used as synonymous with Lapland.' (K.K.)

21 When singing to the accompaniment of a *kantele*, two Finns clasp their hands together, and sway backwards and forwards, in the manner described in the text. Compare Acerbi's *Travels to the North Cape* (1802), I, chaps. xx and xxiii, and the illustration opposite his Vol. I, p. 226.

61 Probably the honey of humble-bees (*Bombus*) is here meant, or the expression may be merely figurative.

63, 64 The metre allows the translation of the names of the cows to be inserted here.

110 Ilmatar, the Daughter of the Air; *tar/-tär* is a feminine suffix in Finnish, and is generally understood to mean 'daughter of –'; in older usage it also indicates the spirit of the phenomenon to which the suffix is attached. In the following passages we have the combined Finnish version of the widespread cosmogonical myths of the Divine Spirit brooding over the waters of Chaos; and the Mundane Egg. In the 1835 *Kalevala*, however, and in many Finnish ballads, an eagle is said to have built her nest on the knees of Väinämöinen after he was thrown into the sea by the Laplander, and the Creation-Myth is thus transferred to him.

229–44 In the Scandinavian Mythology the world was created in a similar manner by Othin and his brothers from the body of the giant Ymir.

289 Vaka vanha Väinämöinen – these are the usual epithets applied to Väinämöinen in the *Kalevala*. 'Vanha' means old; 'vaka' is variously interpreted: I have used 'steadfast' by Professor Krohn's advice, though I think 'lusty' might be a better rendering.

320 The ring-finger is usually called the 'nameless finger' in Finnish.

RUNO II

27 The Bird Cherry (*Prunus padus*).

29 The Mountain Ash, or Rowan Tree, is a sacred tree in Finland, as in Scotland.

83 The Great Oak is a favourite subject in Finnish and Estonian ballads.

117 Finnish and Estonian water-heroes are sometimes described as entirely composed of copper.

211 Compare the account of the breaking up of the *sampo*, and the dispersal of its fragments, in Runo XLIII.

245 The summer ermine is the stoat, which turns white in winter in the North, when it becomes the ermine. The squirrel also turns grey in the North in the winter.

376 The cuckoo is regarded as a bird of good omen.

RUNO III

15 We here find Väinämöinen, the primeval minstrel and culture-hero, the first-born of mortals, living in an already populated world. There seems to be a similar discrepancy in Gen. iv. 14–17.

35 Women were held in great respect in heroic times in most Northern countries.

58 'I will bewitch him who tries to bewitch me.' (K.K.)

72 A gold-adorned, or perhaps merely handsome, sledge.

154 An epithet for the seal.

156 The powan, or fresh-water herring (*Coregonus*), of which there are several marine and fresh-water species. They are chiefly lake-fish of the Northern Hemisphere, and in the British Islands are better known in Scotland and Ireland, and in the North of England, than in the South.

168 The word used here may also mean the elk or ox.

230 The Arch of Heaven in the *Kalevala* means the rainbow.

231, 232 The Sun and the Moon are male figures in Finnish, with sons and daghters.

233 The constellation of the Great Bear.

273 Most of the heroes of the *Kalevala*, except Kullervo, have black hair, and the heroines, except the wife of Ilmarinen, golden hair.

411, 412 A common ransom to propose in Finnish and Estonian stories.

533 Different stories are told of the origin of both Väinämöinen and Ilmarinen, and they are often called brothers.

RUNO IV

4 Bath-whisks are used to heighten the circulation after bathing in the sauna. 'The leaves are left on the stems. The bath-whisks for the winter are all made early in the summer, when the leaves are softest. Of course they become quite dry, but before using, they are steeped in hot water till they become soft and fragrant.' (A.M.)

75 'The store-houses where the peasant girls keep their clothes and ornaments are sometimes very pretty, and the girls always sleep there in summer. There are other store-houses for food.' (A.M.)

121 According to Speke, Central African women are compelled to drink large quantities of milk, to make them inordinately fat, which is considered a great beauty.

206 *Fuligala glacialis.*

295 'Came she to the sea's broad margin. (K.K.)

308 This passage is hardly intelligible. I have heard some people suggest that Aino perhaps took a birch branch to be used as a bath-whisk.' (A.M.) 'The line may also be interpreted as descriptive: the incident took place by the shore.' (M.B.)

377   There are many popular tales in Finnish relating to animals, especially the bear, wolf, and fox, but this is the one illustration of the true 'beast-epos' in the *Kalevala*.

413   'The sauna, or bath-house, is always a separate building; and there Finnish people take extremely hot baths almost every evening.' (A.M.) It is also used for confinements and for the practice of healing spells.

RUNO V

220   Here a human mother, rather than Ilmatar, seems to be ascribed to Väinämöinen. Visits to parents' graves for advice and assistance are common in Scandinavian and Estonian literature. Commentators have also quoted the story of Achilles and Thetis, but this is hardly a parallel case.

RUNO VI

120   This passage is again inconsistent with the legend of Väinämöinen being the son of Ilmatar.

RUNO VII

19   The word used here is 'poika' which literally means a boy, or a son.

51, 52   The original admirably expresses the hovering motion of the bird:

> Lenteleikse, liiteleikse,
> Katseleikse, käänteleikse.

142   In the original 'the song of a hen's child'.

177, 178   Weeping appears no more disgraceful to the heroes of the *Kalevala* than to those of the *Iliad*. Still, Väinämöinen not unfrequently plays a very undignified part when in difficulties.

241   Louhi recognized him, though he would not mention his name.

286   'Virsu is a shoe made of birch bark.' (A.M.)

311   It appears that the magic mill called a *sampo* could only be forged by a competent smith from materials which Louhi alone possessed, and which, perhaps, she could not again procure. Otherwise Ilmarinen could have forged another for himself, and it would have been unnecessary for the heroes to steal it. The chain forged by the dwarfs, according to the *Prose Edda*, for binding the wolf Fenrir was also composed of materials which could not again be procured. 'It was fashioned out of six things; to wit, the noise made by the footfall of a cat, the beards of women, the roots of stones, the sinews of bears, the breath of fish, and the spittle of birds.'

RUNO VIII

3, 4   The daughter of Louhi is never mentioned again in connection with the rainbow; and it is quite incorrect to call her the Maiden of the Rainbow, as some writers have done, for no such title is ever applied to her in the poem.

35   There are so many instances of maidens being carried off, or enticed into sledges, in the *Kalevala*, that it seems almost to have been a recognized legal form of marriage by capture.

57   Finnish magicians profess to understand the laguage of birds; but the passage in the text is probably intended only in jest.

152   In the Icelandic saga of Grettir, the hero mortally wounds himself in the

leg while trying to chop up a piece of driftwood on which a witch had laid her curse.

179   The Finns supposed that if the origin of any hostile agent was known, and could be recited to it, its power for evil was at an end. In Denmark, the naming of any person or thing was an evil omen, and liable to bring about its destruction.

217, 218   Finnish hamlets are sometimes built on a hillside in the manner described.

RUNO IX

35, 36   Here we seem to have an allusion to the first chapter of Genesis and to the second chapter at 43*ff*.

44   The same epithet, Luonnotar, is sometimes applied to Ilmatar, and thus Väinämöinen might literally be called the brother of Iron.

45   'Mothers of the ore of Iron.' (M.B.)

111, 112   Pallas Athene sprang armed from the brain of Zeus; Karna, in India, the son of the Sun, was born with armour and earrings; and Mexitli in Mexico was born with a spear in his hand.

231   Hornets often buld their nests under the eaves of houses.

242   Both frogs and toads exude a more or less poisonous secretion from the skin.

433   Honeydew seems to be meant here.

525, 526   An imaginary mountain inhabited by a female spirit to which the workers of magic professed to be able to banish pain and sickness.

RUNO X

306   Compare the account of the forging of the Gold and Silver Bride in Runo XXXVII.

311   'Ilmarinen first employs ordinary servants, and then calls the winds to his assistance.' (K.K.)

331   In the Icelandic sagas, we read of the sword Tyrfing, forged by dwarfs, which, if ever drawn, could not again be sheathed till it had slain at least one victim.

332   Literally, 'on his best days'.

414   In the story of Ala Ed-Deen Abush-Shamat, in the *1001 Nights*, we read of a magic bead with five facets, on which were engraved a camel, an armed horseman, a pavilion, a couch, etc., according to the use intended to be made of each facet.

RUNO XI

31–42   Salme and Linda are similarly wooed by the Sun, the Moon, and a Star in the Estonian poem *Kalevipoeg* (see Kirby's *Hero of Esthonia* (1895) I, pp. 10–15.

264–6   These names mean respectively Blackies, Strawberries, Cranberries. 'I think Lemminkäinen means that he has no cows, and only calls these different berries his cows.' (A.M.)

306   Lemminkäinen appears to have been afraid that some one else might carry off his wife, if she showed herself in public (especially Untamo, says Professor Krohn).

385   The Snow Bunting (*Plectrophanes nivalis*), a white bird more or less varied with black.

RUNO XII

25   'The lad Ahti, without compare'. (M.B.)

93   The Finns and Lapps often hide money in the ground. The word used in l. 94 is 'penningin' from 'penni', a word common to most Teutonic and Northern languages.

211, 212   Such omens of death are common in fairy tales; as, for instance, the bleeding knives in the story of the Envious Sisters in the *1001 Nights*. The bleeding trees in medieval romance belong to rather a different category of ideas.

233   Lemminkäinen seems to have hidden himself to escape further remonstrances from his mother and Kyllikki.

262   Probably a creature like a kelpie or Phooka.

474   We are not told how Louhi escaped; but she seems to have come to no harm.

RUNO XIII

39, 40, 44, *passim*.   Kirby translates Finnish *lyly, kalhu* and *suksi* (plural *sukset*) by the single term 'snowshoe'. 'Ski' would be more accurate and is the usual translation, The pair of *sukset* referred to in Kalevala poetry normally consisted of the *lyly*, worn on the left foot and used for gliding, and the shorter, broader *kalhu* on the right foot to propel the skier. (M.B.)

105   The part played by Hiisi in the *Kalevala* usually resembles that played by Loki in the Scandinavian Mythology.

109   Animals, etc., are often thus constructed in Finnish, Estonian and Siberian mythology by gods, demons, and magicians. They do not seem able to create from nothing, but to manufacture what they please or what they can from pre-existing materials, however incongruous.

111   I suppose rushes are here intended.

RUNO XIV

33   'Bring the hero to the hillocks'. (M.B.)

47, 48   Mielikki's gold and silver are the spoils of the chase.

69   Honey is sometimes used in the *Kalevala* for anything sweet and agreeable, just as golden is used for anything beautiful.

103, 104   It appears that the hunter's fortune in the chase was foretold by the rich or shabby garments worn by the forest-deities.

142   Finnish women often wear a blouse over their other garments.

216   *Kuningas* (king) is a Teutonic word, which rarely occurs in the *Kalevala*. The heroes are patriarchs, or chiefs of clans; not kings, as in Homer.

248   There is often much confusion of terms in the *Kalevala*. The creature here mentioned is generally called an elk, but often a reindeer, and in this line a camel-foal. 'For Lönnrot's informant the "camel-foal" was a wondrous animal and therefore suitable as a parallel name of Hiisi's supernatural creature; in most variants, however, singers used "tall" in place of "camel".' (M.B.)

304   When the inferior deities are deaf or too weak, the heroes appeal to the higher gods.
308   The reference here seems to be to Gen. vii. 11. 'The whole passage is of Christian origin.' (K.K.)

RUNO XV
7   Compare Homer, *Iliad*, III, 311–14.
498   The constellation of Orion is variously called by the Finns the Moonshine, the Sword of Kaleva, and the Scythe of Väinämöinen.
559–62   This conceit is common in fairy tales (especially in Russian ones) in the case of heroes wakened from the dead. Sometimes it takes a comic form; and sometimes, as in the present case, a pathetic one.
617   'Dirty-nosed' is a common opprobrious expression in Estonia.

RUNO XVI
27   The account of the boatbuilding in 'Hiawatha's Sailing' is evidently imitated from this passage.
128   In Roman times divination from birds was chiefly taken from their flight or feeding.

RUNO XVII
20   Roads of this description are thoroughly Oriental in character.
86   In Icelandic sagas we often find heroes roused from their graves, but this is usually attempted in order to obtain a sword which has been buried with them.
93–104   Hiawatha was also swallowed by the sturgeon Nahma, but the circumstances were quite different.
211   Note the resonance of the line:
        Kuusista kuhisevista.
237   Ahava, a dry cold wind that blows in March and April, probably corresponding to our cold spring east wind.
285, 286   Vipunen here refers to himself as a little man, which I presume is to be understood figuratively, as I have rendered it.

RUNO XVIII
71   'If you are a salmon skerry'. (M.B.)
379   Compare Cuchullain's wooing of Eimer in Irish story.
405   'Thereupon the obedient serf'. (M.B.)
579   'From the corner an old woman spoke'. (M.B.)

RUNO XIX
33   This episode is very like the story of Jason and Medea.
210   'The wolf Fenrir opens his enormous mouth; the lower jaw reaches to the earth, and the upper one to heaven, and would in fact reach still further were there space to admit of it.' (*Prose Edda*)
217   Vetehinen, a malicious water-spirit.
311   'Ukko's bow' here means the rainbow, broken by the fiery eagle. It may be worth noting that in the Scandinavian Mythology, the sons of Fire

(Muspell) are to ride over the rainbow, and break it to pieces, on their way to battle with the gods.
409 'Wherefore dost thou know, oh suitor'. (M.B.)
483 In the Danish Ballads there are several stories of children speaking in their cradles, but generally to vow vengeance against an enemy.

RUNO XX

17 The Great Ox is a stock subject in Finnish and Estonian ballad literature.

RUNO XXI

161 The Glutton or wolverine, a well-known animal in sub-Arctic Europe, Asia, and America.
393 This curious passage may have been partly suggested by the 'coats of skin' and 'the land flowing with milk and honey' of the Old Testament.

RUNO XXII

194 In the Scandinavian mythology the giantess Skadi was required to choose a husband from among the gods by looking at their feet only.
515–22 'There are ricks in every clearing,
      Bins of grain by every brook,
      Alder-woods for bread fields suited,
      For barley fields the sides of ditches,
      For fields of wheat the water lands,
      Stones from the fields are piled like coins,
      Little stones are spread like pennies.' (M.B.)

RUNO XXIII

330 The usual word to express a long time is *viikko*, a week.
469, 470 These infernal damsels played various parts in the *Kalevala*, as boat-women, death-bringers, etc., and here we find them in the character of Furies.
487 The term 'snowy month' is used for the period between 20 February and 20 March. I have rendered it March.
787–92 Perhaps this is only figurative, as in the case of the unpropitious forest-deities.

RUNO XXIV

119 The roots of the marsh arum (*Calla palustris*). The most usual substitute for more wholesome food in times of famine is bread composed of a mixture of fir-bark and rye.
240 Slav peasant women are said sometimes to regard beating as a sign of affection on the part of their husbands, but this does not seem to be the case with the Finns. In the *Kalevala* we read a good deal about wife-beating in theory, but find very little of it in practice; and even the licentious and violent Lemminkäinen never thinks of beating his wife when he quarrels with her.
446, 450, 454 'To move lightly once about thee.' (M.B.)

RUNO XXV

47 According to popular usage, a son is ennobled by being called a brother.

97   In some of the legends of Sigurd and Brynhilda, Brynhilda is represented as lying asleep in a tower of glass, encompassed by a circle of fire, through which Sigurd had to ride to wake her. In this story she is the prototype of the Sleeping Beauty.

157   We often read in Russian folk-tales of revolving huts supported on fowls' legs.

159   The favourite weapon of the Icelander Skarphedin, the son of Njal, was a bell which rang out shortly before any person was to be killed by it.

289, 290   Saxony and Viro are Germany and Estonia.

564   A sort of master of the ceremonies at Finnish weddings, corresponding to the Russian *svat*, or matchmaker.

596   The scoter duck (*Oidemia nigra*).

642   Brows; literally, eyelashes.

646   Her shift-collar.

665, 666   The beautiful Estonian story of the Dawn, the Moon, and the Morning and Evening Twilight will be found in Jones and Kropf's *Folk-Tales of the Magyars* (1889), pp. 326–8, and in Kirby's *Hero of Esthonia*, II., pp. 30–4.

RUNO XXVI

129   Literally, 'his teeth'.

230   In the *Völuspá*, we read of a Hall of Serpents in Naströnd, one of the Icelandic hells, composed of serpents wattled together, with their heads turned inwards, vomiting floods of venom in which wade murderers, perjurers, and adulterers.

271   Literally, 'the toads'. A diabolical creature, half dragon and half frog, is described in a well-known Estonian story.

307, 308   'You swam in all the land-locked pools,
Though overgrown with dog's tongue weed'. (M.B.)

427   *Tetrao tetrix*, known as the Black-cock and Grey-hen.

555   Virsta, a Russian word naturalized in Finnish.

617   This description recalls the serpents of Indian mythology, such as those described in the first book of the *Mahabharata*.

619   Such a passage might have suggested to Longfellow the folowing:
Bigger than the Big-Sea-Water,
Broader than the Gitche Gumee.
Hiawatha, xxi

RUNO XXVII

208   Here commences a magical contest somewhat resembling the transformation scenes in the stories of the Second Calendar, and of Nooreddin and Bedreddin, in the *1001 Nights*.

RUNO XXVIII

15, 16   His horse and sledge seem to have been transformed, like those of Joukahainen in Runo II.

25   'Flash of weapons in the village'. (M.B.)

185   In Finnish and Estonian tales we often find persons transformed into trees and flowers; sometimes for purposes of concealment.

223   'A young man, his face black with soot'. (M.B.)

RUNO XXIX

242 'Grass-widows' are probably intended.

RUNO XXX

175, 187 Literally, 'nails'.

185 Pakkanen, Puhurin poika. Frost, the son of the North Wind.

389 The unmanly lamentations of the heroes over a fate that has not befallen them may remind us of Grimm's story of 'Die kluge Else'. It will also be noticed that the heroes are concerned only about their mothers; and Tiera has as little thought for his virgin bride as Lemminkäinen has for Kyllikki.

RUNO XXXI

1 The tragedy of Kullervo is the favourite episode of the *Kalevala* in Finland, next to that of Aino. The preamble (lines 1–10) is the same as the opening of the Estonian *Kalevipoeg*. The story of the Estonian hero, though he was a king and not a slave, resembles that of Kullervo in so many respects that he must have been the same character originally.

19 I think the change of style, indicative of different authorship, in this episode is sufficiently obvious even in a translation. Many words used here do not occur earlier in the poem.

91–5 The same story is told of the infant Kalevipoeg.

107 Estonians call dwarfs 'Ox-knee people'; i.e. people as high as an ox's knee.

137 Like Simple Simon.

337 It is obvious that some of the youthful exploits of Kwasind (slightly varied, after Longfellow's manner) are imitated from those of Kullervo. (Compare also Runo XXXV: 11–68.)

RUNO XXXII

24 The rye-bread, on which the Finnish peasants largely subsist, is described as baked in very hard round loaves, like quoits, which are strung on a pole. But Kullervo's cake seems to have been prepared to look nice on the outside.

156–62 Does this refer to stories of witches milking cattle?

206 Of juniper wood.

498 Literally, an apple-berry. Probably a small crab-apple is intended.

533 In the Estonian story of the Northern Frog, the monster is secured by an iron stake driven through the jaws. (Kirby's *Hero of Esthonia*, II, 253, 256).

542 These elaborate and ineffectual prayers and incantations may be compared with the prayers of Achilles for the safety of Patroclus, in *Iliad*, XVI.

RUNO XXXIII

40 Wheat is used in the folk-songs as a term of endearment. (K.K.)

61, 62 The Estonian Kalvipoeg was constantly instructed by the voice of birds.

285–90 In Estonia this episode occurs in the story of the Royal Herdboy (*Hero of Esthonia*, I, pp. 279–305).

RUNO XXXV

65 As Kalervo appears to have been a chief in his own right, it is not very clear why, or to whom, he had to pay taxes.

107, 108 The lake of course was frozen.

153   As in several other instances in the *Kalevala*, this does not appear to be abduction in the modern sense, but merely marriage by capture.

343   Sea-beasts are very rarely mentioned in the *Kalevala*, for nearly all aquatic animals referred to are lake- or river-fish. Here the allusion is probably to the story of Jonah.

RUNO XXXVI

80   Literally 'the rest of his flesh'. Having regard to the supposed powers of Finnish magicians, this passage is not to be taken merely as an impudent rejoinder, but as asserting powers which Kullervo actually claimed to be able to exert.

327   This reminds us of Sir Peter's 'Sword of Vengeance' (Prior's *Danish Ballads*, I, pp. 269–75).

341   The Estonian Kalevipoeg was also slain, like Kullervo, by his own sword (*Hero of Esthonia*, I, pp. 140, 141).

RUNO XXXVII

39   'Gold from the sea he gathered'. (M.B.)

56   Literally, their hatless shoulders.

61   Compare the account of the forging of the *sampo* in Runo X

RUNO XXXVIII

94   This might allude to the Viking practice of carving the Blood-Eagle on the backs of enemies; but Professor Krohn remarks that this was unknown in Finland.

255   'With the girl lay as he slept there'. (M.B.) Here it seems that the mere fact of Ilmarinen having carried off the girl, even against her will, was enough to constitute her his lawful wife.

273   Ilmarinen's sword was less bloodthirsty than that of Kullervo; but it will be noticed that there is as little real chivalry in the *Kalevala* generally as in old Scandinavian literature.

RUNO XL

75   'Also past a wizard's shelter'. (M.B.)

274   Literally, 'at the tips of my ten nails'.

RUNO XLI

238   Similar incidents are common in folk-tales. The reader will recollect the decoration of Mama, the Woodpecker (*Hiawatha*, IX).

RUNO XLII

1–3   Here again we notice a difference of expression, indicating a different authorship.

146   Compare Runo XX: 17–118.

295   Literally, his finger-bones.

403   Perhaps the cap had ear-flaps to be worn in bad weather.

RUNO XLIII

37, 38   This seems to be meant ironically. 'It is more likely that the lines reflect a problem unresolved by Lönnrot either here or in various other passages of the *Kalevala*. In combining passsages, particularly as he created composite characters as in the present example, Lönnrot did not eliminate features from one figure which were not in keeping with the character of his composite.' (M.B.)

115–20 This, or something similar, is a common device for impeding a pursuer in European fairy tales.

177 *Pohjan eukko*. Another epithet for Louhi.

RUNO XLV

41 Loviatar represents the evil and destructive powers of Nature, as opposed to the beneficent powers, represented in the *Kalevala* under the twin aspects of Ilmatar and Marjatta.

117 This speech or invocation is not addressed to Loviatar, but apparently to some goddess similar to the Roman Lucina.

168 Dr Russell says that the itch was more dreaded than the plague in Aleppo in the eighteenth century.

181 Pestilence has often been attributed to the anger of gods or demons; and Finland suffered severely from plague till well into the eighteenth century.

200, 201 'Logs brought there on water drifting;
          Water brought in undercover'. (M.B.)

215–18 'Wipe away the holy sparks,
        Put out the holy pestilence,
        Bad vapour drive into the ground,
        The evil vapour send away'. (M.B.)

269, 282, 283 All these names have nearly the same significance, and might be rendered by 'Dolores, our Lady of Pain'.

RUNO XLVI

13, 14 The pestilence having abated at the approach of winter, the wild beasts naturally overran the devastated country. So I would interpret this passage.

81 For an account of bear-hunting in Finland, compare Matti Sarmela, 'Death of the bear: an old Finnish hunting drama', *Drama Review*, 26:3 (New York, 1982). (M.B.)

246 The word here rendered 'charge' literally means 'bundle' or 'package'.

377 A honeyed forest perhaps means a forest abounding in honeydew.

565, 566 These lines are rather musical:
          Kuuluvilla karjan kellon,
          Luona tiukujen tirinän.

RUNO XLVII

15, 16 There is a Finnish ballad relating how the sun and moon were stolen by German and Estonian sorcerers, and recovered by the son of Jumala (*Kanteletar*, III, 2; translated by Mr C.J. Billson, *Folklore*, VI, 353, 344).

37 Compare the story of Maui stealing the fire in New Zealand legends.

214 'Through a glowing ice pick's ferrule'. (M.B.)

Notes 661

RUNO XLVIII
169 Here a different epithet is applied to Väinämöinen.
283 Probably *Polyporus ignarius* or *P. fomentarius*, both of which are much used for tinder.
302 'And then the flame, son of the Sun!' (M.B.)

RUNO XLIX
83 This is Rhabdomancy, or divination by twigs. Tacitus describes the priests of the Ancient Germans doing this, and the Druids had a similar practice.
417 Literally, at the end of our thumbs.

RUNO L
1 'Marjatta, graceful youngest child'. (M.B.) The story in the present Runo seems to exhibit a veneer of Christianity over shaman legends. Even the name Marjatta, notwithstanding its resemblance to Maria, seems to be really derived from the word marja, a berry. An old writer says that the favourite deities of the Finns in his time were Väinämöinen and the Virgin Mary.
199, 200 She already recognizes her unborn son as an Avatar.
289 The word here rendered 'hapless' properly means 'little'.
465 This is the only passage in the *Kalevala* in which Väinämöinen is spoken of as ever having been young; though he is occasionally called young in variants.
465–8 This passage apparently alludes to Väinämöinen having sent Ilmarinen to Pohjola by a trick (cf. Runo X).
471–74 This must allude either to the fate of Aino, or to some story not included in the *Kalevala*.
501 In Estonian legends, Vanemuine is not an Avatar and culture-hero, but the God of Music, who withdrew from men on account of the ribaldry with which some of his hearers received his divine songs (*Hero of Esthonia*, II., pp. 80–5). Longfellow also makes Hiawatha depart in a boat after the conclusion of his mission. So also King Arthur.
613, 614 These expressions remind us of the Buddha 'breaking down the rafters and the roof-tree' preparatory to reaching Nirvana.

Glossary of Finnish names

AHAVA, *the cold spring East Wind.*
AHTI, *a name of Lemminkäinen.*
AHTO, *the God of the Sea and of the Waters.*
AHTOLA, *the dominions of Ahto.*
ÄIJÖ, *the father of Iku-Turso.*
AINIKKI, *Lemminkäinen's sister.*
AINO, *a maiden, Joukahainen's sister.*
ALUE, *name of a primeval lake.*
ANNIKKI, *Ilmarinen's sister.*
ANTERO VIPUNEN, *a primeval giant or Titan, whom some commentators suppose to be the same as Kaleva.*

ETELÄTÄR, *the goddess or spirit of the South Wind.*

HÄLLÄPYÖRÄ, *name of a waterfall.*
HÄME, *a province (Tavastland) in South-Central Finland.*
HERMIKKI (SINEWY), *name of a cow.*
HIISI, *the same as Lempo, the Evil Power, somewhat resembling the Scandinavian Loki in character. His name is often used as a term of reprobation.*
HIITOLA, *the dominions of Hiisi.*
HONGATAR, *the goddess or spirit of the fir-trees.*
HORNA (HELL), *name of a mountain.*

IKU-TURSO, *a water-giant; the name is doubtless connected with the Icelandic word Thurs, which means a giant, and which is also the name of the letter þ, called þa in Old English.*
ILMA (AIR), *name of Ilmarinen's homestead.*
ILMARI, ILMARINEN, *the primeval smith; still used as a proper name in Finland.*
ILMATAR, *the Daughter of the Air; the Creatrix of the world, and the mother of Väinämöinen.*
ILPOTAR, *a name of Louhi.*
IMATRA, *the great falls or rapids in the river Vuoksi in Eastern Finland.*
INGERLAND, *usually known as Ingermanland or Ingria, the area around present-day Leningrad and the south of the Gulf of Finland extending west to Estonia.*

JOUKAHAINEN, JOUKO, *a young Laplander.*
JOUKOLA, *the land of Joukahainen.*
JUMALA, OR UKKO, *God.*
JUOTIKKI (DRINKER), *name of a cow.*
JUUTAS, *a name probably derived from Judas. It is used as a name for Hiisi and lesser evil spirits, and also as a term of reprobation.*

KAATRAKOSKI, *name of a waterfall possibly in Karelia.*
KALERVO, *a chieftain, the brother of Untamo, and the father of Kullervo.*
KALERVOINEN, *epithet of Kullervo.*
KALEVA, *the ancestor of the heroes, who does not appear in person in the Kalevala.*
KALEVALA, *the land of Kaleva.*
KALEVALAINEN, *a descendant of Kaleva.*
KALEVATAR, OR OSMOTAR, *the daughter of Kaleva and brewer of the primeval beer.*
KALMA, *the Grave, Death personified; he is more often called Tuoni or Mana.*
KAMMO, *a rock, the father of Kimmo.*
KANKAHATAR, *the goddess of Weaving.*
KANTELE, *the Finnish harp or zither.*
KANTELETAR, *the Daughter or Spirit of the Harp; name given by Lönnrot to his published collection of Finnish ballads.*
KARJALA, *Karelia in the* Kalevala, *an area in the east; today a large area embracing parts of Eastern Finland and that part of the USSR bounded in the north by the Gulf of Kandalaksha, in the east by the White Sea, and by Lake Ladoga in the south.*
KATAJATAR, *the nymph of the Juniper.*
KAUKO, KAUKOLAINEN, KAUKOMIELI, *names of Lemminkäinen.*
KAUPPI, *a Laplander, skilled in making skis.*
KEITOLAINEN, *the Contemptible One, one of the names of the Evil Power.*
KEMI, *name of a river in Northern Finland.*
KIMMO, (1) *a stone;* (2) *name of a cow.*
KIPUTYTTÖ, *Maiden of Pain.*
KIRJO *(variegated or dappled), name of a cow.*
KIVUTAR, *Daughter or Spirit of Pain.*
KUIPPANA, *a name of Tapio.*
KULLERVO, KULLERVOINEN, *a hero, the son of Kalervo.*
KUURA, *a name of Tiera.*
KUUTAR, *the Daughter or Spirit of the Moon.*
KYLLI, KYLLIKKI, *a maiden of Saari, whom Lemminkäinen carries off and marries.*

LEMMINKÄINEN, *a reckless adventurer.*
LEMPO, OR HIISI, *the Evil Power.*
LOKKA, *the mother of Ilmarinen.*
LOUHI, the Mistress of Pohjola.
LOVIATAR, *one of the daughters of Tuoni, and the mother of the Plagues.*
LUONNOTAR, Daughter of Creation, a name applied to Ilmatar, and other celestial goddesses.
LUOTOLA, *name of a bay.*
LYYLIKKI, *a name of Kauppi.*

MAIRIKKI, *name of a cow.*
MANA, OR TUONI, *the God of the Otherworld.*
MANALA, OR TUONELA, *the Otherworld.*
MANALAINEN = *Mana.*
MANALATAR, *Daughter of Mana.*
MANSIKKA (STRAWBERRY), *name of a cow.*
MARJATTA, *the mother of Väinämöinen's supplanter. She is usually identified with the Virgin Mary.*

MÄRKÄHATTU (WET-HAT), *name or epithet of an unprepossessing cowherd.*
MELATOR, *the goddess or spirit of the Rudder.*
METSOLA, *the Woodlands, from metsä, a forest.*
MIELIKKI, *the Mistress of the Forests, the spouse of Tapio.*
MIMERKKI, *a name of Mielikki.*
MUSTI (BLACKIE), *a dog's name.*
MUURIKKI (BLACKIE), *name of a cow.*

NYYRIKKI, *the son of Tapio.*

OSMO, *a name of Kaleva.*
OSMOLA = *Kalevala.*
OSMOINEN, *an epithet of Väinämöinen.*
OSMOTAR, *the daughter of Osmo and brewer of the primeval beer.*
OTAVA, *the constellation of the Great Bear.*
OTSO, *pet name for the bear.*

PAHALAINEN (THE WICKED ONE), *a name of the Evil Power.*
PÄIVÄTÄR, *the Daughter or Spirit of the Sun.*
PAKKANEN, *the personified Frost.*
PALVOINEN, *apparently the same as Tuuri.*
PELLERVOINEN, vide *Sampsa.*
PIHLAJATAR, *the nymph of the Mountain-Ash tree.*
PILTTI, *the handmaid of Marjatta.*
PIMENTOLA, *a name of Pohjola.*
PISA, *name of a mountain.*
POHJA, *the North.*
POHJOLA, *the North Country; (a) A dark and dismal country to the north of Kalevala, sometimes identified with Lapland itself; (b) The castle or homestead of Louhi, to which the name of the country itself was applied.*
PUHURI, *the North Wind personified.*
PUOLUKKA (CRANBERRY), *name of a cow.*

RUOTUS, *the wicked headman of a village, a Finnish-Karelian corruption of Herod.*
RUTJA, *a cataract in the Far North to which workers of magic banished evil forces, said to be the same as Turja.*

SAARELAINEN (THE ISLANDER), *an epithet of Lemminkäinen.*
SAARI, *an island to which a hero fled to escape vengeance.*
SAMPO, *a magic corn, salt and coin-mill.*
SAMPSA PELLERVOINEN, *the genius of agriculture (from pelto, a field), the servant or agent of Väinämöinen.*
SARA, SARIOLA, *names of Pohjola.*
SAVO (SAVOLAKS), *a province in East-Central Finland.*
SIMA, *a Sound in Pohjola.*
SINETAR, *a nymph who colours flowers blue.*
'SOTKO'S DAUGHTERS', *the protecting nymphs of ducks.*
SUOMI, *Finland.*
SUONETAR, *the nymph of the veins.*

SURMA, *Death, or the God of Death.*
SUVANTOLA *(the land of still waters), a name of Väinölä.*
SUVANTOLAINEN, *an epithet of Väinämöinen.*
SUVETAR, *the goddess or spirit of Summer.*
SYÖJÄTÄR, *an ogress, the mother of the serpents.*
SYÖTIKKI (EATER), *name of a cow.*

TANIKKA'S FORTRESS, *Tallinn.*
TAPIO, *the God of the Forests.*
TAPIOLA, *the dominions of Tapio.*
TELLERVO, *the daughter of Tapio, but in some passages apparently identified with Mieliki, the spouse of Tapio.*
TERHENETAR, *the goddess or spirit of the Clouds.*
TIERA, *Lemminkäinen's comrade in arms.*
TUOMETAR, *the goddess or spirit of the Bird Cherry.*
TUOMIKKI, *name of a cow.*
TUONELA, OR MANALA, *the Otherworld.*
TUONETAR, *the daughter of Tuoni.*
TUONI OR MANA, *the God of the Otherworld.*
TUORIKKI, *name of a cow.*
TURJA, *Lapland; also name of a cataract.*
TURJALAINEN, *a Laplander.*
TURSAS, vide *Iki-Turso.*
TUULIKKI, *a daughter of Tapio.*
TUURI, *name of a god, apparantly borrowed from Scandinavian Thor, the god of thunder.*

UKKO (OLD MAN), *usually identified with Jumala, the God of Heaven, with special authority over the clouds.*
ULAPPALA *(the country of the open sea), apparently the same as Tuonela.*
UNTAMO, UNTAMOINEN, *(a) the god of Sleep and Dreams; (b) a turbulent chieftain, the brother of Kalervo.*
UNTAMOLA, the dominions of Untamo; sometimes used for Untamo himself.
UNTO, *short for Untamo.*
UNTOLA, *the dominions of Unto.*
UVANTO, UVANTOLAINEN, *names of Väinämöinen.*

VÄINÄMÖINEN, *the primeval minstrel and culture-hero, the son of Ilmatar.*
VÄINÖ, *short for Väinämöinen.*
VÄINÖLÄ, *the dominions of Väinämöinen (=Kalevala).*
VAMMATAR, *the Daughter of Evil.*
VELLAMO, *the goddess or spirit of the Sea and of the Waters, the spouse of Ahto.*
VIPUNEN, vide *Antero Vipunen.*
VIRO, *Estonia.*
VIROKANNAS, *used as a proper name; apparently meaning the Wise Estonian.*
VUOJALAINEN, *a name of Lyylikki.*
VUOKSI, *an important river which rises in Eastern Finland and flows into Lake Ladoga.*

Further reading

Without the opportunity to visit libraries in Finland, the study of Kalevala poetry and tradition is no easy matter. Unless by good fortune the reader has ready access to a national library, even the few works written in English, French or German are usually more easily available in Finland than in the countries where those languages are spoken. The works recommended below will certainly be held in most national libraries and possibly also in larger university and provincial libraries.

An overview of the background of the *Kalevala*, Lönnrot's composition technique and the epic's influence on Finnish life and culture are provided in John I. Kolehmainen's *Epic of the North* (New York Mills, Minnesota, 1973). The appendices and critical apparatus provided by Francis Peabody Magoun, Jr, in his *The Kalevala or Poems of the Kaleva District* (Cambridge, Mass., 1963) and *The Old Kalevala and Certain Antecedents* (Cambridge, Mass., 1969) contain a rich source of material about Lönnrot's life and times and the men who inspired and guided him. Professor Magoun's two books make available translations not only of the 1835 and 1849 editions of the *Kalevala* but also of Lönnrot's earlier folklore writings and the relevant work of von Becker. Together, Professor Magoun's books provide an excellent starting point for study of the evolution of the epic.

To see the *Kalevala* in context of the history of folklore study in Finland, the reader should consult Jouko Hautala's *Finnish Folklore Research 1828–1918* (Helsinki, 1969). The role played by the *Kalevala* and Finnish folklore studies in Finnish political and cultural life, especially in the twentieth century, is the subject of William A. Wilson's *Folklore and Nationalism in Modern Finland* (Bloomington, 1976).

For the analytical study of the *Kalevala* the reader is recommended to Professor Hans Fromm's magisterial Commentary to his German translation of the epic, *Kalevala Kommentar* (Munich, 1967). The material from which the *Kalevala* was compiled can be studied in the original dialects with English translation in *Finnish Folk Poetry: Epic*, selected, edited and translated by Matti Kuusi, Keith Bosley and Michael Branch (Helsinki, London, Montreal, 1977); the introduction to this book provides an overview of the Kalevala poetry tradition, while the evolution of the individual poems is analysed in a commentary (companion volumes on lyric and magic are in preparation).

Very few examples of Kalevala lyric poetry are conveniently available in English. In 1900, Charles J. Billson published a pamphlet entitled *The Popular Poetry of the Finns*, which contains a résumé of the *Kanteletar* and some translated passages. More recently short selections of poems from the *Kanteletar* have been translated into French by Jean-Luc Moreau, *La Kantélétar* (Paris, 1972) and into German by Erich Kunze, *Kanteletar: Alte Volkslieder und Balladen aus Finnland* (Helsinki, 1976); both works provide short but informative introductions.

Finnish magic poetry is better provided for in English. The interest in the beliefs and practices of 'primitive' peoples that grew up in the second half of the nineteenth century found in Finnish poetry a rich source of material for conjecture about the nature of religion and culture. Much of the introduction to the first English translation of the *Kalevala*, by John Martin Crawford (New York, 1888), is taken up by an analysis of the religious beliefs of the Finns. A sizeable corpus of Finnish magic poetry together with analysis and commentary is available in John Abercromby's two-volume *The Pre- and Proto-historic Finns both Eastern and Western with the Magic Songs of the West Finns* (London, 1898). A succinct overview of the subject is provided by Anna-Leena Kuusi (now Siikala) in a chapter entitled 'Finnish Mythology', published in *Ancient Cultures of the Uralian Peoples* (Budapest, 1976).

For detailed information about specific motifs and themes relating to Kalevala poetry and about its composition and performance the reader should turn to the two main research series, *Folklore Fellows Communications* and *Studia Fennica* (both published in Helsinki). Together these series comprise several hundred monographs, some of which, especially the more recent publications, are in English or German, or are provided with résumés in those languages.

The reader who wishes to go further with the study of Kalevala poetry on the basis of materials in English, French or German should consult the relevant sections in Hilkka Aaltonen's *Books in English on Finland* (Turku, 1964), Sulo Haltsonen's and Rauni Puranen's *Kaunokirjallisuutemme käännöksiä: Livres finnois en traduction* (Helsinki, 1979), and the bibliographical guides published from time to time in *Studia Fennica*.